Dio Chrysostom

Politics, Letters, and Philosophy

EDITED BY
SIMON SWAIN

OXFORD
UNIVERSITY PRESS

OXFORD

UNIVERSITY PRESS

Great Clarendon Street, Oxford OX2 6DP

Oxford University Press is a department of the University of Oxford.
It furthers the University's objective of excellence in research, scholarship,
and education by publishing worldwide in

Oxford New York

Auckland Bangkok Buenos Aires Calcutta Cape Town Chennai
Dar es Salaam Delhi Hong Kong Istanbul Karachi
Kolkata Kuala Lumpur Madrid Melbourne Mexico City Mumbai Nairobi
São Paulo Shanghai Singapore Taipei Tokyo Toronto
with an associated company in Berlin

Oxford is a registered trade mark of Oxford University Press
in the UK and in certain other countries

Published in the United States
by Oxford University Press Inc., New York

© Simon Swain 2000
The moral rights of the author have been asserted
Database right Oxford University Press (maker)

First published 2000
First published in paperback 2002

British Library Cataloguing in Publication Data
Data available

Library of Congress Cataloging in Publication Data
Dio Chrysostom : politics, letters, and philosophy / edited by Simon Swain.
p. cm.
Includes bibliographical references and index.
1. Dio, Chrysostom.   I. Swain, Simon.
B557.D35 D56 2000
885'.01—dc21   00-025841
ISBN 0-19-925521-0

1 3 5 7 9 10 8 6 4 2

Printed in Great Britain
on acid-free paper by
T.J. International,
Padstow, Cornwall

ACKNOWLEDGEMENTS

It is a pleasure to acknowledge the help and advice of Donald Russell, Ewen Bowie, and all the others who attended the 'Dio Day', which was the origin of this volume. All Souls College provided intellectual, financial, and nutritional support according to its customary standards. Corpus Christi College kindly supplied sustenance. The Department of Classics and Ancient History at the University of Warwick has been supportive and keen throughout. H. Jordan and J. Swain have contributed at all times. Last but not least Hilary O'Shea, Jenny Wagstaffe, and Georga Godwin at OUP have been extremely helpful and accommodating. I should also like to thank Graham Sells for his excellent translation of Chapter 2.

S.S.

Shotteswell
June 1999

CONTENTS

Note on Contributors   ix

Dio's Life and Works   1

PART ONE: INTRODUCTORY

1. Reception and Interpretation   13
   Simon Swain

PART TWO: POLITICS

2. Dio, Rome, and the Civic Life of Asia Minor   53
   Giovanni Salmeri

3. City and Country in Dio   93
   Paolo Desideri

4. Public Speech and Community in the *Euboicus*   108
   John Ma

5. Marriage, Gender, and the Family in Dio   125
   Richard Hawley

PART THREE: LETTERS

6. Some Uses of Storytelling in Dio   143
   Graham Anderson

7. Dio's Use of Mythology   161
   Suzanne Saïd

8. The Dionian *Charidemus*   187
   John Moles

PART FOUR: PHILOSOPHY

9. Plato in Dio   213
   Michael Trapp

10. Dio, Socrates, and Cynicism   240
    Aldo Brancacci

Contents

11. Dio on the Simple and Self-Sufficient Life   261
    Frederick E. Brenk

Bibliography   279

Index   305

NOTE ON CONTRIBUTORS

GRAHAM ANDERSON is Professor of Classics at the University of Kent. He has written several studies on the ancient novel and on the literary culture of the Second Sophistic. He is currently completing a book on fairy-tale in antiquity.

ALDO BRANCACCI is Professor of Ancient Philosophy at the University of Rome. He has published widely on classical and post-classical philosophy, including books on Dio (1985) and Antisthenes (1990). He is especially interested in Socrates and the Socratic tradition, Plato, Cynicism, and the Second Sophistic.

FREDERICK E. BRENK is Ordinarius Professor for the History of the New Testament at the Pontifical Biblical Institute, Rome. He has published extensively on the religion and philosophy of the early Roman Empire, and is interested *inter alia* in self-sufficiency in Hellenistic philosophy.

PAOLO DESIDERI is Professor of Roman History at the University of Florence. He has published widely on Greek and Roman historiography and intellectual/cultural history, including his book on Dio (1978). He is also interested in south-eastern Anatolia and in 1990 published a book on Cilicia with A. M. Jasink.

RICHARD HAWLEY is Lecturer in Classics at Royal Holloway, University of London. He has published on gender and the family in antiquity, including *Women in Antiquity: New Assessments* (1995, co-edited with Barbara Levick). He has a particular interest in imperial Greek prose, especially biography.

JOHN MA is Fellow and Tutor in Ancient History, Corpus Christi College, Oxford. His research interests bear on the post-classical *polis*, Greek epigraphy, and Asia Minor. These three areas are combined in his book, *Antiochos III and the Cities of Western Asia Minor* (Oxford University Press, 2000; paperback 2002).

JOHN MOLES is Professor of Latin at the University of Newcastle. He has published on ancient biography and historiography, ancient philosophy, especially Cynicism, Augustan poetry, and later Greek literature. His first (and best) article was on Dio, who has remained a constant interest.

SUZANNE SAÏD is Professor of Classics at Columbia University, New York. She is interested in mythology, literature, and the history of ideas, and has published on Homer, tragedy, comedy, history, Lucian, and the Greek novel.

GIOVANNI SALMERI is Professor of Latin Epigraphy at the University of Pisa. His many publications concentrate on the history of the Greek world under the Roman Empire (including a book on Dio published in 1982) and the history of classical scholarship.

SIMON SWAIN is Professor of Classics at the University of Warwick. His interests span literature and history and he is well known for his work on Hellenism and the Second Sophistic. He is currently director of a Leverhulme research project on the transmission of Greek thought to Islam.

MICHAEL TRAPP is Reader in Later Greek Literature at King's College, London. He has published on Dio, Plutarch, Athenaeus, and particularly Maximus of Tyre. He is interested in Platonizing elements in later Greek writers, and in philosophy as a constituent of general culture in Graeco-Roman antiquity.

Dio's Life and Works

Dio Chrysostom (*c.* AD 45–115) is one of the leading figures of the Second Sophistic, the name we give to the renaissance of Greek culture and politics during the High Roman Empire. His surviving writings comprise some seventy-six essays and speeches on a wide range of topics (see the list of works, including *spuria*, at the end of this Preface). They are united by a common interest in the legacy of classical culture and the problems and prospects for Hellenism under Roman rule. In the last thirty years or so there has been a marked increase in the study of later Greek literature and life. This has been driven by the quality and variety of the writing that survives from the period. In this regard Dio Chrysostom has much to offer. His work, like that of his contemporary Plutarch, is relevant to historical, literary, and philosophical researches. He offers prime evidence to historians interested in civic life, relations between Rome and the provinces, and the aspects of the social history of families and minorities. His ability to maintain complex narrative puts his best work on a par with classical literature. To the ancient philosopher he provides valuable evidence of the development of the Hellenistic philosophies of Stoicism and Cynicism, and of the literary and moral authority of Plato.

Much good work has been done on Dio in recent years, but there is no single volume which illustrates the distinctiveness and variety of his writing and its relation to the historical developments of his time. We hope this book will go some way to filling the gap. It contains ten original essays on key areas of Dionian thought which have been prepared by well-regarded experts in the field. The introductory chapter serves to set the essays against the major scholarly trends in which Dio has been involved since the age of Italian Humanism. English-language readers will thus be able to see current work on Dio in the light of the long and respectable tradition of mainly continental scholarship (which this volume itself further exemplifies).

Naturally we do not all share the same views of the material we examine, and readers will want to make up their own minds about many of the key issues and debates.

At the end of the first chapter I shall say a few words about the succeeding essays in the volume. Here I outline aspects of Dio's background which are relevant to our choice of themes. We begin, after the introduction, with four contributions on Dio in his socio-political context. In recent years students of classical Greece have come to recognize that the traditional way of dividing Greek studies between 'history' and 'literature' is unproductive. Cultural activities in literature and art cannot be separated from politics, warfare, and the economic and religious background of society, and have a very large input into these formations in their turn. In the time of the Second Sophistic the interconnectedness of the cultural and politico-economic-religious worlds is, if anything, more obvious and dynamic than before. The relationship between forms of cultural production and the society in which they arise is never easy to determine. In this period we can at least establish without difficulty that the cultural-intellectual renaissance went hand in hand with a noticeable revival in many other areas of urban life. The peaceful conditions of the Roman Empire under the Julio-Claudians and the Antonines brought about an economic resurgence in the Greek world. For whatever reason, polytheistic religion flourished. The emperors allowed the local aristocracies to rule themselves and kept interference from Rome within tolerable limits. The result was a superficially stable social system where unrest from have-nots was easily containable and inter-elite tensions and rivalries, which were rife, could be dissipated through readily identified channels before Rome need become involved. The system operated most successfully in the wealthy cities of Asia Minor, from one of which (Prusa, modern Bursa, in Bithynia) Dio himself came. It is visible to us in the material record of these communities—the evidence of new public building, communal celebrations and rituals, public giving on the part of the well-off (the phenomenon of 'benefaction' or 'euergetism'), and a very widespread desire to record through inscriptions and statues honour and glory given and bestowed at local or imperial level by or on any who mattered. Although the Greek city continued to prosper till the end of antiquity, the great reduction after 250 in the epigraphical evidence that is our best window on civic culture (and by inference, then, of the whole nexus of giving, display of honour, and communal play) points to a change of gear in the life of the city after this period. The Greek city did not disappear as an institution; but the pattern of civic life became less rich. That is why we talk of the Second Sophistic as a phenomenon of the High Roman Empire.

Intellectual culture during the Second Sophistic follows a similar course. Major figures whose works, like Dio's, have come down to us through generations of copyists are no more than the foremost representatives of a vast production of oral and written literature, most of which is lost. It is attested both in the surviving literary works and in other related texts that are still available to us, such as the lexicons and handbooks which prepared men like Dio for a life of public speech and writing. Literary production must be seen as part of the pervasive 'logocentrism' of a society which placed a premium on command of the language and thought of Hellenistic and especially classical Greece. This cultural system is linked with the socio-economic, political, and religious systems because the actors in all of these came from the same families, were friends, or were identical. In all cases, the Greek past sanctioned and authorized present-day interests and aims. After the middle of the third century Greek culture begins to drift. When it re-emerges into certainty, the classicizing glue that had kept it together has lost its strength. The state-sponsored Christianity of the fourth century and later still needed to display traditional Greek learning and education; but its focus on a radically different set of values and histories served to sever these from their traditional roles within pagan society. Most of the great literature in Greek in the fourth century and later is written by Christian authors. The result was a world which Dio would not have understood, though his works continued to be read by both pagans and Christians (cf. below).[1]

It is particularly important to situate Dio in his society because he was an active politician, at home and abroad, as well as an intellectual. Virtually all of his literary works (which are conventionally known as 'orations') illustrate the civic values of his age. Dio thought and talked hard about the politics, the social environment, and the physical infrastructure of the Greek city (which for him always means city and territory), and the city's role in the Roman Empire. He was a communicator between different interest groups (emperors and

---

[1] See Brancacci (1985) chs. 3–4 for Themistius, Julian, and esp. Synesius (on the latter, see also below, pp. 22–5).

subjects, governors and cities, elites and populace, Greeks and non-Greeks), broadcasting a message of co-operation and stability within the Greek world (see esp. *Orr.* 31–51) and between Greece and Rome (see esp. *Orr.* 1–4). That not a few of his political orations (esp. 42–51) attest to disputatious, devious, and arrogant public behaviour on his own part will not surprise anyone who has observed or participated in political life. Dio was not a politician who wished to practise his principles at the expense of power, however small that power might be. The negotiations and compromises of a real life are one of the main reasons why his work continues to be interesting.

Dio is continually discussing power. His great city speeches to Rhodes, Alexandria, Tarsus, Nicomedia, and the Bithynian cities, are reasonably well known, at least to historians. To them are joined a large number of what might be called 'socio-political' works, that is, the many short pieces, some mere fragments, on such subjects as slavery, beauty, glory, and law. These are Dio's thoughts, almost certainly in some cases recorded by others from lectures, on the values assumed in the public life of the community, and Dio's advice on public policy in his major speeches reflects them. The difference between Dio and Plutarch here is instructive. Plutarch wrote a series of essays advising his peers on their individual conduct with one another. The sphere of operation is largely socio-political, but the accent is firmly on the individual's set of rights and obligations, not his community's.[2] Dio, on the other hand, looks at social questions from a communal point of view. Thus, for example, *Or.* 21 *On Beauty* is not about personal appearance, but about community perceptions of male beauty, and has a very contemporary resonance, since Dio is probably thinking about how far the statues which dominated civic centres and buildings should be ideal in form.[3] Again, *Or.* 66 (*On Glory* I) focusses on *doxa* ('repute') and *philotimia*, that 'love of honour' which characterizes the aims of the elite in their striving for status and rank. Plutarch often refers to these qualities in his work. But Dio seems to go further by discussing *philotimia* as a contemporary social phenomenon. He thinks globally as the essentially quietist and academic Plutarch for the most part did not.

Dio's thoughts on political organization have survived because he was taken as a model of good style after his lifetime and for the rest of antiquity and the Byzantine era (hence his nickname, Chrysostom,

---

[2] Cf. Swain (1999c).   [3] Cf. Smith (1998).

'Golden Mouthed'). Dio the writer is the focus of Chapters 6–8 of this volume. The admiration of later generations was not just a literary matter. Dio's readers had themselves to deliver speeches and needed models of good style to practise from. Moreover, the appeal of Dio's morality was always an important factor in the continued reading and use of his work in ancient times.

Second-sophistic literature looks, of course, to the massive legacy of literature from Homer onwards. Literary imitation (involving style and register as well as content) can sometimes go too far and result in poor-quality productions without much sparkle or freshness; but for the most part it was a spur to new writing with original ideas and contemporary concerns. Poetry, it is true, is rather poor: plenty of verse was written, but what there is, is too dependent on the classics and is not especially memorable for its own sake.[4] Prose, how-ever, shows much vigour and innovation, even where the quality is low, as it is in some examples of the great new invention of this age, the romantic fiction of the Greek novel.[5]

Dio himself makes particular use of the long-established speech and dialogue forms, though he was too interested in his own opin-ions to be overly beholden to classical models. It is difficult to know to what extent real speech is involved in any one instance. How-ever, the point to note is that Dio especially needed to project himself as being listened to. This is not simply a familiar case of intellectuals needing an audience. Oral communication was *the* mode of communication in the ancient city. The elite had at all times to address and convince the citizen body as a whole. Thus Dio's city speeches are often set before the assembly, real or imagined (as so nicely in the reported assembly speeches in *Or.* 7, the *Euboicus*). The elite had also to speak to itself. This is part of a widely observed need to evaluate and chart social behaviour in a society where codes of conduct were becoming ever more self-conscious. Language was one of the best guides to status, for set occasions had now begun to require a classicizing version of the usual educated speech and individuals' ability to display classical knowledge here was constantly tagged. It is no surprise to find that talk came to occupy an insti-tutionalized space of its own with the development of the formal, rhetorically prescribed 'chat' (*lalia*), which would be held in the numerous lecture halls that grew up in city centres. These venues

---

[4] Cf. Bowie (1990). [5] Cf. Swain (1999a).

are the contexts for Dio's socio-political pieces. The dialogue or reported dialogue form of many of them was perfect for rehearsal on such occasions. That is not to deny the possibility that a wider audience listened as well; but the range of literary allusion and the intellectual content of such speeches show they were primarily for the delectation of Dio's peers.

Dio plays his own special part in the rise of Greek fiction during this period. The message he bore had to be worth hearing. Thus storytelling, anecdotes, and fiction of all kinds are a hallmark of his discourse. These stories can become the dominant focus of a work, as in the *Euboicus*, where the lengthy and elaborate tale of what happened to Dio after his shipwreck on Euboea was used, at least in the surviving form of the oration, to introduce one of his hardest-hitting disquisitions on labour, employment, and social morality. He also drew on a stock of stories and anecdotes in common circulation. The most important group of these is without doubt the tales of Greek myth. Paul Veyne's famous little book, *Did the Greeks Believe in their Myths?*,[6] drew heavily on later Greek sources to answer a question that was posed essentially from the perspective of a timeless Classical Greece (stretching indeed as far as our own times). There are particular factors that made myth relevant to Greeks of the Second Sophistic. The world of myths and heroes was the oldest stage of Greek civilization. As I have remarked, Greek identity in Dio's day was more than ever grounded in the authority of the past. Thus myth came into its own as a prime source of social power and constituted an internally rational and logical account of Greek values and civilization in the new world of the Roman Empire. There is a civic dimension to this too, since the mythological wanderings of the Greek heroes provided ready-made claims to Greekness for cities whose paternities were not clear as well for those whose ancestry was quite secure (cf. e.g. *Or.* 33 to Tarsus).

As a creative and original writer Dio manipulated known mythological stories for his own purposes (the *Trojan Oration*, *Or.* 11, is a spectacular example in which the history of the Trojan War is totally rewritten). He also made up myths. This power of invention is especially important in his philosophical writings, where the interrelation of *muthos* and *logos* (myth as a rational account offering truth) is particularly clear. In these writings Dio is largely concerned to explore

[6] Veyne (1988).

the role of humankind in the universal scheme of things. The allegedly Zoroastrian narrative of the earth's periodic destruction and rebirth in *Or*. 36 (*Borystheniticus*) is probably the best-known example of his own myth-making (whatever its particular inspiration). *Or*. 30 (*Charidemus*) is another very good example, and indeed a richer one, since Dio here invents three *logoi* which offer interlocking but competing accounts of the meaning of life and death, the second short and the third long account being particularly good examples of his positive, humanizing Stoicism. The skilled construction and real force of Dio's prose at its best can only be appreciated in such pieces by careful textual explication.

Dio's self-presentation varied over the years according to his given aims and audiences. After his exile he settled on the image of the philosopher for his public persona. What sort of philosopher was he? What did people expect when he presented himself thus? The final chapters of this volume explore these questions. Of the three technical divisions of philosophy (ethics, physics, logic), Dio was not to our knowledge interested in logic nor in physics except at a general level.[7] Ethics, i.e. moral and political philosophy, is his concern. In Dio's age the pride placed in education, or the claim to it, meant that the description *philosophos* ('philosopher', 'philosophical') was part of the general currency of intellectual self-advertisement.[8] But the perception that the philosopher was technical, academic, irrelevant, and above all a hypocrite who did not live by his own moral code, made the term suspicious.[9] Philosophers had another problem which was an ineradicable trait of second-sophistic society (cf. above) and in this case was too visible for comfort: an absence of vitality caused by their competitive adherence to the creative philosophers of the past. First- and second-century philosophy is more concerned with exegesis and commentary than originality (which is not to deny that interesting and original developments took place). Philosophers tended to stand apart from society and emphasized this by the use of a symbolic display of simple clothes and 'poverty'. It was this very lack of appeal that was seized on by the politically astute Dio who sought to realize the untapped power of the philosopher

---

[7] *Or*. 12 (*Olympicus*) and *Or*. 36 (*Borystheniticus*) make use of (the ideas of) Stoic physics. Cf. below, Introduction, p. 45 n. 104.

[8] Cf. below, p. 24 n. 42.

[9] These allegations are most easily seen in the witty parodies of philosophical values and lives by Lucian (*c*.125–90).

to shock and reform his hearers, if they could be brought to believe in his sincerity. Dio's mask of philosophy was a risky act of political entrepreneurship. Sincerity was asserted by claiming as his models men who were recognized as having lived their lives beneficially or who had displayed true wisdom: the heroes Heracles and Odysseus, the martyr Socrates, the free-thinker Diogenes. It is as interesting to enquire into the intellectual origins of Dio's thought as into the literary structure in which he encases it. His models of philosophy in action are Platonic or perhaps rather Socratic (he particularly admired and used the writings of Plato, but Antisthenes and other Socratic writers were used in intellectual contexts) and (through the legacy of Antisthenes) Cynic, and it remains a debated question as to where his sympathies really lay. Stoicism (which also saw itself as ultimately Socratic) is another important strand of Dio's thought on the social life of the community and the constitution of the universe. In the end it is important to emphasize that Dio's philosophy constitutes a sophisticated, but at least in public contexts probably defensive, strategy of communication: had he been a more successful politician, he might not have needed to put on a mask at all. At the same time his approaches to human and social organization represent real-life developments of the philosophers' enquiries.

Ultimately there is an ambiguity about Dio. It is this that makes us feel we are confronting a complex personality who was responding to varied circumstances. We can never be sure where the author and the intellectual part from the counsellor and the politician. That is why Dio needs—and will go on needing—reinterpretation and study.

TITLES OF ORATIONS IN THE *CORPUS DIONEUM*

1–4	*Kingship Orations/Orations on Kingship*
5	*Libycus/Libyan Myth*
6	*Diogenes, or On Tyranny*
7	*Euboicus/Euboean Oration*
8	*Diogenes, or On Virtue*
9	*Diogenes, or Isthmian*
10	*Diogenes, or On Slaves*
11	*Troicus/Trojan Oration*
12	*Olympicus/Olympian Oration*

13   *In Athens, On his Exile*
14–15   *On Slavery and Liberty* I–II
16   *On Distress*
17   *On Greed*
18   *On Training for Public Speaking*
19   *On Pleasure in Listening*
20   *On Withdrawal*
21   *On Beauty*
22   *On War and Peace*
23   *The Wise Man is Happy*
24   *On Happiness*
25   *On the Daimon*
26   *On Deliberation*
27   *On the Symposium*
28   *Melancomas* II
29   *Melancomas* I
30   *Charidemus*
31   *Rhodian Oration*
32   *Alexandrian Oration*
33   *First Tarsian/Tarsic*
34   *Second Tarsian/Tarsic*
35   *To Celaenae*
36   *Borystheniticus*
37   *Corinthian Oration*
38   *Nicomedian/To the Nicomedians, On Concord with the Nicaeans*
39   *Nicaean/On Concord in Nicaea*
40   *On Concord with the Apameans*
41   *Apamean/To the Apameans, On Concord*
42   *Address in his Fatherland*
43   *Political Speech in his Fatherland*
44   *Speech of Greeting to his Fatherland*
45   *Defence of his Relationship with his Fatherland*
46   *Before a Philosophical Career, In his Fatherland*
47   *Public Speech in his Fatherland*
48   *Political Speech in the Assembly*
49   *Refusal of Office before the Council*
50   *On his Deeds, before the Council*
51   *To Diodorus*
52   *Aeschylus, Sophocles, and Euripides, or the Bow of Philoctetes*

53   On Homer
54   On Socrates
55   On Homer and Socrates
56   Agamemnon, or On Kingship
57   Nestor
58   Achilles
59   Philoctetes
60   Nessus, or Deianeira/Nessus
61   Chryseis
62   On Kingship and Tyranny
63–5   On Fortune I–III
66–8   On Glory I–III
69   On Virtue
70   On Philosophy
71   On the Philosopher
72   On Dress
73   On Trust
74   On Distrust
75   On Law
76   On Custom
77–8   On Envy[10]
79   On Wealth
80   On Freedom

NB *Orr.* 37 and 64 are by Dio's pupil, Favorinus.[11] *Or.* 63 is also inauthentic. It is likely that one or two more of the shorter pieces are falsely attributed.

---

[10] *Orr.* 77 and 78 have been accepted as a single work since Emperius (1840).
[11] Cf. Amato (1995).

PART ONE

Introductory

Introductory

I

Reception and Interpretation
SIMON SWAIN

Dio Chrysostom's contributions and responses to the culture of his time form the principal focus of this volume. The purpose of this introduction is to allow readers to set modern views of Dio in the context of a long history of Dionian commentary and scholarship, beginning with the Humanists of the fifteenth century.[1] By looking at some of the aims of Dio's past editors and translators we shall better understand our own approaches and interests today.[2]

POLITICS AND LETTERS[3]

The first of the Italian Humanists to turn his attention to Dio was the celebrated Franciscus Philelphus (Filelfo; d. 1481), one of the great transmitters of Greek culture to the West. As a young man Filelfo journeyed to Constantinople as secretary to the Venetian consul and returned in 1427 with numerous manuscripts, including copies of Dio. On the sea-journey home, as he records romantically in his letters, he sketched out a Latin translation of Dio's notorious retelling of the Trojan War, the *Trojan Oration* (*Or.* 11), which he finished the next year.[4] The translation was addressed to Leonardo Bruni,

---

[1] See Brancacci (1985) for the reception of Dio up to this period.
[2] It should be stressed that this survey is not comprehensive and naturally reflects my own interests.
[3] The following standard works have been consulted in this section and the next: *Allgemeine deutsche Biographie*; *Archivio biografico Italiano*; Brockhaus, *Enzyklopädie*; *Deutsches Literatur-Lexicon*; *Dizionario biografico degli Italiani*; *Enciclopedia Italiana*; *Grand Dictionnaire Universel du XIXᵉ siècle*. One area of Humanism which would repay further work is the reading of Dio before he was printed in his entirety (i.e. before *c*.1550); cf. here below in text on Filelfo and n. 8 on Politian.
[4] Calderini (1913) 287–9.

Humanist himself and recently elected Chancellor of the Florentine Republic, where Filelfo soon settled. It evidently made an impact in learned circles, since it was eventually printed at Cremona in 1492 (and reprinted three times shortly after).[5] In the afterword Nicolaus Lucarus expresses his gratitude to Borsius Cavitellus for restoring 'the almost extinct memory of Dio of Prusa' in the translation of Filelfo. Filelfo himself in his preface recounts his interest in the poetics of fiction—he naturally turned to Dio, because Dio had approached the saga of the Trojan War as a philosopher concerned to find the truth. But the dedication is quite as much political as cultural. Filelfo goes on to recall that Dio had been a confidant of Trajan. Leonardo Bruni, he implies, will be his patron. It is somewhat ironic that Filelfo's life was henceforth spent in unsuccessful political intrigue and a lengthy banishment from Florence owing to the hostility of the Florentine Humanists and Cosimo de' Medici himself, for Dio's own relations with his Roman patrons led to his exile under Domitian and even after his return, when he could claim the support of Trajan, brought little lasting political success.

The printed version of Filelfo's translation is not the first printed Dio. That honour goes to Franciscus de Picolhomineiis (Piccolomini) of Siena (very briefly Pope Pius III). Not long after the introduction of printing into Italy he published at Rome the Latin translation of Dio's famous *Kingship Orations* (*Orr.* 1–4) by Publius Gregorius Tifernas (Tifernate), which had probably been done two decades before.[6] In prefatory remarks dated 1469 Piccolomini addresses Maximilianus, the young son of the German emperor, and remarks in words that recall Dio that princes will derive much benefit from listening to what Dio has to say (with the obvious implication). Tifernate in his introduction points out to Pope Nicholas (V), Humanist founder of the Vatican Library (d. 1455), the relevance of Dio for modern princes. Nicholas was one of the great restorers of the papacy, turning it into a centre of diplomatic activity, with a firm eye on the glory of ancient Rome. This age of alliance and diplomacy, between the long wars of the first half of the fifteenth century and the predations of foreign invaders at its end, was clearly a perfect setting for the ingenious statesmanship of the *Kingship Orations*.

---

[5] See Filelfo (1492).

[6] De Picolhomineiis (1471); 1471 is the accepted date for the printing. It is possible that Tifernate was directed to Dio by Filelfo, who was to secure him an appointment at the court of Francesco Sforza in Milan.

The second printed Dio (at least, probably the second[7]) is *Or.* 53 *On Homer*, a short encomium of the poet which had the honour of being included in the *editio princeps* of Homer, published in Florence in 1488, and several other early Homers as well.[8] The combination of politics and high culture against the backdrop of Italian history is evident again in the fourth publication of Dio some five years after the printing of Filelfo's *Troicus*. The revival of the papacy brought foreign interest to Rome and eventually full-scale invasions in the decades of unrest that began with the temporary ousting of the Medici from Florence in 1494 during the French invasion of Charles VIII. It was during these events that C. Valgulius (Carlo Valgulio) published in translation at Brescia in 1497 a volume of several socio-political tracts from the second century AD. Two works of Plutarch (*On Moral Virtue, Advice on Marriage*) and Cleomedes' cosmological treatise, *On the Circular Motion of the Heavenly Bodies* (reflecting the Neoplatonic-Boethian interests of the learned circles of the age) are addressed in turn to the Borgia pope Alexander VI and his sons, Juan and Cesare (for whom Valgulio acted as secretary). There is also a translation of Aelius Aristides, *To the Rhodians, On Concord*, together with Dio's 'ad Nicomedios de concordia cum Nicenis componenda' (*Or.* 38) and his short *On Concord in Nicaea* (*Or.* 39).[9] The translations of Dio's speeches are prefaced by very personal remarks about the state of Italy. Valgulio cites the French invasion as a general context and specifies the deluge of civic and familial strife it threw up as Italians sided with French or Spanish interests against their own.[10] The dedicatee is none other than Francesco Piccolomini, who was now well established as an honest statesman and diplomatist. However, the relevance of ancient works

---

[7] The Greek edition of Dio by Dionysius Paravisinus, allegedly published in Milan in 1476, is attested only by the personal communication of the 18th cent. bibliophile, Antonio Simonetta, to the Milanese bibliographer, Sassi (see Sassi (1745) p. dlxvi with p. 4). There is no reason to be totally sceptical (Dionysius Paravisinus certainly existed: he was the first man to print a work in Greek, in Milan in the same year); but the great 19th cent. bibliomane Dibdin is probably right in saying that it 'must not be entitled to a moment's attention' ((1827) 1: 491–2 n.).

[8] For Politian's use of *Or.* 53 and *Or.* 36 in his introductory lecture on Homer of 1486, see Wilson (1992) 102–3. He was apparently criticized for using his source unacknowledged, perhaps indicating a reliance on Dio's unfamiliarity.

[9] On Dio's concord speeches cf. below, p. 42.

[10] The actual occasion of the publication of the translation was the visit to Brescia of the cultured Catherine Cornaro, titular queen of Cyprus (which was by this time, like Brescia, under Venetian control): Valentini (1903) 12.

of advice, which was predicated on the existence of still largely self-governing city-states, diminished rapidly from this time onwards. The early years of the sixteenth century saw new types of political writing. Niccolò Machiavelli's *The Prince* and Baldassare Castiglione's *The Courtier*, both in Italian, mark not only the end of the Latin phase of Humanism but also a new sort of political advice for a world of local despots and foreign kings.

LITERATURE AND BOURGEOIS CULTURE

Scholarly interest in Dio begins in the mid-sixteenth century with the first complete Greek edition by Federicus Turrisanus (Torresano), probably in 1551.[11] The dedicatee, Cardinal Rudolphus, will want to read Dio for his style, his language, and his philosophy. Dio has been lurking in the dark; but *studiosi* will be all the more grateful to discover his abundant and pleasant fruits after so long. Rudolphus will be his first patron, and Dio will remind him of 'our' services. At about the same time there were various (mostly translated) editions of Dio's speeches by the French printer, Wechel(i)us (André Wechel), and the German Humanist and theologican, Camerarius (Joachim Kamm(er)meister).[12] There is also the important, complete Latin translation by the Hellenist and Reformer, Thomas Naogeorgus (Kirchmeyer, Kirchmair, etc.) in 1555. Kirchmeyer's Latin was reissued at Venice in 1585 by Hieronymus Zenarus. The background to this is once more, and for the last time in Italy, political. The second half of the sixteenth century was another period of relative stability for the Italian states. After 1590 this stability became increasingly precarious. Dio was eminently suitable, says Zenarus, for a man of distinguished political ancestry such as his addressee, Franciscus Barbarus, ambassador of Venice and son of the illustrious M. Antonius (Marcantonio Barbaro), famed negotiator with the Ottoman court. Moreover, Dio's philosophy is superior to Plato's 'entire *Republic*' and 'all of Aristotle's *Ethics*' because he was a man

---

[11] The edition can be placed securely only between 1550 and 1553: Renouard (1834) 151.

[12] See Bibliography svv., and for the editions of Wechel, cf. Maittaire (1741) 5. 1: 342. Camerarius dedicated his edition to Johannes Mylius (apparently the professor of Greek at Jena of that name; d. 1575), whose son (?) Andreas Mylius edited *Orr*. 1–5 (cf. Fabricius (1796) 135).

of action, exiled by Domitian, aided by Trajan, a benefactor of his homeland, a victim of political enemies and an ungrateful people. Only Xenophon and Isocrates are better. His idea of God's care for men makes his religion very similar to Christianity. Thus kings and 'moderators' must read him.

Zenarus was already out of date when he wrote this. In the East the Ottomans sapped the declining strength of Venice, while in the West the accession of Henry IV of France in 1589 and his successful restoration of religious harmony at home spelled more trouble for Italy. It was in Henry's reign that the next milestone in the history of Dio is reached, the Greek edition of the royal printer, Féd. Morel, in 1604. Morel had already tried his hand at editing Dio.[13] Now he presented the 'lectori Dionophilo' with a Dio restored to health after years of neglect, his cloak almost rent apart from old age. This Dionian imagery is in keeping with what Morel says to his dedicatee, Pomponius Bellievraeus (Bellièvre), recently appointed as Henry's chancellor. Bellievraeus will find Dio 'en redivivus auriloquus orator, Regumque amantissimus'. It is not just Dio's career that is relevant (Bellievraeus's long political service had been rewarded with exile by Henry III), but also the sophisticated social level at which Dio and his readers live. Both Bellievraeus and Dio are eloquent, both have sons with public careers, both love kings. And just as Dio was so approved of by Trajan that he once rode in the emperor's car, so (the implication deafens) is Bellievraeus approved of by Henry.[14] Morel was a scholar before he was a courtier. He casually attacks the Venetian edition and improves his own with familiar scholarly devices—Kirchmeyer's Latin set parallel to his Greek, the discussions of Dio by Synesius and Photius, an index, explanatory/textual notes, and the *Diatriba* of the great Hellenist, Isaac Casaubon.[15] The *Diatriba*, a collection of literary and textual notes, is addressed to the equally famous Henri Estienne (Le Grand; d. 1598). Stephanus had himself dabbled in the editing of Dio.[16] Casaubon tells him of his excitement when he received Morel's 'chartas': he read the volume in one go, and Morel received his comments so well that

[13] Morel (1589); (1598–9), Latin and Greek editions.

[14] Henry, however, removed Bellievraeus's seals of office only a year later, prompting the chancellor to remark that he was like 'an apothecary without sugar' (*Grand Dictionnaire Universel* s.v.). The anecdote about Dio and Trajan comes from Philostratus: see most recently Schmitz (1996).

[15] Casaubon (1798 [1604]) (cited from the edition of Reiske).

[16] Estienne (1577).

he had them printed with his text and notes. The attention given to Dio by these scholars in the ambit of the court reflects, of course, the status of and utility of classical studies. What Casaubon says of Or. 31 (*To the Rhodians*) is true of the rest (and typical of his comments): *tirones* should attend carefully to the 'subtlety and abundant arguments with which Dio has treated a noble theme'.

Interest in Homer always ensured a continuing interest in Dio's *Trojan Oration*. In its second-century context the speech works on several levels. It is a rhetorical *tour de force*, a 'refutation' (*anaskeuē*) of an accepted set of facts (the Greeks' victory in the Trojan War, the sack of Troy), which shows the orator's prowess. It is part of a widespread *Homerkritik*, which is not 'criticism' of Homer, but is rather a part of the constant re-examination of the sources of Greek culture and of the identity which was grounded in them, and serves to vitalize rather than diminish, to illuminate rather than obscure, its principal elements. It is also elaborate praise of the city of Ilium in the Troad, where at least one version was delivered (the one which is the source of most of the transmitted text). More than anything it is designed to entertain by teasing the intellectual elite who formed Dio's audience. The first scholarly edition (with translation, commentary, and explication of the technical rhetorical matters) was produced by the German Hellenist (and accomplished epic poet in Greek), Rhodoman(n)us (Lorenz Roseman), in Rostock in 1585. He reprinted it in his edition (the second ever) of Quintus of Smyrna's *Posthomerica*.[17] The existence of Rhodomannus's edition no doubt made the work better known. The Jesuit polemicist François Garasse used it in his stinging attack on the high status of Homer among his contemporaries (1626).[18] Thereafter it attracts attention in the second half of this century in Germany, beginning with Christophorus Adamus Rupertus's *Observationes* (1659) on the universal history of Christoph Besold (publ. 1626). Criticizing the acceptance of Homer as a source for early Greek and world history he summarizes Or. 11 with evident approval and remarks, 'Unus repertus est *Dio Chrysostomus Coccejanus . . .* qui tantae multitudini se solum objecit; et quae magno consensu recepta erant, multis rationibus refutavit.' Dio knew what he was talking about because he relied on ancient Egyptian records.[19] The *Troicus* is next noted,

---

[17] Rhodomannus (1604).   [18] Hepp (1968) 53.
[19] This reliance is of course part of Dio's fiction.

albeit briefly, in d'Aubignac's *Conjectures académiques ou Dissertation sur l'Iliade*.[20] This work, which was written between 1666 and 1670 but not published till 1715, is of some importance in Homeric scholarship, since its interest in the problem of composition allows it to be recognized as a precursor of Wolf's *Prolegomena to Homer*.[21] D'Aubignac's examination of the problem (which he was not the first to raise in modern times)[22] was, however, premature and lacks Wolf's scientific elegance. Meanwhile several German scholars of the later seventeenth century cut their teeth on the *Trojan Oration*. A certain Matthias Linck disputed the historicity of the Trojan War 'propalam Jenae'.[23] He praises Dio, and Rhodomannus for bringing Dio to light, and has plainly read his Rupertus. Shortly after G. H. Ursinus delivered an extraordinarily florid speech to the scholars of Regensburg, expressing mock indignation that anyone should have believed the lies told by Dio (that great orator) about Homer (he singles out Rhodomannus and Rupertus as culprits).[24] He is followed within a decade by Christianus Krayerus's defence of Homer against Dio.[25] This is a far more careful, scholarly piece, paying tribute to Dio for his *persona* and his fiction, and tracing its own ancestry back to a hint in Casaubon's *Diatriba* that Homer should be defended by someone.[26]

It is not irrelevant to mention here the place of Homer, and Dio's thoughts on him, in the so-called 'Querelle des Anciens et des Modernes', the battle about the merits of classical and modern culture that beset late seventeenth- and early eighteenth-century France. The 'Querelle d'Homère' was a tributary of this, in which Homer was the vehicle of a bitter dispute between Mme. Dacier and her opponents concerning the definition of a moral culture.[27] Dio's praise of Homer in *Or.* 53 *On Homer* is cited in her *Life* of the poet. The *Troicus* has no part to play (except inasmuch as it is mentioned in d'Aubignac's *Conjectures*, which was published as part of the quarrel). And when Homeric scholarship took a professional turn from the 1730s onwards, antiquity's views of Homer ceased to be of much importance.

[20] D'Aubignac (1715) 58 (Magnien's pagination).
[21] See Magnien's patriotic introduction to d'Aubginac (1715).
[22] Magnien p. xxxvii ff. citing Camerarius in 1558.   [23] Linck (1674).
[24] Ursinus (1679).   [25] Krayerus (1687).
[26] Casaubon (1798 [1604]) 461 'ut in eius [*sc.* Homeri] gratiam velit Dioni ὁμόσε χωρεῖν.'
[27] Hepp (1968) pt 4, ch. 3.

Dio was neglected during (at least the first half of) the eighteenth century according to the first of the two major scholars to have worked on him during that era.[28] In 1752 de Bréquigny published a French translation of the three speeches (*Trojan, Euboicus,* first *Kingship Oration*) which best represented the three categories ('philological', 'philosophical', and 'political') into which Dio's writings fell.[29] These are accompanied by a life, an essay on Dio's oratory and philosophy, and a survey of his works. The study of Dio formed the second volume of a projected series on the Greek orators (volume 1 is on Isocrates), and Dio is justified as a subject because, despite his quality, he is 'très-peu lû' (even for an age which neglects Greek).[30] De Bréquigny, an aristocrat and well known intellectual, represents a summation of scholarship up to his time. He is thus somewhat old-fashioned, as can be seen from his disquisition on the truth of Dio's *Trojan Oration*.[31] He had, he says, been tempted to believe Dio along with other moderns; but he has come to realize that the speech is a mere 'jeu d'esprit'.

De Bréquigny was also troubled by the state of Dio's text. Others were directed to this problem. An Englishman, William Piers (Peirs), and a German, J. Chr. Wolf, both contemplated complete editions. Their proposed readings, along with the notes of the famous seventeenth-century lawyer and scholar, John Selden, found their way into the first respectable edition of the text, that of the great German classicist and Arabist, J. J. Reiske. Reiske's text was published after his death by his wife, Ernestine, in 1784 and then revised in 1798. Its preface strikes a forthright note. Morel's edition was saved only by the inclusion of Casaubon's *Diatriba*, since Morel was probably better qualified to do anything other than edit a text.[32] Reiske does single out for praise the emendations of Henri de Valois (d. 1676), which were published in 1740.[33] His own *tirocinium* had been served in the *palaestra* of Dionian Greek and he is in no doubt of his own competence as an editor.

---

[28] Note the short entry in Fabricius's *Bibliotheca graeca* (1st edn. 1708).

[29] The last part of the *Euboicus* is, however, omitted to spare his readers details of 'certaines professions destinées à servir les passions des hommes' (p. 335).

[30] For awareness of earlier neglect of Dio de Bréquigny cites *inter alia* the *De jure Belli et Pacis* (publ. 1625) of the statesman-jurist, Hugo Grotius (who makes good use of Dio).

[31] de Bréquigny (1752) 21 f., 163–76.

[32] Cf. de Bréquigny (1752) 5 for a polite notice of Morel's failings.

[33] Valesius (1740) 43–79. Valois too represents a purely scholarly approach to Dio (hence an intense rivalry with Casaubon).

THE RISE OF PROFESSIONALISM

Reiske, with his confident, intuitive style of emendation, may be considered the last of the scholar-gentlemen editors. The next century was to bring a sea change to Dionian studies, both in the editing of the manuscripts and in the importation of more sophisticated methods and approaches.[34] These culminate in the edition and study by von Arnim. The first names to mention are the Dutch scholars, Geelius and Emperius. In his 1840 edition of *Or.* 12 (the *Olympicus*) Geelius (Geel) was among the first to try to 'pénétrer dans la forêt vierge' of Dio's text.[35] He was not, however, interested in a scientific appraisal of the relations of the manuscripts. Today his edition is remembered as a commentary with a mine of information that in itself set new standards. Adolphus Emperius is the first scientific editor. His textual *Observationes* (1830) tells us something of the status of Dio in his day. Reiske's edition, he says, is full of typographical errors (a possibly diplomatic comment). More than this, a new edition (by Emperius) can be justified because Dio is not one of the heavily re-edited school texts—indeed, people only ever read the first half of the *Hunter* (*Or.* 7).[36] Emperius published his text in 1844, but died before completing a volume of commentary.[37] The 1857 Teubner edition of Dindorf, whose tardiness Emperius had already reproved,

[34] An interesting footnote to eighteenth-century scholarship is the life of Dio (with a *catalogue raisonné* of his works based on Fabricius) by the poet, Giacomo Leopardi. It was written in one month during the sixteenth year (Cugnone, intro. to Leopardi (1814) p. vi) of his notoriously repressed and unhappy childhood. The study was accompanied by similar treatments of Aelius Aristides, Fronto, and Hermogenes (himself a *bambino prodigio*). Cf. n. 36.
It is as well to record here the rare 1810 edition of Neophytos Dukas (*non vidi*), which was to be used for the education of Greek children, plainly in a romantic, nationalist context, as his other editions of ancient texts reveal: Sonny (1896) 136, Μεγάλη Ἑλληνικὴ Ἐγκυκλοπαίδεια vol. 9: 509; cf. already Patousas (1744). Note also the interest in Dio attested by vernacular translations into German by Reiske's wife Ernestine in 1778, and into English by the scholar and anti-war, anti-Pitt polemicist, Gilbert Wakefield in 1800 during his incarceration in Dorchester gaol for political libel (the selection clearly reflects his political vision).
[35] François (1922) 10 (referring to Geel's appendix of 'Adnotationes in Dionis Chrysostomi orationes').
[36] The lack of interest in post-classical Greek was true of most of Europe, though in Italy 'la preferenza per la grecità ellenistica e tarda fu . . . normale . . . fino a dopo il 1860', Timpanaro (1978) 16 *à propos* of Leopardi (cf. n. 34).
[37] See the short essay on Dio's exile—Emperius (1840)—for an indication of his wider interests. It makes the suggestion, which has been almost universally accepted since, that the cause of Dio's exile was the fall of Flavius Sabinus, the cousin of Domitian.

made no advances. The construction of the text used today was not achieved before the labours of von Arnim, and that story (which is part and parcel of his great study of Dio's 'life and works') must be postponed for a while yet.

For the period from 1860 marks the beginning of Dionian scholarship in other ways. Important in spirit, if disappointing in content, is the 1864 article by the great Swiss Humanist historian, Jacob Burckhardt, on Dio's value for historians.[38] For Burckhardt the *Kenntniss* that Dio offers to students of his time comprises religion and literature as well as historical and cultural knowledge. What makes Dio worth reading is that his life coincided with the *Glanz* of the reign of Trajan, the last 'clear day' before the empire of magicians and theurgists that began with Hadrian. Even so, this world is in decline, and Dio deplores the dissolution of his own race in the territory of a great empire. Eventually his pessimism infects Burckhardt, who concludes that only the *Euboicus* is worth anything. There is much here that is repeated by von Arnim, who saw his own study of Dio as a means of studying Dio's age. Von Arnim was also influenced by the picture of Dio in a book published the following year, which was well-regarded over the next half-century, Martha's *Les Moralistes sous l'empire romain*. Martha proposed to recall to attention the valuable and concordant pagan and Christian morality of the Empire, a task he hails as 'fait surtout pour nous-même'. He studies Dio, on whose philosophical activity he had written an uninspiring dissertation,[39] in a chapter entitled 'La Prédication morale populaire'. The title shows how much Martha assumes, and from what angle. This Dio was a popularist preacher. His preaching was characterized by 'l'énergique recommandation de la propaganda populaire'. Moreover he was a convert from the idle life of the sophist. He spoke to the people as 'l'homme du peuple', as a 'sermonnaire païen' fighting 'tous les vices de l'Europe et de l'Asie' (this on *Or.* 32, the *Alexandrian*). It was men like him who prepared the people to listen to Christian homily (252 f.; Martha cites St Paul on the Areopagus in Acts 17). Martha does not characterize Dio as a Cynic,[40] but the idea that he was a Cynic preacher, which arises a little later, obviously owes much to his reformulation.

Martha took his cue for Dio's conversion from the essay by Synesius, the bishop of Cyrene and Neoplatonist *littérateur* of the

---

[38] Burckhardt (1864).   [39] Martha (1854).   [40] Cf. Martha (1854) 39.

early fifth century.[41] In his *Dio* Synesius takes issue with Philostratus' presentation of Dio in his *Lives of the Sophists* (487–8). This dispute is of great importance in the shaping of modern scholarship. What was it about? Philostratus wrote his biographies of the sophists in the 230s. 'Sophists' is the name he gives to the elitist cultural and political group who were the most distinguished teachers and exponents of rhetoric in his time. He undoubtedly overuses the term in his work; but his desire to connect his subjects with the sophists of fifth- and fourth-century Athens (hence his description of his age as 'the Second Sophistic') reflects a dominant, perhaps the dominant, mode of consciousness of the Greek culture of the High Roman Empire with regard to the sources and foundations of its authority. Among these sources Athens reigned supreme. Philostratus categorizes Dio in a special category of philosophers whose eloquence has earned them the name of sophist—'though they were not sophists in fact'. In his other main work, *In Honour of Apollonius of Tyana*, a quasi-biography written in the 220s about a first-century AD holy man, Philostratus presents Dio as an opportunist orator and a political trimmer. In Book 5 of the work Philostratus stages a debate before Vespasian between Apollonius, the Stoic philosopher Euphrates, and Dio on the subject of the future constitution of Rome. Apollonius speaks in favour of monarchy pure and simple (Philostratus writes with an eye on his own position at court). Euphrates proposes the restoration of republican government. Dio hesitates between republicanism and monarchy, and Vespasian/Philostratus concludes that it was regrettable that he had sided with Euphrates: he was a brilliant display orator whose rhetorical talents made him argue for the sake of it (5. 37).

Like many commentators Synesius was anxious to make his subject a wholly serious one. To this end he put Dio in a straitjacket. Dio had been a sophist, but 'he was made into a philosopher'. Thus his works were to be classified as 'before the exile or after the exile— not only those in which the exile is apparent, as some have already done, but every one'. The common thread between Dio's sophistic and philosophical writings was his forceful nature—whatever he did, he did to the utmost. It would be unsatisfactory to say that Synesius'

---

[41] He was also influenced by de Bréquigny's earlier Synesian presentation. The main section of Synesius' work is reprinted in the last volume of the Loeb Classical Library edition of Dio, Cohoon and Lamar Crosby (1932–51) 5: 364–87. On it see Treu (1958), Desideri (1973), Aujoulat (1992), Cameron (1993) 62–9, cf. 265–71.

picture of Dio's conversion is simply 'Christianizing'. Rather, to understand the two presentations we have to think about the cultural gulf between the two authors. During the later third and the fourth centuries Platonism became the dominant philosophy. This Neoplatonism was extremely exclusive. At a time when Greek culture was undergoing major change as it adapted to Christianity, philosophy became increasingly introspective and academic. The situation in the Second Sophistic was in some significant respects quite different. In this period more than before or after, social and political reasons pressured many, perhaps most, among the leading classes of the Greek world into claiming and advertising a high degree of classical education and culture. One manifestation of this is the widespread use of cultural labels such as *philologos* ('lover of words/ literature'), *philokalos* ('lover of beauty/good things'), or *pepaideumenos* ('cultured/educated'). These advert to social status as much as educational attainment. The term 'philosopher' could also be employed as a marker of social/cultural distinction in the eyes of the wider community.[42] For Philostratus the double labelling of Dio was unproblematic. But he regards the labels as different, indeed as concurrent. Dio, he says, was too quarrelsome to be a true philosopher (*Lives of the Sophists*, 488). Moreover he finds Dio's experience of suffering under Domitian, which Synesius makes the cause of his conversion, quite unedifying. Whereas Dio himself explicitly refers to his 'exile' (*phugē*; cf. esp. *Or.* 13), Philostratus says 'he was *not* ordered to go into exile', but dropped out of sight 'owing to fear of the tyrants in the City [i.e. Rome], who were persecuting all philosophy'. The implication is clear. The finale of the *Apollonius* has Apollonius confronting the 'tyrant' Domitian on behalf of philosophy: Dio had ducked his responsibilities. He was not a committed philosopher, but a talented orator who pronounced on serious and non-serious subjects indiscriminately. Many scholars today would hold that there is a good deal of truth in Philostratus' presentation, barring the tendentious denial of the exile.[43] But Martha's

---

[42] See e.g. *IGR* 4. 1359 'Menecrates . . . physician and philosopher, hero, *logistēs*, general, gymnasiarch, *prytanis*, agonothete', cf. 457, 468, 1324, 1403, etc. See Hahn (1989) 160–4 (esp. on the combination 'philosophical, patriotic . . .' in honorary inscriptions).

[43] See Jouan (1993*b*) for discussion of the fictionality of Dio's presentation of his exile. It is surprising that no one has taken Philostratus' denial (which is aimed at *Or.* 13. 1) more seriously.

own Christianizing attitude was better served by Synesius' parti-
tioning, and Dio's conversion was enshrined in all later work (with
the exception of Hirzel) until recent times.

Martha was writing at the beginning of one of the great historical obsessions of the late nineteenth and early twentieth centuries:
the establishment of 'oriental' cults in the Roman Empire and the
victory of the oriental religion *par excellence*, Christianity. Dio could
be used in two ways here. With Martha he could be presented as a
pioneer of Christianity from within a pagan culture that met Christianity half way.[44] Alternatively he could be seen as preparing the
way for Christianity from without by having publicized the new
religious lore of the East. This latter use of Dio focused on *Or.* 36,
the *Borystheniticus*, in which Dio tells a 'Magian myth' that seems
to show extensive knowledge of Zoroastrian/Mithraic doctrine.
This reading had been the subject of occasional criticism or acceptance by orientalists,[45] and had been accepted in an 1884 article by
Haupt on Dio as a historian.[46] No less a figure than Franz Cumont
regarded the myth as precious evidence for the Hellenized reception of Mithraic lore.[47]

Dio was also used as a mine for early Cynic thought. The start of
this approach, and the discovery of the Cynic Dio (who employed
Martha's 'sermonizing' diatribes), is marked by Ferdinand Dümmler's
1882 dissertation on Antisthenes (focusing on the *Diogenics*, i.e. *Orr.*
6, 8–10).[48] This was followed up in a lengthy study by Ernest Weber
(1887). Things had gone too far. An important Kiel dissertation by
Paul Hagen in the same year sought to give a more rounded picture
of Dio as a man of wide interests and wide influences. Hagen wrote
on Dio as a collector, interpreter, and inventor of myth (esp. the
'Magian myth' of *Or.* 36), a commentator and critic of Homer, and
(a hitherto neglected area) 'De Dione artis aestimatore' (with reference to *Or.* 12). While he stressed Dio's familiarity with classical
letters (especially Plato), he was concerned to show that he was more

---

[44] Martha's romanticism reaches its acme in the fantasies of Dill (1904) 21–3 (Dio
recalls for us the 'shy companies of men and women meeting in the early dawn to
sing hymns to One who . . . had taught a similar gospel of love').

[45] Meiners (1778) 72 '[Dio a] shameless imitator of Plato'; Windischmann (1863)
309–13 (genuine).

[46] On the basis of Dio's Zoroastrianism in *Or.* 36 Haupt attributed to him a *Persika*
assigned by the Suda to Cassius Dio.

[47] Cumont (1896–9) 1: 24 'L'origine . . . certainement iranienne', 2: 60–4.

[48] Cf. Desideri (1978) Appendice II 'Sul cinismo di Dione'.

than a repackager of classical thought, including Cynicism. The question of Dio's classicism had been broached.

In the same year as Hagen's dissertation Wilhelm Schmid published the first volume of his monumental examination of the Greek prose of the Second Sophistic, *Der Atticismus in seinen Hauptvertretern*. 'Atticism' is the (ancient) name for the stylistic and linguistic imitation of a variable canon of classical authors centred on the great Athenian orators such as Lysias and Demosthenes. It refers to the elevated Greek used in speech and writing for such genres, subjects, or occasions as were felt to require it. Its hallmarks were phonological, grammatical, and syntactic structures that were no longer in existence in the contemporary Greek of the educated elite (let alone in the language of less favoured classes). It was an intrinsic part of the classicizing identity that was so successfully adopted by Greeks or those who thought of themselves as Greeks and claimed Greek ancestry or membership of the Greek cultural commonwealth. Schmid (and his contemporaries) placed the real beginnings of Atticism in the second century. Nevertheless Dio was used in the first volume to demonstrate the development of a classicizing Greek in the later first century.[49] Schmid correctly recognized Dio's strong feeling for the Greek past and demonstrated his reliance on the language of Attic authors, especially Plato and Xenophon.[50] He also stressed Dio's capacity for independent, unstilted writing and his freedom from pedantry.

In keeping with the attitudes of Hagen and Schmid are the three Göttingen dissertations of Capelle, Hahn, and Wegehaupt which were published in 1896 under the direction of Wilamowitz. All three were concerned to restore Dio's Cynicism to Dio and, especially in the case of Wegehaupt (who was heavily influenced by Schmid), to characterize the literary integrity of Dio's writing and its contemporary relevance. In a work of very much greater importance in the history of scholarship, *Der Dialog*, Rudolf Hirzel had put many of these points more elegantly in the previous year.[51] Hirzel adopted a very Philostratean approach to Dio. Philosophy was used by Dio 'zur Schau'. He was eclectic. As for Cynicism, he used and abused its doctrines. Worse, Dio's use of dialogue form was not philosophical —it reflected educational practice and the 'schoolboy' was easily

---

[49] Schmid (1887–97) 1: 72–191.
[50] Cf. Geyr (1897) on Dio's final clauses (classical, but with innovations).
[51] Hirzel (1895) 2: 84–119.

discernible in the grown man. Nor did Dio properly employ the diatribe form, the conversation between a philosopher and a few listeners which traced its origin to Socrates. Dio's 'diatribes' were all fictitious. He spoke to no one. Indeed, had he been a real philosopher he would have made more use of Socrates!

Hirzel's view of Dio was soon to be disputed violently in von Arnim's *Leben und Werke des Dio von Prusa*, published in 1898. This remained the only book-length treatment of Dio till 1978. Before coming to it, something must be said about von Arnim's edition of a critical text, which he published in 1893–6. Emperius had identified thirty-eight manuscripts in which some or all of Dio's works were transmitted. Von Arnim was able to add only one more (the Estensis) to these. His contribution lies rather in establishing the history of the text and in determining which manuscripts editors should rely upon.[52] He showed from common errors and lacunas that all the manuscripts descend from a hypothetical archetype (labelled α) which was datable to the late eighth or early ninth century, the period of transference from uncial to minuscule script. The 'book of Dio with eighty speeches' summarized by the ninth-century patriarch and bibliophile Photius was the first known examplar.[53] Von Arnim divided the manuscripts into three classes.[54] To construct his text he relied principally on a combination of V (valuable for its freedom from interpolation but incomplete) and M from the second class with P, the head of the third class (which, he argued, offered genuinely ancient readings). A consequence of this was the retention of the 'logical' order of the speeches found in VM, the order known in fact to Photius,[55] whereas the order of printed editions since Turrisanus had been that of UB from the first class.[56]

[52] In addition to the preface in vol. 1 of the text see von Arnim (1891).

[53] Photius, *Library* cod. 209 (repr. and trans. in the Loeb edition, above n. 41, 386–407).

[54] These are represented by (1) U (Urbinas 124; 11th cent.) and B (Parisinus 2958; 14th cent.); (2) V (Vaticanus gr. 99; 11th cent.) and M (Meermannianus Lugdunensis 67 = Leiden B.P. 2c; 16th cent.); (3) P (Palatinus gr. 117; 15th cent.) and H (Vaticanus gr. 91; 13th cent.).

[55] This groups the works by subject, so far as possible (the numbers refer to the familiar order): (i) speeches on kingship (*Orr.* 1–4) with *Or.* 5 (the 'alternative ending' to *Or.* 4); (ii) the *Diogenics* (*Or.* 6, 8–10), moral philosophy using the *persona* of Diogenes of Sinope, originator of the Cynic movement; (iii) political affairs outside Bithynia (*Orr.* 11–13, 7, 31–7); (iv) Bithynian politics (*Orr.* 38–51); (v) the rest (*Orr.* 52–80, 14–30), a mixed bag of literary/art criticism, moral/philosophical commentary, encomia.

[56] Turrisanus based his *editio princeps* on a descendant of U—which one is not clear—but he also knew readings from the second class: Amato (1995) 30–1.

Von Arnim's reconstruction is certainly not free from objection. The Kievian scholar Sonny published a detailed analysis of the manuscripts in the first chapter of his *Analecta* (1896) as a prelude to a new Teubner edition which he was unable to complete. He argued that the ancient readings in P were actually the work of a clever copyist, that the second and third classes were in fact quite close, and that the text should be founded on a combination of V and U. The differences between von Arnim and Sonny are reprised with subtlety by François in his discussion of the history of the text before his edition and translation of *Orr.* 4–5.[57] His conclusion is that Sonny was too ingenious and that von Arnim's text could not be much improved. This is both true and false. A fresh examination of the tradition and of the relations between the manuscripts, which are not as clear-cut as von Arnim wanted, would undoubtedly clear up a number of lesser problems and highlight some neglected readings.[58] Recently an Italian scholar, Eugenio Amato, has brought forward two hitherto neglected manuscripts from Toledo, which do not, however, add much to our knowledge.[59] In a way, though, this is beside the point. For 'much of what troubles us is not small-scale scribal error but major stumbling blocks in the structure and coherence . . . due to the circumstances of delivery and preservation of the speeches in ancient times. Such difficulties are very unlikely to yield to any new evidence (except perhaps a papyrus find).'[60] Von Arnim himself was acutely aware of this major problem and devoted a good deal of his study of Dio to resolving it.

Von Arnim was born of an aristocratic Prussian family in 1859.[61] *Leben und Werke* is dedicated to his teacher, Wilamowitz, and many of the master's interests are apparent in it. He is writing, he says, because knowledge of the past demands 'die lebendige Vergegenwärtigung bedeutender Persönlichkeiten'. As we shall see, he also had empathy with Dio and a feeling for the times he lived in. The book is built around the idea of Dio's *Entwicklung*. This 'development' is very simple: Dio began as a sophist, became a philosopher during his exile, a local politician immediately after his return to Prusa,

---

[57] François (1922), esp. 37–41; see also de Budé (1916–19) 1: pp. iv–viii. See von Arnim (1897) for a somewhat tetchy reply to Sonny.
[58] Cf. Wenkebach (1944) on the validity of von Arnim's families of MSS.
[59] Amato (1995) ch. 3.   [60] Russell (1992) 24.
[61] Radermacher (1931), with photograph, and Meister (1933) offer rather thin obituaries.

and was finally a cosmopolitan politician who embodied all of his previous experiences and manifestations as an adviser to emperors and cities and a possessor of true wisdom. It is obvious that this picture goes back to Synesius. Synesius' division between Dio the sophist and Dio the philosopher is itself firmly rooted in Plato's attacks on the sophists of classical Athens. Understanding the development of the long battle between rhetoric and philosophy after Plato was in von Arnim's view the key to understanding Dio's *Entwicklung*. This is why he begins his study with a monograph-length history of the topic.

The contemporary resonance of von Arnim's approach may be illuminated by turning for a moment to Wilamowitz's famous article on 'Asianismus und Atticismus', published in 1900. One of his starting points was Philostratus' claim in the *Lives of the Sophists* that rhetoric had almost died before it was revived by Nicetes, the first sophist of the Second Sophistic.[62] Wilamowitz allowed (as he had to) that the term 'sophist' came back into vogue during the Second Sophistic; but he contended that this development could only be comprehended by taking account of the gradual victory of rhetoric over philosophy in the previous half-millennium. This task had been made easier 'by the profound first chapter of Arnim's *Dio*'.[63]

Von Arnim's basic argument in his study of the relations between rhetoric and philosophy is that sophistic rhetoric started (in the fifth century BC) with good intentions, but quickly degenerated into mass education (*Volksaufklärung*). This extension of high culture soon encompassed philosophy too, which should have remained exclusive. With the political decline of the Greek world the final result was a rhetoric that had no function and a philosophy that did no thinking. The scene was set to explain the 'paradox' of why a serious young man like Dio should ever have become a sophist. Von Arnim could assume that 'all my readers' have 'Rohde's *Greek Novel*' before them.[64] Both he and Wilamowitz followed Rohde's book in holding that the Second Sophistic marked the lowest point in the battle between philosophy and rhetoric and (in von Arnim's

---

[62] With regard to Nicetes Wilamowitz (and von Arnim and Rohde) suffered from an important error in Kayser's standard text of Philostratus (*Lives* 512), reading Νερουὰν instead of Νέρωνα, and thus dating the first sophist some four decades too late.

[63] Wilamowitz (1900) 16.

[64] Rohde (1876). On this work see Swain (1999a) 12–20.

formulation) the lowest *Bildungsideal,* which forced the Greeks to
retreat into an unhealthy and unreal classicism.

Thus von Arnim turns to Dio's sophistic works, moving immediately to his abiding interest in Dio as the province of the textual
critic. His study of *Or.* 11, the *Troicus,* is a good example of a style
of writing which is far from light. He refers confidentially to 'my
edition' in raising the problem of the doublets which beset interpretation of this speech. After a valuable excursus on the widespread
practice (of which Dio complains himself) of illicit publication of
works from notes taken down shorthand during performances (this
is the most important explanation of the state of our text), the doublets themselves are discussed in minute detail. This is the sort of
thing von Arnim enjoys.[65] His conclusion is in keeping: *Or.* 11 is
worthless as a piece of literature.

The comments on the next stage in Dio's life, his exile, illuminate
von Arnim's empathy with his subject. He stresses the fact that
Dio retained his property in Prusa rather than selling up and severing
himself, and remarks, 'To divorce oneself from an old family estate,
with which you have felt yourself grow from childhood, is always
difficult' (p. 235). It was experience that made Dio a philosopher
('purely human motives'), together with his 'veracity . . . and deep
modesty' (pp. 239, 242).[66] To this Synesian reasoning is joined a sort
of Nietzschean sententiousness (which is not incompatible with
the fair sprinkling of clichés and proverbs throughout the book).
Under certain conditions societies suffer *Erstarrung* ('torpor'). Many
view today's society in this way. Like Dio they seek freedom in
Declassirung—the recourse to a lower social level—for in such times
as these they think that the 'naive *Gesittung*' of the lower class is
preferable to their own fake pseudo-culture. Dio learnt the bless-
ings of bodily toil. He rejected a culture that had turned its back
on *eudaimonia* and aimed at a free, happy, human life. 'Rückkehr
zur Natur ist die Losung' ('The watchword is Return to Nature').[67]
So Dio became a Cynic.

An analysis of the 'Cynic' diatribes follows. Von Arnim sides with
those who studied these works as Dionian creations. The diatribes

---

[65] A little later, on *Or.* 31, he is so carried away by similar arguments that he cries
out, 'Nun woh!' (212).
[66] Even at points like these von Arnim is far from the cloying praise of Dio in
Breitung (1887) esp. 21–3.
[67] 243–5.

are all taken from genuine oral performances. It is crucial to his belief in Dio's sincerity that Dio did hold forth during his exile and teach on subjects such as fame and virtue on which he could air and confront a 'popular' view in informal discourses. Hence in Dionian mode von Arnim suddenly launches a virulent attack on Hirzel for harbouring suspicions of Dio: he must oppose 'die Ansicht des Gegners' (pp. 281–98).[68] He bases himself on *Or.* 13. 31 'by twos and threes' (that Dio says 'I did *not* take them by twos and threes in palaestras and porticoed walks, for it was not possible to associate thus in that city [Rome]' is not the only manipulation of the evidence).[69] A *Sammler* collected these talks and published them (hence, again, the problems of the text). Though his tone is too triumphalist, there is a good deal of sense in what von Arnim says. But he might have paid more attention to Hirzel's realization that dialogic exchanges once again became a feature of literature in this period, a realization that was taken up with great influence in Rudolf Bultmann's work on the preacher Paul (in which Dio was one model of the new type).[70] As to his sentimental generalizations about the lower class as a repository of true culture, here we should be suspicious, for von Arnim's Dio ends up decidedly *bourgeois*.

All in all von Arnim's critical approach to the text contrasts with a rather simple faith in Dio's picture of his own blameless life, especially regarding his plans to beautify Prusa and his friendship with Trajan. These matters are the subject of chapter 4, where for the first time von Arnim attempted to order the Bithynian speeches in a chronological sequence. He is more at home in his thoughts on the *Kingship Orations*, for here again a major part of the analysis is text-critical, especially on the serious structural problems of *Or.* 3. In this period (after 103) von Arnim's Dio becomes an adviser of Roman government. On his return to Prusa he enters the fully blended part of his life. He resorts to a sophistic style again to speak about religion and ethics (*Orr.* 12, 36). He posits a utopian society in *Or.* 7, the famous *Euboicus*, where the rural life is contrasted with the evils of urbanism. Von Arnim signals the importance of this programme by uniquely citing the work of a contemporary writer,

---

[68] Cf. 412 on Hirzel's 'anonymous' attack on him.

[69] For the ideal, cf. *Charidemus* 42 'talking one to one, or peers in groups of twos or threes'.

[70] See especially Bultmann (1910); cf. Nestle's review in *BPhW* 1912: 931–3; more generally Geffcken (1909).

the American utopianist Edward Bellamy, whose *Looking Backward: 2000–1887* (1888) enjoyed great success in its day. Bellamy's fantasy advocated social equality through the erection of a totalitarian state for which all people would work. Dio's aim, and it is a laudable one in von Arnim's view, is the creation now of 'einen artbeitsamen, einfach lebenden Mittelstand' ('an industrious, moral middle class'). He is in the end an essentially *moral* politician (pp. 504–5).

Von Arnim's strength—aside from his text-critical labours—is his detailed, coherent, sensible picture of Dio's life based on Dio's works. There are aspects in which he is not overly interested: the sources of Dio's thought, religious developments, local politics, literary criticism, *Nachleben*. Some of these were taken up in the three decades following the publication of his book, a period which in general offers 'fine tuning' of von Arnim's ideas and detailed recon-siderations of his views on particular speeches. Among others may be mentioned: Hermann Dessau's review of some of von Arnim's dates and von Arnim's reply;[71] Asmus (1900) on Synesius' imitation of Dio; Callander (1904) on the political background of the Tarsian Orations; Binder (1905) on Dio's debt to Posidonius; Thomas (1909) on the Stoic-filtered Cynicism of the *Kingship Orations*; Meiser (1912) on the *Charidemus* (*Or.* 30); Mesk (1920–1) on the rhetorical basis of *Or.* 11. More original is Valgimigli's 1912 study of Dio as a lit-erary critic (important on *Or.* 12) and François's 1917 article on Dio as a Stoicizing critic of art in *Or.* 12. François is the author of two monographs on Dio, which are essentially in the orbit of *Leben und Werke*. His 1922 Paris thesis has already been mentioned for its clear introduction to the history of the text. His 1921 Paris thesis is an intelligent study of the sources of Dio's religious and moral thought, consciously examining an area von Arnim had ignored (p. 5).[72] Overall he combines von Arnim with the source criticism of those who preceded him fairly successfully. His work is certainly more interesting than Lemarchand's 1926 monograph (the last till modern times) on Dio's works 'before his exile', in which the only positive thing to be said about an author whose speeches are choked by 'invraisemblances' is that, though from Asia, he behaves like a Greek 'de pure race'.

---

[71] Dessau (1899); von Arnim (1899).
[72] For example, the Mithraic basis of *Or.* 36 and the Stoic sources of Dio's social and political thought.

Von Arnim's attempt to put Dio in his historical context was based on a dominant view among Hellenists that the Second Sophistic was a period of decline (though not without redeeming features). The corresponding period at Rome was viewed as a genuine classical age. It needed an historian, and a Roman historian in particular, to look at Dio afresh and positively. That historian was the Russian Mikhail Rostovtzeff, whose *The Social and Economic History of the Roman Empire* (SEHRE) appeared in 1926.[73] This work is a massive celebration of the bourgeois-liberal civilization of the High Roman Empire. In this it reflects, of course, Rostovtzeff's own political views and wishes.[74] Rostovtzeff was interested in using the writings of Greek intellectuals—especially Dio and Aelius Aristides—to support the picture of the epoch that he drew on the basis of the material evidence. Success was built upon the ever-increasing extension of citizenship,[75] the fair distribution of wealth along the social scale through the key mechanism of euergetism (i.e. provision by wealth-holders of public buildings, recreational facilities, festivals and feasts, distributions of money),[76] and the very power of civic-political structures and civic amenities. Dio's speeches on achieving concord between the cities of Bithynia, his plans for a *sunoikismos* in the territory of Prusa (i.e. an amalgamation of the smaller communities with Prusa), his plea for the enfranchisement of the linen-workers at Tarsus in *Or.* 34 (the second *Tarsic Oration*), and his ideas on honourable employment for the proletariat in the *Euboicus* contributed to the characterization of him as 'a liberal and a philosopher' (p. 257). Rostovtzeff was especially persuaded by the *sunoikismos* proposed in *Or.* 45, choosing to read the plan as the extension of citizenship to the rural population.[77] Into this picture of social inclusion was fitted Dio's philosophical activity as a Stoic and Cynic. His philosophy originated in the aristocratic philosophical opposition to the Flavians. This opposition caused his exile. Rostovtzeff fantasized about

---

[73] I cite from the second edition (1957), which is based on the revisions made by Rostovtzeff in the Italian translation of 1933.

[74] Shaw (1992); cf. Salmeri (1998).

[75] Cf. esp. (1957) 125. This model, made even more influential by Sherwin-White's *The Roman Citizenship* (Oxford 1939; 2nd edn. 1973), is only now being challenged.

[76] Cf. (1957) 126 n. 32 for a eulogy of the 'self-denying service' of Dio and others who lavished their personal resources on their homelands.

[77] Cf. Salmeri (1982) 33 n. 109. On the meaning of 'liberal' in Rostovtzeff see below n. 90.

Dio 'preaching everywhere the new Stoic-Cynic gospel which now became his creed' (p. 119). This 'gospel' was about true kingship (*basileia*).[78] After the exile the *Kingship Orations*, which were 'repeated . . . in the most important cities of the East,[79] probably at Trajan's wish, formulated the points of Stoic doctrine which the principate accepted' (p. 121).[80]

This view of Dio as a real politican with 'liberal' policies, an adviser and emissary of a progressive Trajan, who like other Greek intellectuals 'worked for the consolidation of Roman power in the East' (p. 126), had a far-reaching influence on later interpreters. It is far away from the textual Dio of von Arnim, and also from the Dio of political theory alone, an area which was re-examined at the time of *SEHRE*'s publication by Rostovtzeff's fellow-Russian Valdenberg.[81] It is interesting to note that at the end of his work Rostovtzeff shies away from the model he had so painstakingly built and muses pessimistically on the insoluble problem of extending higher civilization to the 'masses' without debasing it.[82] The Dionian ideology of the Principate had failed.

MODERN WORK[83]

There is a dearth of work on Dio between the mid-1920s and the early 1970s. In the intervening period there are only two areas which receive extensive study, the *Euboicus* and Cynicism. Scholarship on the *Euboicus* divides into those who were attracted by its liberal morality and those more sceptical historians who dismissed its worth as

---

[78] Thomas (1909) is given as the source of this interpretation.

[79] An allusion to von Arnim's idea about multiple publication.

[80] Contrast de Ste Croix (1981) 372 the Kingship Orations give 'not the constitutional theory of the Principate, but . . . a correct description of its practice'.

[81] Valdenberg (1926–7), (1927).

[82] Rostovtzeff (1957) 541, cf. (1919) 9. Rostovtzeff has in mind, of course, the Russian Revolution and perhaps specifically the 'proletarian culture' advocated by men like his cousin, Lunacharsky (cf. again Rostovtzeff (1919)). His remarks about Dio's new 'gospel' of the Principate, quoted above, may contain more than an echo of Lunacharsky's neo-Romantic conception of the new creed of socialism (for which see Kolakowski (1978) 2: 446 f.).

[83] The positions taken in this section inevitably reflect the chapter on Dio in Swain (1996) 187–241, which presents Dio, his relations with Rome, and his conduct in the Greek world, from (what is taken to be) an Hellenic perspective.

economic evidence (which it was never Dio's intention to provide).[84] The important 1973 article by Brunt on Stoic social thought may be mentioned here, since it also focuses on *Or.* 7 as evidence of Dio's more enlightened views. These are compared with the Roman Stoic tradition exemplified by e.g. Cicero's *De Officiis* (from Panaetius), an interpretation which is also consistent with Dio as counsellor of the emperors.[85] Dio's Cynicism is subject to two different approaches, Dudley (1937) 148–58, which sensibly takes him, as Hirzel had, as an eclectic, and the more personal, complex study of Höistad (1948), which takes the *Kingship Orations* as a source of an imaginary positive Cynicism, and rejects the evidence of the *Diogenics*. The connection between Cynic 'preaching' and the early Christian message was advanced rather mechanically in a volume of parallels collected by Mussies (1972).

For the rest, largely silence, which may be seen on the one hand as part of a general reduction of interest in later Greek authors among Hellenists, and on the other as due to the domination of prosopography and epigraphy among Roman historians striving for a more scientific history.[86]

The modern era begins in earnest with three works published in 1978, John Moles's article on the 'conversion' of Dio and the books of Christopher Jones and Paolo Desideri on Dio's relationship with Rome and his role in the Empire. I start with Desideri because his long study may be regarded as the most original and comprehensive treatment of Dio to date. *Dione di Prusa. Un intellettuale greco nell'impero romano* is a very personal book. It is governed by a strong political axis, though there is nothing remotely crude about the

---

[84] Morality: notably Reuter (1932); cf. above on von Arnim, p. 31; there are elements of this approach in Rostovtzeff (1957) 370, and in the economic histories of Mazon (1943) and Kahrstedt (1954); contrast de Ste Croix (1981) 200. Sceptics: Larsen (1938) 479–81, Day (1951).

[85] Note also the literary approaches to the *Euboicus* by Highet (1973), comparing it with New Comedy, and Jouan (1977), adducing parallels in the Greek novel. In the context of Dio's imagined communities mention should also be made of Treu's 1961 study of the *Borystheniticus*.

[86] The exception to highlight here is Momigliano's short lecture of 1950—which was not published till 1969: his Dio is a Rostovtzeffian provider of a 'new [Greek] political philosophy' for Rome, but he has no understanding of the Empire and his civic orations are 'politically frivolous and immature' (barring the call to Greek dignity in the *Rhodian*; cf. Momigliano (1975)). Note also Vielmetti (1941) on the Bithynian speeches, Cytowska (1952), a detailed study of clausulae and hiatus, and Treu (1961) as in n. 85. Mention should also be made of the 'good' Loeb edition of Cohoon and Lamar Crosby (1932–51).

abundant ideas it brings forth. Indeed, it is written in a very literary style (which is not easy for slow readers of Italian like myself).
It contains a fantastic volume of information. Some of the major the-
ses are familiar from the history of Dionian scholarship, particularly
those relating to the social diffusion of second-sophistic culture and
the role of popular philosophy. Desideri is very aware of his forerunners. This comes out not in the text as such but in two crisply
written appendices, the first on Atticism and Asianism and more
generally on the new system of communication established by the
rhetorical culture of the High Empire, the second on Dio and Cynicism. In a way these are the key to understanding the whole book.

Desideri's basic position is that of an Italian Marxist intellectual.
His premiss is that the intellectual is always in the service of power.
Ideas of resistance or independence are inconceivable. Dio is a 'con-
trollore del messaggio imperiale', a messsage which is concerned
with the stability of social relations (p. 91). His Hellenism, which
Desideri stresses, cannot be taken as a challenge to Roman rule or
even as an attempt to do something for Greeks. Rather, anything
that accords with what Romans want must be pro-Roman. What is
new about Dio is his desire to extend this imperial message as widely
as possible (cf. Rostovtzeff). As for Dio's development, Desideri
proves to himself that he was always a philosopher by his careful
dating of *Or.* 32 (*Alexandrian*) to the time of Vespasian.[87] *Orr.* 31,
32, 33, 35 are also pre-exilic.[88] Already Dio is using Cynic techniques
(e.g. his call for 'naturalità' at Tarsus, *Or.* 33), but he takes care to
reposition the ideological struggle by removing it from real Cynic
street-preachers. Dio's exile is handy for Desideri because a number of 'depressive', anti-social works can be hidden in it. It is
argued that these were produced before Dio consulted the Delphic
oracle and was told of his wisdom (*Or.* 13 *In Athens, On his Exile*;
a good example of Dionian image-building). They include the attack
on tyranny and the Greek agonistic ethic in *Orr.* 6 (*Diogenes, or
On Tyranny*), 8 (*Diogenes, or On Virtue*), 9 (*Diogenes, or Isthmian
Oration*), the apparent questioning of the Aristotelian notion of
natural slavery in *Orr.* 10 (*Diogenes, or On Slaves*), 14 (*On Slavery
and Liberty* I), 15 (*On Slavery and Liberty* II), and the attacks on

---

[87] Agreeing with Jones (1973) against Kindstrand (1978). On this speech note recently
Barry (1993).

[88] Ch. 2. According to Desideri *Orr.* 33 and 35 are linked to *Or.* 32 by
'mimetismo'. Cf. Swain (1996) Appendix C.

doxa, the 'glory' or 'fame' that is the end product of the civic politics of the age, in *Orr.* 66–7 (*On Glory* I–II), and social trust in *Orr.* 73–4 (*On Trust, On Distrust*). There is in fact, of course, no evidence to date any of these speeches for certain: if we wish to psychologize their negative tone, it is equally possible to place most of them[89] at the end of Dio's political career when, as we know from *Letters* 10. 81–2 of Pliny the Younger, he was beset by serious political enmities in Prusa; or we might well hold that political philosophy can be produced at the same time as records of political action which inevitably disclose compromises and discrepancies.

Desideri's post-oracle Dio is concerned with the regulation of power and wealth in society, wishing to stop the poor from agitating by producing demagogues and to prevent the rich from making their wealth too obvious. His first move after restoration by Nerva is to deliver *Or.* 3 *On Kingship* to that emperor (ch. 4). Dio specifically says (for what it is worth) that he was unable to meet Nerva before the emperor's death (*Or.* 45. 2). Desideri dimisses this because he needs Dio to set out his idea of a new relation between emperor and intellectual at the very start of the new regime. The basis of the new relationship is the emperor's dependency on the intellectual. Desideri is not interested in the sources of the arguments Dio puts into the mouths of his *dramatis personae*: this is a literary Dio who can set out his own rules of conduct which will regulate the emperor's relationship with the ruling classes as well as intellectuals (cf. again Rostovtzeff). All of this is a well-reasoned, if subjective, reconstruction. Dio's ideas are further explored through *Or.* 36 (*Borystheniticus*). Again, the immediate context dominates discussion. The reason for this is not only Desideri's rejection of approaches led by *Quellenforschung*, but also that he does not accept von Arnim's and Wilamowitz's denial of the practical application of sophistic rhetoric. Indeed he radicalizes his own position by a highly original interpretation of what may be regarded as one of Dio's finest speeches, the *Olympicus, or On the First Envisioning of God*. Dio's rejection here of the violent attributes of Zeus in Homer's *Iliad* is aimed at Trajan's militarism. But since Trajan must be a good leader of soldiers (see *Orr.* 1–2), Dio wants to eliminate not war itself but the dualism of Hellenes versus barbarians. Once more there are shades

---

[89] But *Or.* 66 is very likely to be Domitianic, if the two houses in §6 should indeed be taken as those of the Julio-Claudians and the Flavians (which is now 'in danger').

of Rostovtzeff's liberal behind this radicalization. As Shaw has pointed out, 'liberal' for Rostovtzeff meant a set of political themes combining autocracy for all with freedom for the business and educational elite.[90] But Desideri's Dio is not quite Rostovtzeffian. He is certainly working for Trajan (he was 'una scelta quasi-obbligata' because he was untainted by the Flavian regime). On the other hand, the old teleological view of the Roman will to ethnic aggregation (Sherwin-White; Mommsen himself) is wrong (p. 421), and Dio's desire to augment Prusa (entailing the participation of non-Greeks) is part of a plan to strengthen the provincial elites against the real Roman intention of sucking them into the centre. The same policy is clear in *Orr.* 11 (*Trojan Oration*: East meets West) and 34 (the indigenous population at Tarsus).

The last chapter is entitled 'Techniques of Popular Preaching: Towards a Dionian Rhetoric'.[91] This is perhaps Desideri's most original turn. Most commentators would have started this subject with *Or.* 18, *On Training in Speech*. There has been a long debate about the addressee of this short work which gives advice on the authors to read in preparation for public speaking. Von Arnim thought it was addressed to a Greek politician. For Desideri it is addressed to Titus, hence pre-exilic, hence of no interest now. Nor is he interested in Dio's literary-critical analyses (or fragments thereof), *Orr.* 52 (*Aeschylus, Sophocles, and Euripides, or the Bow of Philoctetes*), 58 (*Achilles*), 59 (*Philoctetes*). Running through his book is a strong interest in Homer as the reference point (cf. p. 485) for Dio's thoughts on the ideal king. In this last chapter Desideri maps out the 'common territory' between speaker and audience that is formed by their mythical and historical inheritance. Several times Dio speaks of rationalizing myth for moral purposes (see esp. *Orr.* 5 *Libyan Myth*, 60 *Nessus, or Deianeira*). In the case of Homer Desideri may well be right in arguing that the task of rationalization was seen by Dio as crucial.[92] This task culminates in the *Trojan Oration*. Here the old Homeric myth of a divided world must be replaced by a new one, a process which Dio acknowledges will be painful to his audience (11. 1–5). The new message is of the harmony of East and West in a philo-Roman framework.

---

[90] Shaw (1992) 223.

[91] 'Tecnica della predicazione popolare: cenni di oratoria Dionea'. Cf. Desideri (1991*b*).

[92] For details of Dio's citation and use of Homer see Kindstrand (1973).

If there is something faintly 'Christian' about the idea of Dio as the bearer of a new message to a broad public, that is because Desideri has certainly been influenced by older work on Cynic preaching and popularization. He goes beyond this in his novel approach to the Second Sophistic as a whole. In his Appendice I he relies heavily on Higgins's 1945 attempt to prove that the distinctive features of atticizing Greek, especially the use of the optative, were actually very close to the 'living' language observable in papyrological texts.[93] In reality the optative was long dead by the time Dio used it and what we see in the papyri is simply an echo of what was being retaught to people like Dio in the schools: sociolinguists see no sharp division between the high and low varieties of a language, but rather a continuum in which the spoken and written languages of any individual will fluctuate according to social and educational constraints and aspirations. Atticism was elitist, but that is not to say that low social groups could not understand high style. Further, if we wish to see Dio as someone who desired to 'realizzare il massimo di capacità communicativa' (p. 536), we could envisage the possibility that the language in which his speeches were delivered was easier than that in which they were published (by Dio or by his editors). However, that is to miss the main point: did Dio deliberately seek out and address the *popolo minuto*? Desideri has posed the central problem of the nature and the extent of communication between mass and elite in this age better than anyone else. He links this to the further problem of how pagan culture was transformed into 'una civiltà pagano-cristiana' (p. 526). If, he says, classicizing rhetoric was the sphere of a self-serving elite in decline (the view of Rohde, etc.), Christian culture had to start again; if classicizing rhetoric was firmly rooted in real political practice and in particular functioned as a vehicle for communicating with the masses, we can maintain a continuity between pagan and Christian discourse. Differences aside, both elites wished to 'realizzare un'egemonia culturale sulle masse, di senso fondamentalmente normativo' (p. 536).

The mythical-historical thematic is a key element in the practice exercises of the schools which prepared members of the second-sophistic elite for public communication. This thematic also plays a key role in real political oratory; the chapters on political rhetoric

---

[93] For a summary of Higgins and his opponents, esp. Gerhard Anlauf, see Reardon (1971) 80–96.

in Plutarch's *Political Advice* are proof of this, if it is needed.[94] But
the complex, allusive, and frequently ironic sets of ideas Dio places
on the back of this thematic regarding liberty, slavery, wealth,
beauty, fame, trust—the subjects Dio 'preached' on—surely make
it rather likely that he was addressing social peers. To try to understand what Dio might have been doing in the *Trojan Oration* (say)
is the province of the educated, ancient and modern. Most scholars
would agree that there are many close parallels between the pagan
and Christian thought worlds, which do not however allow us to
suppose a convergence. Nor for that matter is there clear evidence
of a desire on Dio's part to transcend the traditional Hellene–barbarian opposition (which is partly an economic division). So far as
we know he never pronounced on the subject.

Desideri's Dio is a political-ideological animal. Christopher
Jones's Dio is on the surface at least a politician without ideology.
Rather Dio's interest in political philosophy as (briefly) a Cynic and
later a Stoic is subordinate to his role as a guide to his times and
especially to the life of the Greek cities in which he lived and spoke
('the theater of most of his public activity', p. vi). The intellectual
formation of *The Roman World of Dio Chrysostom* owes much to
the disciplines of prosopography and epigraphy, which have dominated Roman history during the last half century and more. The
prosopography of Dio is in fact exiguous; scholars are reduced to
arguing about the identity of the prominent Roman whose down-
fall caused Dio's exile: Flavius Sabinus or (as is now felt more likely)
Salvius Otho Cocceianus?[95] It is the *Tendenz* of prosopography that
is relevant here. Prosopographical history was developed by Roman
historians interested in the career patterns of Roman senators,
equestrians, and military ranks. These interests reflect the nature of
the evidence. The result is to emphasize Roman links, and in some
cases this may well distort overall attitudes and beliefs of individuals and groups. Jones's 1971 study of Plutarch, which his *Dio* 'complements', is a good case in point. Hence Jones is not interested in
Dio as a Greek or in his Hellenism or in the political thought that
may be the manifestation of this. At the same time, the Roman emphasis gives the book considerable strengths and ensures its value as an

---

[94] Cf. Swain (1996) 164, 167–8.
[95] For the latter (Pliny the Younger reports Dio's name as 'Cocceianus Dio' at
Letters 10. 81. 1) see Sidebottom (1996). For another (less likely) candidate see B.
W. Jones (1990).

examination of the workings of provincial cities and of the contacts between the cities and Rome. The principal source of evidence for provincial imperial and local government is a very large number of civic inscriptions. The greatest student of these texts, Louis Robert, is a constant presence in Jones's footnotes.

Jones, then, is not interested in advancing the sort of ideas suggested by Desideri; but many would say his book is better for it.[96] His examination of the civic life of the Greek city proceeds in tandem with Dio's own life. The exile constitutes a major division (Jones sensibly denies any philosophic conversion). The book starts with the time-honoured problem of Dio the sophist. One of the demerits of prosopography is the pressure to put individuals in productive relationships. Thus Dio's attacks on philosophers, as reported by Synesius, lead Jones ineluctably to assume that he became a 'courtier of the Flavians' (p. 14). Fortunately the scope for such reconstructions is limited. The brief comments on the *Trojan Oration* again reveal the method's limitations: there is no epigraphical context to fasten on, hence a rather important speech is more or less ignored. By contrast the strengths of Jones's approach are immediately clear in chapter 2, which is built around *Or.* 46 (traditional title: *Before a Philosophical Career, In his Fatherland*). From what Dio tells us of his family this speech must be early. Jones's interest is in its subject-matter, Dio's response to a bread-riot, which is a good jumping-off point for the mechanics of food distribution and other aspects of the 'life, thought, and language of a Greek city of the first century' (25).

Jones's method of teasing out this information via a detailed summary of a given speech is repeated in the following chapters for *Orr.* 31 (*Rhodian Oration*), 32 (*Alexandrian*), where his belief in a pre-exile date determines the content of the analysis, 35 (*To Celaenae in Phrygia*), Dio's sarcastic look at the imperial cult and provincial jurisdiction, 33–4 (the *Tarsian Orations* I–II), speeches in Bithynia (esp. *Or.* 38 *To the Nicomedians, On Concord with the Nicaeans*) and at Prusa illustrating in detail the internal political life of a Greek city. All of this is done very well. Yet there is always a sense that Dio himself is somewhat peripheral. The chosen method certainly does not work with the *Euboean* (*Or.* 7) and the *Borystheniticus* (*Or.* 36), which are studied in chapter 7. These speeches are central to Dio's

[96] Cf. Reardon (1983).

conception of urban life and especially the correct spiritual values of the human community as a reflection of the divine. On one level Jones may be praised for refusing to rehearse old arguments about Dio's attitudes to the lower classes or the influence of Mithraic lore. Yet the relatively small quantity of historical background material that can be extracted from the speeches is unsatisfying on its own and it would have been interesting to have put his very different, Roman world view together with the traditional focuses.

The concord speeches, *Or.* 38, 39 (*On Concord in Nicaea*), 40 (*On Concord with the Apameans*), 41 (*To the Apameans, On Concord*), and part of *Or.* 34 (second *Tarsic Oration*) are Dio's most appealing addresses to the cities. Concord (*homonoia*, literally 'like-mindedness') is a widely used political slogan at this time. It appears on inscriptions and coins and in the political writings of Plutarch and Aelius Aristides. Jones is very good at explicating the historical background, including the technical terms used by Dio. But his approach tends to remove Dio from the Hellenic context that allows us to look behind the surface of the Greek city. The advertisement of concord was a classic way of maintaining the status quo, both between peers (e.g. between different city-states) and between different classes inside one city (*Orr.* 34, 39). It is not a neutral exercise in political sociology, but a clue to a real network of political attitudes and practices. Some may feel that Jones, who has been one of a few to have discussed the subject at length, misses the wood for the trees.[97]

Ultimately Jones's approaches filter Dio through a Roman prism. The *Kingship Orations* are, to be sure, among the most difficult of all Dio's works. Jones treads cautiously in addressing the major problem of whether they were specifically aimed at Trajan (or even delivered to him) or whether they represent 'eternal norms' against which Trajan must be measured rather than 'a registration of existing facts'.[98] He comes down in favour of actuality, being tempted occasionally to push prosopographical linkages rather too far.[99] In

[97] The same can be said of the important article by Andrei (1981). Kienast (1971), which makes *Or.* 34 into a directive of Trajan, is in the same vein. On concord in Dio see Kienast (1995), arguing against mainstream opinion that precise agreements were involved in concord agreements between states. Note also Bravo-García (1973), Sheppard (1984–6).

[98] Jones (1978) 115 n. 7 citing Rostovtzeff (1926) 120, Momigliano (1969) 263.

[99] E.g. Dio's commendation of hunting at *Or.* 3. 135 must be for the attention of the real, and not an ideal, emperor because Trajan hunted and because Arrian hunted in Baetica whence Trajan came, 120 n. 43.

fact we do not know. There are many possible links. However, the Roman-led approach inhibits another line of enquiry, that the speeches and Dio's alleged friendship with Trajan were (also) vehicles of political praxis at home in Bithynia. One thing is sure: in Trajan's letter to Pliny about Dio, there is no sign of friendship or even acquaintance (Pliny, *Letters* 10. 82).

Leaving Moles aside for one moment and staying with the historians, the next major work to mention is Giovanni Salmeri's 1982 monograph, *La politica e il potere. Saggio su Dione di Prusa*.[100] This has more in common with Jones than with Desideri, since Salmeri is not interested in imposing any ideological model.[101] But it is more successful than Jones because Salmeri does not present Dio through a Romanocentric frame. The first chapter, 'Family, Career, Patrimony', is a very good exposition of Dio's development as a rhetor 'con vaste conoscenze filosofiche' (p. 26). Salmeri adverts to Desideri when he concludes on Dio's political activity, and especially the planned *sunoikismos*, that it would be vain to try to discern 'ampie prospettive politiche e programmi a lungo termine'. Dio's politics are, in a neat Italian metaphor, a 'barcamenarsi', literally 'leading one's boat back and forth' (implying tergiversation), steering a course between local difficulties and opportunities. In the next chapter Dio is used as a springboard to explore the economy and politics of Bithynia. The result is a very successful overall picture, which includes a good study of the *Euboean Oration* (7). In the final chapter, 'The Greek Cities and the Empire', Salmeri concentrates on Dio himself. His politics are informed by a desire to maintain *homonoia* and *eutaxia* ('good order', another slogan of the time). He is close to the mark when he speaks here of Dio's '[v]isione politica ristretta e di conservazione' (p. 95). He is careful to put Dio in the Hellenic context Dio himself stresses (*Orr.* 43. 3, 44. 9, 50. 2). Dio is not an agent of the emperor, nor is he concerned with the extension of the citizen base to non-Greeks. Moreover it is much to Salmeri's credit that for the first time in regard to Dio he questions the idea of a cosy Graeco-Roman unit. Both Plutarch and Dio voice 'harsh words and criticism' against the boorishness and rudeness of their masters. On the other hand there is no 'true polemic' against the Romans, for the references

---

[100] Cf. Salmeri (1980).
[101] The model is rather the historical situation of the *Mezzogiorno* aristocracies and the contemporary pragmatic politics of the late Aldo Moro, especially in response to American pressure on Italy in the 1970s (pers. comm.).

are 'essentially moral in character'. Salmeri quotes with great approval
the verdict of Paul Veyne in *Le Pain et le cirque*: 'Dio of Prusa was
at once fiercely nationalistic and an unconditional supporter of
Imperial authority' (110–12).[102] This leads to a discussion of the
Kingship Orations (which Veyne makes good use of in his study of
euergetism to support various generalizations about the beneficent
emperor).

There is a problem of method here. If the essentially ethical set
of comments in the *Kingship Orations* are believed to have been
addressed directly to the real emperor and therefore have a contemporary political charge, should we not allow that moral disapproba-
tion of Rome, where it occurs, must also have a political charge?
The political meaning of Dio's philosophic rhetoric is the subject
of an important article by Marie-Henriette Quet, published in
1978; its conclusions were used in a further piece published in 1981.
The earlier article uses the evidence of Dio and Plutarch to ask how
stock moral examples, metaphors, and comparisons enabled orators
to 'agir sur l'imaginaire collectif' (p. 56). Dio's images, including his
favoured comparison of the state to a ship (cf. *Or.* 34. 16), may be
plotted in 'une grille culturelle qui donne un autre sens aux actes'
(p. 75). This 'grid' is totally Hellenic. Although Quet is not much
concerned with the *Kingship Orations*, the results may clearly be
applied to them too. This picture is reinforced in the 1981 piece on
the festivals which played so important a role in managing civic
stability and which were among the most tangible benefactions of
the wealthy citizens. Louis Robert expressed the view that Dio the
philosopher's covert criticism of gladiatorial games, especially in *Or.*
66 (*On Glory* I) and *Or.* 31 (*Rhodian Oration*), made him unrep-
resentative of his class because these games were intrinsic parts of
the world of the festival, especially festivals linked with Roman institutions like the imperial cult, and Dio's peers must have accepted
them.[103] In reply to this Quet obverves, '[l]'exemple de Dion de Pruse
me semble témoigner que l'on pouvait alors, sans se sentir incohérent,
parler comme un moraliste et agir à l'occasion comme un évergète'
(p. 62).

What we see in Dio's writings is an ideal, moral politics which
was restricted in its expression for the most part to elite audiences
who understood its value and scope. There is also the pragmatic

---

[102] Veyne (1990) 40 (= (1976) 108).   [103] Robert (1940a) 253.

politics (Salmeri's 'barcamenarsi') of living in a city, dealing with the masses, dealing with Rome. Both styles can coexist with instances of awkwardness kept to a minimum. Dio in fact makes pretty strong attacks on the behaviour of Roman provincial governors (*Orr.* 34. 15, 38–42; 38. 33–8; 43. 11–12; 45. 4–5), attacks which Jones and Desideri ignore or smooth over. He focuses on political interference by the governors for their own ends. It would be difficult to deny that he judges the system itself to be corrupt. He did not dream of overthrowing the Empire: if he accepted the Stoic cosmology he employs in *Orr.* 12 (*Olympicus*) and 36 (*Borystheniticus*),[104] the Roman Empire was arguably an inevitable creation of the divine mind. Moreover, on a pragmatic level he was not such a fool as to attack the Empire or the emperor. He wanted the Empire to advance his class and his culture. The *Kingship Orations* are his main expression of this desire (cf. especially the stress in *Or.* 3 on the emperor's need to draw on the whole Empire for his friends and officials).[105] The message may well have been intended for the centre.[106] It was certainly also addressed to his own kind in the Greek East as proof that the philosopher could persuade the king.[107]

Any reader of the *Kingship Orations* must also be a reader of John Moles's literary studies of them.[108] Moles's first piece on Dio was his 1978 article in which (cf. Jones, Desideri) he rejected by close argument Synesius' analysis of Dio's 'career and conversion', and cogently explored Dio's use of the leading Cynic and Stoic *personae* (Socrates, Heracles, Odysseus) as masks. Nevertheless he took a standard view of Dio as a courtier of the Flavians and adviser to Trajan. The work on the *Kingship Orations* follows from this. Rostovtzeff gives a fair summary of Dio's king: he is selected by Providence, he sees power as a duty, his job is toil rather than pleasure, he is not a master (*despotēs*), but a benefactor (*euergetēs*), his subjects are free,

---

[104] Note also the lost work, *Is the Cosmos Perishable?*, known from the Suda—clearly Stoic (but of course *possibly* anti-Stoic) from its title, but quite possibly rhetorical rather than philosophical.

[105] *Or.* 3. 86–132.

[106] But note again Trajan's 'cool detachment' (Salmeri (1982) 125) towards Dio in his letter to Pliny.

[107] Dio's presentation of himself as a philosopher and his advice to the Roman king under this guise are the subject of Sidebottom's 1990 dissertation, which draws too heavily on cultural anthropology to enliven the topic. For more speculative but traditional historical work see Sheppard (1982) (with Moles (1983*b*)), (1984), (1984–6) on concord (cf. above, n. 97).

[108] See also Charles-Saget (1986).

he is a friend to both civilians and soldiers, he fights wars and promotes peace, and he surrounds himself with noble friends and counsellors.[109] These are the 'eternal norms' to which Trajan had to conform. The interpretation of the *Kingship Orations* depends to a large extent on the problem of Dio's relationship with Trajan. Only the first and third are actual addresses, which are usually held to have been delivered before him at Rome.[110] The other two are dialogues, which could have been sent to him. The flattery of the addressee at 1. 36 and 3. 1–24 makes it easier to believe in delivery. But the critical, admonitory tone of the fourth Oration, a dialogue between Diogenes the Cynic (= Dio) and Alexander the Great (= Trajan), makes perusal by the emperor improbable. Moles's originality lies partly in his redirection of the old debate about the Cynic or Stoic sources of these works. He argues strongly for Cynicism, and in this way seeks to circumvent the problematical candidness of the fourth Oration.[111] But this focus does not detract from a very close reading of the texts themselves and their language, and this is another part of Moles's contribution. His method is the robustly cumulative one of drawing together key words and ideas to build up a picture that brooks no disagreement. The best illustration of this is his 1990 article, which is practically a monograph in itself. The Dio that emerges from Moles's pen speaks with Trajan, not 'eternal norms', in mind. It is only natural that he is rather pro-Roman.[112]

Moles's interest in Dio's Cynicism (and in Cynicism as a whole) is part of a wider modern revival of interest in this philosophy, especially in France and Italy.[113] With regard to Dio,[114] one of the most important contributors has been Aldo Brancacci. He began in a 1977 article on the problems of recovering genuine *Cynica* from the *Diogenics*, sensibly pointing to the literary nature of Dio's blend of dialogue cum *chreia*.[115] These thoughts were advanced and refined

[109] Rostovtzeff (1957) 120.

[110] Cf. 1. 5, 36, 49; 3. 1–3, 25. On Trajan as the addressee of *Or.* 3 (the usual interpretation) see Moles (1984) against Desideri.

[111] Esp. Moles (1983*a*). Others have suggested that the critique was saved for another, later audience (e.g. Lepper (1948) 195–7).

[112] Moles has more recently done an about-turn here: Moles (1995), and cf. below, p. 209.

[113] It is worth noting the vitality of the Christian-Cynic axis in the influential work of F. Gerald Downing: see Downing (1988), (1993).

[114] See Billerbeck (1996) 211–13 for a summary of recent work.

[115] On the futility of searching for authentic Cynic philosophy in these speeches cf. Szarmach (1977), again emphasizing Dio's fondness for *chreiai*.

in a careful 1980 article on the composition of the speeches and in his well-received 1985 book on Dio's *Nachleben*, and in a more recent piece (1992) which argues for Antisthenes as a major source of the third *Kingship Oration* (cf. Moles).[116] Brancacci's book is a thorough examination of the reception of Dio from the second century to the fourteenth, exploring the constitution of the corpus at each stage and following changing interests in Dio as a model of style and, in the Byzantine age, as a useful source of political ideals. It makes it plain that the story of Dio is also the story of the continuing debate between rhetoric and philosophy, at least until Late Antiquity. François Jouan's 1993 chapter in a collection of papers on Cynicism marks an advance on previous work by looking at how Dio characterizes his Diogenes.[117] He is essentially an intellectual agent; shocking details from his life are mostly omitted apart from his 'signature' of public masturbation and defecation (*Orr.* 6. 17–20 and 8. 36). Jouan correctly observes that Dio needed Diogenes because he was a great figure from the past and one with the right values (cf. Socrates, Heracles, Odysseus), even if some of the values dear to Dio do not reflect the real Diogenes (who was never interested in e.g. *eunoia* and *philia*). In sum Dio put Cynicism back on the agenda for 'les milieux cultivés' (p. 397).[118]

The literary Dio has not been entirely neglected in recent work. A word-index was published in 1981.[119] There is a worthwhile monograph by Luzzatto (1983) on *Or.* 52. This short speech is a literary discussion of the three tragedians' handling of the Philoctetes story. Luzzatto explicates it in terms of the stylistic judgements made in the rhetorical handbooks about what literature was worth reading, and the views of the grammarians, which survive as scholia and plot-summaries. A far more important contribution to Dio as literature is Donald Russell's 1992 commentary on *Orr.* 7, 12, and 36, the three speeches which contain the main elements of Dio's Stoicizing thoughts on the relation of the human and the divine community.[120] Russell has done scholars and students of Dio a good turn by making

---

[116] See also Brancacci (1994) 442–55 for a good discussion of imperial Cynic literature, esp. in Dio and Lucian.

[117] Jouan (1993*a*).

[118] Note also Hahn (1989) 157–60, 160–71 on Dio's civic activities as a philosopher at home and abroad.

[119] Koolmeister and Tallmeister (1981).

[120] See also Schofield (1991) esp. 57–64, 84–91.

these important works accessible through a literary and linguistic commentary.[121]

Finally, Dio's views on sex and gender have started to receive notice in recent years. Karin Blomqvist published a reasonable 1989 dissertation on Dio's attitudes towards women. This contains a comprehensive review of the evidence (with particular reference to *Orr.* 7, 11, and 61), and argues that Dio, as a product of his age, portrayed women more positively than many (male scholars) have assumed. Foucault himself did not discuss Dio in *The Care of the Self*.[122] But this extraordinarily influential book has been the starting point for scattered comments in Winkler (1990), Halperin (1990), Gleason (1995), Swain (1994) and (1996), and for a recent important treatment by Houser (1998).[123]

WORK IN THIS VOLUME

This collection begins with four chapters on aspects of the social and political background to Dio's writings. Giovanni Salmeri presents a comprehensive and up-to-date survey of provincial life and Dio's role in it at the turn of the second century. This offers historians a wealth of detailed knowledge of the period and its problems, which is the indispensable basis of interpreting Dio's own views. Paolo Desideri in Chapter 3 reflects his long-standing interest in the development of Dio's ideas. Careful as ever to base himself on the chronology of Dio's works, while alive to the difficulty of so doing, he explores the particular opposition in Dio between town and country and tries to make sense of a set of quite negative remarks about urban life on the one hand and another (later) group of realistic and positive attitudes on the other. The change is seen as part of Dio's response to possible changes in the wider Roman attitude to the Greek city with the advent of the Antonine emperors. Dio, as we have seen, expended much thought on the theoretical formation of the city. Political oratory was his forte. These interests intersect in the imagined assembly debate in the *Euboicus*, which is

---

[121] Note also Whitmarsh (1998) on *paideia* in Dio and his peers.

[122] Foucault (1986).

[123] Houser argues against the (too generalized) view of Swain and others that Dio condemned male homosexuality outright, starting from *Or.* 3. 98–9 (where the assumption that men are interested in both women and boys is surely a simple, illustrative example of Dio's main argument).

the starting-point of John Ma's chapter. The *Euboicus* has been mentioned frequently in the preceding pages. Ma sidesteps the question of reality versus fiction and looks at how Dio imagines real political oratory in action and how we relate his imagination both to classical models and to contemporary epigraphical and papyrological records. His stress on the continuation of real political life in the cities of Dio's era is central also to Salmeri in Chapter 2. Finally, in this section, Richard Hawley surveys Dio's civic community from the key perspective of marriage, gender, and family, bringing out nicely the blend of contemporary observation and classical tradition that is so typical of him. It is plain from Hawley's chapter that there is much more to be done in this area.

Within second-sophistic literature Dio's best pieces are first rate; yet they cannot be said to be well known.[124] The next section of this volume turns to Dio's originality and inventiveness as a writer. Graham Anderson has chosen to look at the way in which Dio constructs stories, especially in his main works (including the *Euboicus*), and at how he confects new versions (for example, in the first *Kingship Oration*) to entertain and, above all, to teach (with consequences for his literary profile). Suzanne Saïd writes on myth as a structuring element in Dionian discourse and one which serves as a vehicle for creative rewriting, for moral disquisition and allegory, and for literary criticism. She exemplifies her conclusions with a detailed study of how Dio handles the saga of Troy in the *Trojan Oration* (and how modern scholars have handled Dio). John Moles takes this further with a study of a complex and neglected work of the highest literary quality, the *Charidemus*. He argues convincingly by means of a Molesian 'close reading' that it reflects very personal experiences of Dio. If he is right, as he surely is, we have a consolatory piece that is extremely moving and ranks in the power of its writing with the *Kingship Orations*, the *Troicus*, *Olympicus*, and *Borystheniticus*, as well as the great political speeches at Alexandria, Celaenae,[125] Rhodes, and Tarsus.

---

[124] Even as sharp a commentator as Goldhill can dismiss Dio in a study of the Greek novelists who were his contemporaries with the aside that 'few would accuse [him] of sharing the sly knowingness of Achilles Tatius' ((1995) 123 on the *Euboicus*): comparison is unfair to both authors, since their aims are so different, but the quality of Dio's writing and the skill needed to read him put him far beyond the Greek novel.

[125] On which cf. recently Zambrini (1994).

I should like to thank Aldo Brancacci for his comments, and esp. for his information on de Bréquigny and Leopardi, and also Rees Davies, George Holmes, and Bryan Reardon.

The pessimism which is evident at the end of the *Olympicus* and through the first part of the *Charidemus* is often countered by a more positive view of human society, especially in the later works, which is part of Dio's philosophical inheritance. His philosophical models have long been debated, and in our last section Michael Trapp and Aldo Brancacci express rather different positions on the sources of one of Dio's principal *personae*, Socrates. Socrates was the 'common property' of Stoics, Cynics, and, of course, Platonists. Brancacci comes at this from a philosophical angle: like Moles and others he emphasizes the Antisthenic, practical colouring of Dio's Socrates. Trapp amply charts Dio's extensive literary debt to Plato and to Plato's presentation of Socrates. Both contain resonances of the great debate about the possibility of using Dio as a source to construct lost Cynic thought. The practical aspects of Dio's philosophy are further explored by Frederick Brenk. He looks at the concept of self-sufficiency (*autarkeia*), the desire and ability to lead a simple philosopher's life, and how far this could be squared with the real life of an urban notable. This goes right to the heart of the problem of how far individuals supply their own needs and how far they depend on community, a problem which is never far from Dio's mind.

PART TWO

Politics

Politics

2

Dio, Rome, and the Civic Life of Asia Minor

GIOVANNI SALMERI

IMPERIAL AND LOCAL SERVICE

The title of a recent study by Greg Woolf, *Becoming Roman, Staying Greek*,[1] eschewing as it does so outworn a term as 'Romanization',[2] may be taken as fairly representative of the approach—showing particular sensitivity to the aspect of 'mentality'[3]—that now seems to be prevailing in studies on the impact that Roman power had on the Greek world from the century of conquest to the third century AD. Nevertheless, Woolf's statement that 'Greeks felt themselves to be Greeks, in a sense that was not wholly compatible with being Roman, while at the same time adopting much Roman material culture'[4] does not, altogether, go much further than the conclusions of previous research which limited Roman influence on the Greek world to the adoption of gladiatorial games and certain types of buildings like the bath–gymnasium complexes.[5] Nor does it seem to give much weight to the significant changes that centuries of Roman control, in areas such as Asia Minor, eventually brought about in the conduct of city politics and in the making and advancement of the ruling class.

---

[1] Woolf (1994).
[2] In this connection, cf. in particular Freeman (1997) 10, who sees the notion of 'Romanization' as 'more an academic construct than an incontrovertible reality', and Webster (1996), who criticizes the rigidly one-way view, i.e. from Rome to the provinces, usually taken in describing so-called processes of Romanization; cf. also Millet (1990), Freeman (1996), Hingley (1996), Alcock (1997*b*), Woolf (1998). There are also a number of interesting works taking the more traditional approach to Romanization, including Gozzoli (1987), and above all Brunt (1976).
[3] Cf. Woolf (1994) 118.   [4] Woolf (1994) 128.
[5] Cf. Robert (1940*a*), Millar (1987) and, in particular for influences in the field of architecture, all the contributions contained in Macready and Thompson (1987).

While it is, of course, true that we find rather less evidence of the
Roman presence in Asia Minor than in the western provinces for
both the Republican and the imperial age—limited use was made of
Latin, for example[6]—there are certainly no grounds for concluding
that Rome had no definite policy, or that it deferred supinely to the
'guidance' of the Greeks and their traditions. Indeed, the economic
importance of the Hellenic East had been clear enough to Rome since
the early second century BC.[7] So it was that, once Attalus III had
bequeathed the kingdom of Pergamum to Rome and the province
of Asia had been constituted, along with the *publicani* came a great
many Italian *negotiatores* to exploit its resources. Indeed, by the year
88 BC, when Mithridates instigated their massacre in the cities of Asia,
they already numbered several thousand.[8] During the imperial age,
moreover, tax revenue from Asia Minor—and from the province
of Asia in particular—represented a significant contribution to the
Empire's budget.[9] Just as Rome was adept at safeguarding its economic

---

[6] Cf. Balsdon (1979) 131–5, Brixhe (1987) 7–11, Swain (1996) 40–1, Rochette (1997).
Indicative of the limited diffusion of Latin in Asia Minor is, among other things, the
fact that, in the time of Trajan, in one of the few Roman colonies in the area, Apamea
of Bithynia, Dio addressed the council and the assembly in Greek (*Or.* 41. 1; cf. Jones
(1978) 93, Pino Polo (1989) 102–5); thus it is hardly surprising that well into the third
century AD the colony of Cremna in Pisidia should have raised statues to Heracles,
Nemesis, Athena, Hygieia, and Asclepius, setting on their bases inscriptions in
Greek including the name of the *duoviri*, following a formula that is certainly not
the canonical Roman one (cf. Horsley (1987), Mitchell (1995) 156–8). Moreover admin-
istrators arriving from Rome in the provinces of Asia Minor consistently used
Greek; this was also the language used before tribunals (although not normally for
sentencing): cf. Balsdon (1979) 133, Kaimio (1979) 110 ff., Brixhe (1987) 7.
[7] The tendency to rule out the idea of a real strategy in Rome's intervention in
the Hellenistic world during the period 229–146 BC marks a limitation in Gruen (1984)
(cf. now Gruen (1998)), although he does have a number of stimulating points to
make, especially when dealing with Hellenistic foreign policy and diplomatic tools
such as *summachia* and *philia*, still vital in the second century BC, and to some extent
able to regulate the behaviour of Rome when it came on the scene. On the work, cf.
Salmeri (1987), Gabba (1987). On the Roman presence in the Greek world subsequent to the period dealt with by Gruen, again taking a non-mechanistic viewpoint
with attention to individual cases, cf. Sherwin-White (1984), down to the beginning of
the first century AD; Kallet-Marx (1995), down to 62 BC. Central to the whole question remains Veyne (1975), who offers a clear picture of Rome's capacity to take advantage of the conflicts between Hellenistic states. For Rome's interest in the economic
aspects, cf. Cassola (1962) 56–71; Gabba (1987), esp. 209, (1988) 93, (1990) 207–8.
[8] App. *Mithr.* 22–5; cf. Sherwin-White (1984) 121–31 (esp. 124), 240, important
for the new chronological order of events in Asia Minor between 90 and 88 BC and
for attention to the behaviour of cities not adhering to Mithridates' line, on which
cf. now Campanile (1996).
[9] Hopkins (1980) 101 ff.; cf. also Duncan-Jones (1990) 191–2, who points up the
difficulties in defining the nature of taxation—in money or in kind?—in the
province of Asia during the early years of the Empire.

interests, it also realized that the system of government adopted in Spain and Gaul would not do for an area like Asia Minor which was marked by robust development and urbanization, especially along the Aegean coast. Taking a line of intervention that might be defined as 'intrusive' or indirect,[10] it let the numerous Greek cities and their political structures live on. In the Republican age Roman intervention often went no further than establishing life membership of the city councils, thus fostering the consolidation of a local ruling class that was loyal to the centre and could take charge of internal law and order.[11] As for the less urbanized—or in other words less Hellenized —areas, broadly speaking, until the end of the Julio-Claudians Rome refrained from direct intervention, entrusting its interests to certain local dynasts who were, however, Greek in culture and urban in mentality.[12]

Thus in Asia Minor Rome was represented not only by the governors but also by the notables of the Greek cities. Building on the structures of the Hellenistic kingdoms, Rome maintained the *poleis* within a wide-reaching framework under a unified administration,[13] which enabled them to shake off some of the isolationist tendencies typical of the classical *polis*. To some extent the ground was prepared for the growth of a united Hellenic consciousness, at least at the cultural level.[14] At the same time, however, given the considerable

---

[10] For distinction between actively 'interventionist' and 'intrusive' imperial policy and for definition of the notion of intrusiveness, cf. Alcock (1997) 2–3.

[11] On the intervention of T. Quinctius Flamininus in Thessaly, Livy (34. 51. 6) tells us, 'a censu maxime et senatum et iudices legit potentioremque eam partem civitatis fecit cui salva et tranquilla omnia esse expediebat'; in the cities of Bithynia, as the province was being formed in 64 BC, Pompey departed from the ancient Greek traditions making the *boule* a permanent body and opening it up to ex-magistrates and citizens over the age of thirty entitled to public appointments: Pliny, *Ep.* 10. 79, 80 (on which see Sherwin-White (1966) 528, Salmeri (1982) 11–12, Woolf (1994) 123). In general, cf. Jones (1940) 171, Ste. Croix (1981) 519–21, Bernhardt (1985) 282–4, Quass (1993) 81 ff., 387–94, Müller (1995). Both Bernhardt and Quass rightly stress the relative continuity in the basic structures of civic political life in the Greek world between the Hellenistic and Roman periods; by contrast Gauthier (1985) sees political life in the Greek cities as still essentially bound up with the old canons of the classical age in the fourth and third centuries BC, considering the formation of a class of notables in the first half of the second century BC as something of a novelty. Some acute perceptions on late Hellenistic political life can be found in Habicht (1995). In the early second century AD Pliny the Younger, in one of his letters to Trajan from Bithynia (*Ep.* 10. 79. 3), explicitly states the guideline followed by the Romans in the formation of a ruling class loyal to them, especially in Asia Minor, namely that it is 'aliquanto melius honestorum hominum liberos quam e plebe in curiam admitti': cf. Salmeri (1982) 37.

[12] Cf. Braund (1984), Gozzoli (1987) 81–2.   [13] Cf. Davies (1984) 304 ff.

[14] Salmeri (1987) 793, (1991) 575.

political responsibility they were entrusted with, the notables of Asia Minor found their ties with their native cities strengthening, and with them the desire to spend the rest of their lives in their homeland,[15] following a pattern unparalleled in the western provinces.

Indicative of this state of affairs is the fact that Narbonensis sent its men to the Senate well ahead of Asia, although the latter had been created a province some years before Narbonensis in 129 BC.[16] By the early second century AD, under the rule of Trajan, the entry of Greeks from the eastern provinces of the Empire into the Roman Senate, whose threshold they had started crossing in meaningful numbers under the Flavians, was at any rate a consolidated process, ratifying the social standing of the dynasts and city notables to whom Rome had looked for support in controlling the area.[17] The process was to some extent fostered by emperors like Vespasian and Trajan, but their intervention and choices cannot be taken as decisive;[18]

[15] Cf. Quass (1982) 188 ff.

[16] The point is discussed—taking into account the various forms of Roman intervention in the two provinces—in Salmeri (1991) 563–9.

[17] Halfmann (1979) 73 ff., Salmeri (1991) 564–5, 571–2. The presence of the Mytilenean Greek, Q. Pompeius Macer (grandson of Theophanes, the historian close to Pompey), in the Senate as early as the age of Augustus does not seem to have set any trend, at least until the age of Vespasian: cf. Halfmann (1979) 78, and below, nn. 18–20. Following on Rostovtzeff (1957) 1: 113–14 and 2: 585 n. 10 and Walton (1929), who approached the subject of the Greek senators from the eastern part of the Empire respectively from the broadly cultural and prosopographical viewpoints (cf. Salmeri (1998) 69 n. 50), Syme (1958) returned to the subject with some extraordinary insights (504–19: 'Tacitus and the Greeks'; cf. Syme (1982*a*) 183: 'Senators from the Eastern provinces, that is a large theme and attractive, a long story') that have stirred a new interest in the culture and political role of the Greeks under the Empire: cf. in the first place Bowersock (1965), (1969), and (1997). Bowie (1974), (1982) approaches the subject from a viewpoint that has more to do with literary than political or social aspects, tending to downplay the influence and significance of Greek intellectuals in the Roman Empire; in this connection see also Brunt (1994). Of recent works, cf. Swain (1996) and Schmitz (1997). With regard to the definition of senators hailing from the eastern part of the Empire as Greeks rather than Orientals as in Walton 1929 (cf. also Syme (1958) 510), cf. Millar (1964) 9 n. 7, 182–3, and Said (1978) on 'Orientalism' in European nineteenth- and twentieth-century culture. Moreover, definition of the senators in question as Greeks is not a matter of geographical origin, and even less of race, but of language and culture, which we see as the most significant aspects for attribution of Greek identity in the imperial age: cf. Swain (1996) 9–11, 192 n. 21; Birley (1997) 228, on the other hand, does not seem to have got the full measure of the problem.

[18] In particular, Vespasian—proclaimed by the legions of the eastern part of the Empire—introduced into the Senate a number of experienced officers and notable citizens of local origin, while Trajan showed particular sensitivity to the glamour of the great dynastic families, an attitude possibly dating from the 70s AD when, still a young man, he accompanied his father who held office first as a legate in Syria,

they should rather be understood in the light of the approach to domination—intrusive in nature—that Rome adopted in the Hellenic East and in Asia Minor in particular.

So it was that the first to leave Asia Minor for the Senate did not hail from the *poleis*, but from the few Roman colonies, and seem to have been of Italian descent, such as the Sergii Paulli of Pisidian Antioch and T. Junius Montanus of Alexandria Troas, *consul suffectus* in 81. Nevertheless, in 92 the same office went to a Greek, Ti. Julius Celsus Polemaeanus, who belonged to a family of priests of Rome hailing from Sardis; entering the Senate under Vespasian, he was subsequently to be appointed proconsul of Asia under Trajan, possibly in 105/6. Celsus' son, Aquila, was also to be made *suffectus* in 110, although he is certainly remembered more as the builder of the famous library his father envisioned for Ephesus. Under Vespasian the Senate also saw the entry of a descendant of a family of the high nobility of Pergamum, C. Antius A. Iulius Quadratus, who was appointed *consul ordinarius* in 105 and proconsul of Asia in 109/10, while under Domitian C. Iulius Quadratus Bassus became a senator. He too was from Pergamum, and of royal blood, but above all was celebrated as a valorous general; he died in Dacia in 117.[19]

Apart from these noteworthy examples, we know of close on ten men who came from Asia Minor to enter the Senate under the Flavians,[20] again from the colonies or from the families of the high nobility. With Trajan this tendency seems to have become well-established: the ranks of senators were joined among others by

and subsequently as proconsul in Asia: cf. Syme (1985) 350. In principle, however, in the historical interpretation of the selection processes bringing new men to the Senate from outside Italy the emphasis should go not so much on the intervention and patronage of the emperor (cf. Millar (1977) 290–300), as on the capacity of the provincial areas to bring forth men of sufficient wealth, efficiency, and culture to take a seat in the *curia*: Salmeri (1991) 561–5. It does not seem very convincing to argue that the will of a single emperor should be the decisive factor in the arrival of senators from the Greek East: cf. e.g. Devreker (1982), who indicates Domitian.

[19] For the senatorial Sergii Paulli, cf. Halfmann (1979) nos. 3–4, and for the family and its estates, Levick (1967) 112 n. 6 and Mitchell (1993) 1: 151 ff., 2: 6–7; for T. Junius Montanus, Halfmann (1979) no. 6; for Ti. Julius Celsus Polemaeanus, Halfmann (1979) no. 16; for Ti. Julius Aquila Polemaeanus, Halfmann (1979) no. 37, and for the library of Celsus, completed under Hadrian, Engelmann (1993) and Hueber (1997); for C. Antius A. Julius Quadratus, Halfmann (1979) no. 17 and Quass (1993) 155; for the Pergamene family of Julii Quadrati, cf. Bowersock (1969) 19, 25, 84–5; for C. Julius Quadratus Bassus, Halfmann (1979) no. 26 and Campbell (1984) 322. In particular, on senators from Pergamum, cf. Virgilio (1993) 104–8.

[20] Cf. Halfmann (1979) 78–9.

the Galatian nobleman C. Claudius Severus, the Cilician dynast C. Iulius Alexander, and C. Iulius Antiochus Epiphanes Philopappus, grandson of the last king of Commagene who had been deposed by Vespasian.[21] All three were of Hellenic culture and mentality. They were also accorded the consulate, thus bringing to eleven the total of Greek senators known to us who rose to this office under Trajan.[22]

Even more significant from our point of view is that, again under Trajan, entry into the Senate took off well and truly with representatives, such as the historian Flavius Arrianus of Nicomedia, of Asia Minor's leading Greek families. After many centuries of administering their *poleis* and functioning—generation after generation, in some cases—as high priests of the imperial cult, it was now time for them to play their part in the administration of the Empire, making a contribution that was to prove of extraordinary importance to Hadrian and his successors.[23]

As examples we may consider the small contingent of senators in the second century who hailed from the cities of Lycia, a region that had—at least formally—enjoyed freedom until the advent of Claudius' reign, and that was in any case reputed to have 'men able to bring wisdom to bear on their political activity'.[24] Not all the best

[21] Cf. above, n. 18. For C. Claudius Severus, cf. Halfmann (1979) no. 39; for C. Julius Alexander, Halfmann (1979) no. 25; for C. Julius Antiochus Epiphanes Philopappus, Halfmann (1979) no. 36 and Baslez (1992). Dubbed 'king' by Plutarch (*Quaest. conviv.* 628a), Philopappus lived in magnificent style in Athens where he was also *archōn*, thus appearing to anticipate the great interest the emperor Hadrian was soon to show in the city, together with many intellectuals both Greek and Latin (cf. Salmeri (1994) 44–7). He had his own funerary monument built on the hill of the Muses at Athens (mentioned by Pausanias 1. 25. 8, without precise indication of the dedicatee) and his name incised on both sides of his statue (*ILS* 845): in Latin, in conformity with Roman nomenclature, indicating his tribe and appointment as *consul suffectus* (in 109); in Greek, with mention of his royal titles and his ancestors. On the friendship between Plutarch and Philopappus, cf. Jones (1971) 59 and Puech (1992) 4870–3. On the monument, cf. Kleiner (1983).

[22] Cf. Halfmann (1979) 86.

[23] Cf. Halfmann (1982) 609–10, Quass (1982) 188 ff. On the career of L. Flavius Arrianus, cf. Halfmann (1979) no. 56, Stadter (1980) 1–18, Salmeri (1982) 39–40, Syme (1982a), Vidal-Naquet (1984) 311–22, Swain (1996) 242–3. Halfmann (1979) 79 holds that Arrian was already a member of the Senate under Trajan, while Syme (1982a) 190 and Birley (1997) 218 assign his entry to early in the reign of Hadrian. On the priesthood of the imperial cult as springboard for a career as *eques* or senator, cf. Campanile (1994) 165 ff.; on the imperial cult in Asia Minor, cf. Price (1984).

[24] Str. 14. 3. 2. On the senators from Lycia, cf. Halfmann (1982) 639–41; on the ruling groups in the cities of the region, cf. Wörrle (1988) 123 ff. On the character of the Lycians, cf. Syme (1982b) 650, Syme (1985) 359 and for the Hellenistic age Le Roy (1987). On Claudius' annexation of Lycia to the Empire in 43 (Suet. *Claud.*

and most ambitious inhabitants of Asia Minor's Greek cities had their sights on the Roman Senate, however; many of the notables, and especially those engaged in intellectual activities, preferred to stay within the bounds of their 'little fatherland',[25] attending to its administration. M. Antonius Polemo, the most renowned master of rhetoric of his time and a descendant of a royal family that was also to include a consul, spent his time between Laodicea and Smyrna gaining the appreciation and respect of more than one emperor, but he never entered the Senate.[26] The Lycian Opramoas, one of the wealthiest inhabitants of the Empire known to us, brought such benefits to his countrymen as only an emperor normally could, yet he does not seem to have acquired Roman citizenship.[27]

This attachment to their cities, regions, and, in the final analysis, to Hellenism itself characterizes a considerable number of senators from the Greek world, and again the intellectuals are a case in point. The Bithynian historian Flavius Arrianus, who served in various provincial posts and showed competence as a man of arms, decided to throw in his senatorial career around 140 and retreat to Athens, where he attended to public affairs and was appointed *archōn*.[28] Another historian, A. Claudius Charax, an erudite Pergamene who pursued a brilliant career to become *consul suffectus* in 147, raised the *propylaea* before the Asklepieion of his city and became *patronomos* at Sparta.[29] Then we have the case of C. Iulius Demosthenes

---

25. 3, Dio Cass. 60. 17. 3), cf. Remy (1986) 34–7. Fundamental evidence on the subject is now offered by the inscription called 'stadiasmos provinciae Lyciae' (*SEG* 44 (1994) no. 1205), not yet definitively published, in which the Lycians, notwithstanding their provincial status, still define themselves as *pistoi symmachoi* of the Romans.

[25] The loyalty of intellectuals like Dio to their 'little fatherland' can be compared, *mutatis mutandis*, with J. Burckhardt's to Basle: cf. Kaegi (1942) 306–14.

[26] Philostratus dedicated one of the longest of his lives of the sophists to Polemo: *VS* 530–44. On his family and activity, cf. Bowersock (1969) 22–4, 26, 44–5, 47–8, 120–3; Syme (1985) 361–2; Gleason (1995) 21 ff.; Campanile (1997a) 221–3, (1999).

[27] Extremely apt is the definition of Opramoas as 'régulier de l'évergetisme' in Veyne (1976) 295–6; cf. also Rostovtzeff (1957) 149, 151. The singularly long epigraphic text recording his acts of liberality can be read in *TAM* ii. 3. 905 (for some relevant notes on the series of legates and *archiereis* of Lycia mentioned here, cf. Letta (1994)). Opramoas of Rhodiapolis was also citizen of all the other cities of Lycia: cf. Sartre (1991) 126. Two new inscriptions from the Letoon of Xanthos containing lists of the munificent deeds of an unknown benefactor are associated with Opramoas in Balland (1981) 175–224; *contra* Coulton (1987) 171–8.

[28] Cf. above, n. 23.

[29] Cf. Halfmann (1979) no. 73, and especially Andrei (1984) 9–35; for the office of *patronomos*, cf. Cartledge and Spawforth (1989) 208.

of Oenoanda, Trajan's procurator in Sicily, who gave up his equestrian career and returned to Lycia to cover the major offices in his
city and in the provincial *koinon*. Back home he endowed a theatrical
foundation that is recorded in a recently published inscription of
great length and importance.[30] However, the most interesting case
of all is that of the Athenian, Herodes Atticus. He was one of the
few senators we know of—just ten or so—from the Greece of the
early centuries AD, but he outshone all the other figures we have
mentioned so far in his devotion to his native city and to the ideal
of Hellenism. Scion of a remarkably wealthy family which traced
itself back to the Aeacids no less, Herodes bought land in Italy, as
Trajan had ordained for provincial senators, and was appointed
consul ordinarius in 143; but he took no interest in Rome or the administration of the Empire, and his thoughts were ever turning to the
Greek world. He spent vast sums of money to adorn its cities with
theatres, *stadia*, and *exedrae* (Athens taking pride of place), while
exercising his powers as a sophist to re-evoke the great moments of
the Hellenic past to the great admiration of his contemporaries.[31]

Against this background of Asia Minor and the Greek world in
general during the first two centuries of the Empire (where the notables remained deeply attached to their native cities[32] and deeply imbued

[30] On the career and life of C. Julius Demosthenes, cf. Wörrle (1988) 55–69. On
p. 61 Wörrle suggests advanced age as the reason for Demosthenes' abandonment of
his career as procurator (AD 114) after his first appointment in Sicily, but we may at
least doubt this explanation if we consider that over ten years after leaving the island
Demosthenes was fully active as Lyciarch (*IGR* III. 487, 500 II. 60) and had much
to do organizing his foundation for a theatrical festival, which was to be called the
Demostheneia and to be celebrated at three-yearly intervals. The inscription referring to the foundation can be read in Wörrle (1988) 4–16 (with German translation):
for interpretation of the inscription, cf. again Wörrle (1988), and also Mitchell (1990)
and Rogers (1991).

[31] For the senators from Greece, cf. Halfmann (1979) 68. On Herodes Atticus the
principal ancient source is Philostratus *VS* 546–66; the epigraphic material regarding
him is listed in Halfmann (1979) no. 68. For interpretation of the man a central place
is still occupied by Graindor (1930); Ameling (1983) is, of course, more up to date
on the epigraphic material and building activity of Herodes, but the interpretation
of his character as lax and frivolous (1: 163–9) is unacceptable. Cf. also Bol (1984)
and Tobin (1997). On the thoroughly Greek character of Herodes' portrait statues,
overshadowing the Roman aspects, cf. Smith (1998) 78–9. On Herodes' estates in
Rome, cf. Coarelli (1986) 54 (Trajan's wish that provincial senators should invest at
least a third of their wealth in the purchase of land in Italy and Rome is recorded in
Pliny, *Ep.* 6. 19. 4). On his consulate, cf. Alföldi (1977) 44–5.

[32] As far as second- and third-century AD Phrygia is concerned, Campanile
(1997*a*) points out the decided preference of the local families of notables to chan-
nel their aspirations in the direction of marriage alliances and imperial priesthoods
in the region rather than of a career as *eques* or senator.

with the common ideal of Hellenic culture even as they sat in the Roman Senate) there stand out the two most significant intellectuals of the period, Plutarch of Chaeronea and Dio of Prusa.[33]

Plutarch seems to show more awareness in his writings than Dio does[34] of the process that brought growing numbers of Greeks to sit in the Roman Senate, and that—as we have seen—was consolidated under Trajan. Although he shows no particular approval of this, no anti-Roman implications need be drawn from his views.[35] Rather, he looks askance at the behaviour of certain inhabitants of Chios, Galatia, and Bithynia who are never content with the fame and power they enjoy in their own cities, but hanker without any real hope after a place in the Senate and, still not satisfied, aspire to a praetorship or even a consulate; he sees this as a threat to *euthumia*, or serenity of spirit.[36] From his traditionalist viewpoint that took the *polis* as a closed entity, and with those Greeks in mind who were ready to leave their native cities and sacrifice the best years of their

---

[33] Bowersock (1969) 110–11, Salmeri (1982) 10. Both Plutarch and Dio were Roman citizens, the former with the name of L. Mestrius Plutarchus (Jones (1971) 11, 22, 48–9), the latter most probably with that of Titus Flavius Cocceianus Dio (cf. below, nn. 67, 176). For the aspects of Plutarch considered in this chapter, see Jones (1971), Russell (1973) (literary aspects), Swain (1996) 135–86. For a chronology of the works of Plutarch, see Jones (1966) and Jones (1971) 135–7. Still worth reading on Dio, and rich in stimuli, are Burckhardt (1864) and von Arnim (1898). See also, with various viewpoints, Desideri (1978), Jones (1978), Moles (1978), Salmeri (1982), Brancacci (1985), and Swain (1996) 187–241 (and above, Ch. 1). Close analysis of Dio's biographical data can be found in Sidebottom (1996), who deftly demolishes certain commonplaces of the rhetor's life and experiences, starting with the idea that he had close connections with the Flavian dynasty. See Desideri (1991*b*) (cf. Desideri (1998) 66–76) for a clear demonstration that Dio's real interests lay in civic life rather than literature, and that his concerns as a writer were essentially of a political and social nature. On Dio's cultural background, which included philosophy as well as rhetoric from the outset, cf. Momigliano (1975) 970 ff., Salmeri (1982) 20 ff., Desideri (1994*a*) 850–3, Swain (1994) 168–9. It is worth recalling here the bust found at Pergamum, probably dating to the period of Hadrian, which defines Dio as a philosopher—see Habicht (1969) 162, cf. Salmeri (1982) 22–3 n. 65, Brunt (1994) 41 n. 67—and thus accords with his chosen self-presentation after his return from exile (cf. esp. Moles (1978), and above, p. 45).

[34] For Dio, cf. below, nn. 184–6.

[35] Cf. Swain (1996) 171. Plutarch's attitude towards Rome, its history, and traditions (especially in the *Parallel Lives*) is characterized by interest and attention, but we should not lose sight of the fact that his roots were firmly fixed in the Greek cultural and political humus—cf. Jones (1971) 88–102; Pelling (1989); Swain (1996) 137 ff., (1997); Lamberton (1997).

[36] *De tranquillitate animi* 470c, on which cf. Jones (1971) 45 and Swain (1996) 169–71, esp. 170 n. 103 for information on senators of Plutarch's time from Galatia and Bithynia.

life in the expectation of a well-paid equestrian office,[37] he puts forward the example of Epaminondas, who

when appointed *telmarchos* by the Thebans out of envy and spite, did not decline the duties of his office; indeed, arguing that it is not only the office that brings lustre to the man, but also the man to the office, he brought splendid dignity to that of the *telmarchos*, whose duties had gone no further than clearing the streets of dung and draining them of water.[38]

Plutarch also offers the example of his own goodwill in this respect: he had not only undertaken the highest duties on behalf of his city, but had also taken it upon himself to supervise the measurement of tiles and the transport of cement and stones.[39] In perfect keeping with a view of political commitment that is restricted to the confines of one's own *polis*, if the ageing Plutarch was indeed ever appointed by Hadrian as procurator of Greece, he must certainly have taken it on as a token office, reserving himself properly for the service of his beloved Chaeronea.[40]

More explicitly even than Plutarch himself, and without the preliminary criticism against the Roman aspirations displayed by the Greeks of his time, Dio extols in his speeches the ideal of service to one's native city. No sooner had he returned to Prusa, probably in the last months of 97, his exile finally over,[41] than he reasserted his loyalty to his city, declaring it his chosen residence, modest as it was

---

[37] *Praec. ger. reip.* 814d *tas polutalantous epitropas kai dioikēseis tōn eparchiōn*; cf. Groag (1939) 146 n. 602. For a full study of *Praecepta gerendae reipublicae* (and Plutarch's other political treatises), see Renoirte (1951), Jones (1971) 110–21, Desideri (1986), and Swain (1996) 162 ff.

[38] *Praec. ger. reip.* 811b (reading *telmarchos* with the eds.).

[39] *Praec. ger. reip.* 811c.

[40] Syncellus (659 Dind.) tells us that in his advanced age Plutarch was appointed by the emperor (Hadrian) procurator of Achaea: this is accepted in Bowersock (1969) 57 n. 6 and 112 and in Jones (1971) 34, while Swain (1996) 171–2 is unconvinced. Little credit can be given to the *Suda* (*P* 1793), which states that Plutarch received the *ornamenta consularia* from Trajan: Swain (1996) 171–2.

[41] Although Philostratus (*VS* 488) represents Dio's exile as voluntary, given the rhetor's own remarks and the virulence of his polemic against Domitian (below, n. 175), there are no good reasons to suppose it was not decreed by the emperor. In *Or.* 13. 1 Dio writes that he was exiled on account of his friendship with an illustrious Roman (long thought to be T. Flavius Sabinus; but Sidebottom (1996) 452–3 now plausibly suggests L. Salvius Otho Cocceianus, almost certainly Cocceius Nerva's nephew), whom he also served as counsellor, and who was put to death by Domitian; moreover, Dio himself tells us that his exile (*Or.* 19. 1)—perhaps better defined as 'relegatio' (cf. Jones (1978) 46)—was from Bithynia, his province of origin; otherwise, he could move and express himself as he wished (cf. *Or.* 1. 50). However, it also appears likely that the rhetor was banished from Rome and Italy. As for his property in Bithynia, it was not confiscated although it fell into ruin during his absence: *Orr.* 40. 2, 45. 10–11.

in dimensions and history alike and despite tempting offers to live elsewhere.[42] It is, however, in a speech delivered in 101 shortly after his return from an embassy to represent the interests of Prusa to Trajan that Dio truly evinces his position: rather than be attracted to court circles and the friendship of the emperor, he asserts that he prefers life in Prusa, notwithstanding its *tarachē* and *ascholia*, and he adds that his endeavours at Rome had had the aim of gaining Trajan's favour for the city rather than for himself.[43]

Given that the rhetor had gone to Rome with the intention of becoming 'counsellor' to Trajan and, moreover, that he does not seem to have met with much success on this count, one might suspect a degree of face-saving in his professions of devotion to Prusa. However, I think we can safely rule this out: Dio's conception of the role of counsellor to the sovereign does not clash with his civic commitment,[44] while his indissoluble ties with his 'little fatherland' are attested in a great many of his speeches, which we shall shortly be turning to. Like the passages from Plutarch cited above, these speeches give full expression to the classical Greek point of view, according to which political engagement in one's city should not be seen as a *Beruf*, and should afford no concrete gains, but must appear a natural activity of men, and virtually their primary duty.[45]

THE POLITICAL WORLD OF DIO

There is no doubt about the fact that the first speech Dio delivered in Prusa dates to the rule of Vespasian,[46] and stands out from the

[42] *Or.* 44. esp. 6–7: for the dating of the speech to immediately after Dio's return from exile, cf. von Arnim (1898) 314, Salmeri (1982) 30, also Sheppard (1984) 162; *contra* Jones (1978) 139 hypothesizes 101, after the rhetor's return from the embassy to Trajan (cf. below, n. 78). However, my impression is that Dio's words (11) do not imply that Prusa had already gained enlargement of the *boulē* together with the privilege of being the head of an assize-district and new sources of income as well as *eleutheria*. The paragraph in question seems rather to be presenting a list of requests to be put to the emperor (Nerva: cf. below, n. 67).

[43] *Or.* 45. 3: cf. Salmeri (1982) 10, Swain (1996) 229. For the dating, cf. Salmeri (1982) 30–1 n. 97, Jones (1978) 139.

[44] Cf. above, n. 25 and below, nn. 187–9.

[45] Cf. *Or.* 47. 2. For Plutarch politics is not an activity of limited duration: *An seni resp. ger. sit* 791c; it must be disinterested: *Praec. ger. reip.* 819e; it gives pleasure such as the gods themselves enjoy: *An seni resp. ger. sit* 786b.

[46] Dessau (1899). With regard to the text we have (*Or.* 46), Jones (1978) 21 rightly points out that on the whole it seems to reproduce the actual speech delivered in consideration of the 'fidelity with which it reflects the circumstances and the language of contemporary city life'.

remaining political speeches of the rhetor, which can be ascribed to
the era of Nerva and Trajan.[47] The speech followed a revolt trig-
gered by a sharp rise in grain prices; the angry mob had set its sights
on Dio's house, apparently suspecting him of manipulating the
cereal market.[48] However, no assault ensued,[49] and the rhetor was
subsequently able to defend his honour in the speech in question,
most probably before the assembly,[50] pleading the tradition of honesty and integrity represented by his father and maternal grandfather, and recalling that, young as he was, he had already performed
arduous liturgies and taken his place among Prusa's most illustrious citizens.[51] He also proposed—or possibly endorsed a proposal
—that 'commissioners of the market' be elected to solve the problem of the city's grain supplies, and made a point of warning his
audience to refrain from rash actions that might reach the ears of
the *meizones hēgēmones*—the Roman authorities.[52] Such advice
affords a certain insight into what were to be the guidelines of Dio's
future political attitude, seeking to settle problems and conflicts without recourse to force, and as far as possible keeping the Romans out
of the affairs of the Greek cities.[53]

At the same time, invocation of family traditions as the foundation and guarantee of political commitment may, I believe, be taken
as evidence of the concrete value attached to the *ek progonōn* formula,
often encountered in inscriptions of Asia Minor which recount the
careers of notable citizens.[54] Faced with all the fury of the Prusan
assembly, Dio sought support not only from his father and maternal
grandfather but also from his family tree, again on the maternal side,
ascending to his great-grandfather and thence to his great-great-
grandfather;[55] the latter had probably witnessed the advance of

---

[47] Cf. below, n. 68.   [48] *Or.* 46. 8–13.   [49] Ibid. 46. 12.
[50] Cf. Jones (1978) 20.
[51] *Or.* 46. 2–6. On the paternal and maternal branches of Dio's family, cf. Salmeri
(1982) 12–18.
[52] *Or.* 46. 14. The text seems to suggest that the proposal to have the assembly
elect a group of people responsible for the supervision of the market (*epimeleisthai
tēs agoras*: cf. Jones (1940) 350 n. 15) did not come from Dio, although we cannot
rule out the possibility that it did. For *hēgemōn* in the sense of governor, cf. Mason
(1974) 52; *meizon* expressly qualifies the governor's office as higher than the local
magistracies. The use of the plural is dictated by the needs of the argument.
[53] Salmeri (1982) 20.
[54] With regard to Bithynia, cf. e.g. *IK* 27. 3, 10, 49 (Prusias ad Hypium). In general, cf. Salmeri (1982) 37 n. 128.
[55] For the enraged assembly: *Or.* 46. 1, 10; for Dio's great-grandfather and great-
great-grandfather: *Or.* 46. 3.

Mithridates into Bithynia after the death of Nicomedes IV, and subsequently the establishment of Bithynia as a province together with Pontus by Pompey in 64 BC.[56] To this period of upheavals in Bithynia and its neighbouring regions can be ascribed the origins of the fortunes belonging to the maternal branch of Dio's family and other families of Asia Minor which were to prosper in the succeeding centuries; suffice it to recall Chaeremon of Nysa and his descendants.[57] As Michael Rostovtzeff wrote, the period of Roman rule in Asia Minor up to the time of Augustus was 'not so much . . . an epilogue, but . . . the prologue to a new chapter in the history of the Ancient World'.[58]

It was this same period in Asia Minor's history that saw the rise of a new type of intellectual who was deeply committed to city politics—the very model for Dio himself: rhetors and philosophers, or personages qualified as both, who plunged into the political life of their cities in the turbulent middle years of the first century BC and gave political life a decidedly 'personalist' appearance.[59] No comprehensive study has ever been carried out on these intellectuals, recorded notably in books 13–14 of Strabo's *Geography*, and I cannot even begin to do so here;[60] but it is worth noting that their type of activity and commitment—essentially in the direction of political oratory—comes closer to Dio's practices than to those of certain of

[56] On the death of Nicomedes IV, in 74 BC, Rome inherited the kingdom of Bithynia: on sources relating to the testament and its value, cf. Liebmann-Frankfort (1966) 73 ff. and Debord (1998) 148; for Mithridates' entry into Bithynia, cf. App. *Mithr.* 71, Memnon, *FGrHist* 434, f. 1 (28. 6 ff.), Plut., *Luc.* 7 (with Sherwin-White (1984) 165); on the constitution of Bithynia and Pontus as a province, cf. Marshall (1968), Sherwin-White (1984) 227 ff.

[57] Salmeri (1982) 12; for Chaeremon, cf. Campanile (1996) 172.

[58] Rostovtzeff (1941) 2: 934. Cf. Bernhardt (1985) 281 ff.

[59] For examples of the type of intellectual referred to we may take Metrodorus of Scepsis (Str. 13. 1. 55: a philosopher who took up politics and practised rhetoric), the *stratēgos* Diodorus, who sought the favour of Mithridates by having the members of the Adramyttium *boulē* slaughtered (Str. 13. 1. 66: he poses as a philosopher of the Academy and a teacher of rhetoric), Hybreas of Mylasa (Str. 14. 2. 24: a rhetor), and Athenaeus of Seleuceia on the Calycadnus (Str. 14. 5. 4: a Peripatetic philosopher). On the 'personalist' aspect of political life in the late Hellenistic period, cf. Habicht (1995).

[60] Cf., however, Bowersock (1965) 5 ff. and Brunt (1994) 35 and n. 41, although the latter possibly draws too sharp a contrast in effective action in local politics between the rhetors and philosophers of the first century BC recorded in Strabo and the sophists of the second and early third centuries AD dealt with by Philostratus in the *Lives*. Brunt takes essentially the same line as Bowie (1982), tending to minimize the political and social importance of the sophists; *contra* Bowersock (1997). On Hybreas of Mylasa (above, n. 59), cf. Noè (1996) and Campanile (1997*b*) 243.

the sophists of the second and early third centuries AD who are presented in Philostratus' *Lives* as preoccupied above all with the business of lecturing.[61]

As we have seen, most of Dio's political speeches in Prusa date to the time of Nerva and Trajan after he returned from his exile.[62] With the new aura of authority that came from having been a victim of the tyrant Domitian, Dio made his political *rentrée* to Prusa with a speech to the assembly explicitly offering his services as the city's guiding light.[63] From the outset he disclaims any desire for statues, honours, or the public proclamations proposed for him, explaining that he is content to enjoy the general friendship and goodwill shown to him.[64] However, he also makes a point of recalling the honours bestowed on his father and all his family,[65] sufficient, as signs of prestige, to ensure him a respectful hearing. Dio goes on to speak of his loyalty to Prusa as his chosen residence.[66] Building on this he grows magniloquent as he calls upon the public to decide once and for all to live together in peace and order. He concludes by reading his correspondence with the emperor—Nerva, according to the chronology here proposed—as if to imprint on his words the seal of the supreme power.[67]

[61] Between the rhetors and philosophers of the first century BC and Dio (bridging the distance, as it were) are the rhetors Dio himself recalls as coming shortly before him (*Or.* 18. 12), and thus including his own maternal grandfather. Dio's grandfather had prepared a speech (*logos*) to address to the emperor he had contacts with (probably Tiberius: Salmeri (1982) 14–15) and who had granted him citizenship at Rome and at the *colonia* of Apamea (*Or.* 41. 6, cf. *Or.* 46. 3), with the aim of requesting *eleutheria* for Prusa. Given the brevity of their relations, however, the speech was never delivered (*Or.* 44. 5). Under the principate *eleutheria* for a Greek city meant essentially freedom from the intervention of the governor in local administration and jurisdiction: for the case of Amisus in the province of Bithynia-Pontus, cf. Pliny, *Ep.* 10. 92–3 and Sherwin-White (1966) 686–9; in general, cf. Bernhardt (1971) 229–40.

On the greater interest Philostratus shows in non-political oratory in the *Lives of the Sophists*, cf. Desideri (1994*a*) 23; of the sophists he mentions, however, some do come fairly close to the Dionian model, such as M. Antonius Polemo (cf. above, n. 26) and Scopelianus (cf. Campanile (1999)).

[62] Cf. above, n. 41. The chronology of the speeches at Prusa (*Orr.* 40 and 42–51) is after Salmeri (1982) 30–1 n. 97; cf. also—with differences—Jones (1978) 138–40 and Sheppard (1984).

[63] *Or.* 44, cf. above, n. 42.   [64] Ibid. 2. Cf. above, n. 42.
[65] Ibid. 3–5.   [66] Ibid. 6–7.

[67] Ibid. 12. The manuscripts conserve neither the letter Dio wrote to the emperor, probably apologizing, with the interests of Prusa foremost in mind, for not having been able to accept the invitation he had received to the imperial court, nor the emperor's reply. With regard to relations between Dio and Nerva after the latter's ascent to the throne, in *Or.* 45. 2 Dio states that a serious illness prevented him

Having re-established relations with his fellow-citizens, Dio delivered in Prusa at least nine of the political speeches that have come down to us—seven before the assembly, two before the *boulē*.[68] These are marked above all by his preoccupation with schemes to beautify the modest city. A tottering workshop that had long been causing red faces on the occasional visits of the governor was pulled down on his initiative,[69] while on behalf of the city, with the promise of funds from himself and other notables, he took it upon himself to build a *stoa*, near completion by 105–6, the year of Varenus Rufus' proconsulship in Bithynia.[70] As work proceeded, however, controversy flared, Dio's political opponents accusing him of destroying the most ancient and sacred vestiges of Prusa and doing just as he pleased, like a 'tyrant'.[71] This ominous-sounding epithet often rang out in the Greek world of the imperial age as leading notables inveighed against hostile colleagues, and Dio must have earned it again some time later, in the second year of Pliny's mission to Bithynia

from meeting the emperor: this probably gave rise to the correspondence in question, reference to which can also be found in *Or.* 40. 5. Again on the evidence of *Or.* 45. 2, where Nerva is defined as a *palai philos*, we may hypothesize that the friendship between rhetor and emperor began under the rule of Vespasian, when Dio—as the name recorded by Pliny the Younger demonstrates (Cocceianus Dion: *Ep.* 10. 81. 1)—must have received Roman citizenship thanks (also) to the intervention of Cocceius Nerva, *consul ordinarius* in 71: cf. Moles (1978) 86. Sidebottom (1996) 453 sees behind the name Cocceianus above all the intercession of the man he takes to have been Dio's patron (cf. above, n. 41), L. Salvius Otho Cocceianus, almost certainly Nerva's nephew. However, Dio's full Roman name seems to have been Titus Flavius Cocceianus Dio: cf. Sherwin-White (1966) 676, Salmeri (1982) 18 n. 49, and below, n. 176. On the subject of Dio's Roman citizenship, I cannot accept Whitmarsh (1998) 199 and n. 35, who implausibly asserts that the rhetor inherited it from his father and mother.

[68] Respectively *Orr.* 40, 42–3, 45, 47–8, 51 and *Orr.* 49–50. As we have seen, the two speeches (*Or.* 44, 46) discussed above were also held before the assembly (above, nn. 50, 63). In Prusa, probably before the assembly, Dio also gave the *Borystheniticus* (*Or.* 36: below, n. 157), which is not included in the count. Cf. Quass (1993) 402–3.

[69] *Or.* 40. 8–9.

[70] Money promised by Dio: *Or.* 40. 3; by other citizens of Prusa, but difficult to recover: *Or.* 47. 19; undertaking by Dio: *Or.* 40. 7; other references to the *stoa*: *Or.* 47. 17, 19–20. In the year of Varenus Rufus' proconsulship in Bithynia—recorded in *Or.* 48. 1 (for its dating to 105–6, cf. Eck (1970) 165 n. 227)—work is said to be near completion: *Or.* 48. 11. In an inscription from Prusa dating to the imperial age (*IK* 39. 8) reference is made to a *stoa*, but there is insufficient evidence to judge whether it is Dio's. For building policy in the cities of imperial Asia Minor, cf. in general Winter (1996). For the system of *pollicitationes*, cf. Garnsey (1971) on Africa.

[71] *Or.* 47. 18, 23–4, cf. *Or.* 41. 3; Dio also associates the notion of 'tyranny' with the behaviour of cities (*Or.* 38. 35) and governors (*Or.* 43. 11).

*c.*110.[72] On this occasion it was his political enemy Flavius Archippus who accused him of failing to respect the plan drawn up for the construction of a library connected to a portico, which had been entrusted to his *cura*.[73] Despite Dio's efforts, however, Prusa never succeeded in acquiring that 'splendid' look that would have entitled its citizens to receive the governor with a touch of pride.[74] Pliny the Younger was to find the city still lacking decent public baths, and a great ruin dominating the skyline.[75]

In accordance with customary practice, Dio went out of his way to obtain such imperial favours and concessions as might raise the status of Prusa.[76] Illness prevented him from presenting Nerva with the list of submissions he had drawn up,[77] but things went better with Trajan. Arriving in Rome on an embassy for Prusa, probably in the year 100, the rhetor gained the new emperor's consent for his city to become the head of an assize-district and to increase the number of its councillors, but the longed-for *eleutheria* proved unattainable.[78]

---

[72] Herodes Atticus also received the epithet of 'tyrant' from the Athenians: Philostr. *VS* 559, cf. Jones (1978) 100–1, Kennel (1997). On the attitude to tyranny in the Hellenistic period, cf. Berve (1967) 1: 476. On the start of Pliny the Younger's mission to Bithynia-Pontus (as *legatus Augusti pro praetore consulari potestate: CIL* V. 5262) in September 109, cf. Sherwin-White (1966) 80–1. Syme (1958) 2: 659 is undecided between 109 and 110.

[73] Pliny, *Ep.* 10. 81. 1, 7. Jones (1978) 114 is inclined to identify the library with the *stoa* mentioned in n. 70; *contra*, preferably, Sherwin-White (1966) 676 argues that it was a different building. The political contention between Dio and Archippus, which eventually became a legal battle, is reconstructed in Salmeri (1982) 50–3. Cf. Sautel (1956).

[74] *Or.* 40. 10. For the 'splendid' face created for Greek cities by the *agora* and monumental buildings: Philostr. *VS* 532.

[75] Pliny, *Ep.* 10. 23, 70.

[76] Cf. *in primis* Bowersock (1969) 43 ff. On Dio's grandfather, who had already written a speech requesting *eleutheria* for Prusa, cf. above, n. 61.

[77] Cf. above, nn. 42, 67.

[78] *Or.* 40. 13 records the embassy sent to Trajan, while conveying the impression that many other, similar groups from the Greek world were also present (cf. Pliny, *Pan.* 79. 6–7). The meeting with Trajan probably took place at Rome, where the emperor was resident from late summer 99 to early 101. *Contra* Millar (1977) 414 f. argues that the embassy from Prusa took place in 98, meeting the emperor out of the capital. On the elevation of Prusa to head of a *conventus*, cf. *Or.* 40. 33 (without using any technical terms Dio refers to it here simply explaining the import of the concession, which meant that the citizens of Prusa no longer had to travel to other cities to be judged by the governor, and that for the same reason the inhabitants of the neighbouring centres had to make their way to Prusa); for the supernumerary members of the *boulē* (one hundred), cf. *Or.* 45. 3–7; for the entry fee they paid, thus helping to fill the city's coffers, cf. *Or.* 48. 11. Basically, this is what Dio had wanted from Nerva: *Or.* 44. 11, cf. above, n. 42; all that is lacking is the *eleutheria*

Despite Dio's interest in Prusa and his own proposal to make it the centre of a synoecism,[79] it would be vain to seek long-term plans or broadly framed policies in his speeches. The rhetor's words limn out a picture with narrow horizons composed of day-to-day problems, the inevitable contention with dull-witted opponents, sheer cussedness, and funds that dry up before plans can be completed. Nor did the building works Dio seems to have set such store by, or even the suits to the emperor for concessions, exceed the agenda of a small town with its petty quarrels and dreams of greatness.[80]

This is not to say that political debate was lacking in the Prusa of Dio or, more generally speaking, the imperial age; indeed, the rhetor's orations evoke a decidedly lively political life in the city, and we should always bear this in mind as a corrective when analysing the numerous inscriptions of Asia Minor in the first three centuries AD which record the doings of the *boulē* and *dēmos*. These tend to play down the importance of the *dēmos*, deny the existence of any serious conflict, and stress a basic immobility.[81]

which his grandfather had also failed to obtain: cf. above, n. 61. In *Or.* 45. 6 Dio mentions an unspecified governor of Bithynia who unsuccessfully interceded to make Prusa the head of a *dioikēsis*, i.e. *conventus* (for the equivalence of the two terms, cf. Habicht (1975) 68 n. 13); with regard to Apamea in Phrygia, in *Or.* 35. 15 Dio refers to the *conventus* with the expression *hai dikai par'etos*—indicating the interval between judicial visits of the proconsul (cf. Burton (1975) 98)—without using technical terms; he also points out, with a touch of irony, the economic benefits involved in being head of a *conventus*, deriving mainly from the increased number of residents when hearings were being held.

[79] Dio's proposal to make Prusa the seat of a 'synoecism' (*Or.* 45. 13) is to be ascribed above all to the need for new sources of income for the city mentioned in *Or.* 44. 11: cf. Salmeri (1982) 33–4 n. 109 and Swain (1996) 223; *contra* Rostovtzeff (1957) 1: 257—followed by Desideri (1978) 443 n. 11—sees it as being dictated by the wish of Dio the liberal to extend Prusan citizenship to the rural population. However, it is surely significant that at Apamea in Phrygia Dio dwelt (*Or.* 35. 14) on the concrete benefits of having numerous subject communities.

[80] Cf. above, nn. 70–3; Debord (1998) 154.

[81] Cf. below, and, further, Ma in Ch. 4 of this volume. In Bithynia, in Dio's times, the activity of the provincial council (*koinon*) also appears to have had a certain importance of its own, and not of a purely formal and institutional nature. Contention between notables in a city would interfere with its work, as also would contention between the cities of the province, whose fortunes were affected by the intervention of the governors but which in turn had some power over their fate after their terms of office. On the cases of the two proconsuls of Bithynia, Julius Bassus (holding office possibly in 100–1: cf. Eck (1970) 157 n. 194) and Varenus Rufus (holding office in 105–6: cf. above, n. 70), who were accused by the provincial council, cf. Salmeri (1982) 54–6; on provincial maladministration in general, cf. Brunt (1961). On the *koinon* of Bithynia and its composition, cf. Deininger (1965) 60 ff. and Mitchell (1993) 1: 109; on the *koinon* of Asia, cf. now Campanile (1994) 13 ff.; in general on the provincial councils of Asia Minor see Sartre (1991) 262–3.

In the case of the *boulē*, by describing its task as being to *pronoein tēs poleōs* ('make provision for the city'),[82] Dio clearly presents it as the city's most important political body, to a large extent in charge of decision-making in the administrative and financial fields. In fact, governors and emperors rarely intervened in the internal affairs of the *poleis* of Asia Minor, and virtually only as a result of serious disorder.[83] Moreover, Dio's accounts of the keen competition marking the election of the supernumerary councillors granted to Prusa by Trajan afford some insight into the real interest there was in holding a seat on the council.[84] Nor were its proceedings always as cut and dried as some suppose, giving excessive weight to the formal language of its decrees; the rhetor actually shows the councillors divided into factions, *hetaireiai*, forming groups around the leading figures in conflict.[85] However, a degree of internal strife did not undermine the predominance of the *boulē* over the assembly in Prusa or any other centre of Asia Minor,[86] but it did add a powerful touch of vim to political life, inducing certain notables gifted with oratorical skills like Dio to seek in the assembly the support they needed to overcome opposition among peers.

---

[82] *Or.* 48. 17: Salmeri (1982) 56. On the role of the *boulē* in the Greek world of the imperial age, cf. Jones (1940) 177, Sartre (1991) 129–30, Millar (1993) 241; with special reference to Asia Minor: Mitchell (1993) 1: 180, 201 ff.

[83] Cf. below, n. 108.

[84] For the supernumerary members of the *boulē* and the entry fee they paid, cf. above, n. 78; for the keen contention to get elected: *Or.* 45. 7–10, cf. below, n. 90. Claudiopolis, another city of Bithynia, also obtained from Trajan an unspecified number of supernumerary members for its *boulē*, again subject to entry fees: Pliny, *Ep.* 10. 39. 5, cf. 10. 112. 1. The *inviti decuriones* mentioned in a thorny passage of a letter Trajan sent Pliny the Younger (Pliny, *Ep.* 10. 113), when the latter was governor in Bithynia, need not necessarily be understood in the sense of decurions compelled to enter the council against their will. Without taking up the emendations to the text suggested by Sherwin-White (1966) 722–3, and accepted in Mynors's Oxford edition, including—notably—the reading of *invitati* instead of *inviti* (on which, cf. Lepper (1970) 570–1), the *inviti decuriones* may, as Garnsey (1974) 232 thinks, rather be seen as citizens wishing to join the council but unwilling to pay the entry fee. This seems rather more plausible than the interpretation that has the local councils of Trajan's Bithynia already subject to compulsory recruitment.

[85] *Or.* 45. 7–10. At Amastris, in Pontus, the members of Lepidus' 'faction' are defined by Lucian (*Alex.* 25) as *hoi peri Lepidon*, and one of them is subsequently (*Alex.* 43) called *Lepidōi hetairos*. On the 'competitive' nature of Greek society in the imperial age, cf. Schmitz (1997) 97 ff.

[86] In *Praec. ger. reip.* 813b Plutarch suggests that in order to keep the *dēmos* (cf. below, n. 93) under control the notables should simulate disagreement at certain crucial moments: cf. Desideri (1995) 118; real disagreement Plutarch held to be admissible only in trivial matters: *Praec. ger. reip.* 813c.

In imperial Asia Minor the assembly may not have had all the freedom and prerogatives we may be led to imagine by a famous passage in Cicero's *Pro Flacco* concerning the mid-first century BC;[87] but neither can it be reduced to a mere token presence in the political life of the cities, as a number of scholars have tended to do following the lead given by I. Levy at the end of the nineteenth century.[88] True enough, it had very limited rights to political and administrative initiative, but it could not always be taken for granted that it would elect the magistrates and approve the proposals of the notables and *boulē* as a matter of course.[89] Dio, for example, not only proposed to the *dēmos* of Prusa the election of 'commissioners of the market' to settle an extremely troubled state of affairs, as we have seen, but also records the election of the *archōn* by the *dēmos* itself, and the somewhat more controversial election of the supernumerary councillors accorded to the city by Trajan.[90] As for the importance attached to the *ekklēsia*'s approval of proposals advanced by notables and the *boulē*, there can surely be no better example than the Oenoanda inscription already mentioned, which records how the city's *ekklēsia* not only went into the details of Demosthenes' foundation, but was also responsible for appointing the ambassadors to be dispatched to the governor Flavius Aper to request fiscal immunity for the festivities, while final approval of the foundation seems to have rested on its confirmation.[91] It is, however,

---

[87] 7. 15–17: on the anti-democratic attitude behind certain negative remarks Cicero made on the *libertas immoderata* and *licentia* of the assemblies of the Greek world in comparison with the order of the Roman *contiones*, especially those of former times, cf. Thornton (1998) 292 ff., esp. 293 n. 85.

[88] Cf. Lévy (1895) 205–18 and *inter alios* Jones (1940) 177 ff., Ste. Croix (1981) 532, Millar (1993) 241.

[89] Salmeri (1982) 57. On the electoral functions of the assembly, cf. in particular Lewin (1995) 24–31; for approval of proposals by acclamation, esp. from the late second century, cf. Roueché (1984), (1989) and Mitchell (1993) 1: 201 and n. 22. On the Ephesian assembly, cf. Rogers (1992).

[90] On the election (*cheirotonia*) of the supernumerary members of the *boulē*, cf. *Or.* 45. 10. It is almost certainly to election to the office of *archōn* by the Prusan assembly that reference is made in *Or.* 48. 17 with the verb *poiein*. On the archontate in Bithynia, cf. Ameling (1984*a*). For the 'commissioners of the market', cf. above, n. 52. For other cases in which the assembly intervened in elections, cf. Lewin (1995) 24–31. The term *dēmos*, commonly used to refer to the assembly in the imperial age, was occasionally thus applied also in the classical and Hellenistic ages, cf. Cagnazzi (1980) 299–301, 312–13.

[91] *Supra* n. 30. Wörrle (1988) 10, ll. 58–9; 14, ll. 98–101; cf. 4, ll. 2–3. Cf. Rogers (1991) 95. In the inscription the term *ekklēsia* is used in preference to *dēmos* to refer to the assembly.

above all the writings of Plutarch and Dio that show the *ekklēsia*
as a far from negligible element in the political life of the *polis* during
the imperial age.[92]

Plutarch draws attention to the people's characteristic behaviour
—quick to anger, hard to control—mainly as a warning that anyone interested in a political career should have courage and powers
of persuasion. He goes on to point out that only simple, natural
eloquence will go down with them and win their assent.[93]

As for Dio, on more than one occasion we find him urging calm
on the assembly of Prusa and seeking their support.[94] When, for example, a proconsul who was considered a great friend of the city
paid it a visit, the rhetor made a point of appealing to the *dēmos* to
behave *sophronōs kai kalōs*, avoiding any bickering and disorderliness
that might antagonize the Roman authorities.[95] On a more serious
occasion, during the meeting of the assembly that followed on the
mob's attempt to raid his house, as we have seen, Dio had to draw
on all his rhetorical skills and prestige to assuage their fury.[96] Not
infrequently he would call upon his audience to curb their impetu-
ous, impulsive inclinations, and not abandon themselves to hatred
and violence.[97] The tone Dio adopts for such admonishments, as
also in dealing with the assembly in general, is invariably one of
superiority,[98] which is not to say that he underrates it, however; he
considers it a sovereign body whose assent is important for the
launch of public works and for election as *archōn* or as one of the
supernumerary members of the *boulē*.[99] Moreover, the rhetor was

---

[92] Salmeri (1982) 57; Mitchell (1993) 1: 201–2.
[93] *Praec. ger. reip.* 799c (cf. 800c), 801c, 803a. Cf. Jones (1971) 111, Swain (1996)
164.
[94] In this connection it is significant that most of the political speeches Dio gave
in Prusa were delivered before the assembly rather than the *boulē*: above, n. 68.
[95] *Or.* 48. 1–2; the proconsul referred to in the text is Varenus Rufus: cf. above,
nn. 70, 81.
[96] Cf. above, nn. 48–53.   [97] Exemplary in this connection is *Or.* 48. 9.
[98] In *Or.* 50. 3, in the context of a speech delivered before the *boulē*, Dio expressly
points out that the fact of having felt compassion for the *dēmotikoi*, when they were
beset by difficulties, does not imply that he considers them any closer to himself than
the council: moreover, he had already had occasion to observe (*Or.* 50. 2) that not
even the Athenian demagogues Hyperbolus and Cleon had gone so far as to view
the Areopagus and the Council of the Six Hundred (as it is anachronistically termed
by Dio, since it was still the Council of the Five Hundred in the times of
Hyperbolus and Cleon, to become the Council of the Six Hundred in 307/6: cf. Rhodes
(1972) 1) with less respect than the assembly.
[99] For approval of the new building plans, cf. *Orr.* 40. 6, 47. 14; for election of the
archontes and the supernumerary members of the *boulē* in Prusa, cf. above, n. 90.

well aware that once the support of the assembly was secured even the fiercest of enemies could be tackled without excessive fear.[100]

A significant sign of the vitality of the Prusan assembly, and of its unpredictable inner dynamics, is also offered by its clashes with *boulē* and notables alike. In particular, it charged the latter with holding on to public funds illegally, and failing in their promises to contribute to the rebuilding of the city.[101] Such clashes were not peculiar to Prusa: in Tarsus Dio himself shows us the most important political bodies of the city—*boulē*, *dēmos*, and *gerousia*—in a precarious state of equilibrium, and often at fierce odds with one another. Speeches or pleas for reconciliation made little headway with them: those who addressed the assembly with the intention of sage counselling were actually refused a hearing.[102]

Clashes between the assembly and the *boulē* are recorded not only in Prusa and Tarsus, but also in Nicomedia, Nicaea, and various other cities in Asia Minor.[103] They may not have been so very widespread, but they certainly cannot be minimized to the point of suggesting that the idyllic atmosphere certain inscriptions conjure up represents the normal state of affairs between the two political bodies.[104] Such errors of judgement are all too easy if we assume that, once Roman rule took over, the road ahead was clearly marked out for the cities of Asia Minor and, while overrating their economic well-being, we almost completely ignore the political aspect.

---

[100] Cf. e.g. *Or.* 43. 7.

[101] *Or.* 47. 19, 48. 9: cf. Salmeri (1982) 59; in general, cf. Quass (1993) 382 ff.

[102] *Or.* 34. 16; on this speech, delivered before the Tarsian assembly (1), cf. below, nn. 112, 126. In *Or.* 34. 21 among the contenders we also find the *neoi* (cf. Str. 14. 5. 14). On the state of political conflict behind Dio's speech, cf. Jones (1978) 80. The process of *symbouleuein* in the Tarsian assembly seem to have been reserved solely for *hoi gnōrimoi kai hoi plousioi* (*Or.* 34. 1), though they were often not given a hearing (*Or.* 34. 6).

[103] Attesting to contention between *boulē* and *dēmos* at Nicomedia in the time of Marcus Aurelius is the *homonoia* coin—with the names of the two bodies—apparently marking the restoration of peace: cf. Pera (1984) 124. Violent internal conflict preluded the *peri homonoias* speech which Dio gave in Nicaea (*Or.* 39); there is also a later coin of the city carrying the inscription *homonoia Nikaieōn*, again referring to a previous state of conflict between the citizens: Pera (1984) 124.

[104] The inscription from Prusias ad Hypium (*IK* 27. 30) recording the honours paid by the *dēmos* to the *boulē*, probably concluding a period of conflict, can certainly not be taken to reflect a constant state of easy relations between the two bodies. It is very interesting to see what Dio has to say (*Or.* 51. 2) on the state of schizophrenia occasionally characterizing political life in Prusa: praise and commendation are reserved to formal meetings of the *boulē* and *ekklēsia*, conflict breaking out in the *agora* and other places where meetings are informal.

Taking this viewpoint, one is also hard put to it to account for the uprisings that broke out not infrequently in Greece and Asia Minor during the imperial age; they are considered as something like feverish fits associated with economic development.[105] If, on the other hand, we give due weight to the assembly and its clashes with the *boulē*, seeing in them one of the possible outcomes of class conflict, the uprisings will no longer have the appearance of gratuitous events but will be seen rather as a virtual continuation and transformation of the ordinary political strife.[106]

In the Greek cities when the have-nots found themselves in dire straits they had nothing to lose if they raided the notables' houses and attracted the attention of the Roman authorities with their riotous behaviour. It was, by contrast, in the interests of the upper classes for harmony and order to reign in the cities; indeed, it was an indispensable condition for them to be able to enjoy their economic well-being, and to prevent the intervention of the Roman governors.[107] Should the governors somehow become involved or forced to deal with the cities' internal affairs, they could render both *boulē* and assembly equally powerless, and deprive the local courts of all authority. Moreover, no one could stand in the way of a governor set on verifying the accounts of a centre like Prusa, and the petition of a single citizen was enough for him to intervene and collect the sums promised for the construction of some building.[108]

---

[105] As, for example, in Gren (1941) 20. On the revolts and urban unrest in Asia Minor in general, cf. Sartre (1991) 187–90, Mitchell (1993) 1: 203. For a balanced account of economic growth in Asia Minor during the imperial age, with attention to the different levels enjoyed in the cities and the rural areas, cf. Mitchell (1993) 1: 257–9.

[106] Cf. Salmeri (1982) 60, and Mazza (1974) 267. Not infrequently urban unrest in the Greek East during the imperial age, once brought back within the political sphere, would be concluded by a meeting of the assembly, culminating in a speech by Dio (at Nicaea: *Or.* 39; for Prusa, cf. *Or.* 46, and above, nn. 52–3), Aristides (*Or.* 24, to Rhodes), or some such orator singing the praises of concord.

[107] On the living conditions of the poorer part of the population, cf. Mazza (1974) 243 ff.; on Dio's concern lest the Roman authorities should learn of disorders at Prusa, cf. *Or.* 46. 14.

[108] Cf. Plut., *Praec. ger. reip.* 814f–815a. In Prusa, most probably following disorder, the assembly was deprived of its right to meet; this was later restored by proconsul Varenus Rufus: *Or.* 48. 1, cf. above, nn. 70, 81, 95; in any case, no one could prevent the proconsul from controlling *ta dēmosia*: *Or.* 48. 2. In *Or.* 47. 19 Dio hints at the possibility that he may appeal to the proconsul to recover sums promised for construction of the *stoa* mentioned at n. 70; and it is again in Prusa that we find Pliny the Younger as governor of Bithynia (above, n. 72) intent to 'revocare a privatis et exigere' funds to be used for construction of baths: Pliny, *Ep.* 10. 23. In this context

Indeed, at the time of Pliny's mission supervision of the finances of the colony of Apamea was in the hands of the legate. Thus the relative freedom enjoyed by the Greek cities could be circumscribed, and much the same obtained when the governor was informed of judiciary cases or civic squabbles that should not have needed his intervention.[109]

Plutarch was highly critical of this practice, with severe words of censure for members of the upper classes who by greed and ambition compelled the *elattones* and their own colleagues to invoke the aid of the Roman authorities. Plutarch's view seems to derive not so much from sympathy for those smarting under the arrogance of petty local tyrants as from the wish to avoid any interference in the affairs of the Greek cities. Anyone whose actions brought it about was blameworthy, but those who called for intervention also had their part of the blame. In short, what mattered most to Plutarch was that the Greek world should retain that degree of autonomy it still enjoyed under the emperors, and cope with its own problems 'unaided'.[110]

As we have seen, Dio feared that the unrest of the mob might drive the governors to intervene, curtailing the rights and jurisdiction of the cities for the sake of law and order.[111] It was above all to avoid intrusions of this kind that the rhetor was unflagging in his appeals for concord, and when things grew seriously embroiled —such as when he suggested granting citizenship at Tarsus to the turbulent and marginalized *linourgoi*—he always had some compromise to propose.[112] Plutarch took the same line: again and again

we may well understand the behaviour of M. Antonius Polemo (above, n. 26) who, in the hope of avoiding intervention by the Romans, sought to settle strife *huper chrematōn* entirely within the city of Smyrna: Philostr. *VS* 532. In general, cf. Mitchell (1993) 1: 65.

[109] For the Apamean finances, cf. Pliny, *Ep.* 10. 47–8, on which see Lepper (1970) 568. Evidence of the tendency to resort to the judgement of the Roman authorities even in trivial cases can be found in Luc. *Demon.* 16. Stahl (1978) 177 overstates the case in arguing the identity of interests and prospects between Rome and the local elites.

[110] *Praec. ger. reip.* 814f–815a, cf. Salmeri (1982) 64–5, Swain (1996) 172–3.

[111] Cf. above, nn. 53, 95, 107.

[112] Cf. above, nn. 95–6. For Dio's advice to the Tarsian assembly (cf. *Or.* 34. 1) to grant citizenship to a group of flax workers (*linourgoi*) who had in many cases been resident in the city for generations and were in possession of the 500 drachmas necessary to become full citizens: *Or.* 34. 21–3. From the context it is clear that the rhetor was hoping that once the workers no longer felt marginalized they would cease their riotous behaviour, eliminating an obstacle to internal order. Convincing in this

in his writings we find appeals to the Greek politicians to settle conflicts within their cities, even at the cost of heavy concessions or, at the worst, defeat. For him as for Dio, the use of force was always to be shunned, and the intervention of the Roman author-ities avoided, grave though the tension might be; the discontent of the urban populations was not to be countered by drastic solutions; if politicians showed a certain flexibility, on the principle of give and take, they could afford to call for concord and order.[113]

Evidently, political activity in the *poleis* of the Empire did not—and could not—aim very high, but had to concentrate on maintaining the existing equilibria through subtle manoeuvres. Quite naturally, therefore, the study of rhetoric was of great importance for the *poli-tikos anēr*:[114] having ruled out the use of force and Roman intervention, he had to develop his skills in cogent persuasion and convincing advice, ever ready with an answer to the fury of the *dēmos*, and never caught napping. The politician had to be constantly prepared to mediate between conflicting sides, although the successes he obtained tended to be short-lived since words could paper over the cracks, as it were, but never remove the causes.

Apart from the ten speeches delivered in Prusa after his return from exile, the years of Nerva and Trajan also saw Dio addressing the inhabitants of the Bithynian cities of Apamea, Nicomedia, and Nicaea, as well as those of Alexandria, Tarsus, Apamea in Phrygia,

---

connection is Jones (1978) 81, who argues that the *linourgoi* of Tarsus were orga-nized in a *suntechnia* as at Anazarbus (*IGR* III. 896), *contra* Cracco Ruggini (1976) 463–5. On the financial qualification to obtain Tarsian citizenship, cf. Jones (1978) 81, Sartre (1991) 126–7. As for the advice Dio offers, it appears to have been inspired not so much by philosophical (i.e. Cynic: Welles (1962) 75) ideas or some, improb-able (cf. below, n. 129) prompt by Trajan (Kienast (1971) 72–3, Desideri (1978) 461–2 n. 6) as by rules of political expediency familiar to the rhetor, and in particular the principle that serious problems can often be settled and greater support won with occasional concessions.

[113] *Praec. ger. reip.* 815a, 818a, cf. *Or.* 40. 20.

[114] In *Or.* 18—a text written for a wealthy, mature Greek notable eager to devote himself to study (cf. von Arnim (1898) 139–40 and Sidebottom (1996) 450; *contra*, with no real evidence, Russell (1992) 8 vaguely suggests some Roman, and Desideri (1978) 137 Titus before becoming emperor)—Dio extols the virtues of eloquence, stressing its importance for politicians as a tool for them to gain respect and influence, and to fill their listeners with courage or fear. Dio also reminds his inter-locutor of the great help a politician can obtain from a perusal of the classics, in par-ticular of Xenophon, whose works—and above all the speeches contained in the *Anabasis*—are of help to the *politikos anēr* in all sorts of circumstances, whether address-ing an agitated public or discussing reserved matters with the governors (14 ff.). Cf. Salmeri (1982) 20–1.

and, possibly, Rhodes.[115] The rhetor himself tells us that as his prestige grew many centres in the Greek world vied to have him as counsellor; with the reputation he had gained for oratorical skills and,
above all, sound wisdom, he was much sought after.[116] Nor is it
particularly surprising that Dio did not confine his oratorical activity to the inhabitants of his city and region, but took it as far as
Alexandria and Tarsus. In fact, he considered no Greek city foreign
to his competence. Living in Prusa was no problem for him; unlike
Arrian, Dio felt no need to reside at Athens and take on the identity of a new Xenophon to be a champion of Hellenism.[117] Such a
champion he proved himself to be, in his own way, with his speech
in Olympia where, through the mouth of Phidias, he entrusted Hellas
to the protection of Zeus,[118] and above all with his earnest appeals
to his fellow-countrymen to live in concord and decorum, without
abandoning the glorious traditions of the past.[119]

Although, of course, it was also a matter of safeguarding Greek
honour, it was in the first place more specifically political considerations that led Dio in his appeals for *homonoia*, which he saw as
a guarantee for the continued power of the notables, his peers, and
for that degree of the autonomy the *poleis* might still enjoy under
the Empire.[120]

So it was that, when invited to Nicomedia and given citizenship
there for his singular competence in advising the community on
what best suited their real needs,[121] he took great pains to make the

---

[115] Dates: *Or.* 41 at Apamea in Bithynia (above, n. 6), cf. Jones (1978) 138 and
Salmeri (1982) 30 n. 97; *Or.* 38 at Nicomedia, probably before the assembly, Jones
(1978) 135 and Salmeri (1982) 74 n. 92; *Or.* 39 at Nicaea, again probably to the assembly, Jones (1978) 136 and Salmeri (1982) 92 n. 11. On the dating of the speeches to
Alexandria (*Or.* 32), Tarsus (*Orr.* 33–4), and Apamea in Phrygia (*Or.* 35), cf. below,
nn. 142, 126, 147 respectively. With regard to *Or.* 31 to Rhodes, possibly delivered
to an extraordinary assembly (cf. Jones (1978) 28), after the attribution by
Momigliano (1951) 151 to the early years of Vespasian (establishing the 'modern
orthodoxy'), Sidebottom (1992) 407–14 and Swain (1996) 428–9 with good reason
propose to date it to the reign of Trajan. Cf. below, nn. 140–1.

[116] *Or.* 42. 3–5, 44. 6, cf. *Or.* 41. 2. Dio makes a point of saying he was called to
Apamea in Bithynia (*Or.* 41. 1–2), Nicomedia (*Or.* 38. 1), and Rome (*Or.* 13. 31).
Cf. Aristid. *Or.* 24. 1–3.

[117] Cf. above, n. 23. Arrian, called the *neos Xenophōn* in the *Suda* (*A* 3868), in *Cyneg.*
1. 4 has no hesitation in drawing a parallel between himself and Xenophon: cf. Swain
(1996) 246–7.

[118] *Or.* 12. 74. On this speech, cf. Desideri (1980), Cellini (1995), Swain (1996) 197.

[119] Cf. below, p. 84.

[120] Cf. above, nn. 107 ff.; Salmeri (1982) 90–5, Sheppard (1984–6).

[121] *Or.* 38. 1.

audience see how much better off they would be if they gave up
contending with nearby Nicaea for the title of *prōtē*:[122] the governors would no longer be able to exploit tensions between the two
cities, and the Romans would lose the object of their sneers.[123] He
also made a point of impressing on his audience the concrete gains
they stood to obtain once Nicaea and Nicomedia entered into
homonoia. They would be able to exchange magistrates, benefactors,
and wise counsellors, the miscreants of one city could no longer take
refuge in the other, while the cities would reap redoubled produce
and wealth on the strength of their close relations.[124]

The main burden of Dio's political speeches outside Prusa as in
his own native city remained the appeal for concord and internal
stability. We may take the cases of Tarsus, Nicaea, and Alexandria:[125]
when the rhetor visited these places he would on occasion—in Tarsus,
for example—give more than one speech,[126] but he never seems to

---

[122] The history of the clashes between Nicaea and Nicomedia, which Dio defined
as 'a war over names' (*Or.* 38. 33), is reconstructed in Robert (1977*b*), cf. also Debord
(1998) 156 ff. Referring to his own times, Dio points out that the two cities do not
contend for possession of land or seas (38. 22), but for the title of *prōtē* (38. 24, 33).
In fact, not content with being the undisputed metropolis of the province of
Bithynia (38. 39) with all the privileges this entailed, Nicomedia also wished to become
the only city bearing the title of 'first', which Nicaea also boasted.

[123] *Or.* 38. 36–8, cf. *Or.* 34. 48.

[124] *Or.* 38. 41–2: the *homonoia* recommended by Dio has no legal aspect. The hypothesis of Kienast (1964) that in Roman Asia Minor the cities were able to conclude
treaties of *homonoia* ('Homonoiaverträge') deriving from the Hellenistic treaties of
isopoliteia does not seem to stand: cf. Jones (1978) 84, Pera (1984) 12–13, Price (1984)
126, all pointing out the lack of any epigraphic evidence. In Kienast (1995) the hypothesis of *homonoia* treaties is abandoned in favour of more generic agreements
('Vereinbarungen'), which do not appear any more acceptable. The *homonoia* coins
of the cities of Asia Minor are analysed in Pera (1984), where manifold reasons for
their origin are identified. Cf. also Kampmann (1997).

[125] Tarsus: *Or.* 34 (above, n. 112 and below, n. 126); Nicaea: *Or.* 39 (below, n.
131); Alexandria: *Or.* 32 (below, n. 137).

[126] It is certain that Dio delivered two speeches in Tarsus: *Orr.* 33–4; there is no
certainty about the other two speeches (*Orr.* 79–80), which the title applied in the
manuscript tradition (not unanimously for *Or.* 79) purports to have been delivered
in Cilicia. For the dating of the former two speeches to the reign of Trajan, and to
the last years of Dio's life (after 105), cf. von Arnim (1898) 443 ff., 460 ff., Jones (1978)
136, Salmeri (1982) 100 n. 40. The second Tarsian speech (*Or.* 34) in particular is of
a distinctly political turn: immediately introducing himself to his public as a philosopher, Dio berates the philosophasters who sow hatred in the city and goes on to
review the city's problems, beginning with its rivalry with neighbouring centres (7–14),
going on to the bad relations with the Roman governor (15), and concluding with
the discord often reigning between the various city organizations and groups (above,
n. 102) and the uprisings stirred up by the *linourgoi* (above, n. 112). Nor does Dio
neglect to mention the shortcomings of the local ruling groups (28–37). Faced with
such a state of affairs, his advice is to show superiority to the demands and provocation

have received any money for his labours.[127] In general he would be given the honour of citizenship and a supernumerary seat in the *boulē*, which of course enhanced his prestige while allowing him to point out to his audience that he was in fact no stranger, but one of them.[128] In the speeches delivered in Tarsus and Alexandria, Dio makes no explicit reference to his local citizenship, but this does not necessarily mean that he was sent there by the emperor. In fact, there is no decisive evidence to support such an assumption, and no reason why the two eastern metropolises should not be among the cities that—in the words of the rhetor himself—requested his counsels and speeches.[129] *Homonoia* and *eutaxia* certainly were close to the heart

of neighbours (47), to be neither servile nor argumentative in relations with the governors (38–41), and to grant full citizenship to the *linourgoi* (above, n. 112). Inspired by principles of moderation and compromise (cf. above, nn. 53, 112–13), these suggestions seem to aim at restoring not only concord to Tarsus (17, cf. 45), but also that *eutaxia* (25), or proper conduct, that constituted the only way for the capital of Cilicia to continue enjoying the many privileges obtained from Augustus (cf. Salmeri (1982) 75 n. 97 and 102 n. 49). Cf. below, n. 137. With regard to the first Tarsian speech (*Or.* 33), cf. below, nn. 149–52.

[127] *Or.* 3. 15, cf. *Or.* 13. 33 and above, n. 45.

[128] In *Or.* 39. 1 (*Egō chairō timōmenos huph'humōn* . . .) Dio is almost certainly referring to the citizenship granted him by Nicaea. In *Or.* 38. 1 the rhetor explicitly states that he has received the citizenship of Nicomedia; while in *Or.* 41. 5 he lets it be understood that he has also received that of the Roman colony of Apamea in Bithynia (cf. Salmeri (1982) 15). Moreover, before the citizens of Apamea Dio affirms that he has received citizenship, a seat in the *boulē*, and the highest honours not only from other cities but also from other—no more clearly identified—colonies that found him 'neither unserviceable to themselves, nor unworthy of being honoured' (*Or.* 41. 2). Cf. *OGIS* 567, and Sartre (1991) 126. Here the case of Dio is a clear example of a point Pliny the Younger makes in *Ep.* 10. 114. 1, stating that at the time of his mission the article of the *lex Pompeia* that allowed 'Bithynicis civitatibus adscribere sibi quos vellent cives, dum ne quem earum civitatium quae sunt in Bithynia' remained a dead letter: cf. Sherwin-White (1966) 724–5.

[129] As already pointed out in Salmeri (1982) 92–3. In the first place, in *Or.* 33. 13 Dio clearly alludes to the fact that his intervention had been requested by the people of Tarsus and, since *Or.* 33 appears to be contemporary with *Or.* 34 (cf. above, n. 126), the latter, too, should have been the upshot of a local invitation. However, Kienast (1971) 68 argues on the evidence of *Or.* 34. 1 (in Tarsus only *hoi gnōrimoi kai hoi plousioi* are allowed to speak in the assembly) that Dio was able to speak in the assembly of the Cilician city only as the envoy of Trajan, ignoring the possibility that the rhetor, without making a point of it, might well have held the citizenship of Tarsus and belonged to its *boulē* (cf. *Or.* 41. 2). Another hypothesis of Kienast's ((1971) 74–7), that Trajan sent Dio to the capital of Cilicia in 113 to restore order before the Parthian expedition, is rightly contested by Jones (1978) 137. Again, Desideri (1978) 109, 118, 166–7 nn. 86–7, argues—on the basis of an identification of the emperor with the divinity said to have sent Dio to Tarsus (*Or.* 34. 4)—that the orator was Trajan's emissary to the city (cf. Desideri (1991*a*) 3893). However, nothing in the passage cited warrants such an interpretation: cf. below in this note some observations on a similar situation recorded in *Or.* 32, and Swain (1996) 217 n. 115.

of the lord and master in Rome, but they were even closer to the hearts of the provincial notables.[130]

It was in particular at Nicaea, in the speech he delivered after rioting had shaken the city, that Dio specifically sings the praises of *homonoia* within the city, describing it as the fairest sight and sweetest sound, a surer guarantee than abundance of buildings, territory, or population.[131] Addressing his own fellow-citizens in Prusa, he looks to the animal realm for images of concord, evoking the life-styles of bees and ants.[132] To the same end he also draws on the doctrines of the Stoics, often offering as a model to his listeners the harmony reigning among the gods, heavenly bodies, and elements, and compares the havoc that would beset the universe, were *homonoia* and *philia* to disappear, to that of a city unable to live in peace.[133]

With regard to Dio's mission to Alexandria (*Or.* 32), Jones (1978) 44 very gingerly suggests that he might in some way have been the bearer of a message from the emperor (Vespasian, according to his dating of the text: but cf. below, n. 142), while adding that there seem to be no other cases of a Greek acting as imperial envoy in a city not his own. Desideri (1978) 105, 109–10, 166–7 nn. 87–8, following the same line, goes much further and decisively identifies Vespasian (but, again, for the dating of *Or.* 32, cf. below, n. 142) with the *daimonion* (Serapis) spurring Dio on to his mission (32. 12), to present the orator as an imperial emissary *tout court*; cf. Moles (1978) 84. However, the fact that Dio claims to have been spurred by the intervention of a divinity does not automatically imply that he was sent by the emperor. Rather, it tends to enhance the sacred aura the author wishes to create about himself—also comparing himself with Hermes sent by Zeus—in order to be able to face the crowd in Alexandria with confidence (*Or.* 32. 21–2). Finally, and again in contrast to the idea of Dio as an imperial emissary, it is worth recalling that in *Or.* 32. 24 he says he wishes to 'be of use' (*ōphelein*) to the people of Alexandria, insisting on that 'utility' that earned him the citizenship of various cities (*Or.* 41. 2, cf. Or. 38. 1). Cf. Salmeri (1982) 93 n. 13, and Sidebottom (1996) 447–9.

[130] For the presentation of Dio as a theoretician of concord, cf. Palm (1959) 31. In particular, in his speech to the inhabitants of Nicomedia Dio sings the praises of concord at length; he also asserts that we owe it to concord that things continue to exist and are not destroyed by the strife men incline to (*Or.* 38. 10–15, cf. *Or.* 33. 28). On *homonoia* in general and its cult in the Greek cities, cf. Thériault (1996).

[131] *Or.* 39. 3–5. Aelius Aristides (*Or.* 24. 4) presents concord as the greatest asset cities can have.

[132] *Or.* 40. 32 (ants), 40 (birds, ants, bees); *Or.* 44. 7 (bees); *Or.* 48. 16 (ants). On such models, cf. Quet (1978) 67, 72.

[133] Cf. *Or.* 36. 22 (concord and perfect happiness reigning among the gods), 30 (the order of the universe); *Or.* 40. 35 ff. (harmony among the elements); *Or.* 48. 14 (disaster in the absence of concord). Still valid is von Arnim (1898) 476–7 on the far from original nature of Dio's Stoicism; cf. also Brunt (1973) and Moles (1978) 94 and n. 130. Specifically on the Stoic roots and political potential of Dio's cosmology in *Or.* 36 (below, nn. 134, 157–62), cf. Swain (1996) 203–5.

There is nothing particularly original about such images and examples, but the rhetor does not disdain using them. It is not his purpose to develop new theories in his speeches: the tried and tested teachings of Plato and the Stoics proved a great help in winning over his hearers.[134] And the fact that the conception of *homonoia* evoked in his speeches seems to echo Aristotle's definition of it as an extension of *philia* between individuals to the city, in no way detracts from the validity of Dio's political speeches.[135] On the contrary, by appealing to the great philosophers and ancient schools he succeeds better than others in giving substance and content to the widely felt need for concord.

Again, we have Dio to thank if *eutaxia* (discipline, good conduct, balance), which we see extolled in so many inscriptions of the Antonine age as an ideal for individual living,[136] takes on a more political connotation. Associating it with other virtues, the rhetor recommends it to the people of Tarsus and Alexandria as a worthy goal, seeking to impress upon them that only through proper conduct could they conserve their privileges and prestige.[137] Narrow and conservative as the vision may seem, the fact remains—as Aelius Aristides acknowledged with lucid realism—that there was nothing left for Greek orators to do under the Empire but urge concord on their listeners.[138]

Alongside appeals for concord, which evoke the turbulent conditions that must have prompted them, Dio's speeches often contain censorious observations on the moral conduct of the Greeks of his

[134] In *Praec. ger. reip.* 803a Plutarch invites politicians to use *gnōmologiai, historiai, muthoi, metaphorai*, as occasion demands, to capture the attention of the audience. In perfect keeping with this, in a speech delivered at Prusa shortly after his return from exile (*Or.* 36, cf. above, nn. 68, 133), Dio recalls a *muthos* on the order of the universe and its creation by the supreme god, explaining how it was sung in secret rites by *magoi andres* (39 ff.). Bidez and Cumont (1938) 1: 92 ff. argue that the fusion of Stoic and Zoroastrian elements to be found in the *muthos* had already been brought about before Dio by Hellenized *magoi*. Nock (1940) 197–8 underlines the 'elevated writing' displayed by the piece, and the presence of Platonic influences. Cf. Trapp, below, pp. 214–19.

[135] Compare *Orr.* 38. 11; 40. 26, 41; 41. 13 with Arist. *EN* 7. 1155ᵃ, 9. 1167ᵃ.

[136] On *eutaxia* as an ideal in the life of individuals in the second century, cf. [Plut.] *Cons. ad Apoll.* 119f; Reinach (1906) 119 no. 41, Robert and Robert (1954) 177 nos. 70–1, Robert (1965) 222. On *eutaxia* as subject of competition in the gymnasiums of the Hellenistic period, see Crowther (1991). Cf. also Panagopoulos (1977) 213.

[137] *Orr.* 32. 37, 95; 33. 48; 34. 25. Here we may also recall the close tie Aristotle draws in *Politics* 7. 1326ᵃ between *eunomia* and *eutaxia*.

[138] Aristid. *Or.* 23. 2–3.

times, notably in the addresses to the people of Rhodes, Alexandria, Apamea in Phrygia, and the first *Tarsian Oration*.[139]

In Rhodes the rhetor begins by immediately warning his audience that, albeit not a citizen, and uninvited,[140] he intends to broach a subject that grieves him. The point was that, in order to honour certain contemporary personages, and Romans in particular, the Rhodians dedicated to them old statues erasing the name of the previous honorands, thus satisfying their needs at little expense—apart from that of their own dignity. In such a way, the last of the inhabitants of the great Greek cities of ancient times which still counted for something were destroying the records of their own past, wiping out the rightful memory of heroes who had sacrificed their lives in order to gain the favour of the lords and masters of the Empire.[141]

In the latter years of his life Dio presented himself to the people of Alexandria in the robes of the philosopher, and as an envoy of Zeus no less,[142] fully aware of the importance of addressing the people of

[139] Cf. below, pp. 84–6.

[140] *Or.* 31. 1. This might also mean that the request to address a speech to the people of Rhodes was made to Dio extemporaneously during a visit to the island (cf. *Or.* 36. 14–15). Having previously (Salmeri (1982) 96) accepted Momigliano's dating of the speech to the early years of Vespasian, I now incline, with Sidebottom and Swain, to ascribe it to the reign of Trajan: cf. above, n. 115. However, this does not affect the interpretation of the text given in Salmeri (1982) 96–7, as a reprimand against the dishonourable treatment the Rhodians accorded their statues (cf. below), together with an appeal to set dignity of conduct before every other consideration, as befits true Greeks. Cf. now Veyne (1999) 541–53.

[141] *Or.* 31. 8–9 etc.; for the statues dedicated to Romans, cf. 31. 43, 105; for Rhodes as the last bulwark of Hellenism in the imperial age, cf. 31. 157.

[142] Dio is addressing the 'people' of Alexandria: *Or.* 32. 2, 4, 24–5, 29, 96; it is worth recalling that the city was not to have a *boulē* until the years of Septimius Severus (Dio Cass. 51. 17. 2–3; *HA, Sev.* 17). For the philosopher's dress: *Or.* 32. 22, cf. *Or.* 34. 2 (above, n. 126). For Dio's self-comparison with Hermes as an envoy sent, against his own will, by Zeus: *Or.* 32. 21–2, cf. above, n. 129. The dating of the speech to the reign of Trajan proposed by von Arnim (1898) 435–8, mainly taking into consideration analogies between the section concerning kings and tyrants (*Or.* 32. 25–6) and the *peri basileias* orations (cf. below, nn. 177 ff.), was almost unanimously accepted until Jones (1973) 302–9 suggested ascribing it to the reign of Vespasian. Jones's arguments are questioned in close detail by Salmeri (1982) 97–8 n. 30, where a dating to the period of Trajan is preferred: in particular, I do not accept Jones's identification (305 ff.) of the relatively unimportant *tarachē* mentioned by Dio (*Or.* 32. 71–2) with the Alexandrian revolt recorded by the Armenian Eusebius and dated to 74/5 (in his *Chronicon* Jerome ascribes it to 73); the Alexandrian revolt seems rather to have to do with the disorders stirred up by certain Sicarii who, after Judaea was subdued, had left the country and made their way to Egypt (Jos. *BJ* 7. 407 ff.). This criticism of Jones's arguments is taken up in Sidebottom (1992) 415–18, who also proposes a Trajanic date. In this connection, cf. also Kindstrand (1978) and Swain (1996) 429. Jones (1997) reasserts attribution to the period of Vespasian.

the second city of the Empire.[143] He was not intimidated by them, however, and proclaimed his discontent with Alexandria and defined life there as a 'wild, ruinous revel of dancers, whistlers and murderers',[144] making particularly scathing animadversions against the mania that gripped the city for chariot races and performances by cithara-players—occasions when anything might happen, from howling and whistling to rioting.[145] All this was undesirable to his eyes, and above all for the Alexandrians, who may have entertained a high opinion of themselves but were not only incapable of exercising command like the Spartans of former times: they did not even know how to behave as good subjects.[146]

At Apamea in Phrygia[147] the rhetor's dissatisfaction came out in ironic remarks on the oratorical tastes of the city's conceited inhabitants, eagerly drinking in the fulsome praises poured forth by the sophists.[148] In his first address to the people of Tarsus,[149] on the other hand, Dio's shaft of censure falls on a characteristic vice of the city, which was to 'snort' all day long. Without wasting his words on the subject, the rhetor simply compares it with the noise made 'when men are drunk, or have gorged themselves with food, or are reclining in an uncomfortable position'; to hear it one would think the city is one huge 'brothel'.[150] Given such a scant description, and

---

[143] For Alexandria as the second city under the sun, and thus in the Empire: *Or.* 32. 35. The care Dio took over the drafting of his speech is aptly underlined in Burckhardt (1864) 120.

[144] *Or.* 32. 69.

[145] *Or.* 32. 41, cf. *Or.* 32. 45, 50, 55–6, 69 ff. The Apollonius of Tyana created by Philostratus, following also Dio's model, was another opponent of chariot races: *VA* 5. 26.

[146] *Or.* 32. 69, cf. *Or.* 32. 52–3.

[147] For dating of this speech (*Or.* 35) to the years after 100, cf. von Arnim (1898) 463 (after 105), Jones (1978) 137, and Salmeri (1982) 102 n. 50.

[148] For an early appraisal of the ironic nature of the speech, cf. Burckhardt (1864) 119, and now Zambrini (1994). The refined oratorical expectations of the inhabitants of Apamea are made fun of in *Or.* 35. 1; the sophists are attacked at 35. 8. In the conclusion of his speech, or at least the last part that has come down to us, Dio declares with evident hyperbole that only the mythical Indians (*Or.* 35. 18 ff., cf. Luc. *VH* 2. 6–16) and those men who amass hoards of gold stealing it from the fabled ants (*Or.* 35. 23 ff., cf. Hdt. 3. 102–5) are happier than the inhabitants of Apamea. Such unlikely comparisons are all part of the author's way of mocking the credulity and conceit of his audience, while taking off the sophists they are so fond of. Cf. Jones (1978) 69–70 and Salmeri (1982) 103.

[149] For dating of the first Tarsian speech (*Or.* 33), and indeed the second (*Or.* 34), to the reign of Trajan and the final period of Dio's life, cf. above, n. 126. Desideri (1978) 423 prefers to date the first Tarsian speech to the period preceding Dio's exile.

[150] *Or.* 33. 33; for Tarsus as a 'brothel': 33. 36, 60.

considering the hostility to homosexuality permeating the speech, some have identified the 'snorting' with the groans and grunts of sexual intercourse.[151] Perhaps Dio simply meant the snorting as a symbol of the bad conduct of the people of Tarsus, but his dissatisfaction with the city—an ancient colony of Argos—remains unmitigated.[152]

In the face of the undignified behaviour displayed by so many communities of the Greek world in his times, Dio evoked the past glory of that same world. Admittedly, none of the surviving orations commemorate specific events in the ancient history of Greece, but they show a rich sprinkling of references to Pericles, Epaminondas, Plataea, Leuctra, and Thermopylae—in short, that heritage of memories that Greeks cultivated with growing interest under the Empire, and which marked them out distinctly from the Gauls and Britons, subjects of the same monarch.[153] And while Plutarch saw recollections of the Hellenic past in the speeches of the politicians of his day as a means to attune themselves with their audiences, to guide and correct their conduct,[154] Dio held out the protagonists and episodes of ancient Hellas as models in his orations, urging his contemporaries to emulate them in dignity, or at least to mend their ways.[155] Moral admonitions take on political overtones, Dio's approach emerging clearly in a speech delivered in Prusa:

---

[151] Swain (1996) 214–16, esp. 214–15 n. 99; cf. Gleason (1995) 82, Houser (1998).

[152] The possibility that the 'snorting' had a symbolic significance is suggested in Jones (1978) 74. The Argive origin of Tarsus is recalled in *Or.* 33. 40–1, as also in Str. 14. 5. 12, but cf. Ruge (1932) 2416 and Robert (1977*a*) 107.

[153] Salmeri (1982) 104–7. Pericles: *Orr.* 12. 6 and 55; 25. 4; 49. 6; 51. 7; 73. 5; Epaminondas: *Orr.* 22. 2–3; 43. 4; 45. 13; 49. 5–6; Plataea: *Orr.* 11. 145; 56. 6; Leuctra: *Orr.* 15. 28 and *Or.* 22. 2–3 (contrast Aristides' five orations on the subject, *Orr.* 11–15 Lenz–Behr). Thermopylae: *Orr.* 31. 18; 78. 40. As an admirer of Xenophon (*Or.* 18. 14), while associating Athenians and Spartans as models (*Orr.* 44. 11 and 50. 2), Dio shows a greater appreciation for the constitution of Sparta, including such important figures as the ephors (*Or.* 56. 6); for his criticism of the Athenians' democratic constitution, cf. *Orr.* 7. 108; 48. 12–13; 50. 2. (On Xenophon as Dio's major source for Sparta, cf. Tigerstedt (1974) 201–6.) On references to the Greek past, use of rhetorical maxims, etc. in Dio and Plutarch, cf. Quet (1978) 56–62.

[154] *Praec. ger. reip.* 803a, 814a–c (here the point is stressed that subjects which may excite the public should be avoided): cf. Swain (1996) 166–7.

[155] Cf. above, n. 153. We may add that, apart from Xenophon (above, n. 114), Dio considered it important for the *politikos anēr* to be acquainted with historians like Herodotus, Thucydides, and Theopompus (*Or.* 18. 10). Moreover, the speeches given in Rhodes (*Or.* 31), Tarsus (*Or.* 33), and Nicaea (*Or.* 39) show that Dio was well acquainted with the foundation legends and the variegated histories of the cities (cf. Salmeri (1982) 106 n. 65), using both to urge dignity of conduct on his listeners. I cannot accept the interpretation advanced by Bowie (1974), esp. 203–9, that

If therefore, you find me making use of examples from ancient Greece, as is my wont, do not jeer at me; indeed, I do not think ill of our city, nor do I hold you incapable of understanding such things, nor regard the assembly or the council as ignorant. But what I most desire is that you have a truly Greek character, and that you be neither ungrateful nor foolhardy. If, however, this is asking too much, it would certainly do you no harm to listen to these words and receive their fruits which, I believe, may improve your characters.[156]

It was again to this end that Dio on his return from exile gave his fellow-citizens a 'fabulous' account of the valiant conduct he had observed during his stay at Borysthenes, the ancient Milesian colony on the northern coast of the Black Sea.[157] Under the constant threat of barbarian attack and incursions, it was, unlike the rest of the Greek world, ever ready for war, to the extent that its inhabitants, *philēkooi kai tōi tropōi Hellēnes*, went in arms to listen to Dio's speech, anticipating a sudden assault.[158] The result of this state of affairs was a modest tenor of life in Borysthenes, but one free of corruption and contentiousness,[159] and as such a possible model for

re-evocation of the past in the Greek authors of the second century AD was a way for them to elude, at least verbally, their dependence on Roman power: cf. Gascó (1992). On the use of the past to consolidate the (Greek) identity of the 'groups' authors like Dio addressed, cf. Schmitz (1997) 193–6.

[156] *Or.* 43. 3, cf. *Or.* 44. 10, 50. 2.

[157] For the dating of the *Borystheniticus* (*Or.* 36) to the period following Dio's exile, cf. Jones (1978) 135 and Salmeri (1982) 28 n. 88. The interpretation adopted here is that of Salmeri (1982) 107–10. A commentary on the text can be found in Russell (1992) 211–47. On the *muthos* of the order of the universe and its creation by the supreme god, cf. above, n. 134. Borysthenes is defined by Dio as *archaia* and *hellēnis* (*Or.* 36. 18), and is recorded as a colony of Miletus (*Or.* 36. 8); the rhetor adopts the name Borysthenes for literary purposes, the name most commonly used for the city at the time being Olbia: cf. Belin de Ballu (1972) 20–2 (however, on the inaccuracies to be found in this volume see Braschinsky (1977)). Jones (1978) 63 is sceptical about the veracity of Dio's representation of Borysthenes, above all underlining the idealization of the inhabitants; with an eye on the archaeological evidence Braund (1997) 126 ff. argues that Dio overstates the isolation the city found itself in during the imperial age.

[158] Borysthenes takes to war: *Or.* 36. 8; suffers barbarian raids: 36. 15; listens to Dio in arms: 36. 16. Although Dio does not hide the fact that the Greek spoken in Borysthenes is not pure *dia to en mesois oikein tois barbarois* (36. 9), he seeks to assert the Greek character of the city, thus tending to pass over the barbarian presences within it, now revealed by archaeological investigation: Braund (1997) 129.

[159] *Or.* 36. 5, 25. Indicative of Dio's propensity for the life-style of Borysthenes is the fact that in the speech he recalls a distich by Phocylides (fr. 4 Diehl)—which has thus come down to us—asserting that a small town perched on a rock is, if it keeps order, preferable to foolhardy Nineveh (*Or.* 36. 13). Themistius also cites the distich (*Or.* 24. 307C), but his source is evidently Dio.

the inhabitants of the many Greek cities afflicted with internal strife.[160] Of course, this does not mean that Dio's words were in any way aimed against the peace of the Empire.[161] Despite his dissatisfaction with the manners and morals of the Greeks of his time, he did not wish war upon them as a general condition to lead them in the direction of virtue,[162] nor did his praise of warlike Borysthenes mean that it should be a model to imitate *in toto*; rather, he sought to keep the image of the true Hellas alive among the citizens of Prusa, as a spur to overcome strife and vices.

DIO AND ROME

Apart from the strictly educative aim, recollection of the past glories of the Greeks in Dio's orations is also dictated by the sense that the customs of his people were more ancient than the Romans' own,

---

[160] Salmeri (1982) 110. Acknowledging that the message Dio wished to impress on his audience in the *Borystheniticus* was in part of a political nature, i.e. to urge on them the practice of wise government, Swain (1996) 83–5 also points out certain ironical touches in the description of Borysthenes as an ideal city. On the spatial play in *Or.* 36, delivered in Prusa but dedicated to the evocation of a journey to a distant outpost of the Hellenic world, cf. Trapp (1995) 165–7.

[161] Salmeri (1982) 109–10, cf. Sidebottom (1993) 251–2 and below, n. 164.

[162] On the association between peace and corruption of the spirit, and between war and nobility of soul, so evident in Dio and often recurring in the Greek and Latin culture of the first century AD, though dating back hundreds of years before, cf. Salmeri (1982) 109–10 nn. 76–9. A passage significant for Dio's attitude towards war appears in the *Olympicus* (*Or.* 12): arriving in Olympia from the Danube and the regions of the Getae, Dio asserts he had gone there—as *eirēnikos polemou theatēs* (note the play of words)—driven by the wish to see 'men who fight for dominion and power, and on the other side other men fighting for freedom and their native land' (20). Bearing in mind that the *Olympicus* most probably dates to 105 (cf. von Arnim (1898) 405–7, Desideri (1978) 279 n. 49, Salmeri (1982) 36 nn. 119–20, Russell (1992) 16, 171), the reference here can only be to the second Dacian war (105–6). The tone Dio adopts, when referring to his own presence in the encampment during the preparations, does not suggest great enthusiasm for the event, and he is moreover unequivocal in describing the Roman action as aggressive and imperialist. However, I fail to see Dio going any further than this 'objective' assessment, to the point of openly espousing the cause of the Dacians and supporting wars of liberation against the Romans. Rather, the rhetor's judgement is in perfect accord with the context of the *Olympicus*, which suggests some Roman responsibility in the decline of Greece. As for the Getae, in *Or.* 48. 5 (probably written soon after the *Olympicus*: Salmeri (1982) 36), showing no sympathy Dio defines them as *echthroi* and *kataratoi*. In particular, for interpretation of *Or.* 12. 20, cf. Sidebottom (1993) 255–6, (1994) 266; Moles (1995) 181–4; Swain (1996) 202.

and indeed superior to them.[163] He certainly had no aspiration to overthrow the power of the emperors,[164] but he also had no qualms about pointing out certain crude, uncivilized aspects of the behaviour of the Roman masters.

Referring to the origins of Rome, Dio[165] describes it as inhabited by a mob of poor, wild men, its very existence jeopardized by the harshness and cruelty of Romulus.[166] Moreover, he speaks with horror of the right ancient Roman fathers enjoyed of condemning their children to death without trial or evidence,[167] and takes a decisive stance against the cruelty of gladiatorial games.[168] Indeed, it may well have been thoughts of Rome's murky past that rankled most with Dio when he saw the Rhodians attributing statues of Heracles or Tlepolemus, or the sons of Helius, to some obscure Roman Caius or Sempronius.[169]

---

[163] Cf. Bowie (1991) 195–204, Schmitz (1999) 85. Compare the case of Plutarch: much as he appears, for example, to appreciate Flamininus' famous declaration of Greek liberty, he tends to keep his distance from the Romans and defines them as 'foreigners' in the same passage: *Flamin.* 11. 7, cf. Swain (1996) 140, 147–8, (1997) 172. Unlike Plutarch, Dionysius of Halicarnassus had as one of his main aims in the *Antiquitates Romanae* that of demonstrating the Greek origin of Rome and Roman life: cf. Gabba (1991) 97, 107–9, 134–8.

[164] On Dio's acceptance of the peace brought by the Empire, cf. Veyne (1976) 108.

[165] Hahn (1906) 206 defines Dio as less 'rombegeistert' than Plutarch.

[166] *Or.* 25. 8, cf. Dion. Hal. *Ant. Rom.* 1. 4. 8, where it is recalled that many Greeks were in the habit of making negative remarks about the origins of Rome: cf. Gruen (1984) 1: 354. In the same passage cited Dio has the subsequent *eudaimonia* of the Romans derive from the intervention of Numa, who gave them laws, gods, and a constitution. The king, albeit somewhat doubtfully, is presented in *Or.* 49. 6 as a follower of Pythagorean doctrines. In short, according to the ancient Tarantine tradition (Gabba (1991) 13–14) that Dio appears to accept, it was Greek wisdom that lay at the origin of the future developments of Rome. The tradition of Numa as a pupil of Pythagoras is rejected as anachronistic in Liv. 1. 18. 2; Dion. Hal., *Ant. Rom.* 2. 59; Cic. *Tusc.* 4. 1. 3; in Plutarch's Life of Numa the association of the Roman king with Pythagoras is also considered anachronistic (1. 3–6), but is accredited as having a deeper truth, cf. Rawson (1989) 235–6. Other references to Numa in Dio are in the paragraphs preceding *Or.* 25. 8 and in *Orr.* 56. 4 and 80. 3.

[167] *Or.* 15. 20: here the Romans are not named explicitly, but the reference is clear.

[168] *Or.* 31. 121–2. The philosopher who criticizes the Athenians for their insane passion for gladiatorial games in this passage is probably Musonius Rufus, cf. Jones (1978) 32.

[169] *Or.* 31. 93. The passages so far examined, containing unfavourable references to the Romans, are listed by Schmid (1887–97) 1: 38 n. 13. In *Or.* 36. 17 Dio refers contemptuously to the only inhabitant of Borysthenes who shaves off his beard as a sign of adulation and friendship towards the Romans, criticizing not so much the Roman habit of shaving (dominant before Hadrian) as the fawning attitude towards Rome, cf. Swain (1996) 217.

However, none of this points to any real polemic against the Romans on the part of Dio; nor does his carping at the vices and degeneration displayed by the capital of the Empire rise to the level of true invective.[170] A certain polemical *vis* does, however, seem to emerge[171] when the rhetor, dwelling on the theme of *eutuchia*, tells the Rhodians it was only valour that saved their city from collapse, while Rome owed its fortunes to good luck as well as valour.[172]

Behind these words we may discern the old historiographic tradition that sought to cut Rome down to size and strike a blow at its arrogance by attributing a leading role in the city's conquests to *eutuchia*.[173] However, the sense of superiority displayed by the Greek Dio never, let us repeat, resolves itself into defiance of the Empire.[174] Jealous a guardian as he was of the margins of autonomy left to the Hellenic cities, the rhetor nevertheless realized that his fortunes, no less than those of any other notables in the Greek world, rested on the peace generally obtaining throughout the Roman world. True, Dio launched formidable accusations and violent tirades against Nero and Domitian, but never with the apparent intention of calling imperial rule into question, his aim being rather to denounce tyrannical degeneration.[175]

---

[170] *Or.* 13. 33–4, 36, cf. Jones (1978) 128–9. A more radical interpretation can be found in Moles (1995) 180 and Swain (1996) 212.

[171] It may possibly be detected also in the *Olympicus* where Zeus is extolled as the god of peace, while the Romans are presented by Dio as given to wars of conquest: *Or.* 12. 20, cf. above, n. 162. For Zeus as god of peace, cf. *Or.* 12. 74.

[172] *Or.* 31. 68, cf. *Orr.* 11. 142 and 41. 9 (but in these two passages reference to *eutuchia* does not actually appear to imply criticism).

[173] Cf. Fuchs (1938) 14–15, Gabba (1974) 637, Bernhardt (1985) 260.

[174] Cf. Veyne (1976) 108, Salmeri (1982) 112–13, and now Schmitz (1999) 85. For similar assessment of Aelius Aristides, cf. von Staden (1996) 160, Pernot (1997) 10. Here it should be noted that in *Or.* 41. 9 (cf. above, n. 115), where he addresses the inhabitants of the only Roman colony of Bithynia, Apamea, and urges them on to concord with his Prusa, having asserted that Rome is distinguished from the rest of humanity by virtue of its fortune (*eutuchia*) and power (*dunamis*), Dio goes on to add that it excels even more in moderation (*epieikeia*) and humanity (*philanthrōpia*), thanks to which it generously extends its citizenship, laws, and offices to those who are worthy of them, while at the same time guaranteeing just treatment to all. Evidently, the rhetor sets out to win over his audience with these words, offering them (10) a model of the open, well-disposed attitude to be adopted in relations with Prusa, but he also shows understanding of imperial Rome's behaviour. However, this is at the level of mere insight, and does not appear to be followed through in Dio's work. Cf. Desideri (1991*a*) 388*9*.

[175] Cf. Gabba (1959) 369. For Dio's attacks on Nero and Domitian, cf. Salmeri (1982) 113–14 n. 97, and also Szepessy (1987) and Cuvigny (1986).

Indeed, it never seems to have occurred to Dio, or Titus Flavius Cocceianus Dio, to give him his full Roman name,[176] that the world he knew could be ruled in any way other than monarchically, and by the sovereign who had his seat in Rome. However, in the four *Kingship Orations* he wrote for Trajan,[177] the rhetor and notable of Prusa takes a decidedly different view of the Empire's administration and recruitment of its ruling class from that voiced by Tacitus in the *Agricola* or in Claudius' speech in the eleventh book of the *Annals*.[178] Starting out from the traditional attitudes of Hellenistic philosophy and political culture towards monarchy[179] and not, as did Tacitus, from the centuries-long process constituting Roman history, he places the notion of 'friendship' at the basis of relations between emperor and ruling class, defining it as the 'fairest and most sacred' of conditions that may befall a sovereign, and the best defence of his fortunes. If a monarch succeeds in worthily fulfilling all his duties and satisfying all his needs, it is his friends he has to thank—the indispensable assistants and collaborators of one who rules over vast dominions.[180] Metaphorically represented as extraordinarily powerful eyes, ears, tongues, and hands, it is such friends that empower a master to keep all his lands under control.[181]

[176] On Dio's Roman name, cf. above, n. 67. It is worth recalling here that a fragmentary inscription from Prusa (*IK* 39. 33) mentions a certain *Titos Phlaouios Diōnos huios*, a *Titos Phlaouios Phaidrou huios*, a *Diōn* and also a *Kaleidia*; the inscription might have belonged to the funerary monument Dio had built for his wife and son (Pliny, *Ep.* 10. 81. 2).

[177] *Orr.* 1–4. General interpretation of them is beyond the scope of this paper; cf. Salmeri (1982) 35, 114–23 and, with various points of view, Jones (1978) 115–23, Desideri (1978) 283–316, Moles (1990), Swain (1996) 192 ff. For the dating of the four orations to the early years of Trajan's reign, and in particular of *Or.* 1 to late 99/early 100, following von Arnim (1898) 325 ff., 402 ff., cf. especially Salmeri (1982) 35 and nn. 114–18 and Moles (1990) 360–1; for a more precise dating of *Or.* 3 and 4, cf. below, n. 187.

[178] Cf. specifically Salmeri (1991) 553–61; in general, on the different viewpoints taken by the Latin historians and authors on the one hand, and their Greek counterparts on the other when considering the Empire, cf. Gabba (1984). The speech by Claudius in favour of admitting certain of the magnates of the Tres Galliae to the Senate is to be found in *Ann.* 11. 24; on the speech, also taking into account its epigraphic version (*ILS* 212), cf. Syme (1958) 1: 317–19, 459–60 and 2: 624; De Vivo (1980); Griffin (1982). A certain consonance between the fleeting intuition of *Or.* 41. 9, discussed in n. 174, with the speech by the Tacitean Claudius does not justify placing Dio himself in the line of Tacitus.

[179] Cf. Brunt (1979) 170, Salmeri (1982) 116 ff.

[180] *Or.* 3. 86–7 (the reordering of the text by Emperius and von Arnim here is not followed). Cf. Salmeri (1982) 121–2, and now Konstan (1997).

[181] *Or.* 3. 104–6, cf. Arist. *Pol.* 3. 1287[b].

On the nature of the relations that should exist between sovereign and friends Dio is most explicit: they cannot be based on the law, but must be rooted in loyalty (*eunoia*). Only thus can a sovereign enjoy security, and ward off the treachery and plotting against which *nomos* is impotent.[182] Dio sees the monarch's choice of friends as the decisive factor in the development of such relations: it can neither be taken casually, nor light on the first to appear, but must be made among the best and most gifted subjects, namely the free men (*eleutheroi*) and the nobles (*gennaioi*). In short, just as the best horses will be fetched from the Caspian area, and the best dogs from India, so from Rome the sovereign must cast about in all his lands for those who are to be his *philoi*.[183]

Dio's insistence that the emperor seek out friends in every corner of his dominions can be associated with the process by which, from the reign of Vespasian, the elites of the Greek East followed upon those of the West in gaining increasingly significant roles in the Senate and administration of the Empire, as we have seen above.[184] However, the rhetor of Prusa went no further than urging the need to recruit the Empire's ruling class from a vast geographical area; from his Graecocentric position he does not even seem to have formed a very clear picture of the way the Roman state worked.[185] While never mentioning senators or *equites* in his *peri basileias* orations, he suggests to Trajan as a model for his collaborators the figure of the *philos*, which had functioned perfectly well in the governing structures of the Hellenistic kingdoms but could not match up to the complex administration of the Roman Empire, deeply rooted as it still was in the Republican tradition.[186]

Moreover, with his gaze still fixed resolutely on the past—with such models as Agamemnon and Nestor, Alexander and Aristotle, Pericles and Anaxagoras before his eyes[187]—Dio believed that on the

---

[182] *Or.* 3. 88–9.

[183] *Or.* 3. 89, 129–31, cf. Pliny, *Paneg.* 45. 3. For the preference the sovereign should accord to 'free men' and 'nobles', cf. *Or.* 1. 33. On the emperor's choice of *amici* in general, cf. Brunt (1988).

[184] Cf. above, nn. 16 ff.

[185] Cf. Salmeri (1982) 122 n. 137; on Dio's lack of interest in Latin culture, cf. Desideri (1991a) 3885.

[186] Cf. Salmeri (1991) 560. On the figure of the *philos* in the Hellenistic courts, cf. (still) Corradi (1929) 318–43, and Habicht (1958), Herman (1980–1), Savalli-Lestrade (1998). In general, on the Hellenistic *basileia*, cf. now Virgilio (1998).

[187] *Or.* 49. 4, 6. This speech was delivered in Prusa shortly before a journey (15), probably the one that was to see Dio performing before Trajan with at least two of the *peri basileias* orations (*Or.* 3 and 4), and which was then to take him to the arena

strength of his learning, and without severing his ties with Prusa, he was the right man to take on the role of educator and counsellor to Trajan. This was the very role that, in the long history of relations between Greek intellectuals and Roman masters, had for brief periods and in exceptional circumstances been taken up by Polybius and Panaetius with Scipio Aemilianus, Posidonius and Theophanes with Pompey, and by the philosophers Areius and Athenodorus with Augustus.[188] Dio does not seem to have had much success with Trajan, however, not only because the emperor took no particular interest in culture and philosophy, but above all because the times were no longer those of Scipio, nor even of Augustus, when the Greek intellectuals could enter into contact with the Roman leaders without any particular formalities, and without any estrangement from their own world.[189] After Dio's failure two other notables from Bithynia of intellectual bent, Flavius Arrian and Cassius Dio,[190]

of operations between Romans and Dacians (above, n. 162): cf. Salmeri (1982) 34 n. 110 and 35 n. 118, and for a different view Jones (1978) 139. He dedicates much of the piece to reviewing relations (cf. Rawson (1989), and below, n. 188) between philosophers and men of culture (3: *pepaideumenoi*) on the one hand, and monarchs or men of power on the other, as if alluding to the real purpose of his journey: cf. Salmeri (1982) 125. Dio dwells on the influence Nestor had on Agamemnon in *Or.* 56, which Jones (1978) 137 argues should be associated with the *peri basileias* orations in date.

[188] Cf. Salmeri (1982) 5–10. Minimize as she might, not even Rawson (1989) can deny the existence of relations between Greek intellectuals and Roman masters, although we should heed her warning to verify such relations case by case, without automatically taking them to be permanent, and to beware of their idealization, notably by Dio and Themistius.

[189] Cf. Salmeri (1982) 35, 125–6. The only evidence we have suggesting cordial relations between Dio and Trajan is a passage in Philostratus (*VS* 488) showing the latter in ecstatic appreciation of the words proffered by the former as he is borne on the triumphal chariot (not, of course, during an actual triumph), but this is very probably a 'culturalist' construction of the author's: cf. Swain (1996) 195 n. 33, 397; Anderson (1986) 99–100; and Rawson (1989) 250; Fein (1994) 231–6 follows Philostratus, however. Cf. also Schmitz (1996) and Whitmarsh (1998) 207–11. In contrast, evidence of scant relations between Dio and Trajan can be found in the cool detachment marking a letter from Trajan to Pliny the Younger (*Ep.* 10. 82)—for the date, cf. above, n. 72—where he considers the accusations made against Dio by his political enemy Flavius Archippus: cf. Salmeri (1982) 125–6, and also Swain (1996) 237 and Sidebottom (1996) 454 n. 62. On the relatively unrefined culture of Trajan, who knew Greek, however, cf. Jones (1978) 115–16 and Moles (1990) 300–1. For an attempted typification on chronological grounds of relations between Roman masters and Greek intellectuals, cf. Salmeri (1982) 5–10. To be rejected is the thesis—defended among others by Mazon (1943) 56—that presents Dio (in the *Euboicus* : *Or.* 7. 33–7) as a propagandist of the emphyteutic policy of Trajan: cf. Salmeri (1982) 82–7.

[190] On Arrian, cf. above, n. 23. On Cassius Dio, from Nicaea, whose career spanned the late second century and the early decades of the third, the classic texts remain Gabba (1955) and Millar (1964); cf. Ameling (1984*b*), Aalders (1986), and Swain (1996) 401–8.

seeking optimal scope for their ambitions, apparently saw the Senate, magistracies, and provincial governorships as the structures most likely to assist them. For his own part, however, Dio had already taken full cognizance of the vital role the Roman Empire played in sustaining the fortunes of the local elites in the Greek East. As Paul Veyne put it, Dio was 'farouchement nationaliste' as well as a 'partisan inconditionel du pouvoir impérial'.[191]

---

[191] Veyne (1976) 108. Note that Dio is somewhat less of a *partisan* in Veyne (1999). Cf. in general Pernot (1998).

3

City and Country in Dio
PAOLO DESIDERI

THE HISTORICAL CONTEXT

I hardly need to recall here that Dio of Prusa was, together with Plutarch, the first author, and one of the most important ones, of the so-called Greek Renaissance in the time of the High Roman Empire.[1] Just a little less obvious, perhaps, is the fact that this Renaissance itself took place in a completely different political world from that which had been the theatre of classical Greek and

Thanks are due to Philip Stadter for improvements to the English of this chapter.

[1] The first modern occurrence of this expression in an (as it were) technical sense that is known to me is in W. Schmid's now virtually forgotten inaugural lecture at the University of Tübingen, *Über den kulturgeschichtlichen Zusammenhang und die Bedeutung der griechischen Renaissance in der Römerzeit* (1898). Just one year later, the fifth volume of the *Histoire de la littérature grecque* by Alfred and Maurice Croiset was published, which repeatedly uses the expression 'renaissance hellénique', in particular in the title of the third chapter of the second part (devoted to the Greek literature of the Roman period): 'Débuts de la renaissance hellénique au second siècle'. At the beginning of his lecture Schmid himself referred to the scholars he considered his forerunners in his appreciation of second-century Greek literature and culture: Giacomo Leopardi, the Italian 'poet and philosopher'; Jacob Burckhardt (the author of *Die Zeit Constantins des Grossen*, first published in 1853); Friedrich Nietzsche (especially for his *Antichrist*, written in 1888); and, above all, the great German scholar, 'Nietzsches Waffenbruder' (Seillière), Erwin Rohde, the author of *Der griechische Roman* (1876), to whom Schmid's lecture is dedicated. It is impossible (even if it would be well worth doing) to expound on these connections now, which lead to the very heart of European cultural life in the nineteenth century (see my own sketch in Desideri (1978), 524 ff., though it urgently needs to be updated and rewritten); but it is relevant to our present purposes not to forget that it is precisely in this context that the still most important modern book on Dio was conceived: H. von Arnim, *Leben und Werke des Dio von Prusa* (1898). The very idea of a renaissance of Greek oratory has recently been questioned by Brunt (1994), who would rather speak of a renaissance of Greek philosophy (p. 46); but the case of Dio is a good warning against any too strictly terminological approach to historical phenomena. According to Reardon (1984) 35, the emergence in this period of a new Greek literary prose could be better defined as a 'revolution' rather than a 'renaissance'.

Hellenistic culture. Octavian's victory at Actium had not only marked the end of a long period of Italian civil strife, but also of any independent political government in the East, and especially of any Greek civic tradition. It was due to an incredible underestimation, not to say misunderstanding, of the real significance of the events that had happened, that Dionysius of Halicarnassus could dare to declare in the introduction to his work *On the Ancient Orators* that a splendid new era was beginning. This was simply not true, not even from the strictly technical point of view of oratory, which was his main concern at that moment. He was perhaps right when he said that, as a consequence of Roman success, 'apart from a few Asian cities, where the progress of culture is impeded by ignorance, the world has ceased to admire vulgar, frigid and banal oratory'. He was far less right when he added that,

this state of affairs has led to the composition of many worthwhile works of history by contemporary writers, and the publication of many elegant political tracts and many by no means negligible philosophical treatises; and a host of other fine works, the products of well-directed industry, have proceeded from the pens of both Greeks and Romans, and will probably continue to do so.[2]

We may wonder about the existence of these admirable writings, at least as far as Greek literature is concerned. Even if one supposes that Dionysius is thinking of Strabo's *Geography* or his own *History of Early Rome*, the fact is that these works mark the end, not the beginning, of an era; and no new era was really to start until the end of the first century AD.

If one asks oneself the reasons why what was in fact to be a long and deep cultural crisis took place, one can immediately find an answer in the famous last chapter of Pseudo-Longinus *On the Sublime* (a work which is now dated to the first half of the first century AD).[3] Summing up the positions expressed in that chapter, we meet first that of the 'anonymous philosopher'. His point is that the universal peace which the Romans brought to the world put an end to the free political life of the cities and provoked a sort of general slavery;

---

[2] *De Ant. Or.* 3 (trans. Usher). Many scholars have examined this *Introduction* in the last few years, among whom I may mention Dihle (1977) 164 ff.; Desideri (1978) 78 f.; Bowersock (1979) 59 ff., 76 f.; Gabba (1982) 44 ff.; Swain (1996) 25 f. For the general outlook, from Dionysius' point of view, see esp. Gabba (1991) 24 ff.

[3] Gabba (1991) 42 n. 55 (with bibliography).

and from slavery neither oratory nor any other form of art or literature can be derived. The author himself does not share the philosopher's ideas, which presume a sort of primacy of politics: according to him, it is rather our own vices which are responsible for the crisis. Both the author and the philosopher, however, are convinced that they are living in an age of decline, at least as far as the Greek world is concerned; which, *pace* Dionysius' optimism, seems to be the current opinion in this century. It is Dio's (if not Plutarch's) opinion too, in spite of the fact that he himself is one of the key figures in the Renaissance.

Leaving Plutarch aside, I would like to suggest that most of Dio's body of thought on town and country may be considered as his way of envisaging the contemporary decay of the Greek world. In fact, the main thesis I will expound in the first part of this chapter is that the cities, and their inhabitants, were in Dio's opinion no longer (if they ever had been) the centre of the social and cultural experiences of human beings. Far from it: they were the place where one could find the worst of humanity. It is rather in the country, and among the country-dwellers, that one could find, according to Dio, a kind of moral and intellectual preserve of true human values. But Dio's works do not always hold to this belief: the Bithynian speeches, in particular, appear to be more optimistic as regards the possibility of acknowledging some positive meaning to civic life and its accomplishments. So, in the second part of my essay, I will examine these different positions, which surely date to the last years of Dio's life, and I will try to explain the reasons for what can be called a partial overturning of his previous way of thinking. It is precisely in this change of Dio's mind that one can find, as I suppose, a sign of the beginning of that Greek Renaissance which was to burst forth in the second century, alongside the characteristics and the limits of this Renaissance as well.[4]

THE CITY

Let us begin with the texts, and first with a passage from the *Alexandrian Oration* (32). I still believe that this oration was

---

[4] It is evident that I am not interested here in the *Realien* of the economic, administrative, or even cultural, life of the Greek towns themselves during the first centuries of the Roman Empire; I limit myself to referring to the recent sketch by Millar (1993).

pronounced in Vespasian's time,[5] and the arguments I will develop here could be seen, in a way, as a confirmation of this belief.[6] In general terms, Dio observes that the urban dimension not only makes individual defects appear macroscopic, but radically changes their nature as well. Speaking of the passionate love of songs and horse-racing, which enslaves the inhabitants of Alexandria, he says that

> while such experiences are doubtless terrible even in the case of individuals, they are altogether more disgraceful when they happen to a people. For indeed all other afflictions, as long as they affect a single person, receive no great or awful label; but when the visitation becomes general, then it is called a plague. For, on the whole, all varieties of human weakness might be discovered anywhere at all, and drunkards, perverts, and woman-crazed wretches are present in every city; and yet not even that condition is disturbing or beyond endurance; but when the malady becomes prevalent and a common spectacle, then it becomes noteworthy and serious and a civic issue. (32. 91)[7]

The obvious implication is that the cities, precisely because they are places where so many people live together, are particularly well disposed to the outbreak of sudden and unrestrainable moral and political diseases.

This concept is clearly formulated in another of the speeches directed to the inhabitants of the great eastern cities, *To Celaenae* (35), a speech where irony, not to mention sarcasm, plays a dominant role, as a young Italian scholar has recently shown.[8] Dealing with the pretended advantages which Phrygian Apamea could avail itself of as the head of an assize-district of the province of Asia, Dio says that a lot of people convened there, and a lot of money as well; in the same way as 'the district in which the most flocks are quartered proves to be the best', he comments, 'for the farmer because

---

[5] Desideri (1978) 68 ff. (based on Jones (1973) 302–9; Jones (1978) 36 reasserts the early dating). The alternative hypothesis of a 'Trajanic' dating, going back to von Arnim (1898) 435 ff., seems now to enjoy the favour of the majority: see Sidebottom (1992); Brunt (1994) 41 n. 70; Swain (1996) 429. I would like to reaffirm anyway that the only correct way of facing most of the problems which emerge from Dio's corpus is to try to fix—as far as possible—a chronology of its parts; that is, to consider Dio's texts as strongly connected to the author's experiences of life: see Desideri (1991*b*) 3928 n. 125.

[6] However, I am considering the possibility of a new discussion of the problem.

[7] This, like all the other Dio translations are (with some slight variations) those of Cohoon and Lamar Crosby (1932–51) in the Loeb Classical Library.

[8] Zambrini (1994).

of the dung, and indeed many farmers entreat the shepherds to quar-
ter their sheep on their land' (35. 16). It is evident that Dio is strongly
censuring the consequences of moral disorder which derive from the
congestion of urban life. And he adds with even greater sarcasm,
'nothing in the city is out of work, neither the teams nor the houses
nor the women' (35. 15). Here we can trace the same idea of the
impossibility of finding honourable jobs in a city that is present for
the bulk of the second part of the *Euboean Oration* (*Or. 7*, on which
see below).

The real problem appears to be, both in the Alexandrian and in
the Celaenaean discourses, the huge dimensions of the city, which
derive from its wealth, and the corruption it produces in the moral
values of its people. One can guess that, for Dio Rome itself, the
most important, the wealthiest, and the largest city of the Roman
Empire, is a sort of prototype of this situation. In fact, one of Dio's
discourses, *In Athens, On his Exile* (*Or. 13*), contains what can be
defined as a moral description of Rome, which corresponds exactly
to what might be expected. At the end of the speech (which is not,
however, preserved intact) Dio, who is speaking at Athens, affirms
that he is reproducing the issues he had been accustomed to
expound to the Romans as he tried to turn them away from their
obsession with making money and encourage them to a simpler and
happier way of life.

For only then, I continued, will your city be great and strong and truly
imperial, since at present its greatness arouses distrust and is not very secure
(13. 34) . . . and the houses in which you live will be smaller and better, and
you will not support so great a throng of idle and utterly useless slaves
. . . and the whole multitude that is now being supported in your city will
be much smaller. (13. 35)

It is clear that, apart from considerations of a moral nature, Dio was
denouncing the social risks of a situation in which a great amount
of wealth was assembled in one and the same place, amidst a mass
of underprivileged people. 'The situation', he said,

is similar to that in which Achilles, after heaping high the pyre of Patroclus
with many logs of wood, with many coverlets and garments, and also with
fat and olive oil in addition, summons the winds, with libations and the
promise of sacrifices, to come and set it afire and burn it. For such possessions as yours are no less likely to kindle the wanton spirit and licen-
tiousness of human beings. (13. 36)

Despite the differences in the contexts of the two speeches, the same ideas are recognizable in the previously mentioned Alexandrian discourse, where Dio exclaims, 'For on the whole it is better to behold a desert, or no more than fifteen substantial citizens, than an innumerable horde of wretched, raving creatures, a sort of concentrated dunghill piled high with the sweepings of every kind' (32. 87).[9] But the blame attributed to the city, as a kind of human settlement, can be even more radical in Dio's texts. In the speech *On Freedom* (80), proclaiming his right to live alone, apart from politics, 'conducting a popular assembly all by himself' (80. 2), Dio puts forward a general principle, according to which it is actually the towns themselves that deprive men of their freedom, even if the lawgivers say that they guarantee it.

On the contrary, after they had gathered within the compass of their city walls slavery without bound or limit, thereupon with ramparts and towers and missiles they tried to protect themselves against the chance that slavery might make its entry among them from without . . . Accordingly, just as it is said that the Trojans for Helen's sake endured siege and death, although she was not at Troy but in Egypt, just so has it been with these men—on behalf of their freedom they fought and struggled, when all the while they had no freedom.   (80. 4)

Along this same line of thought, in one of the so-called *Diogenics* —presumably to be dated in the period of Dio's exile—and specifically in the *Diogenes, or On Tyranny* (6), where Diogenes talks about life according to nature, the invention of the city appears as one of the most shocking symbols of human stupidity. 'Men crowded into the cities to escape wrong from those outside, only to wrong one another and commit all sorts of the most dreadful misdeeds as though that had been the object of their coming together' (6. 25). In one of the Bithynian speeches, *Before a Philosophical Career* (*Or.* 46)—the only one of the Bithynian speeches which was composed before Dio's exile—we can find the best comment from this perspective, derived from Dio's personal experience. Dio is speaking after a popular mutiny in Prusa, during which he and his relatives have risked their lives; they survived, Dio says, only because the mob assaulting their house did not dare pass through a very narrow lane which went around the house itself. 'If that is what saved me', he observes,

[9] In this passage I prefer to follow von Arnim's, instead of Lamar Crosby's, text.

it is high time from now on, as if the city were an armed camp, to occupy the difficult terrain and the lofty or precipitous positions! And yet, God knows, not even in armed camps does one soldier seek a safer spot than his neighbour in which to pitch his tent; no, their precautions are aimed at the men with whom they are at war. (46. 13)

Here too, as in Rome, the town reveals itself as a place where competition, or even strife, among the social classes reaches its peak, just because the demographic concentration, far from producing a sense of solidarity among men and fellow-citizens, intensifies mutual quarrels and makes them degenerate into outright hate. In situations like these it was the Roman troops, of course, who ultimately re-established order, protecting the well-to-do (46. 14); but when a Roman intervention took place, it was simply the open admission of the insecurity and precariousness of civic life, incapable of auto-nomously solving its own problems.

To sum up, civic life does not seem to offer respectable people any reason why it should be preferred to any other way of living and acting. This really marks the end of an ancient and authoritat-ive model in the Greek (and Roman) mentality. We are very far —going back to what I said at the beginning—from Dionysius' optimism.

THE COUNTRY

We shall not be surprised to find in many significant passages of Dio's works a sort of idealization of the rural, as contrasted with the urban, way of life. The most important of these passages is indeed an entire speech, the *Euboean Oration*. As everyone knows, the *Euboean* (or rather, its first part) is a discourse of great artistic value, but this does not prevent it from being at least as important from an ideological and cultural point of view as well. As a matter of fact, I would say that there is no need to polarize, as if they were mutu-ally exclusive, a literary and a historical approach, especially as regards texts like this one, which was intended for a large audience. This oration declares frankly its educative ends:

Now I have not told this long story idly, or, as some might perhaps infer, with the desire to spin a yarn, but to present an illustration of the manner of life that I adopted at the beginning and of the life of the poor, an illus-tration drawn from my own experience for anyone who wishes to consider

whether in words and deeds and in social intercourse the poor are at a dis-
advantage in comparison with the rich on account of their poverty, so far
as living a seemly and natural life is concerned, or in every way have the
advantage. (7. 81)

This passage fully justifies an ideological way of reading the entire
text.

There is no need here to recall the story, but I would like to underline some points which are fundamental to our topic. First, the city
appears to be a place where too many people live together, which,
among other things, provokes contention and conflict; this aspect
emerges especially in the hunter's tale of his visit to the Euboean
unnamed town, where he takes part in a popular assembly (7.
22–63). Secondly, the town is also the realm of the monetary economy, where it is impossible to survive in a natural way, that is
without money; this is particularly evident in the second part of the
discourse, where Dio examines the extremely scanty opportunities
of life which a town can offer to the poor.

Suitable work may perhaps be hard to find in the cities, and will need to
be supplemented by outside resources when the poor have to pay house-
rent and buy everything they get, not merely clothes, household belongings, and food, but even the wood to supply the daily need for fire . . . so
perhaps we shall be forced in our discussion to banish the respectable poor
from the cities in order to make our cities in reality cities 'well inhabited',
as Homer calls them, where only the prosperous dwell, and we shall not
allow any free labourer, apparently, within the walls. (7. 105, 107)

Both these points confirm what we have already observed in other
discourses of Dio. In fact, even if in the second part of the speech
Dio tries to suggest jobs which the 'respectable poor' can do, what
really results is the opposite, that is, a long and boring list of shameful jobs, which the poor of course were not to be allowed to do.

Third is the role of the country. In the *Euboean* at last we find
the idea openly expressed (which is indeed implicit in various contexts we have examined so far) that the country, as opposed to the
town, is the only place where men can lead a free and natural life,
earning their living in honourable ways, respecting morality and traditional values, in a spirit of authentic religious devotion. I shall avoid
retracing here the single elements of this picture, which are well
known. It will be more useful to mention some other, perhaps less
familiar, passages, where these same, or similar and compatible, ideas

are at work. First of all, we have to keep in mind an obvious bio-graphical fact, that during his exile Dio presumably spent most of his time in the countryside and among peasants, devoting himself to popular preaching; even Philostratus, who did not believe he was exiled in a technical sense, said that Dio 'vanished from men's sight, hiding himself from their eyes and ears, occupying himself in vari-ous ways in various lands' (*VS*. 1. 7). In fact, we cannot help think-ing that Dio intended to underline the profound meaning which was to be attributed to his wanderings in the most isolated and remotest places of the Empire. In the first *Kingship Oration*, speaking of his life in this period, he says expressly that he kept 'quite aloof from the cities, spending his time in the country' (1. 51), and along, or outside, its margins too. It is quite possible to advance the idea that we are in fact faced with a highly ideologized and at least partially fantastic reconstruction of his previous life, which Dio proposed after his exile.[10] However, what is really significant in the present con-text is that immersion in a rural landscape is considered equivalent to the regeneration of one's own life, to the possibility of escaping its environmental and historical conditions and dreaming of the future. In this way we can better understand episodes like that of the rus-tic prophetess, which we find in the first *Kingship Oration*; or that of Dio's visit to Borysthenes, a dying Greek colony in Scythian territory, which introduces the *Borystheniticus* (*Or.* 36). In the former the prophetess, who dwells in one of the most out-of-the-way places of Arcadia, proposes to Dio, through the myth of Heracles' choice between tyranny and royalty, what is indeed a political model of kingship, and engages him to report it to the 'mighty man, ruler of very many lands and peoples', whom he would meet shortly (1. 50); in other words, she gives a sort of divine endorse-ment to Dio's intended intellectual activity as a ruler's counsellor. In the latter oration Dio places thoughts about cosmic order, expressed both in a philosophical and in a mythological form, in the context of an outpost of 'civilization' faced by overwhelming num-bers of barbarians. This implied a refocusing of the importance of political phenomena, as compared with divine providence, and a rethinking on this basis of the meaning of human experience.

[10] See Moles (1978). In fact, from *In Athens, On his Exile* we learn that in this period Dio was able to speak in Rome, and from 19. 1–2 that he could approach, but not cross, the Bithynian border. On the special character of his exile see Desideri (1978) 192 ff.

THE BARBARIANS

In a general sense the country appears to be a metaphor for liberty, just as the town is a metaphor for slavery. From this point of view, the country can be considered as something similar to the barbarian world: both represent, in fact, an alternative to the urban way of life. Barbarians, moreover, could play the role of a political alternative to the Roman Empire—which is a world of cities—as well. In fact, it is by no means surprising that in the period of his 'resistance to tyrants' (*Or.* 50. 8; cf. 45. 1 etc.). Dio preferred, as far as we know, to live on the margins of the 'civil' world, dwelling in the country and in barbarian lands—just what the oracle had suggested to him: 'until thou comest to the uttermost parts of the earth' (*Or.* 13. 9). This is the right time to introduce the most important of Dio's references to the world of barbarians, looked at as the one still existing guarantee against the dominant urban life-style of the 'civilized' world. This reference is in fact at the end of the introductory section of the *Olympian Oration* (12. 16–20), which probably dates to 105 (or 101).

I have just finished a long, long journey, all the way from the Ister and the land of the Getae, or Mysians . . . And I went there, not as a merchant with his wares, nor yet as one of the supply-train of the army in the capacity of baggage-carrier or cattle-driver, nor was I discharging a mission as ambassador to our allies or on some embassy bearing congratulations (16–17). I went 'unarmed, with neither helm nor shield nor lance' [*Iliad* 21. 50], nor indeed with any other weapon either, so that I marvelled that they brooked the sight of me . . . (18); for I (who was completely useless from the military point of view) came among men who were not dullards, and yet had no leisure to listen to speeches, but were high-strung and tense like race-horses at the starting barriers . . . Quite alone I appeared in the midst of this mighty host, perfectly undisturbed and a most peaceful observer of war, weak in body and advanced in years . . . desiring to see strong men contending for empire and power, and their opponents for freedom and native land. (19–20)

It is hardly necessary to point out that the world of the barbarians is still defined as the world of freedom (whereas the Romans', that is the 'civilized' world, is imperialistic).

It is a pity that we can no longer read, among others of Dio's works which have not survived, an essay entitled *On the Getae*, which, according to Philostratus, 'proved that he had also a talent for writing history'. However, the pure and simple fact that he wrote something of this kind, regardless of the possibility of finding its remains in Jordanes' *De origine actibusque Getarum*, shows the interest Dio had in a barbarian people, which presumably echoed the spirit of the reference to the Getae in the *Olympian Oration*. In the same way we would very much like to know what he had to say in another of his lost works where, according to Synesius, he 'praised the Essenes, a community of complete happiness, situated beside the Dead Sea in the interior of Palestine somewhere near Sodom itself'. We may suspect that Dio greatly valued this community precisely because it was composed of a small number of members: that is, because it respected at least one, perhaps the most important, of the indispensable requirements of a well-organized city that Dio himself enunciates in several of his speeches. But this is, of course, pure speculation.

THE HOMELAND

Perhaps a work like the one on the Essenes, which evidently implied, after all, an acknowledgement of the possibility of the existence of a 'well-inhabited town', represents the best possible way, from the theoretical point of view, to bridge the gap between the previously examined concepts and those ideas which Dio formulated especially in the Bithynian speeches (*Orr.* 40–51), which come from the last period of his life, with the exception of the already mentioned *Before a Philosophical Career*. It is appropriate to emphasize the chronology of these speeches, not so much because in most cases it is absolutely certain, as because in this way we can point out useful elements in the development of Dio's way of thinking and try to trace its historical motivation.

The fact is that at a certain readily identifiable moment, namely the time of Domitian's death, Dio's conditions of life suddenly changed. Whether or not he had been an exile (as I consider highly probable), Dio had certainly led a difficult and wandering life of poverty up to that moment. Starting from Nerva's, and especially Trajan's, reign, he appears on the contrary as one of the most influential and authoritative persons in the Empire, as far as both general and local politics are concerned,[11] continuing nevertheless

---

[11] Sidebottom (1996), esp. 454 n. 62, thinks that the importance of this role has to be reduced, basing himself on the general premises of Bowie (1982).

to practise his intellectual job of preacher and lecturer, for which he had been known from the beginning. The first noteworthy novelty is his return to Prusa. Dio did not arrive alone. He brought with him a sort of constitutional packet—presumably obtained from the emperor Trajan—which was intended to promote and develop civic life in the town.[12] As he said at the end of his *Speech of Greeting to his Fatherland* (*Or.* 44), delivered to his fellow-citizens (and repeated many other times), the city would benefit from the increase in the number of the town counsellors and would become the head of an assize-district in the province of Bithynia (thereby gaining certain revenues from outside);[13] it was even possible, Dio concluded, that it would obtain *eleutheria* (44. 11). On this last point Dio made an extremely interesting comment:

Rest assured that what is called *eleutheria* [which I would translate 'liberty', or 'freedom' rather than 'independence', as Lamar Crosby has it], that nominal possession which comes into being at the pleasure of those who have control and authority, is sometimes impossible to acquire, but the true *eleutheria*, the kind which men actually achieve, both the individual and each *polis* obtains from its own self, if it administers its own affairs in a high-minded and easy-going manner. (44. 12)

What we have here, in my view, is a sort of palinode of the general statements which Dio had previously made about the irredeemable lack of liberty in urban life, the symptom of its absolute negativity. Even if he denounced the unavoidably artificial character of an *eleutheria* which the Romans had the power to grant—or not grant—to the cities of their Empire, he admitted, none the less, the possibility, for each of them, of achieving a just administration, which is the mark of true liberty. Here indeed is the new spirit, thanks to which Dio engaged himself after his exile in reorganizing the moral and political life of his city and proved besides awareness of the importance of the social and economic aspects of civic life. This is not the right place to examine once again the vicissitudes of the last of Dio's experiences, the political one. Rather I would like, first, to recall briefly the arguments he uses to defend his choice of political involvement;

[12] On the connections between Trajanic politics and Dio's activity in Prusa, see Desideri (1978) 382 ff.

[13] It is interesting to notice the difference between this way of evaluating the institution of the assize-district, and the contempt shown towards it in the *To Celaenae* (35) cited above.

and secondly, to question the possible reasons for such a change in his attitude towards the city.

Concerning the first point, it is easy to find, both in the Bithynian and in other discourses presumably dating back to this same late period of his life, passages where Dio maintained that, as he says in *Refusal of Office before the Council (Or.* 49), 'the function of the real philosopher is nothing else than to rule over human beings'. In particular, he added there,

if a man, alleging that he is not competent, is reluctant to administer his own city when it wishes him to do so and calls upon him, it is as if someone should refuse to treat his own body, though professing to be a physician, and yet should readily treat other men in return for money or honours, just as if his wealth were a smaller recompense than another kind; or again, it is as if someone who claimed to be an able trainer of athletes or a teacher of letters should be willing to teach the sons of others, but should send his own son to someone else of less standing. (49. 13)

Considerations like this one are very common in the speeches of this period.

As for the second point, the possible reasons for the emergence of such ideas, one can say that they are undoubtedly of Platonic and Academic origin, or even older than that, but all the same are in plain contradiction to his previous position on such topics. It is useful to remember, I believe, that in this period, that is, at the beginning of Trajan's reign, or not far from it, we can find these same, or very similar, ideas expressed in some of Plutarch's essays, especially in *Political Advice* and *Should an Old Man Engage in Public Affairs?* Moreover, it had been a very long time since anyone in the Greek world had expressed like thoughts; or rather, since anyone had applied them to contemporary Greek states, not to say city-states. In fact, one is confronted with what we may call a new formula of political involvement for 'intellectuals'—I use a general term like this to avoid getting involved in a hair-splitting discussion about philosophers, sophists, rhetors, and so on.[14] The ultimate goal of this formula was to try to make the traditional Greek concept of the political liberty of the city compatible with the new—though by now firmly established—reality of overall Roman domination. The Greek intellectual who was thinking of political involvement could of course follow the traditional role as the counsellor of the prince, a role which dated

[14] Cf. Anderson (1994) 3–4.

back to the time of the Hellenistic monarchies and which had been all too often practised on Romans (Dio himself in his *Kingship Orations* is one of the best examples of it). But, from this time onwards—that is, from Dio and Plutarch onwards—this same intellectual had a newly recognized, that is, theoretically founded, option: he could legitimately operate as a political figure in his own city, his local fatherland.

It is absolutely clear, both from Dio's and from Plutarch's texts, and it is even made explicit by them, that one cannot speak of political freedom.[15] But even in the rather narrow space which the Roman authorities left to local autonomies, the best citizens had the right and the duty to engage themselves—this is the new watchword— in the task of reviving the tradition of the political life of their city, however limited its range of action may be. We can leave aside now the problem of which contribution, if any, the Romans themselves made to the revival of political life and interests in the cities of the eastern part of their Empire—even if Dio's biographical experiences strongly suggest the possibility of connections between the central and local levels of Roman administration and politics. The fact itself of this revival, in the second century at least, does not seem easy to deny, especially as far as the Anatolian regions are concerned. Dio's and Plutarch's texts reveal their authors' confident belief that the urban context may after all be considered the most appropriate place for an accomplished man to spend his life and energies, regardless of the personal risks in which his engagement could involve him. This fact appears to be the best independent confirmation one could hope to obtain for the huge mass of epigraphical and archaeological evidence. As for Dio, moreover, who in many of his previous writings had been so resolute in exalting rural, and even barbarian, living against life in the city, we might even go so far as to say that we see the germ of a new theorizing about civic engagement which comes after a lengthy period of silence on this topic in Greek (and Roman) political literature. Bringing forward this old theory now meant of course being prepared to recognize the dominant role of the Roman Empire, under whose control civic life was to flow quietly and surely. But at the same time it meant recovering the sense of the importance of the identity of one's own home and fatherland, which was liable to become a strong focus for cultural pride

[15] Desideri (1986), (1994*b*).

and intellectual performance too.[16] In fact, finding and promoting an acceptable compromise between civic self-determination and Roman rule may be considered an important presupposition of the Greek Renaissance—one for whose realization intellectual instruments were required especially, looking forward to the not so far distant time when the true Romans would be the Greeks.

[16] Gascó (1998). For a reassessment of the iconographical aspects of this cultural phenomenon see recently Smith (1998).

4

Public Speech and Community
in the Euboicus
JOHN MA

INTRODUCTION

A complicated little social drama: an assembly-meeting in a Greek *polis*. The actors and the events are familiar enough: *rhētores* speaking before the assembled people; the assemblymen's great roar of disapproval, clamour of praise, harsh, mocking laughter; the generation of *psēphismata*, decrees proposed by speakers at the outcome of the debate, and voted on by the assembly; the close interrogation of a citizen by speakers and magistrates before the people. Familiar as they are, a detailed description of all these features would be interesting enough in the pages of a classical historian. But the present summary is drawn from a second-sophistic author, who transmits what purports to be the extended description (admittedly by a bemused witness) of a contemporary assembly-meeting: in this context, the scene is highly intriguing and deserves further thought.[1]

The text is of course Dio's *Euboicus*, and specifically the first half (1–80) with its story of shipwreck and salvation, complete with the tale-within-a-tale given by the figure of the hunter. The story illustrates the *bios* of this particular individual, the hunter, and his happiness (66) in the face of poverty. In spite of its moralizing elements, it has often been adduced in relation to the social and economic history of Greece under the Roman Empire. Eduard Meyer considered that the portrayal of small-town life, empty countryside, large

---

[1] For the purposes of the present chapter, I consider Dio and Plutarch to be part of the 'Second Sophistic', as broadly conceived (i.e. the Greek culture of the eastern provinces in the late first, second, and early third centuries AD).

estates, was factual;[2] later interpreters have offered more nuanced views, in their awareness that the portrayal of depopulation (*oliganthrōpia*) and decline are stereotypes documenting perceptions rather than realities.[3] In the case of Euboea, where Dio sets his tale, survey archaeology does reveal, as in the rest of Greece, a decrease in the number of rural 'sites' (though how we interpret this phenomenon is still unclear); on the other hand, contrary to what Dio's tale seems to imply, Carystus (possibly the setting) may have been a prosperous urban centre in the relevant period, notably because of the proximity of quarries, which fed the Roman liking for coloured marble.[4]

It is necessary to go one step further. The tale in Dio's *Euboicus* cannot be used as an immediate source for the socio-economic conditions in Greece, for a more important reason than its reproduction of *topoi* about Roman Greece. The elements usually quoted (depopulation, urban disrepair, rural desolation) do not come from Dio's or the huntsman's narrative, but are arguments deployed in a speech performed by a rhetor in the assembly.[5] Neither Dio nor the huntsman vouch for the accuracy of the statements; even if they are made by the speaker whom the hunter believes to be respectable (*epieikēs*), there is no assurance that he is not exaggerating or recasting facts for political purposes. Dio's account is not about the *polis*, but about images of the *polis*, and the use of such images to talk to the *polis* about itself; the tale in the *Euboicus* belongs to a set of texts in Dio treating the idea of the city—a major theme in his work.[6]

Rather than using a political speaker's statements to talk about realities or perceptions in second-century Greece, we might pay attention to the context of public speech: speech before the community, and about the community, in the institutional setting of the assembly, gathered in the theatre of a small city in late Flavian or early Antonine Greece. The topic is of interest, because of the presence of a source portraying ecclesial rhetoric in action (rather

---

[2] Meyer (1924) 1: 164–8.   [3] Day (1951); Bertrand (1992); Alcock (1993) 30.

[4] Alcock (1993) 39 (decrease in rural sites); 101 (civic building in Carystus), with 111(qualifications, because of the unclear economic relationship between imperially owned quarries and local communities).

[5] Day (1951) 213–14.

[6] Bertrand (1992) is an essay on the *Euboicus* as 'political myth' about utopia and the city: the political implications of place. See esp. the *Borystheniticus* for an explicit disquisition on models of the city, with Schofield (1991) 57–64; also Salmeri, in this volume, above pp. 85–6.

than the one-sided, and often fragmentary, view we get from Dio's own public speeches), and because it concerns politics (if not the reality of politics, at least the possibility of conceiving it) in a world which has sometimes been seen as depoliticized: the post-classical city and the Greek East under the Roman Empire. G. de Ste Croix spoke in broad terms of the death of democracy in this period, owing to a variety of factors (Roman intervention, institutional change, the increasingly entrenched position of the rich); Paul Veyne focused on the emergence of an elite of *notables*, who came to dominate the Greek cities especially because of the natural apathy of the masses in communities run by direct democracy.[7] But our vision of the *polis* (at least the classical *polis*) has changed in recent years, focusing on the importance of language and rhetoric (combined with institutions) in creating democratic identity and practice, mobilizing involvement, mediating between elites and masses.[8]

Is this new 'classical-democratic' approach inappropriate for the Graeco-Roman city? The tale in Dio's *Euboicus* raises the possibility of reading such political and democratic themes into the period. At least, it provides a perspective from which we may interpret Dio's tale of a tale about an assembly-meeting, in order to offer broader conclusions about the writing of political history (in the sense of the history of political community and language), about the post-classical *polis*, and about the political culture of the Second Sophistic, and even its cultural politics. It is obviously impossible to read the story as 'factual' in any simple way. Dio's artful protestations of autopsy (1) combine with the various signs of fantasy, such as the huntsman's Homeric hairstyle (actualizing what Dio, in a learned aside, considers to be a Homeric joke at the Euboeans' expense, 4). The story is permeated with themes found in New Comedy, 'pastoral' poetry, or the Greek novel, such as shipwrecks and wandering, trial-scenes, rural idyll.[9] A sign of artificiality is the huntsman's narrative itself: our rural Candide is capable of accurately recalling unfamiliar events, surroundings, and words.[10] The huntsman is accused of *eirōneia*

---

[7] De Ste Croix (1981) App. 4, Veyne (1976) 201–9; Schmitz 1997—drawing on Quass (1993)—is based on this premiss.

[8] Loraux (1981); Ober (1989).

[9] Jouan (1977), Highet (1973); and part 2 of Anderson's chapter in this volume, below, pp. 145–50.

[10] Anderson (previous note) underlines the implausibility of the hunter's accurate reproduction of political oratory, which he had supposedly never encountered before.

by one of the speakers in the assembly; perhaps the word could be applied to Dio's own elaborate, multi-layered account of the whole affair, written with its grain of disingenuousness. Yet I propose to bypass these issues of fictionality for the moment, to provide a first reading of the huntsman's narrative.

SPEAKING BEFORE THE COMMUNITY

Throughout the huntsman's account, the crowd plays a visible role: his first impression is that of 'a great crowd, gathered in the same place, and an irresistible shout and clamour' (23). Actions in the assembly are immediately followed by a vocal reaction: approval, threats, mockery.

Sometimes they all shouted kindly and joyfully, in praise of some men, sometimes loudly and angrily. This anger of theirs was terrible; and straightaway they terrified the men whom they shouted at, so that some were in great fear and ran around, others threw down their *himatia* out of fear. For my part, I once almost fell over under the force of the clamour, as if a wave or thunder had struck. Other men, some going forward, others standing up in the middle (*ek mesōn*), spoke to the multitude, some saying few words, some many. And they listened to some for a long time, but were angry at others as soon as they spoke and did not even let them squeak.   (24–6)

All the elements, as told with ethnographic detachment and physical immediacy by a puzzled witness, are familiar from our standard accounts of the practice of the Athenian assembly: the initiative and freedom with which the assembled people manifests its feelings, by vocalizing them, interrupting the speakers, and even shouting speakers off and shutting them up.[11] This sort of collective inter- action manifests the people's will immediately, as a response to the speakers' words which it directly controls, and sometimes cuts off; less institutionally, the huntsman's description brings out the threatening physical power of the crowd, compared in its noise and its clamour to elemental, natural forces or a savage beast (33)—thus echoing, in his own words (or what Dio purports to be his own words), descriptions of the people by anti-democratic writers of the Classical period.

---

[11] Hansen (1991); Ober (1989) 104 on collective *parrhēsia*; see as a good example Xen. *Mem.* 3. 6.

Other elements are also strikingly reminiscent of classical (i.e. Athenian) democratic institutions. It seems that any person (in classical terms, *ho boulomenos*) can speak; some go forward, presumably to speak in the orchestra of the theatre, just as Athenians went up to the *bēma* in the Pnyx; others make their point from the midst of the crowd, *ek mesōn* (26, 53). A speaker twice proposes a decree to the people, as *ad hoc* proposals relevant to the circumstances and the evolution of the debate in the assembly, and not as part of a fixed agenda controlled by the council or a college of magistrates. The city is a place where decisions are still generated by debate in the decision-making assembly, as it was in the strong democracy of classical Athens, and the spontaneous decrees in the *Euboicus* recall some of the wilder amendments attached, without obvious relevance, as riders to some Attic decrees.[12]

These institutions—collective expression by the crowd, the right of citizens to speak, the generation of decisions in the assembly—form the background to the little drama recounted by Dio's huntsman. All the actions in the tale are interactions with, or before, the assembly (*ho ochlos, ho dēmos*), public speech in action; the various shapes this takes, and the themes, assumptions, and ideology behind it deserve closer attention, especially since they evoke the classical orators.[13]

Thus the first speaker (27–33), in attacking the huntsman, gives voice to class resentment against a (perceived) member of the city's wealth elite, who has grown rich off public resources and, by allegedly avoiding liturgies and *euergesiai*, has refused to play the redistributive games which made economic inequality tolerable in a society of political equals.[14] As a specimen of the 'bad rich', the huntsman may be accused of *hubris*, and hence of being beyond the pale: the rhetor equates him with animals (*thēria*), the refuse from purification, a *katharma* (both usages echoing classical Athenian rhetoric);[15] he further imagines the huntsman and his neighbour as leading a gang of wreckers, luring ships to their doom and pillaging the wrecks, a metaphor for asocial activity by which some men live off the destruction of their fellow men. More than the comic exaggeration of the vehement, demagogic speaker, and the epic echoes in the theme of the wreckers (located in the Capherean Rocks, where the hero Nauplius wrecked the Greek fleet),[16] what matters is the coherence of the assumptions

---

[12] Sinclair (1988) 88–101.   [13] As pointed out by Russell (1992) 9.
[14] Ober (1989) ch. 5.   [15] Russell (1992) *ad* 29, 30.   [16] Jouan (1977).

underlying the stereotypes the speaker projects on to the huntsman. These stereotypes (such as the bad rich man) concern the relations between individuals and community, and recall the moral and polit-ical vocabulary of fourth-century Attic rhetoric. They are revealed the more transparently and comically for being inappropriately applied to a bewildered, genuinely poor, 'quiet Carystian'.

The same analysis can be offered for the second speaker, who defends the huntsman (33–40). The second speaker is more moder-ate than the first. His concerns are less popular and more public in their focus: the city's territory, the dignity of its urban centre. Yet even he plays the game of democratic politics. The images of rural desolation lead to a discussion of urban desolation, with wasteland at the city's gates and crops being grown in the town itself. The point of this shift soon becomes clear: the speaker is attacking the first rhetor, who denounces the 'hard-working' farmers of Caphereus, but is not concerned with people grazing their cattle in the *agora* —as the first rhetor himself does. In fact, a certain permeability between rural and urban was a normal feature of ancient cities; the second speaker, for all his reasonableness, is probably exaggerating this feature, presenting an alarmist picture to prolong his arguments on rural desolation, and attack the credibility of an opponent (40). The rhetoric is different from that of the first speaker; the strategy is the same, the establishing of the speaker's persona and credit before the people, by publicly attacking a rival. Both engage in the con-struction, by public speech, of the relations between the speaker, the criticized figure, and the community.

The huntsman himself gets a chance to speak, only to find him-self closely interrogated about his resources and his willingness to make gifts to the people: at one point a magistrate bluntly asks the huntsman if he and his neighbour are willing to give one Attic talent each (44); at another moment the first rhetor intervenes to suggest that the huntsman has buried his money, literally hoard-ing it away from the community. Asked about his wealth in grain and wine, the huntsman gives a pathetic inventory of his meagre possessions, and declares his willingness to give it all up, as long as the city finds him a place to stay, as is his right *qua* citizen. He denies being a wrecker, and claims to have saved many shipwrecked men, a claim dramatically vindicated by the testimony of Sotades, the assemblyman whom he had earlier saved and generously sheltered. The second speaker, not missing a beat, proposes another decree, to

honour the huntsman with a public meal, the grant of the public land
he now occupies, a tunic and cloak, and a gift of 100 drachmae, which
the speaker promises to give *huper tēs poleōs*, thus establishing his
own euergetical generosity and public-spiritedness.

The whole episode, as I have paraphrased it, implies a coherent
ideology and practice, reminiscent of that of classical Athens. By
cultivating public land, the hunter has unwittingly involved himself
in the world of the *polis*, of participatory politics and communal
values enacted in ecclesial speech. In this world, both words and
deeds imply a strong sense of public, or even popular, sovereignty
over men and things: a magistrate can ask 'Are you each willing to
give an Attic talent?' as a natural question to put to a man suspected
of being rich, and a rich man refusing communal involvement and
redistribution can be publicly vilified as asocial and non-human. Both
the first, demagogic, speaker and the second, moderate, speaker
show the same awareness of the public realm and the special nature
of public interests. This awareness is displayed before the people in
rhetoric: in the public space of the assembly, deeds and words concern popular welfare and interests, and are judged in relation to them.
Speakers strive to establish credibility before the people, by offering
versions of the popular interests: for instance, seeing to the redistribution of wealth by zealous denunciation, or promoting the city's
welfare and reputation by trying to palliate rural desolation and urban
disrepair. Establishing credibility entails savaging rivals and perceived
public enemies, as a matter of course.[17] 'Are you willing to give an
Attic talent?': beyond the redistributive intrusion and casual assumption of the rich man's availability to the community, what is striking,
and perhaps slightly chilling, is the focus on willingness rather than
ability—the answer will reveal publicly what attitude you have
towards the public, and what sort of man you are.[18]

At this point it is worth remembering that this picture is part of
a critique of the *polis* by Dio; he later makes the point explicitly:
his description of the hunter's life concerns the following aspects
of the life of the poor—words, deeds, and *koinōniai pros allēlous*,
relations with each other (81). The assembly scene cannot be read

[17] Though Sotades, who has less at stake in his speech, is content to say 'I am a
citizen, *hōs iste* (as you know)'.
[18] Cf. 29: the first speaker assumes that the hunter must steal public monies
amelei ('without a doubt'), since he occupies public land free of charge; public speech
assumes consistency of character and transparency of action.

in isolation from the rest of Dio's tale; rather than a satire on 'urban corruption', or 'urban vices', the whole story is a challenge to the central claims of the *polis*. To the claims of public interest, Dio's narrative opposes a different reality: the *polis* is not the community embodied, but a purely urban phenomenon, which does not concern the huntsman. The city believes it acts to discover whether the rich are hoarding wealth, and to force redistribution through institutional channels such as taxation and liturgies; but the huntsman's experience of the process is that of the countryman faced with the predatory town, which sends a strange man to take him before a crowd, which threatens to take away all his meagre belongings for no clear reason. This perception is not a fantasy: a striking passage of Galen attests how in times of shortage, a town could simply confiscate the grain from the country-dwellers, leaving them to subsist off roots and vetches until the next crop.[19]

If the hunstman lives far from the city, where everything is strange to him, the city's perception of the countryside is just as skewed: in his attacks on the huntsman, the first rhetor shows no understanding of the rural landscape, its people, or its economy. This lack of understanding between the town and the countryside overturns one of the foundations of *polis* ideology, the close bond between the urban centre and the rural territory, the union of which creates the *polis* as territorial entity. Finally, the city is untrustworthy; the huntsman's view of ecclesial rhetoric, with its ideological exaggerations, is simple: lies and nonsense such as in a dream (42). When Sotades, in this city of lies, stands up to testify to having been saved by the huntsman, the latter's first reaction is fear and the naïve apprehension that this man, too, will attack him with lies (53). The city, in the huntsman's experience, far from being a rational political body,[20] is disturbingly irrational: the huntsman is first accused of living off public land, as if he were a *euergetēs*; he is then offered the chance to keep his plot of land, for a favourable price; he then believes that he must give up all he has and move to the city; and finally, he is rewarded by the grant of the very plot he is now occupying, since it turns out that he himself is in fact a *euergetēs*. In the theatre of assembly politics, the same man is cast in several roles in quick succession; the process, with its mechanical changes, its concomitant popular reactions

---

[19] Galen, *On the Properties of Foodstuffs*, 6. 749 f. Kühn.
[20] Murray (1990).

(anger, praise, inexplicable bursts of laughter[21]), is bewildering and alienating, and the huntsman's final reaction is bitter and unforgiving. When the hunter greets Sotades with a kiss, the *dēmos* laughs aloud; the hunter comments 'then I knew that in the cities, they do not kiss each other', *en tais polesi ou philousin allēlous* (53). The expression also means 'they do not love each other', and is a direct challenge to the ideology of civic love, prevalent at least from the Hellenistic period onwards, and manifested in dedications of statues of Eros in the *agora* as well as in Stoic political philosophy.[22] All these challenges are presented as natural, since they come from a supposedly naïve observer, to whom Dio attributes such 'natural' observations as the fierceness and fickleness of the crowd, or the dignity of the second speaker, an *epieikēs* man as even the huntsman can tell from his demeanour and from the ease with which he controls the crowd rather than excites it. Standard oligarchical positions are expressed by Dio's huntsman, which should alert us to the ideological nature of the whole exercise.[23]

In the other parts of the hunter's own tale and in Dio's description of the hunter's *bios*, Dio proposes a vision of a non-poliadic world, inhabited by men who have reverted to nature. This state is symbolized by the huntsman's garb, an animal pelt (which he tries to wear on top of the tunic and cloak the city gives him, 62–3); it also is alluded to in the huntsman's observations on his father's hounds, who from gruel-fed cowherd dogs gradually turned to meat-eating, blood-drinking, hunting dogs (16–17), a process which is both the

---

[21] E.g. 48: when the hunter replies to the first rhetor that he has not buried his money, because it does not grow, the people burst out laughing; the hunter assumes the laughter is directed at the first rhetor, though his uncertainty betrays his uneasiness and surprise.

[22] Robert (1969) 254–62. These examples raise the possibility that Zenon of Kition's conception of Eros as essential for the *polis*, in addition to being a reworking of the classical Spartan model (Schofield (1991) ch. 2), could have been influenced by the ambient ideology of the Hellenistic city.

[23] Barry (1993) claims that the *Euboicus*, in its sympathetic portrait of the hunter, shows empathy with the poor and hence dates from a different period of Dio's life than the aristocratically biased depiction of the crowd in his *Alexandrian Oration*; on this view, the speech to the Alexandrians dates to before Dio's exile, and the more compassionate *Euboicus* to the post-exilic period. But the *Euboicus* exhibits the same aristocratic prejudices about the crowd as does the *Alexandrian Oration*; sympathy for the poor huntsman is compatible with, and indeed completed by, criticism of crowd politics. Hence there is no reason on this basis to date the Alexandrian oration before Dio's exile, since Dio was quite capable of expressing aristocratic, anti-democratic views after his return. The Trajanic date is preferred by Swain (1996) 428–9.

result and the metaphor of the process undergone by the huntsman's father when he settled in the mountains after having to fend for himself, when he lost his socialized position and became a herdsman instead of a rich landowner. This natural state is not one of savagery, but gentleness. There is love, in the romance between the hunter's daughter and his neighbour's son, in contrast to the city where 'they do not love each other'; there is gentle, teasing laughter, in contrast to the mocking, terrifying laughter of the assembly; there is, in this *locus amoenus* removed from the alienating public spaces of the city, a beautifully kept, private garden. The only decision taken here is the date of the wedding: *edoxe . . . tauta* (79); the similarity in expression to formulas for civic decrees underlines the absence of politics in the hunter's own world. As a function of his natural gentleness, the hunter is hospitable and generous, assisting those saved from shipwrecks, like Dio or the two citizens who testify for him in the assembly, and many others; when an official appears from the city, the hunter's impulse is to give him a meal and gifts of hospitality (22), responding to the demand for money and social involvement with gestures of private hospitableness. He does not need an honorific decree to make him help other men, as the 'hortative clause' in the second decree passed by the city puts it (61); this juxtaposition raises the question of how the city, with its political institutions and practices, can actually ensure the virtuous behaviour which the hunter shows without prompting, as part of his state of nature. The hunter's poverty is less about deprivation than the absence of money, and hence of dealings with a complex, organized society like that of the *polis*. The picture is finally anti-Aristotelian: man does not need to live in a *polis* as the best form of existence, but can exist happily at the level of individuals and their families, with at most a village as the higher form of social organization (such as the village the hunter and his family occasionally deal with). When shipwrecked, the narrator in the *Euboicus* reflects that he does not know to which city he may turn to be saved (3); in the end, salvation comes, not from a city, but a gentle, individualistic hunter, living a natural *bios* far from the city.

REALITIES OF THE GRAECO-ROMAN *POLIS*

What, then, are we to make of this story? This critical picture of the *polis* seems to let itself be analysed in politicizing terms appropriate

for the classical city and in fact developed to study the strong democracy of classical Athens—not just one speech, such as we find (with
the odd exception) in the works of the declaimers, but a pair of
speeches set within a whole world, with its own logic, its working parts
and working ideology—what is the significance of this? Of course, the
story is a fantasy. A first reaction, then, would be to pursue elements
which disqualify the hunter's tale as being just a tale. When the hunter
speaks of his sons growing up as potential soldiers for the city (43),
and the reasonable speaker argues that the hunter should be rewarded
just as a man who has shielded a wounded citizen in battle (60), it is
easy to think such touches betray the 'declamatory' unreality of the
story. Further, absences can be listed: the increasingly oligarchical
institutions of the Graeco-Roman city, the presence of permanent
councils often chosen on timocratic criteria, the transferral of initiative and authority to the magistrates;[24] the Roman Empire, provincial
administration, the supervision of local communities by *logistai*, ruler
cult, and the imperial ideology of monarchical beneficence directed
at the whole world;[25] the love of festivals, oracles, public buildings;
the culture of performers of all sorts (athletes, rhetoricians); the
obsession with the past, the learned language, and conventional, con-
formist values of contemporary inscriptions and rhetoric.[26]

And yet if we take the feature which looks the most like fantasy, the
mention of war and soldiers, it is worth remembering that Thespiae
sent volunteers to fight with Marcus Aurelius, and that, around the
same time, the Elateans, under the guidance of an Olympic victor
(as in the archaic period) fought and destroyed a band of barbarians;
when the general, Mnesiboulus, died in the fight, he was commemorated by a statue in the city's *agora*. Both examples are commented
on by Fergus Millar, pointing out how Apuleius' *Golden Ass* suggests the cities were largely left to themselves, and were capable of
violent, organized self-help.[27] This capacity may have been more than

---

[24] Lévy (1895), de Ste Croix (1981) App. 4.

[25] *Logistai*: Robert (1940*b*) ch. 4. Imperial cult at Carystus, *SEG* 3. 758, one of
countless examples of the phenomenon in the eastern Roman provinces: Price (1984).

[26] Robert (1965) 223; Sheppard (1984–6). The assumption of elite dominance in
the Graeco-Roman city plays a crucial role in the argument offered by Schmitz (1997),
at 39–41, 212–14—namely, that the literature of the Second Sophistic reflects and constitutes this elite dominance.

[27] Millar (1981) 74 on Pausanias 10. 34. 5. Some cities also had paramilitary forces
of citizens patrolling their territory: Robert (1937) 97–108 (admittedly for Roman
Asia Minor).

just a contingency response to emergencies, and an essential part of the city's identity: it marked its descent from, and identity with, the fighting organism that was the classical *polis*. The declaimers' obsession with citizen soldiers, and the casual references to the theme in Dio's tale, might reflect how the Antonine city still imagined its members as military, or militarizable, in a reflection of the classical *polis*, and is perhaps a deliberate attempt at civic self-fashioning in that image.

Likewise, the portrayal of ecclesial rhetoric and events may be less fanciful than it seems at first sight, since Dio's knowledge of civic assemblies did not only come from a knowledge of the Attic orators, but also from his own life as a notable in Prusa. The corpus of his speeches preserves several civic speeches from his home town, allusive and often incomplete, and hence probably identical or close to versions delivered before the citizens there (*Orr.* 42–51). These 'political' speeches (*Or.* 46 is an especially telling example) show him establishing his credentials before them (on the basis of his services to the community, and his father's services, as well as his learning), defending his position, declining honours, dealing with accusations of grain hoarding in time of shortage, and even of tyranny,[28] scolding the people for unrest against its notables, and generating a proposal (in this case, to hand over to the council the supervision of business concerning the *agoranomoi*; this sort of delegation is attested at Athens, and need not be particularly oligarchical or aristocratic).[29]

Outside of Dio, documentary evidence also suggests the persistence of 'democratic' institutions and ideology.[30] On Euboea the Chalcidian inscription *Syll.* 898 (third century AD) shows the people passing, by acclamation, the proposal for an honorary decree put to it by the council—in language which strongly echoes the second decree proposed

---

[28] *Orr.* 43 (defence against accusations, with explicit Athenian references), 44 (declining honours), 46 (grain), 47. 23–4 (tyranny). On these speeches, see Salmeri in this volume, above pp. 63 ff.

[29] *Or.* 48. 10, 17.

[30] So already Russell (1983) 32: the declaimers' obsession with tyranny is not just a melodramatic fantasy, but reflects the reality of tyranny throughout the history of the Greek *polis*, down to the Hellenistic and Roman periods. Recent work has emphasized the persistence of *polis* institutions and ideology in the Hellenistic and Roman periods; Sartre (1991), Gauthier (1993), Millar (1993), all three drawing on the work of Louis Robert. On the crowd in the Graeco-Roman city, and the crowd's importance in public life, cf. Millar (1981) 71 (concerning the phenomenon, at least as it appears in Apuleius' 'magical-realist' novel).

in the assembly in Dio's tale. The vehemence of debate portrayed by Dio warns us against assuming that florid official language and acclamation necessarily mean an inert, formalized politics. The Mylasan decree *OGIS* 515 (now *I. Mylasa* 515), passed under the Severans (date: AD 209–11), is often quoted for its emphatic language and adherence to imperial ideology, and the fact that the assembly, rather than just voting, passes the decree with acclamations, noted in Latin, *succlamatum est*. Yet the document is a complex piece of legislation aimed at repressing abuses by money-lenders in the *agora*, controlling the economic in favour of the communal: the drafters of the decree explicitly declare their purpose to be the protection of the *polis* from those who 'trample' on it, and the checking of those who 'take away the common things', *aponosphizomenōn ta k[oina]*. The sonorous, learned language should not hide the sentiment, which is not far removed from that of the first speaker in Dio's *Euboicus*, nor from democratic ideology in Attic rhetoric. The assembly scene in the *Euboicus*, or indeed the nervousness with which Dio addresses the assembled people of Prusa in *Or.* 46, help us imagine the rhetoric of denunciation that might have been deployed when the Mylasan decree was proposed and passed.[31] Other documents are even more explicit: a well-known papyrus of AD 192 shows a public meeting in an Egyptian town, devoted to negotiations about the magistracies which a notable, Achilleus, is willing to undertake; the proceedings are interrupted by one Ammonion, who points out that Achilleus had struck him, an act he qualifies as *hubris*: over the centuries the word echoes similar dealings, fraught with democratic ideology and class tension, in fourth-century Athens. In both contexts, the feeling is voiced that such matters—what a rich man can get away with—are relevant to politics and should be aired at a public meeting when discussing suitability for office: social eminence does not sanction physical violence against men who are social inferiors but political equals by virtue of their citizen status.[32] There is no evidence from Euboea that is so explicit about the survival of democratic politics; but, suggestively enough, Carystus, which was possibly the scene of the hunter's tale, kept the strong democratic institution of sortition for its council down at least to the time of Hadrian (*IG* 12. 9. 11).

---

[31] On Dio's political speeches as evidence for vigorous popular politics and the assembly's sense of its own sovereignty, see Salmeri's contribution to this volume, above pp. 71–4.

[32] P. Ryl. 66, ll. 32–47, in A. S. Hunt and C. C. Edgar, *Select Papyri* 2, no. 241.

More details could be adduced to parallel institutional details in the huntsman's story, which have often been signalled as realistic (the *emphuteusis* decree,[33] the *epangelia* of money by the second speaker; the hortative clause in the honorific decree). The imaginary tale might not be so imaginary after all, and reflect less the conventions of rhetoric and declamation as socio-political realities and ideologies current in the contemporary *polis*. The experiences of Dio's huntsman might point to features of public life in the assemblies of cities in Greece and Asia Minor in the first two centuries AD: rhetorical exchanges in the assembly, couched in a political language concerned with mediating between notables and community, and predicated on the assumption that the crowd will profit from and judge the excellence of the elite;[34] the harshness of certain euergetical transactions, which may have been less about 'social distance' and aristocratic display and more about forcible redistribution of hidden wealth to the crowd;[35] the drama of recognition and testimony, leading to formulaic honorific decrees.[36] At the very least, the potential closeness to reality of the huntsman's tale must force us to wonder if in studying the post-classical cities, our attention has not been excessively mesmerized by the elite of notables ('Honoratioren'), and civic pride and self-image ('la gloire et la haine'), and not focused enough on interaction

---

[33] Bertrand (1992) 88 n. 54; Russell (1992) *ad* 37.

[34] This idea, so essential to our analyses of classical Athens, is expressed (with alarm) e.g. in Dio *Or.* 38. 34–5, and Plutarch, *Political Advice* 799a, 822a.

[35] 'Social distance' is the notion developed by Veyne (1976) to explain euergetism, though he is well aware of public pressure, often informal, on the rich.

[36] Many such decrees are gathered in Bielman (1994), for honorands who saved citizens from pirates or captivity. From the huntsman's account of the various speeches (54–8, 60–1), we may imagine another narrative, such as would appear on an honorific decree: [– – –] ἐπειδὴ [– – –] πολίτης ὢν ἡμέτερος ἐμ πᾶσι καιροῖς χρείας παρεχόμενος τῇ πόλει διατελεῖ [– – –] καὶ Σωτάδης [– – –] ου διεμαρτύρησεν ἐν τῇ ἐκκλησίᾳ ὅτι διαφθαρείσης τῆς νεὼς περὶ τὸν Καφηρέα καὶ παντελῶς ὀλίγων σωθέντων [– – –]· ἵνα οὖν καὶ τοῖς ἄλλοις προτροπὴ γένηται δικαίοις εἶναι καὶ ἐπαρκεῖν ἀλλήλοις· δεδόχθαι τῷ δήμῳ· ἐπαίνεσαι μὲν [– – –] ἐπὶ τῇ προαιρέσει ἣν ἔχων διατελεῖ πρὸς τὸν δῆμον· καλεῖσθαι δὲ αὐτὸν εἰς ξένια εἰς τὸ πρυτανεῖον· συγχωρῆσθαι δὲ αὐτῷ καὶ τοῖς ἐγγόνοις δωρεάν καρποῦσθαι τὸ χωρίον ὃ ἔχει ὡς εὐεργέτῃ ὄντι τοῦ δήμου· διδόσθαι δὲ χιτῶνα καὶ ἱμάτιον [– – –], 'Since [So-and-so], being our fellow-citizen, continuously renders the best services to the city . . . and since Sotades has given testimony in the assembly that, when his ship was destroyed against cape Caphereus, and very few men saved . . . in order therefore that there be an incentive for others to be just and to help each other; let it seem good to the people: to praise [So-and-so] for the disposition which he has towards the people, and to invite him to a public meal of hospitality in the *prytaneion*; to grant him and his descendants the right to cultivate, for free, the land which he has, since he is a benefactor of the people; to give him a *chitōn* and a *himation*. . . .'

between elite and community, and on the crowd as a political actor in these cities; if we have not focused too much on elite normative texts, describing consensus and conformism rather than conflict and political negotiation; if we have not been too willing to dismiss political rhetoric such as Dio's *Euboicus* portrays, functioning with virulence and liveliness in the assembly.[37]

IMAGINING POLITICS, IMAGINING THE *POLIS*

There is a second, related, approach to Dio's tale: rather than thinking about the realities that might have underlaid or shaped the narrative, we might reflect about what is implied in the fact that Dio was capable of writing this story at all, imaginatively, consistently, accurately portraying a democratic world. Whatever the correspondences with the complex realities of the day, the themes and the language in the story are classical, or classically inspired. This is not astonishing for a literary production of the Second Sophistic, a classicizing age, when the high literary culture of the elite was turned towards models from the fifth and fourth centuries BC, in most genres, and indeed much of higher education, in its rhetorical aspects, drew its themes and expressions from the classical period.[38] Recent work, rather than deploring the period as retrograde and sterile, emphasizes its vibrancy and complexity. Ewen Bowie has drawn attention to the implications of this attitude: pointed detachment from the unpalatable realities of the Roman Empire, nostalgia for the past; Simon Swain has studied the dynamic affirmation and renegotiation of Greek identity and culture in a Roman world.[39]

The reading I have offered for the first half of Dio's *Euboicus* indicates another characteristic: attention to, and commentary on, the themes and the ideology expressed in the classical texts. At least, that is the conclusion we might draw from the fact that we can detect the same *lignes de force* in both the classical models and

[37] See Salmeri, in this volume, above pp. 69 ff.

[38] On the classical inspiration for *meletai*, declamations, see Russell (1983), ch. 2, and 106–9; Swain (1996) 92–6; Schmitz (1997), 112–13. Russell (1983) 107 points out that the largest number of themes comes from the age of Demosthenes, the time when political rhetoric played a crucial part in democratic Athens and is best attested; Ober (1989).

[39] On linguistic purity, Swain (1996), ch. 2; Schmitz (1997), ch. 3. Generally, Bowie (1974); Swain (1996).

the second-sophistic texts themselves. These themes, derived from fifth- and fourth-century drama, history and historiography, rhetoric, philosophy (notably Plato), are centred on the *polis*: the nature and behaviour of the good citizen, the relation between good citizenship and goodness, the best sort of community. Plutarch's *Political Advice* discusses issues such as the role of rhetoric and gift-giving in dealing with, and hopefully controlling, the people; the importance of enjoying a good place in the people's memory and *eunoia*: what sort of friends to have in politics; what place to give honours from the people (Plutarch criticizes and downplays the civic honours, like crowns or decrees, thus attesting their traditional importance for elite politicians).[40] Plutarch's practical precepts are illustrated with examples, some Roman, most drawn from classical history, which he knows intimately (for instance, he discusses the Athenian amnesty decree of 403): this close knowledge of Greek history is considered directly relevant, more so than the well-known Marathon, Eurymedon, and Plataea (which, incidentally, he attests are frequently used in public rhetoric to excite the people).[41] Plutarch's politician is moderate, rather Periclean, and (as often pointed out) aware of Roman domination; none the less, the terms of the debate, and the assumptions that city politics are defined by interaction with the people (*hoi polloi*), are identical to those of the classical period he draws his examples from. Similarly, the narrative in Dio's *Euboicus*, though devoted to a critique of the notion of the *polis*, is an informed criticism, taking and subverting themes of democratic ideology; to do so, it must be aware of this ideology and its functioning, from the inside, and admit to its prevalence: alienation and the fantasy of a non-poliadic individualistic idyll can only take its force against a pervasive poliadic model.

In the preceding pages I have tried to suggest that Dio's portrayal of not just speeches, but speeches in their full context before the assembled *dēmos*, was not that far removed from certain realities of the post-Classical city, and that the latter was still the scene for real popular politics. Against this context, I have pointed out how issues of community, citizenship, and proper behaviour defined in classical literature and philosophy were still present in the Second

[40] On this text, see the close analysis in Swain (1996) 161–83.
[41] *Mor.* 814a.

Sophistic. Together, these two analyses combine to offer a new perspective on the literature of the Second Sophistic, or at least a new
perception of its central concerns. As is well known and has been
examined with increasing subtlety in these last years, the Second
Sophistic was obsessed with classical literature and philosophy.
However, I would insist that because these were produced by a highly
politicized age, concerned with issues of community, politics, and
democracy (whether to extol, qualify, or criticize), the cultured elites
of the first and second centuries AD, in adopting classical literature
as their source of cultural capital, allowed classical views to shape
their own representations, debates, and ideologies. High culture
lent social distinction to the elites: this aspect has been amply commented on by scholars of the Second Sophistic.[42] This culture was not
just about escapist, fantastic references to a prestigious past, or the
erudite recreation of Attic language and text; it was also a politicized
set of debates and issues concerned with the community. The content
of high culture necessarily involved the elites in their communities,
where poliadic and democratic institutions both gave an appropriate
context for the playing out of a political imagination derived from
the classical, and in turn were sustained by this political imagination of the elites. This is how my two approaches to Dio's *Euboicus*
converge: the realities of politics in the Graeco-Roman *polis*, and
the democratic, political themes in Graeco-Roman high culture
co-operated in ensuring the reproduction and interdependence of
both. The reading I offer of the *Euboicus* (but the approach could be
attempted for other texts, from declamation or the novel) suggests
that the heritage of the Greek *polis* in the second century AD was
not inert, but rather a live cultural phenomenon.[43]

---

[42] Swain (1996); Schmitz (1997), exclusively devoted to showing, in terms derived
from Pierre Bourdieu's work, how high culture in the Second Sophistic legitimated
and expressed the elite's domination.

[43] I would like to thank the following collegaues for help with this paper: Robert
Kaster, Larry Kim, Josh Ober, Simon Swain, Heinrich von Staden, Christian
Wildberg, Froma Zeitlin.

5

Marriage, Gender, and
the Family in Dio
RICHARD HAWLEY

Dio has proved an excellent source for historians interested in the politics, philosophies, and ideas of the first two centuries of the Roman era, and there are many studies of these areas.[1] However, there is not even a basic collection of Dio's views on family relations, a crucial topic in social history. This essay attempts to fill that gap. How one conducted oneself in private, behind the doors of one's house, with one's family and friends had long been a commonplace of social philosophy, from the pithy apophthegms of the Seven Sages to the elaborate abstract theoretical webs of Aristotle or Cicero. Dio lived in an exciting time of cultural rediscovery and renaissance. Traditional, classical texts were dusted off and represented to Greek communities who derived great comfort from seeing their glorious past commemorated and celebrated. Dio and his contemporaries (e.g. Plutarch, Lucian, Philostratus, the novelists) all worked in the same literary environment, drawing on the same founts of classical thought, enjoying and exploiting the same literary traditions and conventions. It is therefore not surprising that they share many attitudes towards private social behaviour. I shall show here how Dio receives these traditions. My aim is primarily to collect the references in Dio's corpus on this topic in what is necessarily a preliminary study which others may use as they will. Limitations of space mean that any theoretical considerations must be limited to a short conclusion.

I divide my discussion into subsections to allow easier handling of my material and to make my observations more readily accessible to readers interested in specific areas of social ethics. I start with

---

[1] See Chs. 1–4 in this volume.

Dio's treatment of women, and proceed to marriage, love, children, parenthood, and finally effeminacy.

WOMEN AND WIVES

Briefly put, Dio's treatment of women is remarkably consistent with the earlier Greek literary tradition, which itself was composed of several strands, both favourable and unfavourable towards women.[2] Where his contemporary environment does affect his view of women,[3] for example as regards their education (esp. *Or.* 61), it results in a picture that is very similar indeed to that offered by Plutarch or Musonius Rufus.[4]

Let us start with some examples of traditional treatment, and with the very first oration on kingship. Here Dio rounds off his text with a *muthos* related to him by an anonymous old woman of Elis or Arcadia, who is not a manic, possessed priestess, but who spoke 'with self control and moderation' (*enkratōs kai sophronōs*). The vagueness of her characterization is deliberately designed to throw into greater relief the vivid, contrasting images of the named person-ifications that Heracles is shown. Dio is playing with the famous and oft-imitated Choice of Heracles propounded by Prodicus. Here Prodicus' Pleasure and Virtue are transmuted into Tyranny and Kingship. Personified female abstractions are a traditional part of Greek thought which Dio exemplifies on several other occasions.[5] Here we may note a couple of interesting features. Both Basileia and Tyrannis are given a bevy of appropriate 'feminine' attendants (*Or.* 1. 74, 82), but Basileia, the 'goodie', is also accompanied by Nomos, or Logos Orthos, without whom, we are told, the others

---

[2] Blomqvist (1989) 1 observes that 'Dio's views on women were not entirely con-sistent'. But traditional Greek views on women were not consistent either, and I would prefer to see Dio taking on board, 'passively' as Blomqvist might say, the tradition's ambiguous and rhetorically flexible attitudes. Blomqvist notes the tradition in which he works (e.g. 258), but fails, I believe, to accord it sufficient weight.

[3] Cf. Blomqvist (1989) 240–54.

[4] For Plutarch see the disappointing Le Corsu (1981), which focuses solely upon the *Lives* in isolation. For studies which integrate the views of the *Moral Essays* and *Lives* on marriage and family life, see Hawley (1999) and the other essays in the same volume.

[5] Cf. Apate, *Or.* 4. 113; the complementing contrast of masculine Nous and feminine Akrateia at the banquet of life, *Or.* 30. 36–8; Fortune, *Or.* 65 *passim*; Furies and Fame *Or.* 66. 29. For a discussion of this phenomenon in Dio: Blomqvist (1989) 208–12.

are not allowed to act or even think of acting (74). Of course one may say that these personifications are female because of the feminine gender of the abstract noun in Greek, but this process itself may reflect subconscious gender stereotyping. I certainly think it striking that we have a masculine moderator here, which must surely imply a subliminal message about gender and power (*pace* Blomqvist (1989) 211, 221). This 'masculine' moderator may remind us of the role of the *kurios* in classical Athens, without whom no respectable woman could act in public. Tyrannis, the 'baddie', is given appropriate characteristics of deceit (78), disorder (79), an inability to sit still (80), even multicoloured clothing to match her fickle character (81). Blomqvist, again, does not see in these personifications any attitude by Dio towards women in general, but these characteristics are quite typical of earlier Greek thought on women, especially in Semonides' poem *On Women*.[6]

Equally traditional are Dio's remarks on women's physical weakness in contrast to the stronger male.[7] Women are expected, as in classical texts, to remain indoors and to concern themselves with household duties.[8] Even the usually intimidating Amazons are described as easy to overcome for Alexander (*Or.* 4. 73).[9] Other traditional motifs which occur incidentally are: women's role in divination (*Or.* 13. 2), in lamentation for the dead (*Or.* 38. 19); Thessalian witches (*Or.* 47. 8, *Or.* 66. 16);[10] the inability to trust women (*Or.* 74. 6, 8, 14, 19);[11] the weakness of women's minds and their prohibition in classical Athens from any deal involving more than a bushel of barley (*Or.* 74. 9–10), which may also echo the Roman legal concept of a woman's *imbellicitas animi*.[12]

However there are departures from tradition, or more accurately diversions from it, that cover a broad range of interests shared by many of the *pepaideumenoi*: religion, ethnography, tragedy. We are told, for example, that the Greeks worship female more than male deities (*Or.* 37. 33), and that the Thracian women (familiar from Herodotus)

---

[6] Disorder: the sow woman (lines 2–4); restless movement: the bitch woman (14); fickleness: the sea woman (27–42).

[7] E.g. contrast of male/female, *Or.* 3. 34; women's weakness like a boy's, *Or.* 66. 23 (citing *Iliad* 11. 389–90, which highlights the consistency of outlook).

[8] Women's jobs: *Or.* 3. 70 contrasted with men; *Or.* 7. 114; women of Celaenae at work, *Or.* 35. 15.

[9] Cf. Blomqvist (1989) 219.   [10] Cf. Aristophanes, *Clouds* 749–52.

[11] Cf. Blomqvist (1989) 213–14.

[12] See Gardner (1986) 21; Schulz (1951) 181–2.

wear marks to show their status (*Or.* 14. 19). We are informed of ancient examples of famous women (*Or.* 64. 2–4), including Herodotus' Semiramis, who is described surprisingly as a lustful old woman eager for toyboys (*Or.* 47. 24; cf. *Or.* 64. 19, 22). As regards tragedy, we find detailed analysis of Deianeira's motivation for killing Heracles (*Or.* 60),[13] focusing on the logic and probability of the story, although Dio does throw in for good measure a traditional remark that women are by nature tricky and cunning (60. 7). In *Or.* 74. 20 we are told that Clytemnestra murdered Agamemnon, not just because she was a woman, but because she was a wicked woman. The text here continues with a discussion of animals who attack in revenge or defence. This bestial context reminds one of the archaic catalogues of women as beasts in Semonides and Phocylides.[14]

Even the attractive Libyan Myth in *Or.* 5 contains many traditional elements (cf. Lucian, *True Histories* 2. 76).[15] The description of feminine beauty conforms to traditionally admired parts of the body: the face, breasts, neck, and eyes. In most Greek societies, these were visible or nearly visible when women walked in public and so become the fetishistic focus for desire in literature from Homeric epic, through tragedy and Hellenistic epigram, to the *Picture Galleries* of Lucian and the Philostrati.

One aspect of feminine characterization (to which I shall return later when discussing effeminacy) which Dio exemplifies more than is traditional is an interest in women's speech and voice.[16] Moral character is betrayed by speech. The speech of *hetairai*, for example, is crude, and abusive (*Or.* 40. 29).[17] In an interestingly 'progressive' passage (*Or.* 33. 38) Dio notices that men and women have different voices, but that this does not make any one sex less human than the other. This oration has as its *leitmotiv* the strange sound of the 'snort' made by the men of Tarsus. Dio imagines a scenario where men's voices become feminine: this is horrendous, he says, but still human. Eunuchs, he adds, make that sort of sound. The snort is a sign of a woman's wantonness (51). Their talk is in keeping with their gait and eye movements (51). Voice, glances, posture, all reveal character,

---

[13] Cf. Blomqvist (1989) 180–91.
[14] Cf. Electra (*Or.* 74. 6), Medea (*Or.* 66. 16; 74. 8), Olympias (*Or.* 2. 16–17).
[15] Cf. Blomqvist (1989) 169–79.
[16] For a general discussion of the importance at this time of voice and speech as gender signifiers, see Gleason (1995), esp. 82–130.
[17] Cf. Aristophanes, *Assemblywomen* 877–937.

as do haircuts, gait, the elevation of the eye and the inclination of the neck. Even a sneeze can reveal a man's true character to one skilled in such matters (54). Effeminate men end up uttering sounds that are not even those of the common prostitute (60–1). The impropriety of blurring or altering vocal sexual difference is a striking aspect of the social ethics of Dio and his contemporaries which is developed with special vehemence against effeminate males (see below).

But what of woman's primary roles in Greek society, those of wife and mother? Again Dio offers a very traditional picture, albeit a collage of colours drawn from several different literary traditions. The narration of marriage customs formed a typical part of ancient ethnographic writing, as in Herodotus and even Thucydides, and they were of great interest to Dio's contemporary Plutarch, when wearing his moralizing historian's hat in several of the *Lives* (e.g. Spartan customs in the *Life of Lycurgus*). Dio's *Euboean Oration* devotes considerable space to discussion of the Euboean peasants' marriage and family relations.[18] They may marry each other's relatives (10, 20, 47), but most other elements are highly traditional. At the feast the wife sits near her husband, with the daughter of marriageable age serving food, while the boys prepare the meat (65). The young blushing lovers (67, 69) parallel the initially tentative heroes and heroines of Greek romance and of those love stories recounted with sugary sentimentalism by Hellenistic writers in both prose anthologies (e.g. Parthenius) and verse. In Dio's idyllic portrait of family life we may note that the wife also replies to Dio's questions: this relative equality at the table reminds one especially of the women of Plutarch, but it too harks back to classical models, for example Xenophon's *On Household Management* or Lysias 1. However, even here Dio uses traditional motifs of feminine characterization: out of respect neither the wife nor the daughter are named and the young girl, who is not yet married, never utters a word. This anonymity may also be a device to lend universality to the moral example, but it is strikingly classical in its treatment.

The relative equality of wives, or the image of the wife as a husband's co-worker and helper are again traditional (especially in Stoicism) and recur in Dio,[19] as are the ideas that wives are highly

---

[18] Cf. below and Blomqvist (1989) 47–89; Swain (1994) 170–2, (1996) 125 f.

[19] E.g. the wife of the ideal king as a helper, *Or.* 3. 122, possibly a reference to Trajan's wife Plotina (Blomqvist (1989) 19 n. 10).

prized and worth protecting,[20] and that marriage can be a means of political and social alliance.[21] Marital relations themselves are also presented in a familar way, with a difference between public and private conduct. Wives and husbands may often fight, although outsiders do not know (*Or.* 11. 20); wives may behave wantonly at home but they should behave differently in public (*Or.* 32. 32), covering themselves (*Or.* 33. 48–9). It is a scandal to force respectable wives to appear in court in torn clothing, as in the grain riot (*Or.* 46. 12). A prosperous man is truly fortunate when his wife and children are alive (*Or.* 27. 8). Dio also treats the by now traditional debate as to whether statesmen or philosophers should marry. True orators, politicians, and philosophers should work for the good of the state, which includes the duties of marriage and running a household (*Or.* 22. 2–3).[22]

Dio's remarks on other aspects of household management are otherwise scarce, but complement, for example, Plutarch's and Seneca's stress on domestic harmony in relationships with slaves. In *Or.* 10, on having servants, Dio notes that a wife might get annoyed at a servant, so it is best if she look after the husband herself. This would also prevent children being pampered into laziness. A household with no servants leads to more 'manly' children (12–13). Dio also praises *homonoia* and *homophrosunē*, *homonoia* characterizing good marriages as *dichonoia* does the bad (38. 15). Dio here shares his contemporaries' interest in domestic, and by extension, civic harmony. Its importance in Plato, Xenophon, Aristotle, the Stoics, and Cicero evolves to a new level in the world of the Greek imperial elite and has a particular parallel in Plutarch's civic and domestic ethics.[23]

CHILDREN AND PARENTHOOD

Like Plutarch, Dio makes his philosophical precepts more palatable by sugaring them with pleasing and immediate analogies from everyday

---

[20] E.g. a wife is listed with a priesthood as something not to be sold, *Or.* 31. 49 (contrast the sale of wives in *Or.* 7. 49); a wife is listed among valuable things to contend for, *Or.* 32. 75; a man should protect his wife and children, *Or.* 73. 3.

[21] E.g. *Or.* 11. 46–48, 51; *Or.* 40. 22, 27; *Or.* 41. 10.

[22] For the rhetorico-philosophical *thesis ei gamēteon*: Musonius Rufus 14; Russell (1979).

[23] Cf. Goessler (1962); Hawley (1999); Swain (1996c) index *s.v.* 'concord', (1999).

life.²⁴ As with Plutarch, these often playfully compare mankind with children, thus offering social historians touching sidelights on an aspect of family life often ignored in mainstream classical literature. The importance of parenthood is paramount for Dio: the friendship of parents and children is the first and greatest (*Or.* 40. 41).²⁵ Dio presents himself as loving his family: after the grain riot in Prusa, he contemplates leaving the city with his wife and baby (*Or.* 46. 13).²⁶ His affection for his wife and family appears genuine. We learn a fair amount about them, especially his feelings for his magistrate son.²⁷ These sidelights are far more engaging than, for example, Plutarch's references to his family, which appear too rhetorically adapted to the role of moralizing teacher.²⁸

Further glimpses into private life include the relationship between nurses and children: they may tell them stories to comfort them after a whipping (*Or.* 4. 74), or tell stories that both amuse and teach (*Or.* 72. 13). However, what is especially warming is the immediate involvement of the parents directly in the lives of their children. They worry and weep for them when they undergo surgery, even though they know it is in the children's best interests (*Or.* 50. 4). They may use terrifying images to deter them (*Or.* 5. 17); they even teach them to talk (*Or.* 38. 8).²⁹ Children's character is illuminated: they may have innate *eunoia* (*Or.* 12. 42–3), and love their parents in their dreams (*Or.* 12. 61), or they be so foolish that they hesitate to make up after quarrels (*Or.* 38. 21). Rebellious children are no benefit to parents (*Or.* 38. 15). Clearly drawing on contemporary Roman practice, Dio openly deplores children who ignore their true parents to fawn on the more wealthy (*Or.* 49. 13), and contrasts the duty children owe natural parents with that they owe adopted ones (*Or.* 41. 45). Orestes' matricide is dreadful (*Or.* 10. 27) and those who maltreat parents are impious (*Or.* 31. 15). We also learn of children's games: hoops (*Or.* 12. 37) and the game of King (*Or.* 4. 47–8), so famous from Herodotus' story of Cyrus.

---

²⁴ Cf. Quet (1978).

²⁵ Cf. parents consulting Delphi about childlessness: *Or.* 13. 9.

²⁶ On the grain riot: Jones (1978). 19–25.

²⁷ E.g. ibid. 6–7. Since *Or.* 46 refers to his son as a baby, Jones gives it a Vespasianic date; contrast Dio's son as an adult in *Orr.* 40. 2, 44. 8, 50. 5, 10. Cf. von Arnim (1898) 122–4, 206, 386, 507.

²⁸ See the full discussion in Hawley (1999).

²⁹ Cf. parents' gifts of dolls (*Or.* 31. 153); children's pleasure in worthless things (*Or.* 38. 37).

Once more developing the theme of domestic *homonoia*, Dio sees the role of the father as being that of a kind governor, as Trajan is to his subjects (*Or.* 3. 5), one loved more by his subjects than even their parents and children (112). Indeed here Dio uses the family motif to frame and structure the whole oration. A father, like Zeus, should combine *eunoia* with *philia* (*Or.* 53. 12) to prevent familial conflict (*Or.* 74. 27).[30]

Motherhood gets only a few fleeting references, mostly to its dangers, especially through adultery. For example, Athenian women had sons by non-free fathers (*Or.* 15. 3); a woman's word as to fatherhood is untrustworthy (*Orr.* 15. 3–13, esp. 4, 11; 31. 42), a fear as old as Telemachus in the *Odyssey*; many Athenian women sleep around (*Or.* 15. 5); Clytemnestra and Aerope are common types (*Or.* 15. 6).[31] Adultery is of course condemned, in the same breath as theft (31. 94). The practice of exposing unwanted babies is discussed in *Or.* 15. 9 and referred to on two other occasions: *Or.* 4. 25, where tiaras are said to be left on babies to aid recognition, an image clearly derived from New Comedy; and *Or.* 31. 154 where Dio condemns the Rhodians for accepting the practice of re-dedicating statues while condemning supposititious babies. The women who indulge in such practices are disapproved of by Dio: they may be rich or sterile and take up other people's babies just to retain material comfort (*Or.* 15. 8). A moving appendix is the remark that slave-women often kill their children to prevent the mothers from having a second slavery imposed upon them, namely rearing their offspring (15. 8).

SEXUAL RELATIONS AND LUST

As both Swain and Konstan, for example, have noted, many texts of this period stress the social necessity of marriage and the desirability of conjugal fidelity.[32] Dio's remarks on lust are, not surprisingly, consistent with those of many of his predecessors and contemporaries. Self-control is the key. As we have seen, the ideal marriage is an extension of friendship (*Or.* 3. 98). Without

[30] Cf. Phidias' Zeus (12. 77); a father's power to imprison, sell, or kill his sons (15. 20); persuasion to be used with children (39. 8); the Persian king was pitiable because of domestic conspiracy (6. 35).

[31] Cf. Blomqvist (1989) 215.

[32] Swain (1996) 118–31, Konstan (1994) 14–98.

condemnation, Dio observes how lovers, when alone, discuss their desires (*Or.* 45. 15). It is foolish, Dio remarks, to fall in love with someone whom you have never seen (*Or.* 11. 54–5). Of course sexual desire is human, but we all have different desires, wherever we live (*Or.* 66. 2–4). What is wrong is to let those desires get the better of you. As a result, men and women of loose sexual morals come in for staunch attack from Dio, but whereas classical authors tended to blame women more for their immorality, in Dio (as with many of his contemporaries) men get a decidedly worse press for their intemperance.

The sheer number of references illustrate a contemporary concern. Avaricious men indulge their lusts indiscriminately with women and men (*Or.* 4. 102); absolute rulers make free with women and boys (*Or.* 20. 17; *Or.* 47. 24). Wanton men love wine, wives, and boys alike (*Or.* 66. 1). Sexual indulgence is graphically imaged in the reference to Pan and masturbation (*Or.* 6. 18–20). Brothels and prostitutes are to be expected in a city, says Dio (*Or.* 32. 91), but philosophers do not pay visits there (*Or.* 70. 9) and condemn the lusts of avaricious men (*Or.* 72. 7), for *hetairai* are among the frivolities of life (*Or.* 70. 1). Keeping a brothel is shameful (*Or.* 14. 14); such establishments resound with Dio's hated 'snorting' sound (*Or.* 33. 36). The *pornoboskos* is subjected to a lengthy and virtiolic attack at *Or.* 7. 123–36, in a section positioned to contrast starkly with the idyllic family life of the Euboean peasants (see above). Dio's tirade, which recalls for us similar remarks in Juvenal,[33] condemns prostitution as sex without love, with prostitutes who are slaves and may be barbarian, who are likened to animals. Their acts are impious to the patrons of marriage, Zeus and Hera. The speech then progresses into an attack on men who commit adultery with those who have no citizen rights. In a tone which recalls the closing sections of Lysias' famous speech *Against Eratosthenes* (1), Dio conjures up images of lustful men pursuing chaste wives and thus harming the status of legitimate women and children (139). Wealth is for Dio, as for Juvenal, the deciding factor. Such lustful men may point to the stories of amorous gods as excuses, but this only works among the rich (140).[34] The dramatic tone of Dio's attack is

---

[33] For Dio's and Juvenal's differing treatment of women: Blomqvist (1989) 259. On the *Euboicus* passage itself cf. Houser (1998) 243–53.

[34] For parody of such lustful gods, cf. Lucian's *Dialogues of the Gods*.

deliberate: the vivid and emphatic exclamation *eien de* (148) underlines his exasperation as if he were speaking direct to the 'reader' of
the published version and acts as a transition to the next section on
boys' education and the dangers of growing depravity. Lustful men,
not satisfied with female lovers, soon turn their disgusting attentions
to men: a dramatic conclusion worthy of Juvenal!

EFFEMINACY

While what Dio has to say about women, lust, and family relations
may generally be seen as consistent with his literary heritage, his
persistent reference to the blurring of distinct gender differences
and to effeminacy in men is very much a hallmark of his own time.
The comparison of homosexual and heterosexual love was a commonplace of the classical tradition, though writers of Dio's time treat
the subject in quite different ways, either clearly advocating heterosexual marriage (e.g. Plutarch, *Dialogue on Love*), or revelling in the
scandals of conjugal infidelity (e.g. Lucian, Athenaeus). However,
the discussion of the importance of maintaining clear distinctions
between men and women in their appearance and behaviour is one
which is predominantly post-classical. Certainly there are echoes
of this in the comic *Women at the Thesmophoria* by Aristophanes
of 411 BC or the tragic Euripides' *Bacchants*,[35] but the sheer bulk of
references in later writers, growing with the centuries, is striking.[36]
In the conclusion I draw attention to some theories which attempt
to explain this, but first we must look at what Dio has to say.

His tone is universally condemnatory. Even the gods and famous
literary figures do not remain unscathed. Athena's music is not
effeminate (*malakon*, *Or.* 1. 1), unlike the 'women's songs' of the
dissolute Alexandrians (*Or.* 32. 62). Homer loses to Hesiod in their
famous contest because the farmers to whom he sang were 'pleasure-
loving and effeminate' (*philēdonois . . . malakois, Or.* 2. 12). Songs
of love are not appropriate for kings (*Or.* 2. 28), nor are licentious
language, dances, women, and music (2. 56). The word *malakos*
is associated with slavery to pleasure (*Or.* 3. 56) and with luxury
(*truphē, Or.* 6. 25). 'Real men' do not sit indoors (*Orr.* 6. 11, 70. 2),

---

[35] Cf. Loraux (1995).
[36] For a splendid and detailed discussion of the whole issue, see Gleason (1995).

as the traditional classical Athenian ideology held proper for respectable women.

One figure stands out as Dio's *exemplum par excellence* of the effeminacy he deplored: Sardanapallus. He rears his camp and listless head, or more to the point he does not raise it, right at the start of Dio's first *Kingship Oration* (1. 3), and reappears at intervals. His Nineveh is overdecorated and decadent (*Or.* 2. 35).[37] He imitates women's life-style indoors, which is shameful (*Or.* 3. 72). At *Or.* 4. 102–13 Dio imagines an avaricious man, surrounded by women and their shrill cries, cymbals, and flutes. This degenerate is pale, effeminate in appearance, and self-obsessed. Dio caps his description by referring to a fictitious painting or statue: it is just like Sardanapallus! At the very end of his tirade against pleasure Dio again refers to Sardanapallus (135), just in case we had forgotten. However, Dio's most explicit attack occurs in *Or.* 62. 5–7, where he is comparing kingship and tyranny. Here we see Sardanapallus in the women's quarters on his golden couch, with a voice shriller than that of a eunuch, with effeminate body language, in sum indistinguishable from one of his concubines.

Effeminacy and 'gender-bending' actually form a consistent pattern in Dio, of which a vital component is external appearance. Manners may 'maketh man', but clothes can make a man womanly. One had to wear clothes appropriate (*prepei*) to one's sex (*Or.* 4. 108–9). Homer is praised for giving his men clothes that are not effeminate (*Or.* 2. 49), like some Carian girl's. The *pornoboskos*'s lewd trade is echoed by his shameless costume, like that of his *hetairai* (*Or.* 4. 96). To lead a woman's life indoors and to wear womanly clothes is a degradation for a man (*Or.* 4. 105–6). Dio complains that in his day it is hard to tell the sexes apart. Men and women have similar hairstyles and both use cosmetics (*Or.* 7. 117). One's walk may also reveal one's true character. Dio praises the Rhodians for their modest hairstyle and gait, which confirms their morality (*Or.* 32. 54; cf. 33. 52), and cites lines from Archilochus which criticize an effeminate walk (*Or.* 33. 17, cf. 39).[38] For Dio the first step on this slippery road to sexual ambiguity is taken when one trims one's beard (*Or.* 33. 63–4; cf. 36. 17). Beards had long been held as a true sign of

---

[37] For houses that echo the character of their occupants, cf. Calypso and the effeminate Menelaus and his Asiatic home, *Or.* 2. 41.

[38] On gender and gait: Gleason (1995) 60–2.

masculinity, from the reviled shaven effeminates and beard-wearing women of Aristophanes to classical vase-painting where beards can signify sex, status, and age. However, nearer Dio's time, the importance of the beard as a sign of masculinity was growing, for example in the Stoic writings on sexual difference by Musonius Rufus or Epictetus, or in the writings of Clement of Alexandria.[39]

Owing to the fact that Dio idealizes married heterosexual love, it is not surprising that homosexual love receives only a few fleeting and condemnatory remarks, and those only concerning male–male relations. Boys are jealous, he says (*Or.* 2. 32), of more handsome boys because their lovers are more powerful. Such lovers are weak-minded. A man may kill his male lover and tell himself that he has killed him because he loved his lover too much, when in reality it may only be the result of some irksome trifle (*Or.* 74. 5). Ironically the boy-lover actually comes off better in Dio's discussion of reputation-seekers. Here those who yearn for fame seek universal acclaim, while a boy-lover can be sated with a small fee and one boy (*Or.* 66. 7).[40]

The subtleties of Dio's attitude towards male–male love, and sex in particular, have been the focus of scholarly controversy in recent years, the most recent contributor being Houser (1998). While scholars such as Swain and Russell see Dio condemning such sex *per se*,[41] Houser would refine Dio's condemnation to focus upon the mental attitude of the active partner and on the power relationship between active and passive participants, developing the views of scholars such as Winkler and Halperin.[42] Houser uses Musonius Rufus' Stoic influence upon Dio (especially in *Orr.* 3 and 7) to argue that what Dio is actually criticizing is sexual contact with a partner *of either sex* when the sole motive is personal pleasure or where the act involves *hubris*.[43] While Houser is certainly right to remind us of Musonius' influence, and of the ancient concern with active and

---

[39] E.g. Musonius Rufus 21; Epictetus 1. 16. 9–14; Clement, *Tutor* 3. 11. 60–3 (generally on hairstyles, clothing, etc., appropriate to the sexes) and 3. 3 (on male hairstyles). The beard was also from classical times a symbol of being a philosopher, especially for the Cynics. However, here the beard was a signifier of professional not gender identity. See generally van Geytenbeek (1963) 119–23.

[40] Cf. the beautiful Callistratus and his male lovers, *Or.* 36. 8.

[41] E.g. Swain (1996) 84, 125–6, 214–16; Russell (1992) 150, 157, 216.

[42] Winkler (1990), esp. 17–44; Halperin (1990) 15–40.

[43] Houser (1998) 257–8, 'The important condition is that the agent pursues *eunoia* or acts out of *philia* . . . The biological sex of the partner is not a source of concern.'

passive in sexual contact (which latter, it is true, is perhaps not fully appreciated by Russell and Swain), the broader context within Dio of the discourse of gender construction and the strong idealization of the family (which this chapter argues for) persuades me that Dio held views which are remarkably similar to those of, for example, Plutarch. Neither openly condemns male–male love as disgusting,[44] but their reticence seems to me to be one of reluctant tolerance in a cultural climate where such activity was viewed more and more as out of date and eccentric, and where legal directive, philosophical thought, and social convention seemed to consider positive sexual activity as that which took place between men and women, ideally in marriage.

However, Dio does discuss male beauty and its positive side in a couple of extensive passages, especially *Or.* 21, *On Beauty*.[45] Here he chooses a dialogue structure with an anonymous interlocutor. Perhaps he is recalling Platonic and later dialogues on the related topic of love. The text discusses the increasing value placed on female over male beauty, which leads men of Dio's time into effeminacy. Any beautiful young men are today, he says, ignored or become the victims of degenerate lust (*Or.* 21. 2). The Persian eunuchs provide the extreme example of this trend (4), implicitly recalling the Asiatic Sardanapallus. Dio contrasts favourably the Athenian educational system with the Persian, for the former does not breed effeminacy (5). This then leads him to an attack on Nero's effeminacy and male lovers, explicitly focusing on dress and hairstyle (7), before he returns to praise of male Greek beauty (15), adding some interesting and unusual remarks about racial distinctions (16). He compares Achilles and Hector, observing that Hector is not described as beautiful until he is dead, and then in more detail than other handsome men. This trait in archaic epic's characterization of masculinity is one I have discussed further elsewhere with relation to classical tragedy and comedy, where again male physical description tends to focus upon men in pain or embarrassment, and where male beauty becomes, as in Homer, a means of adding pathos to a dying or dead hero.[46] Dio is also correct in noting how authors focus upon the hair of such young men for pathos. The oration thus combines traditional elements, such as the unfavourable image of the Persians, with more

---

[44] Indeed, as Houser (1998) 257 notes, Dio, unlike Plutarch, never gives a full discussion of his views on love and sex.   [45] Cf. Hawley (1998*a*) and (1998*b*).
[46] Hawley (1998*b*).

contemporary anxieties about physical effeminacy. It is interesting here to note that Dio starts the discourse by describing the beautiful young boy as possessing 'archaic' beauty (*archaion . . . to eidos*, 1). Dio explicitly observes that modern statues fail to preserve these ancient ideals of masculine beauty. This lamentation of falling standards in statuary can be paralleled with the praise of the classical artistic style which we find in Pausanias, even down to the use of the technical term *archaios*.[47]

The second more extensive discussion of male beauty and physical prowess comes in *Orr.* 28 and 29 devoted to the memory of Melancomas, the famous boxer friend of Titus. Jones highlights the traditionality of the themes in the genres of invented funeral orations and athletic *encomia*.[48] Again we find Dio comparing his subject with statues (*Or.* 28. 3–4), whose own beauty is not confined to his clothing, but shines when naked (5–6). Dio sums up Melancomas' good fortune by enumerating his family, beauty, courage, strength, and, last but certainly not least, his self-control (12–13, cf. 29. 16–17). In *Or.* 29 he complements the image of Melancomas, idealized as the most beautiful of all athletes (6), by comparing athletics and war (15 ff.), recalling analogies traditional from Homeric epic onwards. To cap Melancomas' ideal status, he is described as excelling even the fabulously beautiful heroes of myth. Those men were famous only for their physical beauty, whereas Melancomas possessed in addition genuine courage (17–18).

CONCLUSION

My collection of references in this chapter has shown how Dio uses traditional classical ideas about gender and family relations. In this he resembles many of his contemporaries, especially Plutarch. His audiences probably included members of both sexes and of a wide age range. They shared a common Hellenic culture upon which he could draw for his allusions. His moral code, to adopt Blomqvist's term, is essentially practical and relatively conservative. However, as with Plutarch, we see Dio widening his sphere of interest to incorporate and integrate the greater intellectual and public freedom

---

[47] For a helpful analysis of such aesthetic 'age' terminology see Arafat (1996) 58–75.
[48] Jones (1978), esp. 15–17, 164 n. 50.

the women of his day enjoyed over their classical Athenian sisters. Dio's wise women are the articulate wives and daughters desired by Plutarch and Musonius Rufus.

Plutarch and Dio also share a contemporary concern about effeminacy and masculinity which is not present to the same degree in their classical sources. Why might this be? Recent scholarship has tried to offer some suggestions. On the one hand we find Foucault (esp. (1986)) and his followers, who glimpse here a re-examination by the Greeks of Dio's time of their predecessors' constructions of gender and of the problematic role of homosexuality. Foucault's influence has been wide-ranging in studies of ancient gender and cannot be discussed adequately here. For our purposes perhaps one of the best examples of the value of such a perspective can be found in Gleason (1995). Her analysis examines the games which rhetoric plays in the construction of male self-presentation. Dio figures here, particularly when in exile, as an example of a sophist who adopts distancing *exempla* and *personae* to discuss his own experience. Other scholars, however, see less value in the Foucault line. Swain (1996 and 1999c), for example, argues that such theories have a restricted application in the world of Dio's or Plutarch's Greek elites. My own approach, as a social historian approaching family relations from an initially literary perspective, is deliberately eclectic. While accepting the crucial importance of the historical and political context, it is undeniable that the self-examination so well documented by Gleason is underway. However, some of Foucault's argumentation seems to me flawed, too essentialist, and anachronistic. Quite appropriately, his own work and *persona* are currently undergoing their own historiographical re-examination (e.g. Larmour *et al.* (1998)). Theorists will continue to speculate on the reasons why these authors, who elsewhere seem sometimes unimaginatively to follow and imitate classical thought on family relations, depart from them so strikingly in the area of masculinity/effeminacy. I hope that my survey here will aid them in their overview of the Greek writers of this period, among whom Dio has in this respect been a hitherto overlooked figure.

PART THREE

Letters

6

Some Uses of Storytelling in Dio
GRAHAM ANDERSON

INTRODUCTION

Dio of Prusa is normally studied for his role as a moralist;[1] for his political relationships;[2] and for his sophistic talents in the broadest sense. But he is rather more seldom studied for a role which any sophist might be expected to summon, as a narrator and storyteller. In view of the heightened interest in fiction in early imperial times,[3] it seems right to look at this aspect of Dio as well. I have chosen a small group of works with substantial narrative elements, and set out through them to review the author's narrative interests as a whole. The pieces chosen are the pastoral tale that forms the first half of the *Euboicus*, the 'Choice of Heracles' that concludes the *First Kingship Oration*, the *Troicus*, the *Libycus*, and the *Borystheniticus*. Each of these raises its own questions, but one typical trait will be apparent: there is a degree of reticence, and the sense of narrative resourcefulness is held in check by an overriding moral responsibility. We are looking at someone who sees himself as a philosopher or moralist telling stories, rather than as an entertainer telling philosophically coloured ones. We shall also note from time to time what seems like the voice of personal experience, something that is not always readily extracted from early imperial sophistically coloured authors.

---

[1] For the Cynic background in particular, see now Branham and Goulet-Cazé (1996) *passim*.

[2] Notably Desideri (1978); Jones (1978); Moles (1978). On Dio's public persona in general, see most recently Swain (1996) 187–241.

[3] Dio's own case has excited little interest, though one notes the inclusion of the *Euboicus* in Hadas (1953) together with Longus and Xenophon of Ephesus. Donald Russell (1992) offers commentary on two of the fictional narratives grouped together with the *Olympicus*. There is also brief overview by Swain (1994), and by Holzberg (1996).

We can already see an oblique indication of Dio's overall aim if we look at what he himself would have regarded as suitable aims in narrative, when in *Or.* 18 he gives advice to a late learner on authors to be read for their prose style. Herodotus is unsurprisingly noted for the impression of storytelling he gives even when writing history (18. 10); but it is Xenophon who is singled out for his special relevance to a man of affairs (*Or.* 18. 14):

For his ideas are clear and simple and easily accessible to everyone, and the character of his narrative reporting (*apangelia*) is attractive and pleasant and persuasive, with a great deal of authenticity, charm and effectiveness, so that its impression is not only one of verbal cleverness but even wizardry.

We can set out to examine how far such an impression is true of a variety of situations from Dio's own storytelling. My first example is a short and quite incidental historical *exemplum* which Dio shares with an account in Pausanias (6. 11. 5 ff.), but which has potential for considerable rhetorical and indeed sheer entertainment value. In Pausanias' treatment we are told that after an immensely successful career as an athlete, Theagenes of Thasos had been commemorated by a statue. After his death, a rival of his used to come every night and flog the statue. The statue fell on him and so put an end to the outrage, whereupon the dead man's sons indicted it for murder. Having been found guilty, the statue was sunk in the sea. The Thasian crops failed and the oracle at Delphi commanded the Thasians to restore their exiles. Only a chance catch by fishermen brought the statue back. It is now the centre of a cult, as are his statues elsewhere. Thus far the routinely antiquarian version arising out of Pausanias' experience of the statue itself. But it is instructive to compare the same tale as presented a couple of generations earlier by Dio in his *Rhodian Oration* (31. 95 f.):

Theagenes was a Thasian athlete. This man had the reputation of surpassing the men of his time in strength, and three times took the Olympic Crown, as well as many other honours. And when he stopped competing and returned home, for the rest of his life when his body had passed its prime he was a man inferior to none in civic affairs, but as good a citizen as any man can be (*oudenos cheirōn peri ta koina*). And as a result, no doubt, he fell foul of a political opponent. And although while he was alive this man only envied him, when he died he carried out the most mindless and sacrilegious act. He used to flog at night the statue of Theagenes that stood in the middle of the city.

There are a number of differences later on in Dio's narrative: relatives rather than sons bring the prosecution; a plague rather than a famine follows the punishment of the statue; we are given an actual oracle different from and more extensive than the text quoted by Pausanias. Fishermen play no part in finding the statue, and there is no description of a cult. But these differences are incidental compared to what Dio has expanded: here is a *diēgēma* whose details seem totally fixed: one ought to be able to change very little in giving out the bare facts of the story. Yet within a short compass Dio has given the whole business a far more civic resonance. He gives Theagenes a distinguished civic career *after* his athletic performances; Pausanias says nothing to imply that the man who flogged the statue was a *political* enemy, but simply one of his *apechthēmenoi*; nor does he say that the statue was in the centre of the city. By 'planting' both these details, Dio has imported an emphasis on civic virtue into the story. Theagenes is formulated as if he were none other than Dio himself.[4] This reshaping of course serves to reinforce the criticism that the Rhodians are themselves dishonouring the statues of worthy citizens—Theagenes has to have a prominent civic role to give real point to the story. We might be tempted to imagine how such a story would have been treated by Lucian. The cult might well have been back, the statue's revenge a supposed matter of pettiness and superstition.[5] But Dio passes the rhetorical opportunity in order to make a civic point. The example is unimportant in itself; but it is symptomatic of Dio's outlook as a whole. Most of his narrative efforts make sense as an integral part of some larger endeavour; and while he is an undoubtedly efficient storyteller, he exhibits a degree of reticence, and his real flamboyance is reserved for what he sees as more important matters.

THE *EUBOICUS* AND THE LESSONS OF POVERTY

The most ambitious narrative in the corpus, indeed the most ambitious work of any kind, is the *Euboicus* (Or. 7).[6] Dio offers us a

---

[4] And indeed Dio himself figures in a civic controversy towards the end of his life over his erection of a statue of the emperor: Pliny, *Ep.* 10. 81. 7.

[5] Cf. *Philopseudes* 18 ff. (satire of superstitions concerning cult-statues).

[6] For the *Euboicus*, Highet (1973); Jouan (1977); Jones (1978), 56–61; Russell (1992) 8–13; Swain (1994) 166–72. For the civic ideology explored in the work, see Ma, above, Ch. 4.

long tale purporting to be drawn from his own experience, in which he tells of a shipwreck and the hospitality of a small subsistence community in Euboea; the second half of the speech draws appropriate moral inferences and exhortations, on a scale comparable to that of the narrative portion itself. We naturally ask whether this is a fringe production to the novel, or even whether or not it can usefully have a genre label at all; what questions it raises for truth or fiction;[7] and what it might tell us about Dio as an individual or about sophists in general as narrators.

An obvious and much-discussed starting-point is the *Euboicus'* relationship to the pastoral novel, Longus' *Daphnis and Chloe*, which it clearly pre-dates. A number of common themes have been picked out,[8] not least the culmination of both tales in a rustic wedding and the markedly greater sympathy for nature over culture. Both works could reasonably be called 'pastoral romance', a label which neatly bypasses the issue of length. But perhaps there we should draw the line and emphasize the differences. For here we do seem to have a narrative with an air of sincerity, conviction, and experience about it. Or to put it another way, the story is a great deal less stylized than it might have been. Two features seem to speak out against excessive artifice. For one thing, the circumstances of Dio's shipwreck could have been made more of in any fictional narrative; secondly, the long details of the hunter's family and of his in-laws—his father and father-in-law had been grazers till confiscation deprived them of their livestock—might be expected to have little place in the preoccupations of a conventional romantic narrative, with its postulate of aristocratic parentage to make the plot 'respectable'. Indeed, although the term ecphrasis is rightly invoked for parts of the story, even the description of the pastures seems once more to avoid the traditional allure of the *locus amoenus*. Also, the element of romantic adventure seems spontaneous and implied: the two young lovers are maintaining a modest reticence about the whole business; the boy is rearing a pig for the marriage sacrifice without telling his father (though his mother is already in the know); there are no Cupid's arrows or first kisses, and no more than the subtlest hint of the lovesickness so characteristic of even such a simple 'romantic' author as Xenophon of Ephesus. It is as though Dio and his audience are

---

[7] For the problem in general, see now Gill and Wiseman (1993).
[8] Hunter (1983) 66 f.; for comparison with Lucian, Anderson (1976) 94–8.

intruders into a domestic understanding which is private but totally natural. Not that there is no room for narrative artifice of any kind: we should note the convenience of the shipwreck as affording space for reported narrative, just as a shipowner finds exactly the right time for listening to the narrative of Philostratus' *Heroicus* when he is delayed by contrary winds (*Heroicus* 2 p. 1 Lannoy). And it takes precisely the time from the point at which Dio meets the hunter to the arrival at his hut to tell the story of the hunter's life-style. The recounting of the hunter's experience in the city as he fended off accusations of land theft has an air of the satire of rhetoric and litigation. Moreover, it seems improbable that the rustic would remember the speeches in such detail. But even so one is tempted to feel that nothing very much is really happening: the shipwrecked Dio hears a tale of how a simple countryman came to town and protected his inheritance thanks to a good deed, and his daughter is getting married. It is an engaging sketch, but is it really an action? Alternatively, we might see the whole account as an ecphrasis of a utopia: yet again it seems far short of the degree of schematization that Dio gives to the Indians in his *syncrisis* of their nation with the people of Celaenae in *Or.* 35.

One classification might be suggested by Dio's opening words: the claim to have personally experienced the events is close to the heart of the realistic novella in antiquity.[9] If we see the encounter in the city with the accuser as central, that too is typical of the novella, the charlatan being soundly confuted in front of an audience. And again, true to the conventions which B. E. Perry insisted on for the ancient novella,[10] even so ambitious an account is subordinate to a very different sort of whole.

Whatever the framework we choose to assume, Dio manages the tale itself with considerable technique, setting most of the background in the mouth of the rustic hunter who offers the wandering Dio his hospitality: in describing his one single visit to a town, where he is required to give an account of his assets and title to the public assembly, he offers proof of his own rustic perceptions in his attempts to describe a theatre (7. 24). But then he goes on to provide verbatim the speech of his demagogic accuser; a further speech offered by a speaker in his defence; his own contribution; and the testimony of someone recently rescued by him and able to corroborate his account

[9] Cf. Holzberg (1996) 640.   [10] Perry (1967) 83.

of his humble smallholding (7. 27–61). Dio cannot in the nature of things entirely conceal the implausibility that he had just happened to meet nature's most unaffected orator, endowed with total powers of recall—of epideictic speeches of which he has had no previous experience whatsoever! Or perhaps he can suggest that the facts speak so much for themselves that a natural account of the situation has a rhetoric of its own, free from the artifices of educated argument. He has certainly succeeded in sketching not only the peasant's natural naïvety but his natural generosity as well:

Then the archon asked me what we would be able to give the community, and I said 'four deerskins, really good ones'. Most of them laughed at this, and the archon was annoyed with me. The bearskins, I explained, were rough and the goatskins not so good, some old and some small. But I told him 'take these too if you like'. Once more he was annoyed and called me a downright clodhopper (*agroikos*). And I said 'Are you talking about land again? Can't you hear me saying that we don't have any?' Then he asked me if we were prepared to pay an Attic talent each. And I replied, 'We don't weigh our meat; but whatever we have, we'll give you. A little of it is salted, the rest is smoked and nearly just as good, sides of bacon and venison and other high-quality meats.' Then they went into an uproar and accused me of lying. But the archon asked me if we had any grain, and how much. I told him exactly what we had: two *medimnoi* of wheat, four of barley, and four of millet, but only a *hēmiektos* of beans; for we had none this past year. 'So you take the wheat and the barley,' I told him, 'and let us keep the millet. But if you need millet, have that as well.' (7. 44 f.)

Dio has cleverly concealed the artistry of the rustic's account, so that the pitifully little his family lives on disarms the accusations, and at the same time implies a model of Cynic self-sufficiency. The texture of the narrative can be further gauged from the end of the story, as the preparations for the discreet rural wedding are in progress, and we are presented with a scenario some distance in feel from the corresponding end even of the pseudo-naïve Longus:

So he and the boys ran off at once in sheer delight. Meanwhile the girl got up and from another hut brought slices of sorb-apple, medlars, winter-apples, and swelling bunches of fine grapes, and put them on the table, after wiping away the meat stains with leaves and putting clean fern underneath. The boys arrived with the pig, laughing and joking; the young lad's mother came along with them and two small brothers, with white loaves and boiled eggs on wooden platters and roasted chickpeas. And when the woman had greeted her brother and her niece she sat down beside her husband and said:

'There's the victim this boy had been feeding all this time for the wedding, and everything on our side is ready as well: the barley and wheat flour have been done; only we could do with a little extra wine; it won't be difficult to get from the village.' And her son stood beside her, looking at his father-in-law-to-be. The girl's father smiled and said, 'There's the man who's holding us up! Maybe he wants to fatten the pig a little more.' The lad replied, 'I'm telling you she's ready to burst.' I wanted to come to his rescue and said, 'See that this lad doesn't get thin while the pig gets fat.' His mother said, 'Our guest is right: for he's thinner than usual these days; and the other day I noticed that he was awake at night and would go out of the hut.' 'The dogs were barking and I went out to check.' 'No you didn't, you were pacing around at your wits' end. So don't let us allow him to suffer any longer.' And she threw herself round the bride's mother and kissed her; and she said to her husband, 'Let's do what they want.' So they made the decision and said: 'Let us fix the wedding for the day after tomorrow.' And they invited me to stay too for the wedding day, and I was only too glad; at the same time I thought about what weddings and other things are like among the wealthy—the matchmakers, the business of looking at property and family background, the dowries, the bridegrooms' gifts, the promises and deceits, the contracts and agreements, and at the end of it all the back-biting and ill-feeling often at the wedding itself.   (7. 74–80)

It is not difficult to relate the above to literary tradition in plenty: it can be placed alongside any scenario of country hospitality, from Eumaeus' reception of Odysseus to the kind of detail in Ovid's handling of Philemon and Baucis.[11] Later in the tradition Longus can certainly offer the country hospitality which Chloe's parents improvise for Daphnis in the winter expedition (3. 9); for the detail of happy children we might think of the little boy Tityrus who is sent for Philetas' pipes (2. 33); both the latter are considerably more wittily contrived than the scene here. Dio succumbs to the temptations of the rhetoric of *autarkeia* as he describes his own reflections at the end;[12] but his own contribution is carefully distinguished from the simple *euētheia* of the rustic participants. There is a genuinely successful documentary realism here. It is perhaps best realized by comparing the scenario in Heliodorus' *Aethiopica* where the visiting philosopher-priest Calasiris observes the symptoms of lovesickness of Theagenes and Charicleia: Dio's effort is a triumph of under-statement and quiet spontaneity. And on the level of miniature it is

[11] *Met.* 8. 611–724 with Hollis's commentary (Oxford 1970), ad loc., usefully sketch-ing intervening tradition.
[12] Cf. Brenk, below, Ch. 11.

totally free from the sense of learned affectation which parades itself in nearly every line of, for example, Alciphron's rural excursions.[13]

One recent development in the study of Greek topography might cause us to be more suspicious than hitherto about the overall picture of Dio's narrative: Alcock's *Graecia Capta* gives a more optimistic picture of the Greek provinces in the late Republic and early Empire than the picture of the ruined Carystus (or similar location) and the squatters' rights on Euboea; but the overall picture cannot be to used to correct Dio's descriptions in any detail, though again it underlines the ever-present risks in using convincing and spontaneous detail in fiction as free-standing factual evidence.[14]

MORAL ALLEGORY AND ARTIFICE

True to Dio's philosophical persona, several of his most ambitious narratives have a more directly philosophical frame of reference. This is especially clear of his version of the allegory of Prodicus (*Or.* 1. 50–84).[15] Dio does not attribute his tale to Prodicus or to Socrates, but instead claims to have heard it from a wise old priestess in the Peloponnese on his wanderings in the region. He thus anticipates Apuleius in presenting an elaborate moral allegory as an *anilis fabula*, though with a rather greater degree of plausibility. The shrine at which he hears the tale is associated with Heracles, and so a moral myth about him is appropriate; less plausible is the prophecy that Dio is destined to pass on the story to a ruler, i.e. Trajan. The analogy with Diotima's speech in the Platonic *Symposium* as well as details of the *mise-en-scène* of the *Phaedrus* have been established.[16] In this version the two allegorical figures are neatly modified from Virtue and Vice to Basileia and Tyrannis; if they do not speak out in their own person this time, they are at least tricked out with almost obligatory allegorical retinues. Of action in the reported story there is little, as in the *Euboicus*, though the idea of Hermes guiding Heracles to the site of the twin peaks might seem new. Again, in terms of

[13] For the latter see Anderson (1997).

[14] Alcock (1993) 30: 'The general concurrence of the sources in their negative presentation of Roman Greece does not necessarily prove its truth, but rather the degree to which a rhetoric was shared: depopulation and decline had become natural ingredients for representations of a defeated, inglorious Greece'; cf. Brunt (1973).

[15] For the history of the topos, see Alpers (1912).

[16] In particular by Trapp (1990) 143 f.

'wisdom' materials this is probably not the case: we have only to think of the New Testament story of Satan showing Jesus Christ the Kingdoms of the World which he refuses.[17] We should automatically think that the narrow difficult path should apply to justice, the broad one to vice and folly, whereas the opposite is the case:[18] Trajan has been constitutionally set in place, while tyrants have difficulty and risk in obtaining their tyrannies (cf. Xenophon, *Mem.* 2. 1. 21; Cicero, *De Off.* 1. 32).

Much of the description smacks of ecphrasis: 'her clothing was a motley—one thing purple, another scarlet, something else yellow, and there were some patches of white garments showing, since a great deal of her clothing was torn' (*Or.* 1. 80). The 'king of shreds and patches' theme looms large in the next generation in Lucian, where kings represented by sham tragic actors are a commonplace, often in contexts with Cynic colouring; and the description of Tyrannis is used to generate a familiar string of paradoxes: 'she kept her gold to her bosom in the most contemptible manner, then she would throw it all away again in panic, then she would the next moment snatch even the slightest thing that any passer-by had in their possession . . . and one moment she would laugh in the most shameless manner, while the next she would be wailing.' Much of Dio's handling of the situation also repays comparison with Encolpius' visit to the sham king Trimalchio: Petronius produces a realistic fiction, Dio an allegorical fantasy on what is in effect the same vice of power without responsibility. And in both cases the subject invites proliferation of detail with a life of its own: once more Dio is able to offer rhetorical talents more openly in this instance to philosophical ends, in this case a *speculum principis* for an emperor.

One notes the similar array of materials in the *Charidemus* (*Or.* 30), for example, where an elaborate *epitaphios* for a young admirer is turned into an ingenious fusion of *Phaedo*[19] and *Symposium*. It purports to include the deathbed deposition of Charidemus himself, presenting a sequence of metaphors for human life, culminating in that of human life as a symposium offered by a nameless rustic. Here Dio is able to draw on the kind of philosophic allegory familiar already

[17] Matt. 4: 8–10 (with ministering angels succeeding the devil and thus completing the contrast); Luke 4: 5–8.

[18] On this detail see in particular Lucian, *Rhetorum Praeceptor*, developing Hesiod, *Erga* 286–92.

[19] One of the two books Dio took into exile, according to Philostratus, *VS* 488.

in *Or.* 1 and the humour attributed to the rustic narrator in the
Euboicus itself. It is as if the *Allegory of Prodicus* is being once more
re-enacted, this time with two wine-waiters Sobriety and Intemperance for the banquet of Life, through the eyes of a rustic reported
by a young man on his death-bed, a clever and inobtrusive reversal
of the image of Socrates. All this comes complete with the rejection
of more philosophical alternatives: human life as a prison could
scarcely recall the *Phaedo* more explicitly.[20]

PLAYFUL MYTH AND MORAL RECONSTRUCTION

The *Troicus* (*Or.* 11) takes us into a territory directly opposite to
that of the *Euboicus*. Against the claim that the latter narrative really
happened to Dio, we have here a reworking of the best-known traditional theme, presenting the argument that Troy was never taken.
Against at least the plausibility of the *Euboicus*, we here have the
deliberately total implausibility of the thesis Dio is advancing.[21] Here
we have the maximum apparatus of credulity/incredulity:[22] Dio has
obtained his information in the best tradition of the *Timaeus* from
Egyptian priests who claim to have a privileged account of their
own of the events of the war (*Or.* 11. 37). The whole has the air of
academic paradox at the level of *tour de force*. But we need also to
consider here whether the extended narrative Dio tells has some degree
of coherence about it, and perhaps more important, whether it can
be felt to be a tale in its own right.

To some extent the narrator seems hampered by point-by-point
revisionism of the Homeric version so obviously familiar to his
readers. Any romantic possibilities are early stifled by the idea that
Paris won Helen from Tyndareus, Castor and Pollux by political
and economic advantage. It takes a good deal of blow-by-blow narrative and *anaskeuē* to reach what turns out to be the culmination:
not just that Troy was not taken and the Greeks returned home
defeated, but that it was actually Hector who killed Achilles. Dio
clears the decks for a sketch of particularly barefaced *enargeia* at
this point:

[20] On the *Charidemus* see Moles, below, Ch. 8.
[21] For facetious sophistic treatments of Homer, see Anderson (1993) 174 ff.
[22] On the tradition of lying in antique historiographical tradition, cf. now Gill and
Wiseman (1993) *passim*.

Hence it became clear to Hector because of all this that Achilles was an easy victim, thanks to his own martial skills, so that he confidently confronted him in the middle of the plain. First of all he gave way as if in flight—just to test him, at the same time wearing him out by holding his ground one moment, then retreating. When he saw him slowing up and lagging behind, he turned and fell on him, now that Achilles could no longer carry his own weapons; then he closed and killed him and took possession of his weapons, as even Homer has said [*Il.* 17. 75 f.]. (*Or.* 11. 96)

But of course Patroclus was wearing them at the time! Here, in contrast to the situations discussed elsewhere, there is no hidden moral agenda, other than to expose the absurdity of any attempt at *Homère moralisé*. The more Dio insists on an honourable settlement at Troy for the invincible Trojans, the more blatant is the sense that morally preferable outcomes are unlikely to generate great storytelling.[23]

In a similar vein is Dio's working of the story of Paris (Alexander) in *Or.* 20. The theme of the Judgement of Paris would be elaborated in due course by both masters of sophistic narrative, Lucian and Apuleius;[24] and both succeed in bringing individual touches to it some decades after the death of Dio. But there is no less sophistic finesse in Dio's working, which grows out of moral indignation at the capacity of the powerful to realize their absurd fantasies:

I suspect that Paris, for example, when he found himself idle on Mount Ida minding his herds, would fantasize about how lucky and how happy things would be if he had the most beautiful woman in the world as a wife ... and then already he would think about who the woman of his dreams was and where she was and how he might contrive such a marriage ... and finding that there was a supposed daughter of Zeus living with Menelaus in Sparta, ... he felt the urge to have her as his own wife. In any normal circumstances of course he did not consider the prospect at all possible, but if some deity should promise and deliver her, perhaps such a thing could happen. (20. 19–21)

Paris proceeds to imagine that Aphrodite is the best candidate, and that a bribe would be necessary, and that this could best be done if he himself were appointed by Zeus as umpire. Only because Paris is rich and powerful is he able to put into practice the abduction of Helen after merely imagining the rest (*Or.* 20. 21–4). There is an ingenious *adynaton* here: we are accustomed to take it for granted

---

[23] For the *Troicus* see Saïd, below, pp. 176–86.
[24] Lucian, *Dial. Deorum* 20; Apuleius, *Met.* 10. 30–4.

that the Judgement of Paris is among the immutable 'facts' of Greek mythology, just as surely as Achilles' victory over Hector. Dio playfully rationalizes that it is no more than a thought in the mind of a tyrannical nature. Even the most obvious myth is threatened with *anaskeuē*; and the Judgement of Paris is reduced to the daydream of an underemployed herdsman.

Dio is no less innovative in dealing with the events that bring about the opening of the *Iliad*:

For Chryseis . . . was thankful to the gods that she had not been given to any of the less reputable warriors, but to the king of them all, and that he himself had some regard for her. But when she heard about Agamemnon's home circumstances, that there was a difficult situation, and that Clytemnestra was cruel and determined, then she was terrified of arriving in Argos. And although she had been with Agamemnon up till now, and perhaps even loved him, when the war was about to end and word was going around that the Trojans could not hold out any longer, she did not wait for Troy to be taken. For she was aware that victory usually makes men arrogant, and that men have more regard for the gods when they are still at war . . . (*Or.* 61. 8 f.)

The passage underlines once more the two entwined strands in Dio's make-up. On the one hand he is taking on a sophistic reconstruction of the role of Chryseis, arguably the least-known figure in the events of the *Iliad*, and there is almost an air of effrontery about any conjecture as to her feelings. But at the same time Dio's reconstruction is conditioned by the search to make moral points. It is as if the moral crises of Aeschylus' *Agamemnon* are being read back into the subject's perception.[25] The same dual nature is evident in the still shorter miniature on Achilles and Chiron (*Or.* 58): if the handling of the child Achilles' petulance might have belonged in Lucian's *Dialogues of the Gods*, Chiron's stern lecture sees the future Achilles as the kind of character who will mutilate a corpse. This facetious *post eventum* is all part of the fun, but once more Dio explores the middle ground between moral lecture and revitalization of myth.

THE FABULOUS AND THE FABLE

With the *Libycus* we are again in sophistic territory.[26] Here we have a piece short enough to be classifiable as a *lalia*, and close enough

---

[25] Cf. Saïd, below, pp. 75–6.

[26] For the Lamia story see Scobie (1977) 7–10. For the *lalia* as a form, see now Nesselrath (1990) 111–40; for the *Libycus'* relationship to *Or.* 4, see Swain (1996) 194 f.

to Lucian's *Dipsades* to encourage comparison. As we should assume, Dio extracts a philosophical moral from his monster-horror story, where Lucian extrapolates a message of sophistic advertisement from a more realistic sketch of the effects of a poisonous snakebite. In the first place Dio shows a defensiveness fairly uncharacteristic of sophists: this is stated to be a frivolous undertaking (5. 1 'to expend effort on a Libyan myth and wear away hard literary labour on that sort of thing is not a promising task'). But it becomes profitable when the piece is used as a parable: 'and a useful and profitable *logos* does not allow unprofitable *mutheumata* to be told in vain' (3. 1). Dio goes on to push his luck by suggesting that perhaps such stories were actually composed with allegorical application in mind.

The story begins quite literally with a 'once upon a time' (*legetai gar palai pote*), and Dio's propensity for preamble goes even further than before (it has taken four paragraphs of introduction to get him as far as this). The sophistic proclivity for ecphrasis inclines him to give an extended footnote on the Syrtes, right down to the reason for the sandbars. The snake-women are then described—as double-ended hybrids of beautiful woman and snake, allowing still more ecphrasis before a brief statement of how they entice their victims. Only now does Dio draw his moral: these monsters are like the passions which subdue their victims. And there at chapter 18 the story might have ended. It now switches from quasi-mythical narrative to historical legend. A Libyan king (unspecified) tries to clear the country of the pests, but is himself massacred by a remnant of the creatures. It finally takes Heracles to conquer them. Dio tentatively suggests that this too may be an allegory for destroying the brood of lusts, only to be conquered by the residue. But nothing is made of this, for Dio now adopts the manner of the oral storyteller ('do you want me then to add something nice for my younger listeners?'). He adds an encounter by envoys *en route* to the oracle of Ammon, both entrapped by the creature; the tale ends abruptly with the fact that one of the victims was killed but not eaten by it, so that the suppurating body is found but cannot be touched.

It is difficult to be certain about what this narrative is or what it does. It seems to me wholly misguided to suspect Dio of actually having made up the story: since it is implied by Diogenes in *Or.* 4 to be possibly familiar to Alexander the Great, it could hardly be the invention of Dio himself. And in any case the location at the Syrtes suggests that the tale is a variant of that of the Sirens. Lucian's parody of such stories in his Vinewomen and Asslegs in *Verae*

Historiae has long been noted (1. 8; 2. 46). Dio genuinely does treat the story as traditional, and again Scobie is probably right to think of a Lamia-type tale. For the idea of starting a piece with such a story one thinks of the hybrid mermaid at the start of Horace's *Ars Poetica*.[27] Topless female hybrids are good sophistic copy. The easy alternative of instalments of the tale and their *epimuthia* avoids the ponderous effects of preaching, but the ending still puzzles. There may be a third *epimuthion* missing, or even a concluding sentence less awkward or abrupt; or Dio's attempt at the waywardness and inconsequence of the storyteller may simply have been miscalculated.

We can note a similar political nuance when Dio is telling anything so simple as an Aesopic fable, so often the small change of classical storytelling. In the *Alexandrian Oration* (*Or.* 32. 65), for example, he attributes a rather odd fable to a Phrygian kinsman of Aesop. The devoted animals mourn the death of Orpheus, especially the sheep and the birds, and are to be transformed to human form after his death; they turned into Macedonians who settled in Alexandria. This explains the Alexandrian proclivity for music. Dogs in particular had applied themselves to music and while owing some of their education to Orpheus they accounted for why the music of the harpists of Alexandria remained canine in character. Unlike the last example this story comes perhaps closer to the essence of narrative in Dio. The fable has some affinity with the reincarnation into appropriate animals in *Republic* 10; considerably closer analogues might be suggested by a fable from the *diēgēseis* of Callimachus (Perry, *Aesopica* 431): animals are punished by losing speech given to men (*Aesopica* 432); and the nymphs revolt from Apollo and sing out of tune (Himerius, *Or.* 20). The point where Dio differs most obviously from such examples is that he locates the mutant musical animals in one specific city, Alexandria; and it might not be unreasonable to suggest that he has modified a more familiar fable to accord with his current attack on Alexandrian recalcitrance. Here we see Dio's contribution to storytelling at its most characteristic: morally earnest, often eccentric or highly imaginative, and not easy to align with the most obvious analogues; and often, too, a little more reticent than one might expect of a sophist. Himerius goes to town in his fable and gives a lively speech in which Helicon upbraids the nymphs; whereas Dio,

---

[27] See Brink's note ad loc. (*Horace on Poetry. The 'Ars Poetica'* (Cambridge, 1971) 75 ff.).

even in such a flamboyant *tour de force* as the *Alexandrian Oration*, avoids any such effect.

A WANDERERS' MYTH

The *Borystheniticus* is useful for drawing a number of the afore-mentioned threads together.[28] Dio here offers a long tale of his reception in a remote outpost of Hellenism. He describes in some detail the situation of Borysthenes and its present state of decay, offers a rather Platonic scenario of talking with two of its latter-day community, and provides two discourses, on the earthly and heavenly city. There is little puzzle about the *mise-en-scène*: here again as in the *Euboicus* Dio has at least a plausible beginning, and offers us no reason to suspect his handling of the landscape or the description of the town still under threat with its improvised fortifications. It is the myth that he tells about the heavenly city that causes the difficulties. Dio insists that this is a secret myth of Persian *magoi*. Whether we see Dio as serious or playful, or indeed deliberately ambiguous, the work seems to fit uneasily together.

Whether or not this is a genuine Iranian myth, why flaunt it before the Borysthenites, constantly under threat from incursions by the Sauromatae, a people originating from Iran? Russell reminds us that the prevailing theme of the work is concord,[29] but if Dio wishes to promote concord here he seems to be going about it in a singularly eccentric or elliptical way.

Although Russell shows that this piece seems more complete than a number of others, it still seems to have an oddly abrupt ending. There is a disclaimer that if the myth is not entirely satisfactory, this is due to the Borysthenites, who pressed him for it. There is certainly no doubt about the *ben trovato* nature of the myth itself: it is certainly tempting to go for an exclusively Hellenic interpretation, where Dio has blended the celebrated myth of the *Phaedrus* chariot-eer with a very coherent description of Stoic *ecpyrōsis*. But an open mind is needed. One feels that a forgery would probably have been more coherent, and would have demanded less apology than Dio

---

[28] Recent discussion: Jones (1978) 61–4; Russell (1992) 19–23 and *passim*; Anderson (1993) 216–20. See also Trapp, below, pp. 214–19.

[29] Russell (1992) 23.

actually offers. Nor is the relative absence of Mithraic elements a source of disqualification: we are entitled to expect as much variation and variant in Iranian mythologizing as we have in Greek; and the *Shah-Nama*, which claims assemblage from Magian sources, does appear to support Dio's claim. This medieval Persian text has the character of a Persian national epic, and so underlines what is felt to be genuinely and immemorially Persian. In the creation account at the beginning of Ferdowsi's poem there are four elements: fire, wind, water, and earth. Stress is put on the fact that the last has no light of its own: the elements need to be mixed together to produce life and the world as we know it.[30] This motif apart, flying-horse legends are endemic in the storytelling of Asia Minor, whether of Bellerophon or the *Arabian Nights*. We should note too that the simile which Russell feels is characteristically Greek—of the *thaumatopoios* melting the wax images together (51)—could as easily be seen as Persian, if we see the *thaumatopoios* doing the sort of things a Chaldaean miracle-worker might be popularly supposed to do (translate *thaumatopoios* not as 'toy-maker' but as 'wonder-worker').

What contact might Dio have had with real magi? There was an alleged contact between our narrator and Apollonius of Tyana, who had reputedly met some;[31] but I doubt if we need to justify specific lines of communication with magi real or alleged for anyone already a native of Asia Minor. The whole matter must remain open on present evidence, but at the very least there is a convergence of whatever material Dio might have come by with what is characteristically Greek.

BETWEEN MORALIST AND STORYTELLER

Dio's narrative skills do not by any means end with the array of pieces with a high content of narrative in the normal sense. Sophistically trained narrators tend not to lay their narrative skills aside

[30] Translated as *The Epic of the Kings* by R. Levy, rev. A. Banani (London 1967) 1 f. Such a possibility of course rests on the assumption that Persian religious doctrine is static and conservative, and that a medieval Persian epic can act as a carrier of much earlier belief.

[31] Cf. Anderson (1986) 179, 183; little surrounding the figure of Apollonius can be regarded as clear-cut (cf. Swain (1999*b*) for the contemporary resonances of Philostratus' *Life*).

after conversions to philosophy, real or imagined.[32] It is perhaps no coincidence that so often the authenticity of Dio's narratives or their occasions has been called into question. One can only say that Dio's zest for fiction is a good deal less obvious than, for example, Lucian's; and some of the occasions seem a little too complex to be read as patent sophistic hoaxes. We have to make a very strong case on each occasion when we want to bracket Dio with either Lucian or, say, Philostratus. Perhaps the most obvious feature of Dio's storytelling is the deliberate balance preserved between sophist and philosopher in his own persona. The diptych construction of the *Euboicus* might serve as a symbol of Dio's purposes as a whole; and in the *Borystheniticus* we have a similarly balanced contrast between the unusual location and the universality of the myth itself; or in the first *Kingship Oration* the allegory of Heracles serves as a substantial counterweight to the political substance of the rest of the speech.

A characteristic of Dio's narrative is the obtrusive position he himself occupies in it, a factor in which his exile might itself have played no small part. It gives a range of experience relatively unfamiliar to many of his audiences. It is very often the case that Dio takes his inspiration directly from his own life. Dio himself makes the claim in the *Euboicus* that wandering as well as old age makes men garrulous (7. 1). There are certainly times when what appears to be a highly plausible documentary approach is on show, as when he describes or imagines all the occupations that go on in the hippodrome (*Or.* 20. 10), or when he describes himself as athirst to hear sophistic displays (*Or.* 19. 3), or when more specifically he is able to make contact at Cyzicus with friends during his exile (*Or.* 19. 1). The exotic locations seem for the most part to reflect the facts of the exile. Dio juxtaposes the real world of experience with what Jones calls 'ideal communities'. We have a sense of 'how I found Plato in an odd place', and not just in the *Borystheniticus*. Noteworthy also is the self-consciousness with which Dio involves himself in introducing and retreating from his narratives. One is left time and again with the impression that he really wishes to apologize for storytelling. To be sure, Philostratus congratulates him in the *Lives of the Sophists* for striking a good balance and for not hesitating in his paradoxical works to deal with the lighter side of literary *parerga*. But Dio will trim his sails to the winds of civic virtue. This is seldom sophistic

[32] On the issue in Dio, see Moles (1979).

storytelling as it might have been. A good source of contrast to Dio would be Apuleius, who despite his philosophic interests and pretensions seems invariably to manage the balance on the side of entertainment.

With Dio everything is the other way round; and with this we can come back to our original starting-point. Dio's tales are indeed told by a flamboyant wordsmith, but on the whole in a Xenophontic way, and by a writer who reserves his verbal flourish for moral argument rather for the details of narration. We are on a different plane from Maximus of Tyre, who will scatter his *dialexeis* with *diēgēmata* more or less as the fancy takes him, but who loses the personal involvement, the light touch, the ability to convince that he has been there.[33] We should not go far wrong to conclude that in Dio stories are being told towards an end rather than for their own sakes. Dio will not indulge in the luxury of pure narrative if there is a cause to which to apply it. When Philostratus alleges that Dio confronted the legions on the northern frontier after the death of Domitian, he quotes a common Homeric tag to equate him with Odysseus (*VS* 488). In the art of storytelling Dio has the same capacity as his hero to present a story and manipulate it to the purpose in hand with fluency and aplomb appropriate to his personal circumstances.

[33] For a characterization, see Trapp (1997), pp. xvi–lv.

7

Dio's Use of Mythology
SUZANNE SAÏD

One may wonder, as Paul Veyne did some years ago,[1] if, under the Empire, the Greeks believed in their myths. But one cannot deny that they used them, and this is amply demonstrated by Dio's speeches. As an introduction to this study, I propose to examine the characteristics of myth according to Dio, relying mostly on the occurrences of *muthos*, *muthologein*, etc, in his works. After this, I shall first demonstrate his rhetorical skill at manipulating mythological topoi. Secondly, I shall focus on his philosophical use of myth. Finally, according to the unwritten rules of French academic rhetoric, I shall consider his rewriting of traditional stories in the problematic *Trojan Oration* (*Or.* 11), and also in the *Nessus* (*Or.* 60) and the *Chryseis* (*Or.* 61).

INTRODUCTION: THE MEANING OF MYTH

The meaning of *muthos* in Dio's speeches is not easy to determine. There is no neat contrast between *muthos* and *logos*. Far from opposing the two words, Dio often joins them[2] or uses them as synonyms.[3] So myths may sometimes recapitulate and amplify former arguments.[4] Neither is there any systematic opposition between *muthos* ('fiction') and *historia* ('history'). Whereas *muthōdes* is opposed to *historikon* in *Or.* 18. 10, *muthoi* and *historia* as well as *muthologoi* and *sungrapheis* are connected by *kai* at *Or.* 55. 11. Besides, Dio often strings mythical and historical examples together. In the dialogue *On Slavery and Liberty* II, he puts together mythical heroes (Zethos and Amphion,

---

[1] Veyne (1988).   [2] *Orr.* 12. 39, 43, 46; 37. 12; 53. 2.   [3] *Or.* 60. 9.
[4] Moles (1990) 318 on the first *Kingship Oration*.

Oeneus, Eumaeus) and historical characters (the children of the
Athenians held prisoners by the Syracusans and the son of the wealthy
Callias).[5] In *On Trust*, the only distinction between Dionysius
the Younger, Darius or Antigonus, and Atreus or Agamemnon
is chronological.[6] So, Dio sides with the ancient historians who
defined myth as a record of the most ancient times, whereas history
deals with a more recent past and begins either with the Trojan War
(Diodorus) or the return of the Heracleidae (Ephorus following
Hecataeus).

In Dio's speeches, *muthoi* are stories 'about deities',[7] heroes and
monsters as well as 'Aesopic fables', such as the tale of the wise owl
in the first *Kingship Oration* (27–8). They are supposed to come from
elsewhere and are often characterized as 'old',[8] which provides some
support for our modern definition of myth as 'traditional tale'.

These tales are either conveyed by an 'anonymous and unwritten'[9]
tradition or ascribed to 'poets' or 'prophets of the Muses'.[10] This
link between myth and poetry is no surprise: one of the two 'myths'
alluded to by Herodotus in his *Histories* was already associated
with 'Homer or one of the poets of old' (2. 23). In Dio's speeches,
these poets usually remain anonymous. But a tale introduced by a
vague 'they say' may in fact be borrowed from a specific text. For
instance in the *Diogenes, or On Slaves*, when narrating the Laius
story, Dio chooses to echo the Euripidean version by emphasizing
that the consequence of Laius' disobedience was the collapse of the
house,[11] as in the prologue of the *Phoenician Women*,[12] and not the
ruin of the *city*, as in the *Seven against Thebes*.[13]

Sometimes, the poets, as 'prophets and holy men',[14] lend their prestige to myths which played a major role in art, by inspiring sculp-
tors and painters,[15] and in religion by generating rituals.[16]

But in the *Borystheniticus*, the 'poetic tribe' is partly deprived
of its privileges: poets are compared to 'the outside servants of the
mysteries, who stand at the door, ornamenting the entrance and the
public altars, and making other preparations, never entering within'

[5] *Or.* 15. 14–15. See also *Orr.* 10. 24–7; 17. 13–15; 31. 17–18; 32. 88; 45. 13; 47. 24;
49. 4–5; and the comments of Desideri (1991*b*) 3946 on *Or.* 17. 15.
[6] *Or.* 73. 2.   [7] *Orr.* 12. 43; 53. 2.
[8] *Orr.* 7. 143; 33. 58.   [9] *Or.* 12. 39.
[10] *Orr.* 17. 15; 32. 58; 36. 46 poets; 36. 42 prophets of the Muses. As poems, they
may be 'sung': *Orr.* 5. 4; 11. 9; 36. 39.
[11] *Or.* 10. 24.   [12] l. 20.   [13] l. 750.
[14] *Orr.* 1. 57–8; 12. 23; 77/78. 1.   [15] *Or.* 12. 45–6.   [16] *Or.* 15. 10.

(*Or.* 36. 33). And in the first speech *On Glory*, Dio openly ridicules the authority of Euripides and Sophocles, who gave credit to such absurd stories as the tale of the golden lamb.[17]

Echoing the attacks of Plato, Dio also criticizes the poets for being 'the spokesmen and advocates of ordinary people',[18] and argues that their myths are more often than not a mere reflection of the opinion of the masses.[19] They tell 'pleasant' lies,[20] which easily deceive their audience: 'whatever they delight to hear from anyone's lips, they at once consider it to be true' (*Or.* 11. 42).

Muthos and especially its derivative *muthōdes* are indeed pejorative. At worst, 'myth' is misleading and dangerous. At best, it lacks seriousness and is regularly associated, as in Plato's dialogues,[21] with childhood[22] and playfulness.[23] As a result, when Dio introduces the Heracles myth in the first *Kingship Oration*, he carefully avoids the word *muthos* and calls it 'a sacred and edifying utterance (*logos*) which borrows only its form (*schēma*) from myth' (*Or.* 1. 49). Yet he is afraid of being despised as 'a babbler and vagrant' for telling it.[24] Similarly, his Diogenes, Aesop, and Socrates acknowledge that they 'joke' and behave just as 'nurses' admonishing children in a pleasant way, when they use myths.[25]

But Dio is also well aware of the protreptic value of myths, as demonstrated by the introduction to the *Libyan Myth*. When they are 'turned in the right direction and transformed into a parable of the real and the true' (*Or.* 5. 1), myths can provide no small benefit. But this usefulness has to be 'grafted' on to them by the philosopher who transforms a wild and barren plant into a useful one. In the conclusion of the *Nessus*, Dio also emphasizes that it is the philosopher who, like a sculptor (*koroplathos*, literally 'statue-moulder'), 'moulds' (*plattein*) myths, as he pleases, to render them 'useful and suited to philosophy' (*Or.* 60. 9). This is not very far from Plutarch who, in his *De audiendis poetis*,[26] proposes to 'bring in' (*eisagein*) and 'mix' (*katamignunai*) some philosophy into myth.

---

[17] *Or.* 66. 6.   [18] *Or.* 7. 101.   [19] Ibid. 98.

[20] ἡδέως and ἡδονή as well as χαρίζεσθαι are associated with μῦθος at 4. 75; 5. 24, 53. 3, 72. 13. In the same way, μυθώδης was linked to τέρπειν or χαιρεῖν in Thucydides' *History* (1. 22. 4) or in Isocrates (*Ad Nicoclem* 48–9, *Panathenaicus* 1).

[21] e.g. *Rep.* 2. 377a. Cf. Hermogenes, *Progymnasmata* 1.1 (*Rhet. Gr.* 3. 1–3) τὸν μῦθον πρῶτον ἀξιοῦσι προσάγειν τοῖς νέοις, διότι τὰς ψυχὰς αὐτῶν πρὸς τὸ βέλτιον ῥυθμίζειν δύναται· ἔτι οὖν αὐτοὺς ἁπαλοὺς ὄντας ἀξιοῦσι πλάττειν.

[22] *Orr.* 4. 74; 5. 24; 72. 13.   [23] *Orr.* 6. 20; 32. 67.

[24] *Or.* 1. 56. See also *Or.* 5. 1.   [25] *Orr.* 4. 74; 55. 11; 72. 13.   [26] 15 f.

When Dio alludes to the most common attempt to legitimize an allegorical interpretation of the ancient poets—'Perhaps those who composed these tales in the first place composed them for some such purpose, speaking cryptically and figuratively for those who were able to understand correctly' (*Or.* 5. 3)—he is, as here, sceptical. In his essay *On Homer* he only reluctantly refers to Zeno's theory, anticipated by Antisthenes, which held that, 'the poet has written some things according to opinion and some things in accord with reality'.[27] Besides, in the *Trojan Oration*, he criticizes openly those who excuse Homer's descriptions of divine misconduct by saying that 'at such times he is not speaking seriously, but cryptically[28] and figuratively' (*Or.* 11. 17). Obviously, Dio, like Plato, is less interested in saving old myths than in shaping new ones which are a figuration of the truth.[29] His *Libyan Myth* is introduced as a 'symbolic picture' (*eikasma*) of the desires, embodying at the same time their seduction and destructiveness.

As a conclusion to this brief overview of the meaning of *muthos* and its derivatives, it is obvious that Dio's theory of myth fits perfectly well with his self-portrait as a philosopher. But this is only a part of the picture, and Dio's actual use of mythology is far more complex.

MYTH AS RHETORIC

More than once it can be demonstrated that Dio handles mythological references as a typical sophist. Mythology provides Dio first with a convenient repertoire of similes. In order to show the enthusiasm of the young admirers of a sophist, he compares them to Bacchants leaping around Dionysus.[30] The dreadful and composite character of the crowd is vividly borne out by a parallel with hybrid monsters such as 'Centaurs, Sphinxes, and Chimeras'.[31] Pleasure which casts a baneful spell on men is likened to Circe drugging Odysseus' companions.[32]

---

[27] *Or.* 53. 5: ὅτι τὰ μὲν δόξῃ, τὰ δὲ ἀληθείᾳ εἴρηται τῷ ποιητῇ. See also *Or.* 77/8. 16.

[28] With the exception of two references to the 'riddles' of the Sphinx (*Or.* 10. 31), αἴνιγμα and αἰνίττεσθαι are always associated with myth and poetry in Dio's orations (2. 42; 5. 3, 22; 11. 17, 101, 136; 37. 12; 63. 7).

[29] This is in fact the definition of 'myth' given by Aphthonius (*Rhet. Gr.* 2. 21. 2–3) λόγος ψευδὴς εἰκονίζων ἀλήθειαν.

[30] *Or.* 35. 8. [31] *Or.* 32. 28. [32] *Or.* 8. 21.

In addition, mythology is a store of examples.[33] Thus Dio's Diogenes exploits the sack of Troy to illustrate the dreadful consequences of lust.[34] Mythical characters also set a standard against which others are measured. A man who claims to be a good hunter will say that he is better than the two mythical archetypes of the hunter, Hippolytus and Meleager, and the expert in music 'will say that he knows it better than Orpheus and Thamyras'.[35]

More often, and in my view more interestingly, Dio behaves as a 'sophist's sophist'[36] and parodies rhetorical practice.

In the *Euboicus* the (at times) comic imitation of a prosecution speech written in grand style has the poor and hospitable hunter who entertained the shipwrecked Dio likened to Nauplius, the king who lit fires to wreck the Achaean fleet returning from Troy in revenge for the execution of his son Palamedes.[37] In *On Glory* I Dio begins with a plain narrative of the Perseus myth: 'By carrying around the Gorgon's head and displaying it to his foes, Perseus turned them to stone.' Then comes a comparison, which humorously emphasizes the disproportion: 'But most men have been turned to stone just by listening to one word.' And, last, the sarcasm: 'besides, there is no need to carry it [the word] around, guarding it in a pouch'.[38] Further on, in the same speech, he gives a mythical example a final twist which prevents it from being taken too seriously. Of course Heracles paid no heed to public opinion, but perhaps there was no one who dared to criticize him openly, 'since he would promptly have suffered for it'.[39]

To enhance the exceptional character of the young Melancomas, who was at the same time beautiful, courageous, and self-controlled, Dio piles up beautiful heroes and uses them as foils, emphasizing that they lacked either courage (Ganymede, Adonis, Phaon) or self-control (Theseus, Achilles). But what to do with Hippolytus who was not only beautiful, but also a passionate hunter and the very embodiment of *sophrosune*? Dio jokingly disparages his achievement by saying that 'it is not clear whether or not he had manly courage, since hunting is not real proof of it',[40] and distances himself from the rhetorical topic he has just put to use.

---

[33] Cf. Hermogenes, *Progymnasmata* p. 1, l. 42 f. φαίνονται δὲ καὶ οἱ ῥήτορες αὐτῷ [μύθῳ] χρησάμενοι ἀντὶ παραδείγματος.
[34] *Or.* 6. 16.   [35] *Or.* 70. 2–3.   [36] For the phrase, see Anderson (1982).
[37] *Or.* 7. 32–3.   [38] *Or.* 66. 21.   [39] Ibid. 23.   [40] *Or.* 29. 18.

The same combination of humour and cleverness appears in Or. 47, addressed to his fellow Prusans. Dio begins by listing the philosophers who left their own city under no compulsion, because they were aware that only a man possessing the strength and the power of Heracles could endure the difficulties and vexations involved in a life among fellow-citizens. Then he shows that even Heracles did not succeed. To begin with, he enumerates as a foil the hero's achievements in foreign countries. Then he deals with Heracles' benefactions to his two fatherlands—Argos and Thebes—and thereby draws an implicit parallel between himself and the benefactor *par excellence*. Like Dio who built a portico for his fellow Prusans, Heracles was concerned with the well-being of his fellow-citizens: 'he chased the birds to keep them from troubling the farmers in Stymphalus' (4). Yet, like Dio, he was not rewarded. 'Finally, they say, he was sent to Hades. Such was the fairness of his fellow-citizens towards him!' (4). As told by Dio, Heracles' story nicely duplicates his own. But it is only because Dio has seriously distorted the tradition. For all the labours of Heracles, including the last one, his search for Cerberus in the world of the dead, were imposed on him by Eurystheus who is never named, and only alluded to indirectly as 'the fellow-citizen', so that the city seems to bear full responsibility for this unfair treatment.

Heracles/Dio is but one among the many mythological impersonations of Heracles in Dio's speeches. Next to him, there is the Heracles/Trajan of the first *Kingship Oration*,[41] who right from the beginning 'is endowed with Trajanic characteristics':[42] he rules over the whole world, campaigns with an army, and 'becomes the saviour of mankind not because he defended humans from wild beasts, but because he punished savage and wicked men and destroyed the power of overbearing tyrants' (84). There is also the Heracles/Diogenes of Or. 8. 27–35, the 'paradigmatic Cynic',[43] who leads a simple life according to nature, exterminates wealthy and arrogant rulers such as Diomedes, Geryon, and Busiris, and 'fights against common opinion as much as against wild beasts and wicked men' (35).

---

[41] Or. 1. 59–84. On Heracles the king, see also Or. 2. 79.

[42] Moles (1990) 323. For an anaysis of the myth in Or. 1 see ibid. 324–31, and cf. Anderson in this volume, above, pp. 150–2.

[43] Branham (1996) 102.

Dio himself impersonates various mythological characters. He 'makes several direct comparisons between himself and Odysseus'.[44] In the first *Kingship Oration* and in the *Alexandrian Oration* he also becomes Hermes. Acting as a messenger from Zeus, he 'leads' (1. 66, 69) Heracles/Trajan and 'demonstrates' (69) to him the nature of Royalty and Tyranny.[45] Speaking to the Alexandrians, he uses 'the words of Hermes as he is portrayed in the *Odyssey*', while comically stressing the inappropriateness of the comparison.[46] He often plays Nestor,[47] since Homer's Nestor was the wise adviser *par excellence*. Accordingly, Dio's Nestor who is characterized not only by his superior 'intelligence' (*sunesis*), but also his persuasiveness (*peithō*),[48] becomes Dio's duplicate as the best king's best adviser and illustrates the necessary collaboration between philosopher and monarch.[49] He tries to stop Agamemnon's and Achilles' anger, scolds Agamemnon for his mistakes and 'compels' him to entreat Achilles.[50] Besides, he becomes the people's counsellor: deliberately twisting the Homeric narrative of *Iliad* 2, Dio credits Nestor, together with Odysseus, with dissuading the Greek army from flight.[51] *Orr.* 56 and 57 also give to Nestor a central part. In the first, *Agamemnon, or On Kingship*, Dio boldly portrays Nestor as 'the manager of Agamemnon's empire' (8) and pictures the king as always willing to follow his advice, even in his dreams.[52] In the second, *Nestor*, which is a defence of Nestor's self-praise, he is in fact pleading his case when he 'imitates the teaching of Nestor' (10) and reminds his popular audience that on previous occasions he had succeeded in persuading others who were far superior, that is, the emperor himself. Here more openly than elsewhere, his Nestor is endowed with the typical characteristics of the Cynic philosopher and becomes a doctor trying to cure of their conceit and vanity great men who swell with pride.[53]

Dio's rhetorical skill appears in his various ways of manipulating a myth as well. In his speeches there are three references to Ixion, a character well known for his crime (he lusted after Hera herself

---

[44] Moles (1978) 97. See also Desideri (1978) 174–5, Höistad (1948) 94–102, Jones (1978) 46–8, Swain (1996) 201.
[45] Moles (1990) 325–6.   [46] *Or.* 32. 21–2.
[47] See Desideri (1978) 486, Kindstrand (1973) 135–6, and Moles (1990) 323, 342, 362.
[48] *Or.* 2. 20.   [49] *Or.* 49. 3.   [50] *Or.* 55. 19.
[51] *Orr.* 2. 23, 11. 80.   [52] *Or.* 56. 9.   [53] *Or.* 57. 6–8.

and attempted to make love to her image) and his punishment (he
was bound to a wheel by Zeus). Once, in the *Alexandrian Oration*,
Ixion's wheel becomes a foil for the agony of the Alexandrians
watching a horse-race.[54] The other references to Ixion, both in
the fourth *Kingship Oration*, are more serious. In his portrayal
of the Ambitious Spirit, Dio likens it to Ixion whirled round and
round by his wheel and humorously draws the attention of his audience to the fitness of the comparison, which is not inferior to 'the
ingenious similes of the sophists' (123). A little further on, he comes
back to the same myth and proposes an allegorical reading of its
first part. Ixion embracing a dark and dismal cloud instead of Hera
is the demagogue or the sophist desiring reputation at all costs,
instead of being in love with true glory, and the Centaurs, those
useless and monstrous offspring of Ixion's seed, are likened to their
'bewildering and absurd creations' (131). This reading of Ixion's myth
is not without parallels in the literature of the Empire. Plutarch and
Lucian also compare to Ixion those who are in love with opinion
instead of philosophy.[55]

Relying on this example, one would be tempted to stress perhaps
too much the similarities between Dio's use of mythology and that
of his contemporaries. But I think that there are also good reasons
for setting Dio apart, because of his Cynic 'defacing of the currency'
and his satirical use of rhetorical clichés, which I now wish to illustrate briefly.

As we know from the treatises on epideictic oratory attributed
to Menander and from the epideictic speeches of Aelius Aristides,
orators, when praising a city, used to refer to its mythical founders.[56]
Dio himself, at the beginning of the first *Tarsian*, demonstrates that
he is well aware of the expectations of an audience eager to listen
to a eulogy of the city's gods and heroes, Heracles and Perseus.
In fact, both are properly called upon as protecting heroes together
with 'Apollo, Athena, and the other gods who are worshipped
by the city' (33. 45). But immediately after, they are used to bring
shame upon the Tarsians. Instead of visiting their fellow-citizens
and attending their sacrifices, both would, says Dio, become so
horrified by their snorting noise, that the first, Heracles, would rather

---

[54] *Or.* 32. 74–5.
[55] Plutarch, *Agis/Cleomenes* 1. 1; Mor. 766a, 777e; Lucian, *Fisherman* 12.
[56] See Pernot (1993) 1: 209 nn. 467–8.

go and visit the descendants of his worst enemies, Thracian Diomedes and Egyptian Busiris, while the other, Perseus, would use Pegasus' wings to pass over the city in his flight.[57] It is tempting to parallel this satiric use of encomiastic topoi with the *Misopogon*, the 'festive satire' of Julian.[58]

Dio also enjoys ridiculing tragic heroes and turning upside down the usual meaning of mythical comparisons. In *Or.* 10 his Diogenes debunks Oedipus' cleverness and relentlessly stresses the absurdity of his behaviour after being told by Teiresias that he has married his mother. On the other hand, in *Or.* 9, in order to devalue the achievements of athletes (the swiftest runner cannot outstrip a bird), he extols the fate of Procne, the nightingale, and her wretched family (her husband became a hoopoe and her sister a swallow), by saying, 'if the swiftest is the best, it is much better perhaps to be a lark than to be a man. So we need not pity the nightingale or the hoopoe, if they were changed from human beings into birds, according to the myth' (19).[59] Similarly, in *Or.* 23, the men born of the dragon's teeth sowed by Jason surprisingly become models of wisdom. Knowing that man is the most miserable of all beings, they took the only reasonable course of action and killed each other 'through friendship, not through hatred' (4).

The *Alexandrian Oration*, which puts a critical spin on the standard topics of the encomium,[60] is perhaps the best instance of a systematically derisive use of mythological allusions.

The first reference (28), a comparison of the *dēmos* to a multifarious and dreadful monster akin to Centaurs, sphinxes, and chimaeras,[61] is derogatory, but not particularly original. The second (58) is more interesting since it reverses the way in which rhetorical paradigms operate. Paradigms usually lend some credibility to what is said by the orator. But in chapter 58, it is the Alexandrians who, by their behaviour, 'make believable the myths of the poets' and their portrayal of Bacchants, Nymphs, and Satyrs maddened by music. The great mythical musicians such as Orpheus and Amphion are then (61) introduced as foils for the Alexandrian musicians. Orpheus was the son of Mousa, and they are born of Amousia; Amphion fortified Thebes with his lyre, and they are ruining Alexandria by

---

[57] *Or.* 33. 47.   [58] Gleason (1986).   [59] See also *Or.* 23. 3.
[60] Trapp (1995) 168–75.
[61] The comparison with drunk and lustful Centaurs reappears at 32. 95.

their songs; Orpheus tamed wild beasts and made them musical, and they turn human beings into illiterate savages. All this is a mere introduction to a brilliantly innovative myth which explains the origin and nature of the Alexandrians and cleverly stitches together the myth of Orpheus and a nice pastiche of the Platonic myth of the cicadas.[62] Dio starts from the traditional version of the Orpheus myth, with two interesting alterations which will afterwards become meaningful: his Orpheus does not travel only throughout Thrace, he also visits Macedonia and the animals following him are mostly sheep and birds (63). Then he turns upside down the Platonic myth. According to the *Phaedrus* (259b–c), the cicadas were once human beings who were so enthralled by music that they forgot to eat and drink and were granted by the Muses the privilege of singing all the time, without needing food any more. The sheep and birds of the *Alexandrian Oration* are also characterized by their love of music: at the death of Orpheus they wailed and fell into despair. So the Muse begged Zeus to change them into men, but 'their souls remained as they were before' (64)—an ironical echo of the *Odyssey*, where the companions of Odysseus transformed into pigs by Circe 'have the same mind as before'.[63] Then comes the sting, since these enchanted animals became the ancestors of the Macedonians who settled in Egypt. This is the reason why the Alexandrians are so fond of music, but also why they are, like birds, 'vain', and, like sheep, 'stupid'. As for their musicians, they descend from dogs who tried to mimic Orpheus. After being metamorphosed into men, they carried on the same pursuit, but their degenerate music still sounds like barking (66).

This new myth is followed by a play on existing myths. Dio parallels the Alexandrians' love for horses, which may in time bring forth some strange and troublesome offspring and cause their ruin, to the story of Pasiphae, who 'fell in love with a bull' and gave birth to a dangerous and mighty monster, and the myth of the maiden, locked up with a horse and ruined by him (77–9). He also tells them the story of Ajax the Locrian (80–1), which becomes a warning against the Alexandrians' practice of rioting at public spectacles, since Dio establishes a causal link between Ajax's unseemly behaviour as a spectator at the funeral games of Patroclus and his rape of Cassandra at the goddess's altar, which led to his own death and the shipwreck

[62] See Anderson, above, p. 156. [63] *Od.* 10. 240.

of the whole Achaean fleet. But it is difficult to take this lesson very seriously, given the absurd disproportion between the initial mistake and its consequences and the incongruity of the concluding remark: 'There are people like him at Alexandria, except that no one here is able to fight as bravely as he did and capture towns' (81). Then, hard on the heels of this sarcastic *tour de force*, in chapters 88–90, Dio develops the conceit that the moral destruction of Alexandria by real horses is a reprise of the physical destruction of Homer's Troy by a wooden one; the Alexandrians need to appreciate that they are 'captives' in as serious a sense as the Trojans.[64] But here also Dio humorously distances himself from his pun, by stressing right from the beginning that it is 'a platitude' (88).

Thus by his use and abuse of mythical parallels, Dio demonstrates that he is able, like Lucian, to beat the sophists at their own game.

MYTH AS PHILOSOPHY

Dio is also—and at the same time—a philosopher. He uses myths to condemn the useless crafts which serve luxury or to advocate a simple and virtuous life in accordance with nature. He also creates 'new' myths in a Platonic fashion. But the reader cannot forget for a moment that Dio is closely linked to the Cynics and that 'joking, parody and satire are . . . constitutive of Cynic ideology as such'.[65]

Dio's presentation of the two heroes most closely linked to the crafts and the beginnings of civilized life, Daedalus and Prometheus, may illustrate the way in which he puts the stamp of Cynicism on traditional tales.

With the exception of the *Olympicus*, where he is presented as the first famous sculptor and associated with artists such as Phidias, Alcamenes, and Polycleitus,[66] Daedalus always appears in the worst possible light, as an embodiment of the subversive character of crafts. He violated the laws of nature by equipping his son Icarus with wings, which normally belong only to a bird, or by giving the appearance of a cow to a woman.[67] He is also criticized for having built the labyrinth where his fellow-citizens were trapped and killed by the Minotaur.[68]

[64] Trapp (1995) 171–2.   [65] Branham (1996) 93.   [66] *Or*. 12. 45.
[67] *Orr*. 4. 120–1; 21. 4; 71. 6.   [68] *Orr*. 71. 6; 80. 8–9.

Using Diogenes as his mouthpiece, Dio also passes a negative judgement on Prometheus. According to *Or.* 6, the Titan who gave civilizing fire to men did not improve the human condition. On the contrary, he became responsible for the vices linked to civilization such as 'softness' (*malakia*) and 'luxury' (*truphē*) and was justly punished by Zeus.[69] This was to be expected from a philosopher who was pleased to be compared to a 'dog' and 'upheld animals as models of the true life according to nature'.[70] In *Diogenes, or On Virtue* the 'sophist' Prometheus becomes the symbol of vanity and ambition and his punishment is interpreted accordingly: his liver eaten by the eagle during the day and growing back again each night signifies the sophist's dependence on reputation—he flourishes when praised and withers away when criticized.[71] And the killing of the eagle by Heracles means that the Cynic hero put an end to the Titan's arrogance and contentiousness.

Like Plato, Dio also proposes 'new myths'. Given that myths are by definition traditional tales, he attempts to link them somehow to tradition, either by manipulating their content and recycling already existing mythical motifs or by pretending that they have been handed down to him.

Let us look for instance at the *Libyan Myth*, a tale made up by Dio to show the true nature of desires.[72] It successively illuminates their seductiveness (the Libyan monsters are extremely beautiful and overcome men by showing them their breasts) and their destructiveness (they seize and kill them to devour their corpses). The second part of the myth, with the description of the two attempts to destroy these monsters, the first one, by 'a certain Libyan king', the second by Heracles who succeeded in killing all of them, is clearly allegorical and its meaning is explained by Dio himself:

it says that, when the majority of men try to clear the trackless region of their souls, teeming with savage beasts, by rooting out and destroying the species of desires, in the hope of then having got rid of them and escaped, and yet not having done this thoroughly, they are soon afterwards overwhelmed and destroyed by the remaining desires; but that Heracles, the son of Zeus and Alcmene, carried the task through to completion and made his own mind pure and tame. (22–3)

---

[69] *Or.* 6. 25–9.　　　[70] Moles (1996a) 112.　　　[71] *Or.* 8. 33.
[72] Cf. Desideri (1978) 493–6, and Anderson, above, pp. 154–6.

This vivid picture of the monsters who once upon a time inhabited the sands of Libya is obviously indebted to former myths. It is influenced by the female monsters of Greek mythology such as the Sphinx or the Sirens. It is in part modelled on Plato's description of the 'desiring part' (*epithumētikon*) of the soul in *Republic* 9, a monster with many heads like the Chimaera, Scylla, or Cerberus.[73] Its localization is to be explained by Herodotus and his allusions to a part of Libya which is 'full of wild beasts'.[74] Its conclusion gives Heracles his traditional part, for the destruction of the Libyan monsters can be paralleled by the clearing of the birds that infested the Stymphalian lake or the killing of the Hydra, also a composite female monster.

I shall pass over the myth of the magi in the *Borystheniticus* (it 'was once taken . . . as genuine "Zoroastrian" or "Mithraic" lore, and is now better understood as a deliberately colourful product of Greek thought',[75] which borrows many motifs from the myth of the *Phaedrus*, as convincingly demonstrated by Michael Trapp[76]), and move on to consider the way in which these forgeries are introduced and accorded the guarantee of an external authority.

In Dio's speeches, myths—especially the new ones—always come from elsewhere, from people living in the countryside,[77] in a remote and primitive Arcadia,[78] or in barbarian lands such as Egypt,[79] Persia,[80] Phrygia,[81] or Libya[82] (there are indeed traces of a dubious tradition connecting animal fables with Libya[83]). They are often derived from authoritative sources: an old woman who is also a prophetess,[84] the magi who sang them during their sacred ceremonies,[85] a 'very old Egyptian priest',[86] a Phrygian 'relative of Aesop' (since the legendary fabulist originated from Phrygia).[87]

These characters are presented with more or less elaborate introductions, which may echo the Platonic *Phaedrus* in *Or.* 1 and the *Timaeus* in the *Trojan Oration*.

The minimal introduction is exemplified by the beginning of the *Libyan Myth*: 'Once upon a time it is said . . .', where the author of the tale is not even named. Sometimes the first narrator remains

---

[73] *Rep.* 9. 588b–d.   [74] Hdt. 2. 32; 4. 174, 181, 191.
[75] Swain (1996) 198 and the references in n. 46. Cf. and ctr. Anderson, above, pp. 157–8, and see Trapp, below, pp. 214–19.
[76] Trapp (1990) 149.   [77] *Or.* 30. 25.   [78] *Or.* 1.   [79] *Or.* 11.
[80] *Or.* 36.   [81] *Or.* 32. 63.   [82] *Or.* 5.   [83] van Dijk (1997) 106.
[84] *Or.* 1. 54.   [85] *Or.* 36. 39.   [86] *Or.* 11. 37.   [87] *Or.* 32. 63.

anonymous and the circumstances of his telling the story to Dio or his mouthpiece are not precisely described, as is the case for the Orpheus myth in the speech to the Alexandrians: 'I heard this story from a Phrygian relative of Aesop, who paid a visit here' (32. 63). The myth told by Charidemus in the letter he dictated to his servant before his death is presented in the same way as a story he heard 'from a peasant who spoke with a very rustic drawl', a realistic detail which gives more presence to this fictitious character, but also stresses the gap between the polished narrative of Charidemus/Dio and the original.[88] As Charidemus says, 'Perhaps there is no need for us to reproduce his accent and we shall attempt merely to record his thought' (*Or.* 30. 25).

The introduction to the myth of the first *Kingship Oration* is far more developed. Dio records precisely when and where he met the old *mantis*: during his exile, he happened to walk from Heraea to Pisa along the Alpheius (52) and stopped in a grove sacred to Heracles (54), a perfectly appropriate setting for a myth. These details also create 'a pleasant illusion of authenticity'.[89] But the literary background is more important. 'The circumstances of the *mantis*' encounter with Dio are modelled on the encounter between Socrates and Phaedrus in the *Phaedrus*',[90] and the *mantis* as an old woman of Elis or Arcadia is clearly based on Plato's Diotima whose origins are also Arcadian (from Mantinea). But her persona also has some typically Cynic traits. She is 'dressed like a rustic', 'often tends herself' the sheep of her son, uses her gift of divination for the sake of the herdsmen and farmers who consult her and speaks Doric only because 'the Dorian ethos suits the ruggedness of Cynic thought',[91] for this dialect was not spoken in Arcadia.

REWRITING MYTHOLOGY

To appreciate Dio's originality properly, one has to look at his rewriting of mythical episodes. I focus here on the *Chryseis* (*Or.* 61), the *Nessus* (*Or.* 60), and especially the *Trojan Oration* (*Or.* 11), which questions the veracity of the most famous among the Greek myths.

---

[88] Cf. Moles, below, pp. 192, 199 f.   [89] Moles (1990) 320.
[90] Trapp (1990) 143.   [91] Moles (1990) 321.

As an attempt to create out of next to nothing a consistent character, the *Chryseis* is a fine piece of entertainment for the classically educated as well as an oblique criticism of Homer. Starting from Agamemnon's praises of Chryseis' good sense and apparently relying on the Homeric narrative, Dio succeeds in convincing his interlocutor that 'Chryseis was sensible, if it happened as you say' (18). But his final reply: 'Would you rather hear about how it happened in reality or how it should have happened?' suggests that the truth is rather to be found in his own 'plausible'[92] reconstruction of Chryseis' psychology. For Dio explains successively why at the beginning 'she was content to remain with Agamemnon' (8), why after a while she changed her mind and called for her father (9–15), and why she departed without showing her gladness (16).

In the *Nessus*, which is an open polemic against the authorized version of the death of Heracles and its most famous exponents, Archilochus and Sophocles,[93] Dio adopts the same argumentative strategy. He eliminates what is not 'credible' (*pithanon*, 3) and replaces it by a 'plausible' (*eikos*, 3, 5) version. The result is an account which is 'correct' (*orthōs*) and 'appropriate' (*deontōs*), but opposes the general belief, since 'it is inevitable for the one who wants to tell the story correctly (*orthōs*) to speak against popular opinion' (2). But it is convincing enough, as is demonstrated by the reaction of Dio's interlocutor, 'And by Heaven it seems to me not at all a bad account or unconvincing (*apithanos*) either' (9).

While keeping the basic plot (Nessus still tries to seduce Deianeira and is killed by Heracles, who at the end commits suicide by burning himself), Dio transforms the characters. His Nessus, who is no longer motivated by his lust for Deianeira, but by his hatred of Heracles, resorts to trickery instead of violence. He becomes a good rhetorician, able to invent arguments which are 'fit for his victim'.[94] He tells her how to transform a harsh and difficult hero into a good husband —one who will stay at home and be nice to her—and how to get the upper hand over him. There is now no poisoned tunic. A 'dress like that of other men' (7), which replaces the lion's skin and symbolizes his radical change of life-style, will have the same destructive effects. Persuaded by his wife to reject the 'minimal living' and the self-sufficiency of the Cynics, which is symbolized by the lion's skin,

---

[92] εἰκός: *Or.* 61. 5. [93] Desideri (1978) 491.
[94] *Or.* 60. 4 ἐπιτηδείους πρὸς αὐτήν (not 'suited to his purpose', as the Loeb has it).

Heracles adopts the refinements of civilization and experiences all its drawbacks. Ruined by a luxurious life, the manly and healthy hero becomes soft and weak and kills himself from despair.

As he retains the facts, Dio does not need any external confirmation to validate his interpretation of the character of Chryseis or his version of the death of Heracles. But his radical rewriting of the Trojan War in the *Trojan Oration* has to be supported by the report of an eyewitness, Menelaus, whose words were recorded in writing by the Egyptians. This ploy is not new. Herodotus did the same, when he wanted to prove that Helen never went to Troy. After Dio, it would become a common device. Philostratus in the *Heroicus* solicits information from Protesilaus, the first Greek to die at Troy, to complement and often correct the Homeric narrative of the war, since heroes are granted the privilege of omniscience. In Lucian's *Gallus*, Micyllus asks his cockerel, who is a reincarnation of the Trojan Euphorbus, to tell him if Homer's report is true.[95] Later writers will substitute written testimonies for these oral reports. They will invent characters such as Dictys, a Cretan who fought at Troy with Idomeneus and left a diary written first in 'Phoenician characters', then transliterated into Attic, and finally translated into Latin, or Dares, a Phrygian who left a record of the war, also translated into Latin.

Dio clearly derives the introduction of his *Trojan Oration* from Plato's *Timaeus*, which was itself influenced by Herodotus' *Histories*. There are nevertheless some significant changes. In the *Histories*, the story of Helen is orally transmitted: the Egyptian Priests 'told' Herodotus what they had learnt about the Trojan War by asking questions of Menelaus.[96] As for the events which happen in Egypt before (the arrival of Paris together with Helen) or after the Trojan War (the arrival of Menelaus to fetch his wife; his departure to Greece with her), they know them 'accurately',[97] obviously through oral tradition. The transmission of the Atlantis myth is much more complicated. In the *Timaeus* it is mostly oral. At Saïs an old priest tells the story to Solon who brings it from Egypt to Athens. Then the Athenian passes the story to Critias I who, in turn, tells it to his grandson Critias II, 'as he remembered it' (20e). Lastly Critias

---

[95] *Gallus* 17 οὐκοῦν τὰ ἐν Ἰλίῳ μοι πρότερον εἰπέ. τοιαῦτα ἦν οἷά φησιν Ὅμηρος γενέσθαι αὐτά;

[96] Hdt. 2. 118, 119.

[97] Hdt. 2. 119 τὰ δὲ παρ' ἑωυτοῖσι γενόμενα ἀτρεκέως ἐπιστάμενοι λέγειν.

II narrates the tale to Socrates.[98] A written record which has been kept in an Egyptian temple is alluded to as a source, but it merely echoes a former oral tradition.[99] Moreover, it is not this written record which is read by the old priest.[100] What we are given is only an 'oral echo of these written words'.[101] In the *Critias*, however, a Solonian manuscript kept by Critias' family suddenly appears alongside the Egyptian record.[102] In the *Trojan Oration* the oral tradition is systematically presented as an imperfect reflection of a written text. As with Herodotus, Dio repeats a story told to him in Egypt—at Onuphis—by an Egyptian priest (37) who ultimately relies on an oral source, since Menelaus 'told the Egyptians everything just as it had occurred' (38), 'concealing nothing' (135). But subsequently the entire history of earlier times, including of course the story of Menelaus, has been written in part in temples, in part on *stēlai* which had been destroyed. Thus some parts of the story were remembered only by a small number of people, and much of it was disbelieved (38). This complicated presentation, which oscillates from oral to written report, is well suited to an enigmatic text which raises many questions and has been read as a rhetorical exercise, a political message, or a piece of moral philosophy.

Is it a mere 'trifle' (*paignion*) or, more positively, a 'rhetorical tour de force'[103] and an unusually lengthy and brilliant parody[104] of the rhetorical 'refutation' (*anaskeuē*), as Eustathius claimed in his commentary on the *Iliad*,[105] and has been held by Kroll, Mesk, and many other moderns?[106] This is certainly true in part, since the *Trojan Oration*, according to Hermogenes' definition of the refutation,[107] 'questions a well accepted fact'—the capture of Troy by the Greeks—by pointing out the obscurities, implausibilities, impossibilities, and inconsistencies of the Homeric narrative.[108]

---

[98] Each time emphasis is laid on the oral character of the transmission, as is well demonstrated by Brisson (1982) 23–47.

[99] *Timaeus* 23a, 23c, 24a, 24d.

[100] *Timaeus* 23e–24a.

[101] *Timaeus* 27b ἡ τῶν ἱερῶν γραμμάτων φήμη.

[102] *Critias* 113a–b.

[103] Swain (1996) 210, and Anderson, above, pp. 152–3.

[104] Szarmach (1978) 200–1.

[105] *ad Il.* 4. 163 δῆλον δέ, ὅτι καὶ ἠλαζονεύοντο Ἰλιεῖς μὴ ἀφανισθῆναι τὴν κατ' αὐτοὺς πόλιν. ὅθεν καὶ ὁ Δίων ἐπηγωνίσατο ἀνασκευάσαι τὰ Τρωϊκά. καὶ αὐτοὶ τάχ' ἂν ἔχαιρον τοῖς λεγομένοις ὑπὸ τοῦ Δίωνος.

[106] Kroll (1915) 607 ff., Mesk (1920–1), Stanford (1954) 148, Kennedy (1972) 571.

[107] Hermogenes, *Progymnasmata* 5 ἀνασκευή ἐστιν ἀνατροπὴ τοῦ προτεθέντος πράγματος. See also Theon, *Rhet. Gr.* 2. 93 and Quintilian, *Inst. Or.* 2. 4. 18–19.

[108] Hermogenes (ibid.) explicitly commands arguments ἐκ τοῦ ἀσαφοῦς, ἐκ τοῦ ἀπιθάνου, ἐκ τοῦ ἀδυνάτου, ἐκ τοῦ ἀνακολούθου.

J. F. Kindstrand, on the contrary, proposes to read it as a typical piece of Cynic moralizing, assaulting 'infatuation' (*tuphos*) and *doxa* in its two meanings of 'opinion' and 'repute'.[109] As such, it may be paralleled to the attacks launched against self-delusion by Dio himself in the second *Tarsian Oration*, by his mouthpiece Diogenes in the fourth *Kingship Oration*, or by his mythical personae, Heracles in *Or.* 8 or Nestor in the *Or.* 57.[110] This interpretation relies mostly on the introduction and conclusion of the speech. Right from the beginning, Dio opposes the bitterness of truth to the sweetness of lies and harshly criticizes human gullibility and self-delusion: men are so madly in love with fame that they would prefer to be notorious for the greatest misfortunes than suffer no ill and be unknown.[111] Again, in the conclusion, he opposes those who believe a lie because it has been accepted among those of former times and stresses, like Thucydides, that 'most people', even among contemporaries, do not have an 'exact' knowledge and 'merely listen to rumour'; then the second and third generations easily swallow whatever anyone says, being without experience.[112]

Is it a caricature of the traditional methods of Homeric scholarship, as asserted by Marian Szarmach,[113] or a valuable by-product of Homeric criticism which foreshadows to some extent the work of the modern Analysts, as has been claimed recently by G. A. Seeck?[114] Maybe. The question of Homer's reliability as a historian, and also as a geographer,[115] was fiercely disputed among Homer's ancient commentators, whose opinions ranged from the nearly total denial of any truth in Homer (Eratosthenes) to the affirmation of his complete dependability (Crates of Mallos).[116]

Is it a clever piece of Roman propaganda? There is no doubt that Dio, by asserting the Trojans' superiority over the Greeks and opposing their glory and prosperity to the miserable and humble state of Greece (137), indirectly praises the Romans who claimed a Trojan origin. He even alludes once to a *fides Trojana* which is a blueprint of the famous *fides Romana*: it is 'because of their oaths'

---

[109] Kindstrand (1973) 156.   [110] *Orr.* 34. 47; 4. 7, 72, 77; 8. 33; 57. 8.
[111] *Or.* 11. 1–5.
[112] *Or.* 11. 146 οὐ γὰρ ἴσασιν οἱ πολλοὶ τὸ ἀκριβές, ἀλλὰ φήμης ἀκούουσι μόνον, καὶ ταῦτα οἱ γενόμενοι κατὰ τὸν χρόνον ἐκεῖνον· οἱ δὲ δεύτεροι καὶ τρίτοι τελέως ἄπειροι καὶ ὅ τι ἂν εἴπῃ τις παραδέχονται ῥᾳδίως.
[113] Szarmach (1978) 200–1.   [114] Seeck (1990).
[115] Cf. Schenkeveld (1976).   [116] Ibid. 55–6.

(138) that the Trojans decided to rule only over Italy and refrained from conquering Greece right away. He also praises Italy as 'the most prosperous part' (137) of Europe. In his prophetic speech Hector not only promises Aeneas that he will conquer all Europe, but adds that his descendants will rule over the two continents. The praise of Rome is unmistakable. But it is concentrated in a small part of the speech (137–50) and cannot explain the whole of it, as is recognized by Kindstrand, Jones, and Swain.[117]

Is it possible, as is held by Paolo Desideri, to claim that the *Trojan Oration* shows that myth has to be transformed in order to convey a new ideological message in tune with changed times?[118] The Homeric version of the Trojan War, which prevented the Greeks from being afraid of the rulers of Asia, was a patriotic lie which made possible their victory over the Persians. But as there is no longer any fear of an expedition coming from Asia, 'for Greece is subject to others and so is Asia' (150), there is a new 'truth' which can be told now. 'Sotto l'impero romano è più vantaggioso mettere in luce per quanto possibile l'accordo raggiunto a conclusione della guerra tra Achei e Troiani, prefigurazione mitica di un auspicabile processo di solidarizzazione tra mondo ellenico e mondo orientale.'[119] But as Michael Trapp observes in an unpublished paper on 'Troy and the True Story of the Trojan War',[120] 'it seems strained to make a relatively fleeting remark in the final stages of the performance [that is, 147–50] the crucial key to the whole'.

Michael Trapp himself closely relates the speech's performance at Troy to a civic context. The *Trojan Oration*, which 'reminds the Ilian audience of their dual heritage', becomes 'an example of carefully calculated play with local conditions and local sentiment'. But as opposed to the *Alexandrian Oration*, which is aimed only at a local audience, the *Trojan Oration* explicitly addresses other audiences, as stressed by Dio in his introduction: 'I wish to say at the outset that this discourse must be delivered before other people also and that many will hear about it' (6). This may prevent us from reading the whole speech as 'an example of interplay between rhetorical performance and civic self-image'.

[117] Kindstrand (1973) 162, Jones (1978) 18, Swain (1996) 210–11.
[118] Desideri (1978) 496, (1991a) 3887. [119] Desideri (1978) 433.
[120] Trapp (forthcoming). I am grateful to Michael Trapp for sending me the text of this paper.

In fact, if one follows John Moles, who refuses to draw a firm line between Dio's activities as a sophist, a politician, a philosopher, and a literary critic,[121] there is no reason to think that these readings are mutually exclusive. They are all supported by some section of the oration and illuminate at least parts of it. My own view is that the speech should be read as a lengthy, but not necessarily 'boring',[122] refutation of Homer and those who believe him. In a way this is 'play', but really 'serious play', for Dio chose as his target the Poet himself.

Dio begins by exposing the contradictions of the Greeks. They know that beggars tell nothing but lies, yet they trust Homer the beggar (16). They say that Stesichorus, who followed Homer's account, was blinded by Helen because he was a liar, yet they claim that Homer's poetry is true (40). Then he assails their self-delusion by demonstrating that Homer is not a 'maître de vérité', but a mere representative of opinion and its errors. This is indeed the best way of 'defacing the currency' and deflating human—and especially Greek—arrogance. For the Ilians are not alone in thinking that Homer is 'inspired by a god and wise' (16). All the Greeks believe Homer to be 'wise' or even 'godlike in his wisdom'.[123] Alexander, in the second *Kingship Oration*, lavishes extravagant praises on Homer's poetry which is 'really noble and great and kingly' (6).[124] Phidias calls him 'the wisest among the poets'.[125] The Borysthenites 'honour him second only to gods'.[126] But these praises are never fully endorsed by Dio himself or his authorized representatives and can sometimes sound ironic.[127] In the first *Kingship Oration*, Homer is quoted approvingly only because he agrees on the point in question with all other wise and truthful men.[128] In fact, as is well pointed out by Kindstrand,[129] Homer is never used as an authority by Dio himself: there are no 'rein autoritative Homerzitate' in Dio's speeches, but only 'Hilfszitate', when the Homeric text supports Dio's opinion,[130] or 'polemische Zitate', when Homer 'goes beyond actuality or possibility'.[131] As for the two speeches *On Homer* (*Or.* 53) and *On Homer and Socrates* (*Or.* 55), they echo other philosophers' or grammarians' opinions, extol the charm of his poetry, express admiration for a poet transformed into a wandering philosopher

---

[121] Moles (1978), cf. Swain (1996) 190.   [122] Cf. Desideri (1991*a*) 3887.
[123] Cf. *Orr.* 12. 63, 80. 7.   [124] Cf. *Or.* 2. 18, 44, 54, 65.   [125] *Or.* 12. 73.
[126] *Or.* 36. 14.   [127] *Orr.* 14. 22, 23. 5.   [128] *Or.* 1. 14.
[129] Kindstrand (1973) 32–3.   [130] e.g. *Or.* 44. 1.   [131] *Or.* 79. 1.

modelled on Diogenes or Dio himself, or propose a Socratic Homer who hates presumption and embodies self-restraint.

As for the Homeric narrative of the Trojan War, Dio puts it to the test and carefully points out the limits of Homer's reliability: the Egyptians agree that the Greeks first were prevented from landing at Troy, then, after a successful landing, tried to build a wall to protect their ships, but they say that the wall was not finished (74–6). They acknowledge that Hector put on Achilles' arms and slaughtered the Greeks, but that this happened not after his killing of Patroclus, but after his killing of Achilles (96). The contrast with Philostratus' *Heroicus*, which validates Homer's portrayals of Nestor[132] and Hector[133] as well as his narrative of the deaths of Hector, Sarpedon and Patroclus,[134] and praises the poet for telling 'actual and real facts',[135] is striking.

Usually Dio chooses 'to refute Homer from nowhere else than his own poetry' (11), which I would like to take, with Trapp, as a knowing parody of the Aristarchean maxim of 'elucidating Homer from Homer'.[136] Since Homer, like any other liar, is not always able 'to cover up' (*kruptein/apokruptein*)[137] or 'suppress' (*aphanizein*)[138] the truth, he often betrays 'being at a loss' (*aporia*),[139] and traces of the hidden 'truth' may be discovered in his text.

To establish whether something is to be taken as 'an accurate report' (*historia*) or as a 'fiction' (*muthos*) in the Homeric poems, Dio, like many of Homer's ancient readers, relies first and foremost on verisimilitude (*eikos*) and plausibility (*pithanon*), since for him, as for Plutarch, the past is *not* a foreign country,[140] but a familiar one, similar to the present. Dio accepts as 'true' everything which 'resembles actual occurrences',[141] such as the narrative of Hector's exploits, 'for here there is no Aeneas snatched away by Aphrodite, no Ares wounded by a mortal, nor any other such incredible (*apithanōn*) tales' (90), but rejects the Homeric report of Achilles' heroic deeds, since it is 'unbelievable' (*apithanos*, 107). He contends

---

[132] *Heroicus* 3, p. 165K: καὶ ὁπόσα Ὁμήρῳ περὶ αὐτοῦ εἴρηται, ξὺν ἀληθείᾳ φησὶν εἰρῆσθαι.

[133] Ibid. 12, p. 189K. [134] Ibid. 12b, p. 190K; 14, p. 191K; 17, p. 192K.

[135] Ibid. 18 p. 193K.

[136] The attribution of the maxim, doubted by Pfeiffer (1968) 225–7, is strongly supported by Porter (1992) 70–80.

[137] *Or.* 11. 33, 71, 80, 84, 97, 103. [138] *Or.* 11. 103.

[139] *Or.* 11. 32, 74, 86, 87, 107. [140] Cf. Lowenthal (1985).

[141] *Or.* 11. 88 ἀληθῆ καὶ ὅμοια γεγονόσι.

that the wall of the Achaeans has not been finished, because Homer 'has represented Apollo and Poseidon as having at a later time sent the rivers against it and swept it away'. The 'most plausible' (*pithanōtaton*, 76) explanation is that only the foundations of the wall were inundated. He assumes that 'what did happen was a thing that could happen' (139) and denies that events may occur that are beyond belief: what is unlikely is indeed impossible.[142] Dio is not alone in privileging plausibility. In his *Life of Theseus* Plutarch openly chooses the 'more plausible' (*pithanōtera*, 26. 1) version and often relies on 'verisimilitude' (*eikos*) to reject an episode.[143] Lucian in the *Gallus* also corrects Homer by suppressing unbelievable details in his narrative. He maintains for instance that the heroes of the Trojan War had 'nothing extraordinary' about them: 'Ajax was not as big nor Helen as beautiful as they think' (17). Similarly, Philostratus closely links verisimilitude and truth:[144] his Protesilaus condemns the episodes of Polyphemus, Antiphates, and Scylla, as well as the *Nekuiai* and the Sirens' songs, as 'implausible inventions',[145] and considers as a 'fiction' the story of Achilles' immortal horses.[146]

Dio concentrates his attacks on the beginning and the end of the account of the Trojan War. The whole story of the kidnapping of Helen by Alexander is indeed 'silly' and 'absurd', for it was not 'possible' for Alexander (who had never seen Helen before) to fall in love with her (even for love at first sight, there must be a sight!) and succeed in persuading her to follow a foreigner (a married woman does not depart willingly from her husband and family).[147] Moreover, it was not likely (*eikos*, 55) that a sensible father would allow his son to behave in such a way nor that Hector would tolerate such a deed at the outset, since afterwards he heaped abuse and reproach upon Paris for abducting Helen (55–6). Similarly, it was not 'likely' (*eikos*, 59, 69, 70) for a wife like Helen to meet a foreigner and talk to him, when her husband was away from home and it was plainly 'impossible' (60, 70) for her to elope with Alexander without being stopped by anyone, or even to meet him.

---

[142] *Or.* 11. 70 τούτων οὐθὲν εἰκὸς οὐδὲ δυνατόν.   [143] 10. 4, 31. 2, 32. 2.

[144] *Heroicus* 19, p. 198K πιθανώτατα . . . καὶ ἀληθέστερα.

[145] Ibid. 11, p. 185K ἀπίθανά τε καὶ παρευρημένα.

[146] Ibid. 19, p. 204K τὴν μὲν ἀθανασίαν . . . μεμυθολογῆσθαι τῷ Ὁμήρῳ.

[147] *Or.* 11. 54 σκόπει δέ, ἔφη, τὴν εὐήθειαν τοῦ ἐναντίου λόγου, εἴ σοι δοκεῖ δυνατὸν εἶναι πρῶτον μὲν ἐρασθῆναί τινα γυναικός, ἣν οὐπώποτε εἶδεν, κτλ . . . διὰ ταύτην γὰρ τὴν ἀλογίαν . . .

The whole story of Aphrodite giving Helen to Paris is therefore rejected as a 'fiction still more senseless' (54) than the absurdities it tries to cover up.

After the war, the division of the fleet evidently shows that the Achaeans were defeated, since 'it is reasonable to suppose (*eikos*) that successful people are unanimous and mostly willing to obey the king ... but in defeat and failure all such things are sure to happen' (130). 'Also the domestic disasters which befell those who reached their homes are not the least evidence of their discomfiture and weakness. It is certainly not usual for attacks to be made on men who are victorious and successful' (131–2).

In between, Dio points out many absurdities in the Homeric narrative (the behaviour of Achilles sending Patroclus to fight against a much better warrior, Helen becoming the wife of Deiphobus after the death of Alexander, or the ending of the duel between Hector and Ajax),[148] and numerous impossibilities (e.g. the wounding of a goddess, Aphrodite, by a man, Diomedes).[149]

Furthermore, like the modern Analysts, Dio stresses some logical contradictions in Homer's account of the war: how is it that Troy can have become the greatest city of Asia, after having been sacked by Heracles just a few years before (57)? How is it that Heracles, coming with only seven ships, captured Troy in a few days, while the Achaeans who came with twelve hundred ships were unable to sack it (57–78)? How come that the 'swift-footed Achilles' was unable to catch Hector (107)?[150]

Dio also questions the plausibility of Homer's report by demonstrating, for instance, that he could not have had any reliable information about the private conversations between Zeus and Hera, since 'it is not likely (*eikos*), even among human beings, for any outsider to know of domestic rows' (20).

More interestingly, Dio sometimes relies on narrative technique, distinguishing long before modern narratologists the primary and the secondary narrators. He stresses that

Homer does not dare to tell himself the biggest lies, the story of Scylla, of the Cyclops, the magic charms of Circe, and further the descent of Odysseus into the lower world, but makes Odysseus narrate these stories to Alcinous and his court. Here too he has Demodocus recount the story of the horse and the capture of Troy in a song of only a few lines. (34)

---

[148] Ibid. 83, 99, 100.   [149] Ibid. 87, 90.   [150] Cf. *Or.* 9. 17.

In the same way he points out that 'Homer' does not relate Helen's rape in his own person, but delegates the narrative to his characters, Hector, Helen, and Paris (81).

Prefiguring the approach of neo-analysts, who look behind some of the incidents of the *Iliad* for a pre-existing *Aithiopis*, Dio sees behind Homeric 'lies' traces of a hidden 'truth'. Before him Herodotus had already demonstrated through Homeric quotations that Homer knew about Helen's stay in Egypt, while claiming that she was at Troy.[151] Similarly, Dio proves that Homer was aware that Menelaus did not return to the Peloponnese, but remained in Egypt, since the Homeric description of the Elysian fields where Menelaus is said to have been sent in the *Odyssey* squares perfectly with Egypt (here too there is neither snow nor storm, but sunshine and clear weather throughout the year).[152] Philostratus, in the *Heroicus*, would also contend that Homer knew of Helen's stay in Egypt,[153] and will rely on a Homeric quotation to show that Sthenelus was equal and not inferior to Diomedes in strength, as Homer says elsewhere.[154]

Moreover, Dio produces external testimonies in support of his thesis. Had it been obvious that Helen lived in Greece after the war, it would never have been said that she disappeared immediately upon her return, as did Euripides in the conclusion of his *Orestes*. He draws evidence from traditions ignored by Homer, such as the colonization of Italy by Aeneas, the rule of Helenus over Epirus, and 'the dominion of Antenor over the Heneti and the very best land about the Adriatic' (137–9), to demonstrate that the Trojan defeat is a lie, for 'it was not likely (*eikos*) that men driven into exile and crushed by calamities at home accomplished such a thing' (139).

Conversely, Dio relies not only on authority, but also on plausibility to back the 'Egyptian' version of the story. To support his claim that many suitors of Helen—and among them Paris—came from outside Greece, he proves that in the past 'it was the custom' for great houses to form marriage alliances with foreigners and mentions the story of the daughter of Cleisthenes tyrant of Sicyon and the marriages of Pelops, Theseus, and Io (47–8). Thus 'it is much more plausible (*pistoteron*) that Tyndareus willingly gave his daughter in marriage to the kings of Asia' (68). Philostratus, in the

---

[151] *Histories* 2. 116.   [152] *Or*. 11. 135–6.
[153] *Heroicus* 2, p. 163K.   [154] Ibid. 4, p. 169K.

Heroicus, would also prefer Protesilaus' version of Achilles' exploits to Homer's, because it is 'more plausible'.[155]

Dio also points out coincidences between the Egyptian story and Greek traditions which validate the words of the Egyptian priest. The beginning of the story of Helen (her abduction by Theseus, her liberation by her brothers who retaliated by capturing Theseus' mother), as told by the Egyptian, coincides with what the Greeks say and what Dio himself has seen—here also an unmistakable echo of Herodotean autopsy—'I have', he says, 'myself seen at Olympia in the rear chamber of the temple of Hera a memorial of that abduction upon the wooden chest dedicated by Cypselus' (45). The precision of the detail concerning the location of the chest and 'the inscription in ancient characters' which is written on it authenticate his claim.

But Dio the philosopher is not content with exposing Homer as a liar: he also has to explain why he dared to tell such lies and why his lies gained such credit. This happened first, he says, because men are by nature gullible (1–2), as is proved by their beliefs concerning the gods. Secondly, it is because Homer was the first who applied himself to recording these events, after many generations, when a dim and uncertain tradition survived (92).[156] The third reason is that he was addressing a crowd prone to believe a version exaggerating the achievements of the Greeks (92–3). So the *Iliad* became the authorized version of the events, and 'later writers, because they were deceived and the falsehood was now generally accepted, wrote it confidently' (110). After all, the lie was useful, for it prevented the Greeks from being afraid in case of a war between them and the rulers of Asia.

The *Trojan Oration* shows that Dio's criticism of mythology —or, better, of Homer's version of it—has little in common with Plato's condemnation of myths on the grounds that they provide unacceptable models of behaviour. Rather, Dio sides with Lucian and reproaches the poets, beginning with Homer, for using 'fictions' as cosmetics, sacrificing truth to seduction.[157] He tries to 'rationalize the mythical element away'[158] by rejecting everything that looks

---

[155] Ibid. 19, p. 202K πιθανώτερα.
[156] Cf. Diodorus Siculus 4. 1 on the difficulties faced by the historian in the treatment of 'ancient mythologies', where the antiquity of the events prevents him from finding out the truth and writing an accurate record.
[157] Cf. Lucian, *Jup. trag.* 39.   [158] Wiseman (1979) 49.

implausible to him and therefore impossible, as the classical historians Herodotus and Thucydides, and, to a greater extent, the historians and geographers of the Hellenistic and Roman period, did. To better appreciate his originality, it would be useful to see it against the background of the historiography and literary criticism of the Empire and compare it more systematically with texts such as Plutarch's *De audiendis poetis* and *De malignitate Herodoti* or Lucian's *De conscribenda historia*. But this survey of Dio's use of mythology is enough to indicate the breadth of the spectrum he covers.

8

The Dionian Charidemus
JOHN MOLES

The *Charidemus* attributed to Dio Chrysostom ostensibly commemorates a recently deceased pupil of Dio's named Charidemus. As *Or.* 30 in the extant Dionian corpus the piece suitably follows *Orr.* 28 and 29, the two obituary encomia of the athlete Melancomas. On any reading, *Or.* 30 is adroitly conceived and executed and not without pathos. Yet the bibliography, despite recent and forthcoming items, remains inchoate,[1] its growth perhaps stunted by nervousness over the alleged problem of authenticity.[2] Authenticity is indeed not guaranteed by presence in the corpus. Thus *Orr.* 37 and 64 are generally agreed to be by Favorinus, one of Dio's most distinguished pupils. Nor does the piece's proximity to *Orr.* 28 and 29[3] significantly support authenticity: *Orr.* 37 and 64 are also appropriately contextualized. Might *Or.* 30, then, be 'school of Dio' rather than Dio himself? The piece also poses substantial interpretative problems, which have so far eluded resolution.

The general character of the work may best emerge from a summary interspersed with running comment, followed by direct engagement with the interpretative problems. Since the latter cannot

I thank: Simon Swain for inviting me; all who commented at the conference; Tony Woodman for comments on a written version; and Mike Trapp for a copy of his paper, below, Ch. 9.
[1] Hirzel (1895) 2: 111–14, Meiser (1912), Wilhelm (1918), Cohoon (1939) 395–8, Kassel (1958) 48, Moles (1978) 95, Bowie (1985) 671, Giner Soria (1990–1), Menchelli (1997), and Michael Trapp in the present volume makes valuable observations, below, pp. 223–5; Menchelli's doctoral thesis, 'Dione di Prusa, *Caridemo*, edizione, introduzione, traduzione e note, con contributi alla storia della tradizione dionea', is to be published; Giovanni Schiavo is producing an Italian translation.

[2] Hirzel (1895); von Arnim (1898) 283; Nilsson (1961) 2: 401 n. 2; Desideri (1978) 185 n. 19, 248 n. 42; Moles (1978) 95; Menchelli (1997) 67–73; note the uncertainty of Russell (1992): dubious (178), authentic (247).

[3] Wilhelm (1918) 364: 'in Discourse 29 physical, in 30 intellectual, excellence'.

ultimately be detached from the authenticity question and since continual formulation of strictly non-prejudicial comment would be very laborious, the summary will adopt the genuineness of the piece as a working hypothesis and defer formal consideration of the question until the end. There, however, it will be argued that the case against authenticity is misconceived. Moreover, the commentary material will itself provide evidence for the defence. Consequently, the work's presence and position in the corpus, the material in the commentary, and the solutions offered to the problems will constitute a strong cumulative case for authenticity. We shall then be free to appreciate the work's quality without distraction. The discussion will also explore a hypothesis which, if accepted, adds new dimensions alike to the work's emotional intensity, to its literary complexity, and to its philosophical coherence.

THE *CHARIDEMUS*: SUMMARY AND COMMENT

Dio,[4] having heard of Charidemus' death, is condoling with Charidemus' father Timarchus and surviving brother, also called Timarchus, who are both rightly distraught: besides their personal loss, Charidemus would have been of immense benefit not only to his city but to all Greece (1–3). Dio's relations with his pupil were exceptionally close: he feels almost as much grief as do Timarchus father and son (2); the dying Charidemus kept naming Dio and bade his family tell Dio when they met him that he died thinking of him (4); in life, Charidemus had the same philosophical deportment as Dio, whether or not because he imitated him (4–5). Thus Dio already appears as both a lofty external and an intensely internal figure, an ambiguous status that is capable of rich development and one that is familiar from such Dionian works as the first, second, and fourth *Kingship Orations*, the *Euboicus*, and the *Olympicus*.[5]

The opening scene deftly sketches important themes. The elaborate circumstantial grounding in details of travel and informants and in terms such as *akouō*, *epistamai*, *gignōskō*, etc. sets up questions of truth, language, naming, and knowledge (1–2). There is a contrast

---

[4] Donald Russell emphasizes (in conversation) that the name Dio (in contrast to Charidemus and the two Timarchuses) does not appear in the text (the division of the dialogue by names is a modern convenience). But such 'namelessness' is the norm in Dio. Furthermore, it will be argued that Dio's name is *implicit*.

[5] Cf. n. 49.

between the select and the ignorant majority (3). There is emphasis on the role of *phusis*, both nature as a moral standard (here the natural feeling proper to familial relationships) and individual nature or character (3, 4–5); the latter emphasis already suggests that while philosophical teaching and teachers and their imitation have their place, it is the individual's deployment of his *phusis* that mainly determines good or bad moral behaviour. The question whether Charidemus' deportment caused his family *lupē* (5) neatly conveys the points that among all the *lupai* of life, not least are the *lupai* caused by others, and *lupai* can be small as well as great. Charidemus' death, while the source of the greatest *lupē* which human beings have to bear, is paradigmatic of all types of *lupai*. As will become ever more apparent, there are numerous skilful links between the opening scene, the main body of the work, and the final scene.

The question whether Charidemus' philosophical sobriety betokened cheerfulness or gloominess (5) anticipates the key question which informs the structure of the whole piece: did Charidemus die well? But first (6) Timarchus father declares that Charidemus said 'many spirit-like (*daimonia*) things'. On his death-bed Charidemus is between life and death and approaches the mediating character of *daimones*.[6] To the key question, the answer is that Charidemus died cheerfully and courageously, as proved not only by his death-bed behaviour but also by the work of consolation which he there dictated, which at Dio's request Timarchus father now reads aloud (8–44). The structure of the *Charidemus* thus echoes that of the *Phaedo*, Dio's favourite philosophical text, according to Philostratus (*VS* 488).[7] Both works use the device of an outer frame for the last words of a philosopher as reported by a witness or witnesses to a concerned friend or friends. Conceivably, the device of death-bed utterances transmuted into philosophical text may also reflect something of Dio's own knowledge of philosophical heroism at Rome in his youth, that heroism exhibited (for example) in the deaths of Seneca (Tac. *Ann.* 15. 62–4) and Thrasea Paetus (*Ann.* 16. 34–5), which were themselves partly modelled on the death of Socrates as transmitted in Platonic texts, while Seneca dictated to secretaries what were intended to be his last words and these were subsequently published as a separate work (*Ann.* 15. 63. 3).

[6] At least on re-reading, this *daimōn*-emphasis may be regarded as the first, light, evocation of Plato's *Symposium* (e.g. 202e).

[7] For the *Phaedo* relationship cf. further Trapp, below, p. 224.

In the inner text of the *Charidemus* Charidemus affirms calm acceptance of God's will, cites Homer (*Il.* 3. 65) in support of the proposition that all things done by the gods are 'gifts' which should not be cast aside by mortals, and exhorts his loved ones not to yield to grief, since nothing terrible has befallen him, even if one were to 'go for' (*elthoi epi*) *ton duscherestaton tōn logōn* (9): the most difficult, the most disagreeable, of the various *logoi* of the human condition (in effect, the worst-case scenario). This description, which interacts with 8 *duscherōs pherein* ('we must not bear anything brought to pass by God with difficulty/disagreeably'), already suggests the suspect quality of such a *logos*, acceptable only to the *duschereis*: one's personal disposition affects the sort of *logos* of the human condition that one goes for, but some *logoi* are better than others.

Charidemus' own text, therefore, is explicitly presented as a 'consolation' (6) which will consist of a series of *logoi*, providing progressively greater consolation. Scholars customarily speak of the 'myths' of the *Charidemus*,[8] and indeed these *logoi* possess the conventional characteristics of 'myths': they claim to explain huge moral/ theological problems, contain some narrative and much imaginative writing, and freely invoke the divine.[9] But they are formally presented as *logoi* in the first instance because they make greater truth claims than *muthoi* sometimes do,[10] and Charidemus' concern is above all with truth (9). Yet there remains an implicit challenge in the application of the term *logoi* to material which obviously contains at least some elements of the 'mythical', a challenge for which there are Platonic and Dionian parallels.[11]

The first 'account' (10–24), 'difficult' or 'disagreeable' as it is, is recognizably largely Orphic.[12] Thus the influence of the *Phaedo*, itself influenced by Orphism, continues into the inner text of the

[8] E.g. Saïd and Trapp in this volume, pp. 174, 224; Cohoon (1939) 395 ff. translates 'explanation'. I adopt 'account', as suggesting (*a*) rationalist pursuit of truth, (*b*) narrative content.

[9] The Orphic *logos* is particularly 'mythical' in having something of 'the wonderful' about it (10 *thaumaston*).

[10] Although much recent scholarship (both on Plato and 'myth' generally) argues the slipperiness of *muthos* and *logos* as categories, *logos* certainly sometimes makes a stronger truth claim: cf. e.g. Plat. *Gorg.* 523a, *Tim.* 20d, 21a, *Crit.* 108c–d; Dio *Or.* 1. 49 (Moles (1990) 318–19), *Or.* 5. 3 (with Saïd and Trapp in the present volume, below, pp. 163 and 229; cf. Anderson, above, pp. 155–6).

[11] As in the references in n. 10.

[12] Meiser (1912); the much-discussed problematics of 'Orphism' hardly matter here.

Charidemus.[13] According to this first account, humans are descended from the blood of the Titans, the gods hate us, life is a punishment, lifted only by death, and the universe is a prison; so far from its organization demonstrating beneficent divine providence, everything has been designed to punish and torture us, and most only escape into death when they have produced children to be 'left behind' as 'successors (*diadochoi*) to their punishment' (17). This conception of the function of children seems to reverse that of Plato, *Symposium* 207d: there '*mortal* nature' can pursue its quest for *immortality* only through begetting and 'always *leaving behind* something new in place of the old'; here men desire *death* and can only achieve this by *leaving behind* children to take over their punishment in *life*.

We are all in chains, but for a very few good people the chains are light (19). Charidemus now (20) digresses into an explanation of the chain which he once heard as a child from a beggar (*andros agurtou*).[14] The chain is composed of alternating pleasures and pains, great succeeding great, small small; death is the greatest pleasure, the pain before death the greatest pain. This thought obviously has consolatory force, though this is not spelled out. The digression then discusses the chains that are hopes (*pedas/elpidas*): these come at the end of life, control men, and enable them to endure all tortures; they are very big for the stupid, loose and light for the more intelligent. Presumably (though this also is not spelled out), they bear on different conceptions of an afterlife: the stupid have unrealistically big hopes, the intelligent more subtle ones. Again, then, a thought with consolatory force, though hopes are insubstantial things. The digression continues with the idea of the file that is reason (superior to hope), which is hard to find but whose diligent and constant use enables a man to endure and leave his imprisonment easily (24 *eucherōs* contrasts with 9 *duscherestaton* and 8 *duscherōs*). A digression within an 'account' (*logos*) which instates 'reason' (*logos*) as a source of consolation must have *something* 'reasonable' about it.

[13] Trapp below, p. 224.

[14] Translation points: Cohoon's prejudicial 'wandering philosopher' subserves his interpretation of larger questions (pp. 202 ff.); *pais ōn* naturally goes with *pote* and the genitive *andros agurtou* naturally depends on *ēkousa* (cf. also 25), so that Trapp's interpretation, 'the teller of the myth' [characterizes himself] 'as the offspring of some vagabond' (pp. 224–5), is in itself forced; nevertheless, as we shall see, wider considerations give the collocation *andros agurtou pais* teasing additional resonances.

The digression now seemingly rejoins the main account, though the ending of the digression is not formally marked:[15] sometimes the gods actually make the virtuous and wise their coadjutants (*paredroi*) in an afterlife: more solid consolation, though qualified by that 'sometimes'. There is another deft link between the introduction and the body of the work: Timarchus father rarely saw Charidemus laughing *aneden* (5: 'unrestrainedly'): philosophers are 'bound' to observe a certain 'restraint'. The sober picture of Dio himself (4) now finds a place within the overall argument[16] and the image of chains is revalued in a positive way.

Charidemus ends this first account with a provocative and problematic formulation, to which we must return: 'now this was said by a certain difficult-to-please man [*dusarestos* ~ 9 *ton duscherestaton tōn logōn* ~ 8 *duscherōs pherein*], who had suffered many things in his life and only late had attained true education; but it is not true nor appropriate to the gods; there is another account better than this one, which I shall speak with much more enthusiasm' (25).

This better account (26–7) he heard from a worker of the land who spoke in very rustic style (another problematic formulation). This man hymned Zeus and the other gods and declared that they were good and loved us as their kin (herewith an emphatic Stoic rejection of the Orphic genealogy). The hymning of *Dia* is significant in another way. As part of the debate about the relationship between language and truth, the introduction played with the question of right and wrong naming, and the dying Charidemus kept naming Dio (1–2, 4, 8). The suggestive linkage between his own name and that of Zeus is exploited by Dio elsewhere to bolster his moral and religious authority: Zeus, father of all, is particularly the father of *Dion*.[17] Mankind on earth is a divine colony, related to the gods'

---

[15] 19 *huper hōn authis lexomen* seems to be picked up by 24 *ek toutōn*, 19 *epieikeian* by 24 *aretēn kai sophian*, though there is no resumptive *oun* (*vel sim.*).

[16] This answers Donald Russell's observation (in conversation) that 'the philosopher in 4 does not much look like Dio but more like Aristotle's *megalopsuchos*' (cf. *EN* 4. 3, 1125^{a}12–14).

[17] E.g. *Or.* 4. 27 and *Or.* 12. 85 with Moles (1995) 183. I suspect also further punning interaction between *Dia* and *dianoian* (25), especially in the light of the prominence of *Nous* in the third account, with large implications for the ultimate identity of the 'author' of the whole work (pp. 204 ff.); and as the work becomes progressively more Stoic, as *Diōn* himself appears within the 'accounts' (p. 207), and as apparently separate identities become confused (pp. 207 ff.), one might also recall the Hesiodic word play on *Dios/dia* (*Theog.* 465) and the Platonic word plays on *nous, dianoia*, and *daimones* (*Laws* 713c–d).

home city but much inferior. For a time after the foundation the gods themselves visited or sent divine governors; they then left humans to themselves, whence sin and injustice. As a whole, this account is much more optimistic than its Orphic predecessor and already provides more substantive philosophical consolation.

The worker of the land also sang a second song (28–44): the universe is a very beautiful and divine house built by the gods, all its appurtenances designed for man's good cheer; a still more optimistic vision unfolds. This account must obviously be the most congenial to the cheerful and optimistic Charidemus (5) and indeed has been anticipated by his initial appeal to Homer (8). Man's life is like a splendid feast, banquet, or symposium, man's behaviour at which is conditioned by his individual nature (33 ~ 3). The symposiastic emphasis conveys a sly metatextual allusion to the influence on the *Charidemus* of Plato's[18] *Symposium*. The general conception of a beauteous and harmonious creation is acceptably Stoic and both Chrysippus and Epictetus use the symposium as an image for human life.[19] The contrast between porcine devotees of pleasure (33) and sober types who seek to understand the intelligent universe (41) makes a broad contrast between Epicureans (traditionally caricatured as pigs (Cic. *Pis.* 37; Hor. *Ep.* 1. 4. 15–16)) and Stoics. As in Dio's *Olympicus* (36. 7), Epicureanism is polemically misrepresented, and despite the Platonic framework the existential choice of philosophy lies between Epicureanism and Stoicism (as is often the case also in Dio's fellow-Stoics, Seneca and Marcus Aurelius).

Gross sensualists spend their time acquiring possessions and when they have to depart from life 'leave these behind' to others (34). This detail parallels and contrasts with the anxiety of the majority in the Orphic account to 'leave behind a successor to their punishment' (17): there, what is 'left behind' consists of a child; here, what is 'left behind' consists of possessions left *to* dependants. The drink on offer at life's symposium is Pleasure and there are two cup-bearers, Intelligence (*Nous*) (corresponding to reason in the Orphic account) and Intemperance (*Akrateia*). This contrasting pair evokes the two jars of Zeus in the *Iliad* and Prodicus/Xenophon's choice between Virtue and Vice/Pleasure. The majority of humans become drunk

---

[18] Trapp, below p. 224 n. 32, sceptical of any influence of Plato's *Symposium*, hazards an echo of Xenophon's (*Smp.* 1. 26) at 36.
[19] *SVF* 3: 768; Epict. 1. 24. 20, 2. 16. 37, *Ench.* 15.

on Intemperance, thereby insulting the gods' grace; by contrast the good temper their intake of pleasure with intelligence (42) and admire, observe, and try to understand the beauties of the house that is the universe (41). When they depart, they are anxious to be able to make some response to any enquirer about their observations (42).

The implications of this last detail are multiple and thought-provoking. The introduction's apparently trivial enquiry about people's well-being turns into profound philosophical enquiry (42 *punthanoito* ~ 1 *epunthanomen*). The response of the good to this enquiry is obviously exemplified by Charidemus' work within the *Charidemus* and presumably also by the *Charidemus* itself. The situation of the good at the end of their lives corresponds with the situations both of the gross sensualists, who 'leave behind' to dependants mere material possessions (34), and of the majority of humans in the Orphic account who need to 'leave behind' a child as 'successor to their punishment' (17). These parallelisms create a sense that both Charidemus' text within the *Charidemus* and Dio's *Charidemus* itself are their respective 'children', an idea for which there are important Platonic parallels: *Smp.* 209d 'everyone would prefer children of this sort to be born to them rather than human children, looking at Homer, Hesiod, and the other good poets, and envying the sort of offspring they leave behind them' and *Phaedrus* 275e (words have 'fathers'). The hypothesis that the *Symposium* is an important conceptual influence upon the *Charidemus* seems confirmed.[20] Presumably, however, the *recipients* of these texts, which are in one sense the 'bequests' of their 'fathers', are also to be regarded as 'children' or 'successors'.

The discussions of the virtuous recall Socratic dialectic: 'talking one to one, or peers in groups of twos or threes' (42). Further parallels are suggested: with Charidemus' death-bed dialectic with his loved ones (42 *dialegomenoi* ~ 6 *dielechthē* ~ 4 *dialegesthai*); with the Socratic dialogue that is the *Charidemus*; with the *Phaedo*, the Socratic dialogue behind the *Charidemus*; with the initial conversation between Dio and Charidemus' father and brother. And the interplay between Charidemus' *paizein* and *eleutherioi paidiai* (5) now suggests the Socratic/Platonic interplay between *paizein/paidia/paideia* (e.g. Plat. *Leg.* 2. 656c; Dio *Or.* 4. 30). It now becomes clear

---

[20] The *Symposium* similarly provides the framework of the myth in the first *Kingship Oration*: Moles (1990) 319.

that *eleutherioi* also proleptically distances Charidemus from the Orphic account and marks the *Charidemus* as a text conducive to philosophical 'freedom'. This whole series of parallels, including the present exposition of the *Charidemus* to fellow-Dionians, means that to read and interpret the *Charidemus* is itself a philosophical activity: our interpretation of it is part of the business of a right interpretation of human life and living. Such an observation is nowadays almost a truism of Platonic criticism: it remains, never-theless, important, and even more so in the case of a text such as the *Charidemus*, which is concerned not with first-order philoso-phical questions but with useful practical moralizing about the most difficult and painful areas of life.

Appropriately both to their beliefs and behaviour Epicurean pleasure-enthusiasts cling in unseemly fashion to life and have nothing to leave behind them and no hope of an afterlife. By con-trast, the virtuous depart exhibiting Socratic *phaidrotēs*, and those with whom God is particularly pleased (44 *arestheis* contrasts with 25 *dusarestos*) are called by him to be his fellow-symposiasts in an apparently everlasting bout of the nectar that represents the true sobriety. This apparent immortality is not Platonic, since *only* the elect survive, but reflects Stoic orthodoxy, though obviously no soul survives the next conflagration (in which Dio, unlike some contemporary Stoics, actually believed).[21] But in this generalized mythic context allusion to the conflagration would be inappropriate and perhaps insufficiently consolatory. The promise of immortality for the elect corresponds to the final section of the Orphic account (24). Clearly, Charidemus will belong in this company; hence a final consolation for his death (43–4).

Yet Dio's reaction to Charidemus' work is not unalloyed (45–6): while Charidemus has provided a wonderful *epideixis* not of words but of great and true manliness,[22] thereby validating his extraordin-ary promise and providing an inspiring *paradeigma*, Dio feels unable adequately to console his family, being unable indeed adequately to console himself. They all risk succumbing to Orphic pessimism (45 *bareōs pherein* ~ 8 *duscherōs pherein*). Here, as elsewhere, there is a sense that human beings can, as it were, to some extent 'write

---

[21] Euseb. *Praep. Ev.* 15. 20. 6 = *SVF* 2: 809 = Long-Sedley 53W; Moles (1995) 190.
[22] The first *Kingship Oration* works a similar 'redefinition' of *epideixis*: *Or.* 1. 61 ~ 1. 1 with Moles (1990) 326.

their own *logos'* of the universe. While it makes a big difference to the constitution of the universe and to the human condition within it whether God hates us (as in the Orphic account) or loves us (as in the second and third accounts), our own attitudes and behaviour have some effect on the sort of universe we live in. The challenge implicit in describing as *logoi* what are in some obvious senses 'myths' here becomes acute: one of the functions of such a description is to suggest that these 'myths' are to some degree realizable and thus to pose the question: have we the moral strength to flip the categories and turn *muthos* into *logos*?[23]

As for Timarchus father, only Timarchus son can lighten his misfortune by showing himself akin to Charidemus in virtue (the value of genetic kinship is much enhanced by kinship in virtue). Thus again, while Charidemus' virtue is exhibited in, and proved by, his dictated work, that wonderful work does not quite succeed in its proclaimed aim of consolation (6). It is an unsettling ending, the strongly affirmatory characterization of Charidemus (which corresponds to the final words of the *Phaedo*) segueing into only partial philosophical success on the key moral question of how we bear the terrible misfortunes inevitable in human life.[24]

STRUCTURAL AND VERBAL CONTROL

This summary already suggests some of the piece's considerable quality. Clearly, proper appreciation of the work would need to take greater account of its creative adaptation of the *Phaedo*, of its rich blending of Stoic and Platonic (cf. *Euboicus*, *Borystheniticus*, and *Olympicus*),[25] and of its intermixing of genres: dialogue, encomium, and consolation.

More directly relevant to the present enquiry is the piece's structural control, keyed by detailed verbal relationships and their dense interpretative implications. These detailed verbal relationships are

---

[23] The first *Kingship Oration* issues the same challenge: Moles (1990) 335–6.

[24] Menchelli's ((1997) 73–80) interpretation (the moral of the *Charidemus* is Socratic/Dionian *praotēs/epieikeia* in the acceptance of destiny) takes inadequate account of the ending's complexities (of which more below).

[25] *Euboicus*: Moles (1995) 179, Trapp, below, pp. 219–21, Brenk, below, pp. 270–5; *Borystheniticus*: Schofield (1991) 57–64, Trapp, pp. 214–19; *Olympicus*: cf. now Trapp, pp. 227–8; Trapp's chapter is an important contribution to the general topic.

everywhere, but the most marked examples occur between beginning and end, hence analysis of these relationships must form part of the interpretation of the end. Clearly, 45 *Charideme . . . tethnēkas* echoes 1 *Charidēmou teleutēs* and 2 *Charidēmou . . . tethnēkenai*; 45 *hōs polu . . . emelles* echoes 3 *epei kai . . . emellen esesthai* with a significant expansion of context: Charidemus would have excelled not merely in all Greece but among mankind; 45 *megalēs kai alethinēs andreias* echoes 5 *to . . . andreion . . . tou schēmatos* (before merely manliness of deportment, now full manliness of character); and 45 *egō men . . . pherein* echoes 2 *kai oimai . . . adelphou* (here no change: Dio remains inconsolable).

More importantly, 45 *hikanōs* echoes 1 *pro hikanou*, which means 'a considerable time before' but in juxtaposition with *prin humas idein* and in collocation with the travel terminology *parebalon deuri* and the indication of place *en Messēnēi*, suggests the association of *hikanos* with *hikneomai*. Then in 1 the man who knows nothing at all about Charidemus and his brother except their names[26] 'meets with Dio' (*entuchōn*); by contrast in 4 the dying Charidemus 'kept naming Dio' and gave his father and brother a significant message for when 'we should meet him' (*entuchōmen*). Thus the dramatic context of the *Charidemus* is itself the meeting that matters, in contrast to the chance and inchoate meeting of Dio and the man who knows nothing.

Time is similarly redefined: in 7 Timarchus father worries that Charidemus' dictated work may not be right, as having been spoken 'at such a time' (*en toioutōi kairōi*), whereas for Charidemus himself at 9 the fact that he is speaking at the *kairos* of his death gives his words authority. At the end of the work, in 45 and 46, the ideas of significant travel and significant place recur, with the words *hikanōs*, *atopon* and *prosēkōn*. *Prosēkōn* means 'being kin' but it is a travel word ('having arrived'), linking with *atopon* and looking back to the notions of travel and place in 1. Travel and place become metaphors (of course very common) for moral progress; at the end Dio himself has not reached his destination of full philosophical consolation for Charidemus' death (*oude . . . hikanōs*); Timarchus son, by contrast, must put himself in the same moral topos as that achieved by Charidemus: his journey has yet to begin. Of course the

---

[26] *Ou panu* can mean both 'not quite' and 'not at all' (*LSJ* s.v. *panu* 3), but context excludes Cohoon's 'not very well' (the man knows only the names).

text is itself a journey and both a metaphor for, and a means to, the moral progress to which all must aspire.[27] The different temporal perspectives of 45 also have their force: the death-bed recitation of Charidemus was the original *kairos*—the right time, but how should the various parties respond now? How of course also should we respond now? Is this, *now*, the topos, is this, *now*, the *kairos*, when the problems of the *Charidemus* and of human suffering will be resolved? For the moment Dio himself is disconsolate and will be unable to console the Timarchuses; the future for Timarchus son lies in emulation of Charidemus. The control of topography and time is exceedingly skilful and paralleled not only in Plato but in such Dionian works as the first *Kingship Oration*[28] and the *Borystheniticus*.[29]

The ending is indeed extraordinarily well-judged. Charidemus' text does not fully succeed in its philosophical purpose, but Dio's text (the immediate life beyond Charidemus' text) goes on and holds out the possibility that Timarchus son may emulate Charidemus' virtue as established both in Dio's text (the frame) and in Charidemus' own. Timarchus son in fact corresponds to the *diadochos* left behind mentioned both in the Orphic-Pythagorean account and—implicitly —in the worker of the land's account. He has a double aspect: the literal child and the philosophical child. The influence of the *Symposium* is again felt, and in context *tōn kalliston erasthēnai* (46) functions as a signal for the *Symposium*. And life goes on beyond the *two* texts: maybe in the future the combination of the two will bear real philosophical fruit—or maybe not. The ending dramatizes alike the strengths and the limitations of philosophical texts and teachers (cf. 4–5) *and* the possibility both of human philosophical failure (Dio) and eventual success (Timarchus son). And the pain of loss is not alleviated but the possibility is opened that the continuing practice of virtue by those left behind affords some compensation. It is a magnificent ending (about which there is yet more to say) and the richness of the literary conception and the deft skill of its midwifery look very Dionian.

If the complexities of the ending derive largely from the relationships—the potentially oppositional relationships—between text(s) and context(s)/life, those complexities can also be analysed

---

[27] Hence the dead/colourless metaphor 'go for' (9; *LSJ* s.v. *erchomai* B.1, 4) is brought to life. [28] Moles (1990) 322.
[29] Moles (1995), Trapp (1995).

in terms of the relationships between internal audiences and external audiences, in which respect the multi-layered and ambiguous implications of the ending may fruitfully be compared with those of the *Borystheniticus*.[30]

PROBLEMS OF INTERPRETATION

All the interpretative problems interrelate but it is formally convenient to take them one by one.[31]

1. Is Charidemus a real person (so von Arnim, Wilhelm, and Jones;[32] *contra* Bowie and Giner Soria)? Failing cogent epigraphic attestation,[33] the question is formally unresolvable but it remains crucial. Dio had pupils; on the other hand, he is adept at creating fictional situations for the exposition of philosophical doctrine (*Euboicus*, the *muthos/logos* section of the first *Kingship Oration*, etc.). The circumstantiality of the introduction could point towards truth or fiction: is it, like, say, that of the *Symposium*, so elaborate and so emblematic of wider themes as to convey its own artifice? The chances of Charidemus' reality would increase were there a significant disparity, whether philosophical or literary, between his exposition and Dio's own writings (as von Arnim, Nilsson, and Desideri believe there to be).

2. Is there then such a significant disparity? The answer is two-fold: if there is a disparity, it need not be significant (Charidemus expounds but rejects the Orphic account) and there is no real disparity in other respects, as the broadly Stoic colour of the 'worker of the land' section itself suffices to show[34] (there are obvious possible parallels with *Olympicus*, *Borystheniticus*, etc.).

3. Is Charidemus' work the transcript of the independent work that it purports to be? This already looks unlikely, and modern interpretations of parallels such as *Menexenus* and *Symposium* discourage such a simple reading, as do the intricate links between

---

[30] Russell (1992) 22–3, Moles (1995) 188–92.

[31] Cohoon (1939) 395–8 and Menchelli (1997) 67–73 usefully survey the problems.

[32] Jones (1978) 135.

[33] Ewen Bowie once (letter 27/8/80) alerted me to *IGR* 4. 1: K. Lollios Charidemos, who died aged 20 in Tenedos, a *sophistēs* from Byzantium: coincidence, I think, especially as the Dionian Charidemus was 22 (6).

[34] Wilhelm (1918) 364 well adduces parallels both philosophical and literary with Dio's works.

Charidemus' work and the dialogue frame and the correspondence between Charidemus' work and Socrates' last words.

The ground is cleared for a return to the question of Charidemus' reality with probability already against it. Clearly, 'Charidemus' is a significant name, whose associations of pleasure, joy, grace, etc., suit his adoption of the most optimistic account of the human condition, where man and god can interact with reciprocal *charis*.[35] Such a person brings joy to his *dēmos*: his particular *dēmos*, the *dēmos* of Greece and the human race within the *kosmos*. The name-play plus the extensive imitation of the *Phaedo* discourages taking 'Charidemus' at face value. Subtleties in the text reinforce this, as we shall see in connection with the next problem.

4. Should we identify the figures of the 'beggar', the 'certain difficult-to-please man, who had suffered many things in his life and only late had attained true education' and 'the worker of the land' with specific philosophers? Thus Dümmler, Hagen, and Sonny thought the difficult-to-please man might be Antisthenes, late convert to philosophy and gloomy Cynic *ponos* type, while for the 'worker of the land', Dümmler suggested Bion (who certainly used the symposium analogy (fr. 68 Kindstrand)) and Sonny suggested Cleanthes, who made a living by watering a garden and digging earth (Diog. Laert. 7. 168, 169, 171) and famously hymned Zeus. In this vein one might also hazard Musonius, Dio's revered teacher and proponent of the simple country life.[36]

But is the quest for specific identifications right? It is true that Charidemus encourages the idea, not only by the mention of these various figures and their differentiation but also by the seemingly rather banal gloss at 26 on divine colonization. Nor is it an objection that Charidemus in the early second century AD would be listening to philosophers of hundreds of years before: this is the timeless world of myth and such direct contact with earlier generations would reinforce the idea that choice of philosophical belief is much affected by individual personality. There is also the Stoic–Epicurean distinction in the third *muthos*. But that is much more broad-brush. The gloss could be an ironic allusion to pedestrian scholarly exegesis of a text, conveying a sophisticated double-edged irony: the reference

---

[35] Cf. 3 (*charienta*), 10 (first *logos* not *charieis*), 41 (gods' *charis*); other 'pleasure'/'displeasure' words then become relevant too.

[36] Musonius' influence on central aspects of Dio's thought is rightly stressed by Brunt (1973); Russell (1992) 4, and Brenk in this volume (pp. 262–4).

being primarily to Dio's own exegesis of the second account but secondarily to *our* exegesis of Dio.[37] Moreover, the text sometimes blurs who says what when. Chapters 10–24 mostly use *hoti* followed by accusative and infinitives, focalized by the difficult-to-please man and the beggar, with some harmless glosses by Charidemus, but 16 and 24 use straight indicatives: focalized by whom? The end of 19 is *huper hōn authis lexomen*: who sees, who speaks? Certainly not the difficult-to-please man. Moreover, while the beginning of the digression containing the teaching of the beggar is clearly marked, its ending is not, and 20–4 on the file of reason can hardly constitute a genuinely independent element: are the beggar and the difficult-to-please man therefore in some sense the same?[38] Again, Dio says of Charidemus (7): 'I do not yearn to know his style so much as his meaning'; Charidemus says (25): 'There is another account better than that, which I will say much more enthusiastically. I [first-person singular] heard it from a worker of the land in country rhythm and song; but perhaps I/we [first-person plural] do not need to imitate *that*: rather I/we shall try to recall his meaning.'[39] Who speaks? In the worker of the land's second song 39 to the end uses straight indicatives. At the end Dio cannot adequately console the bereaved father and brother; but Charidemus' work was a consolation: was Dio, then, the real speaker?

The question of specific philosophical identities also involves the question of Dio's sources: are the various suggested identities likely sources for their respective sections, or are there other more plausible sources? The latter conclusion would tend against specific philosophical identities.

Wilhelm argued forcefully for overriding (though not exclusive) Posidonian influence. While some Posidonian influence remains likely,[40] more important are Dio's direct use of the *Phaedo* and of the *Republic*[41] in the first account and (I believe) of the *Symposium*

[37] I suspect anyway neat reversal of Plat. *Symp.* 193a2: 'but now, because of our wickedness, we have been de-settled by god, like the Arcadians by the Spartans'.

[38] Cohoon (1939) 396–7.

[39] On the possible interaction of *Dia*, *Diōn* and *dianoia* see n. 17.

[40] Mainstream modern scholarship has rejected elaborate earlier reconstructions of Posidonian material based on extensive *Quellenforschung* in favour of austere concentration on attested fragments (notably Edelstein and Kidd (1972) and Kidd (1988) and in *OCD*[3] 1232). Wilhelm (1918) remains, however, a good example of the earlier approach, with some challenging detail (e.g. that both Posidonius and Dio use *hestiatōr* in the extremely rare sense of 'guest' rather than 'host').

[41] Trapp, pp. 223–5.

in all three accounts.[42] Most of the rest of the material could readily have been composed by anyone familiar (as Dio certainly was) with the comparison of the world to a feast or symposium and with standard arguments for and against design in the universe.

Platonic parallels, as nowadays read, also tell against the search for specific philosophical identities in such elusive figures. It is primarily their thematic functions that matter. Thus the beggar and worker of the land appropriately voice 'country wisdom' (cf. Diotima in the *Symposium* or the Arcadian shepherdess of Dio's first *Kingship Oration*), here reinforcing the damning portrayal of the great of this world, and the worker of the land naturally knows most about the physical world. The character of the spokesmen also underpins the link between personality/experience and choice of belief: the man who has suffered much naturally goes for the account which most emphasizes and least palliates suffering; as 'difficult-to-please', he is the opposite of the elect with whom God 'is pleased'. And the expression of philosophical doctrine through the mouths of representative figures helps to create that sense of distancing irony with which one must advance and regard myths about ultimate realities; irony that is explicit, for example, at 30.

Yet if the quest for specific philosophical identities is misconceived and thematic functions preponderate, the various figures may still be given identifying characters of a different kind. The beggar, author of part or whole of the first account, recalls the 'vagabond' Orphic priests (*agurtai*) of *Republic* 2, 364b,[43] thereby 'signing' the Orphic/*Phaedo* provenance of that account, and when Charidemus retails the Orphic account he may appropriately characterize himself as 'child of a beggar'[44] (with another allusion to the *Symposium*'s idea of 'literary paternity'). Similarly, the worker of the land might evoke Hesiod, since the worker's 'rustic' songs contain many elements which could be regarded as Stoic interpretation of Hesiodic material.[45] An implicit appeal to Hesiod's poetic authority would nicely balance the initial explicit appeal to Homer (8).

The Loeb editor, Cohoon, however, had already made a more radical suggestion which showed a fine feeling for Dio's distinctive thought world[46] (even if the terms in which Cohoon formulated the

---

[42] Trapp notes other Platonic traces, below, p. 224 n. 32.
[43] Noted by Trapp, p. 225 n. 33.   [44] Cf. n. 14.
[45] So Malcolm Schofield in conversation.
[46] Cohoon (1939) 396–8, followed by Moles (1978) 95 and n. 134.

suggestion were too straightforwardly biographical). The suggestion, which falls somewhere in the middle of specific philosophical identities, generalized representative figures, and literary identifications, was that the beggar and the difficult-to-please man recall Dio himself and that Charidemus' work reflects Dio's own religious odyssey (real or alleged). This is surely right. The intensity of Dio's self-projection in other pieces marks the allusion to the difficult-to-please man who had suffered many things in his life and only late had gained true education as typically self-referential: beggary, suffering (the exile), the celebrated late conversion to philosophy (a construct for which Dio himself bears the ultimate responsibility).[47] Closely parallel passages are *Or.* 1. 9: 'a wandering man and working in wisdom by myself, rejoicing for the most part as far as I can in labours and works, and uttering words for the sake of exhortation to myself and to those others whom I periodically encounter' and *Or.* 12. 51 (on the effect of Zeus' statue at Olympia) 'of humans, whoever . . . altogether labouring in soul, having endured in life many disasters and griefs, not even wrapping himself in sweet sleep, even he, I think, standing before this image [as Dio was when delivering the *Olympicus*], would forget all the terrible and difficult things which occur for suffering in human life'. Moreover, in the first *Kingship Oration* (50) Dio describes himself during the exile period as, precisely, an *agurtēs*. Within this sort of scenario he could also be dubbed a worker of the land.[48] All this would make 23 (on the beggar's 'manly' follow-through of the chain imagery) ironically self-referential in a literary sense, but this is a bonus, not a difficulty.

In the context of Charidemus' work the self-allusion suggests a move from Cynic pessimism to Stoic optimism (*mutatis mutandis* this can be paralleled elsewhere in Dio, e.g. in the aforementioned first *Kingship Oration*). The immodesty of such self-allusion would be characteristically Dionian and equally characteristically the self-allusion would not be merely immodest: Dio the seemingly external figure offers a paradigm of great internal relevance to the progression of the moral argument. The same is true in (e.g.) *Euboicus* and the first and fourth *Kingship Orations*.[49] The illogicality of Charidemus,

---

[47] Self-projection and conversion: Moles (1978).

[48] Cf. Philostr. *VS* 488 (with Moles (1978) 95) on Dio's alleged way of life during the exile.

[49] *Euboicus*: Moles (1995) 179–80; first *Kingship Oration*: Moles (1990) 310–12, 319–29; the fourth: Moles (1990) 348–9.

Dio's pupil, referring to Dio in this way is no objection, for, as we have seen, mythical time is not diachronic and the voice of 'Charidemus' is not univocal. Dio's own philosophical progression (real or alleged) powerfully underpins the cumulative and progressive persuasiveness of Charidemus' case. Cohoon also suggests, with some plausibility, that the lingering emphasis in 16–end on the long-lasting effects of disease glosses Dio's own experience.[50] This again puts Dio inside the Charidemus section.

5. How can Charidemus say that the Orphic account was given by a difficult-to-please man who had suffered much and only late attained true education and *then* claim that that account is not true and that there is another better account? There are two answers. First, there is truth and truth: the coda to the pessimistic Orphic account —the section on the file that is reason and on the gods' freeing of the virtuous and wise—adumbrates the fuller, more joyous, union of god and man promised by the worker of the land in 44; even the most pessimistic account gropes towards the truth. Secondly, since the description of the difficult-to-please man reflects the entire philosophical progression of Dio himself, the writer of the dialogue, the true education is represented not by the Orphic account but by the conclusion of Charidemus' work, the Stoic affirmation of God's goodness and man's potential for virtue and happiness.

THE DIONIAN *CHARIDEMUS*

The presence of Dio's philosophical progression in the text makes it reasonable to hypothesize another connection with Dio's life. This hypothesis has already been published by Ewen Bowie[51] but merits full-scale, if to some extent speculative, development.

The *Charidemus* looks like a late work: Dio is the great philosopher, widely so recognized, he has a pupil, who died aged 22. He alludes elliptically to his celebrated, if fraudulent, conversion. In

---

[50] The emphasis is characteristic: Moles (1978) 95.

[51] Bowie (1985) 671: 'if Charidemus is fictitious, we may suspect that the tender pathos of the introduction derives its power from the attested early death of Dio's own son'. My battered second volume of the Loeb Dio has a pencilled 'Dio as father!?!' on p. 401, a scholion inserted on a Skopelos beach in August 1976, but neither Ewen nor I can remember who first advanced the hypothesis in our conversations about Dio in the 1970s.

his late post-exilic phase Dio was old (60 or more) and sick (cf. 16). Like the difficult-to-please man he had suffered many *lupai*. Despite everything, he maintained his Stoic belief in divine goodness and providence and man's capacity for virtue and happiness (*Olympicus*, *Borystheniticus*). In, or before, 110 his wife and one of his (probably two) sons died (Plin. *Epp.* 10. 81–2). We do not *know* that this was the son who had been an archon in Prusa in 102 (*Or.* 50. 2), that is, that son, then over 30, in whom Dio had had such great hopes and whose nature and virtue he claimed as equal to his own (*Or.* 40. 2), but, for reasons that will emerge, we may strongly suspect it. Disdaining the Roman imperial cult, Dio buried his wife and son in a building beside a statue of Trajan (Plin. loc. cit.). To commemorate and eulogize his son and to console himself he wrote the *Charidemus*, which was one of his last works. But as a fundamentally good man (for so I increasingly believe), he wished to help others as well as himself (to 'leave something behind'), hence he tried to transmute his personal grief into a universalizing exploration and explanation of the human condition in all its suffering in the shape of a literary work whose imaginative creativity and interpretative complexity would give pleasure as well as comfort, pleasure, indeed, that would itself reinforce the case for a fundamentally optimistic reading of life.

Thus the *Charidemus* is at once intensely personal *and* universalizing and objective, and it is this doubleness of perspective which gives it its special poignancy and explains some otherwise puzzling emphases. On the one hand, are Dio's externalness and the transformation of his son into a *meirakion* of 22, poised between youthful promise and mature fulfilment, the extreme untimeliness of whose death maximizes the pain of loss and poses the theoretical question of human suffering in its acutest form, but whose fictional name offers true hope.

On the other hand, are Dio's intense internalness and the hints that he is suffering like a peculiarly close member of the family: 'I think that I myself was not much less pained than you; for to say "more pained" would not be right or proper for me, if someone loved him more than you, his father and brother did' (2); or at the end (45): 'I for my part do not know how to console you, bereft of such a man, so as not to bear it hard; for I am not able sufficiently to console myself for the present. You, Timarchus, alone can lighten the burden of this father'. 'This father': in a work so skilful in its blurring of focalization, this father can also be Dio. So, too, the dying Charidemus' anxiety to leave a message for Dio and his self-characterization as 'child of a beggar' (20); the persistent (and not very Stoic) concern of the *logoi* with the possibility of immortality for the virtuous;[52] and the final inability of Charidemus' work to provide complete philosophical consolation; instead, the consolations of family and kinship, even if kinship reinforced by kinship in virtue. Thus Dio the philosopher sought ultimate consolation in his surviving son, who he hoped would fulfil the promise of the dead one. There is some move from philosophy to life, though philosophy is not abandoned.

On this hypothesis, Charidemus must be Dio's elder son, who must have died when Dio was away from Prusa, hence Dio's absence from the death-bed of 'Charidemus', a circumstance which must greatly have increased Dio's distress. Timarchus son must represent Dio's younger son. Charidemus: a significant name; Dio, too, a significant name. Why 'Timarchus' father and son? It would help if an inscription turned up showing that Dio's second son was called Dion;[53] other than that, Charidemus obviously needs a dramatic father; and since as a *meirakion* he can hardly have a legitimate son of his own, a younger brother is the next best thing; in terms of the 'logic' of the *logoi* it is important that he should have a *diadochos* of some kind, but this younger brother is also Dio's younger son, Dio's sole remaining genetic *diadochos*. Hence, just as Timarchus son is both a literal and a philosophical child, so 'Charidemus' is both the work of that name which is one of Dio's philosophical children and the literal son whom he had lost (doubly therefore 'child of a beggar'). The *Symposium* again underpins the implicit argument. Timarchus the father also of course (!) represents Dio the father of two sons. All this might seem to make the *Charidemus* like a 'soap' which has spiralled into absurdity under the progressive revelation of ever less plausible personal and family relationships. But such fusion/confusion of roles is not self-confuting:[54] witness the first *Kingship Oration*, the *Olympicus*—or the *Aeneid*.

As for the name *Timarchus*, Timarchus father tells Dio at the beginning (4): 'Charidemus seemed to me to *protiman* [to honour more or before] you even before me, his father, not only before other

---

[52] This is insufficiently explained by Socrates' arguments in the *Phaedo* for the immortality of the soul, especially given *Charidemus'* restriction of immortality to the virtuous.   [53] But cf. Salmeri, above, p. 89 n. 176.
[54] Moles (1995) 183 n. 23.

people ... and he did this till the very end'. Dio at the beginning and end of the work; at the beginning and end of Charidemus' life; Dio the philosophical beginning, the philosophical ruler, the philosophical writer, the genetic beginner of his own son. Dio, but also Zeus (*Dia*/*Diōn*): in a Stoic *kosmos* Zeus is 'author' of *everything*. But Dio himself is also a 'Timarchus', because he Dio, philosophical *archōn*, genetic and philosophical son of Zeus, *honours* the rule of the gods (27 *archontas*). Gods and men are kin; the gods inevitably superior; human beings akin to one another in the shared kinship of humankind may also be akin in the genetic kinship of families; they should strive to promote the kinship of virtue which will maximize their shared kinship with God. Within these interlocking relationships, both horizontal and vertical, Dio is the great mediator (*Diōn*/*Dia*).[55] As always, his arrogance is superb (it is one of his most attractive qualities), but this arrogance also subserves the need to establish the essential relationships between man and God and to activate the links between them. And the arrogance is also tempered by the grief of a father for his son and by the larger allegorical implications.

Thus the hypothesis that Dio wrote the *Charidemus* in response to the death of his son is not simply an interesting external factor which might help to explain the work's intensity: the death of his son is inscribed in the text.

Such an allegorical interpretation does not restrict these allegorical figures to the personal and individual: they are all also generalized allegorical figures representing different aspects of a positive human response to God. Dio is also the representative of Zeus; Charidemus is also simultaneously Charidemus, a dramatic character in a Platonic dialogue; a latter-day Socrates; the messenger between god and man; 'Everyman'; Timarchus is also the honourer of *archē* in various senses. And given the general influence of the *Symposium* on the *Charidemus*, the names *Dio* and *Timarchus* must also be fragmentations of *Dio-tima*: this further name-play signalling not only the influence of the *Symposium* but the divine authority and the thoroughgoing piety of Dio's great text.

Yet the identification of Dio as the real grieving father at the end of the work enormously enhances its emotional power. Ideally, we should accept the optimistic Stoic account of the human condition,

---

[55] Cf. also n. 17.

but for real-life suffering humans the practical implementation of that account remains fitful and problematic. Even Dio, the great philosopher, the representative of Zeus, the almost mythic figure, whose philosophical biography underpins Charidemus' progressive exposition, even this Dio must suffer loss and pain like any human being, must find them hard to bear, yet strive to endure. Nowhere did Dio, master of the art, create a more persuasive or moving *persona* or *ēthos* than at the end of the *Charidemus* and it is per- suasive and moving precisely because it is true.[56] And when Dio wrote of the inheritance of Timarchus the son and the future death of Timarchus the father, he must have been conscious that his own death was near at hand. Thus Charidemus also represents Dio him- self, 'father' of the discourse, and we, its readers, are his 'children', challenged as he himself is in the outer text, to translate philosophical text into moral reality in our own lives.

There is, however, another, intensely humanizing, factor in play.[57] Though the ending suggests some philosophical failure, there is also a sense that such *lupē* is natural and to a degree justifiable. For at the start of the work, which, as we have seen, rings with the end, the Opuntian's[58] cold reaction to the loss of his son, who is like Charidemus in being both *charieis* and *kompsos*, is roundly con- demned. That is the sort of reaction commended by Dio's steely fellow-Stoic Epictetus.[59] Thus on another level, Dio moves away from the austerities of orthodox Stoicism to a more practical and humane Panaetianism. The travel imagery of 45–6 glosses Panaetian *prokopē* (moral 'progress'), which is intrinsically ambiguous: alike formally second best to full Stoic *sophia* and the real moral locus of life. Earlier ideas in the text, for example that different person- alities accept different doctrines and that individual nature produces different behaviour, and the appeal to *to prepon* (25) help to put Panaetius potentially in the frame from the very beginning. So if the ending exhorts us to translate philosophical text into moral reality, there is some doubt about which text we should be reading, that

[56] This principle is sometimes recognized in ancient literary criticism, e.g. Arist. *Po.* 9, 1451[b]16.

[57] The *Charidemus* is one of several Dionian works which challenge the judgement of Jones (1978) 130 that 'Dio was not by nature warm or sympathetic'.

[58] Donald Russell finds the text's allusion to *touton ton Opountion* (3) problematic; but if so, it is problematic irrespective of the authorship of the *Charidemus*, and in any case it is explicable as the sort of studiedly untidy detail which promotes realism.

[59] E.g. 3. 24. 85–6; 4. 1. 107, 111; *Ench.* 3, 11.

which expounds Stoic perfectionism or that which gives full dignity to the moral struggle. This, I repeat, is a wonderfully rich ending to what is surely a great work.

There is yet another aspect to the work's moral integrity. Dio was for decades the friend and adviser of powerful Romans, perhaps even of Roman emperors,[60] and his attitude to Roman power has been much discussed, not least in Simon Swain's magisterial recent study.[61] It might seem eccentric to canvass this question here. But the *Charidemus* is at once a universalizing text, concerned with the whole human condition, so that worldly power inevitably comes into the theoretical frame, and an intensely personal text, which should give us access to what Dio 'really thought'. But the text is solidly Greek and when Dio reflects on what Charidemus might have achieved, it is in the context of his city or all Greece; yet Charidemus was going greatly to surpass the men of his generation, which must include non-Greeks (45 ~ 3). Moreover, the third account registers sharp contempt for worldly power and imperial struggles (35 (allegorized)). Thus in the time of his grief for his son Dio felt nothing for the Roman Empire and rejected its militaristic ethos, and he implicitly commended these attitudes to his readers (Roman as well as Greek).

* * *

On this analysis the *Charidemus* is as good as anything that Dio wrote, in fact very much better than most of Dio's surviving works (at least as preserved):[62] it is of the same calibre as the first, second, and fourth *Kingship Orations*, the *Euboicus*, the *Olympicus*, and the *Borystheniticus*, the works on which Dio's claims to greatness, or sublimity, rest. Indeed, to my taste, in its sheer courage, its philosophical grip, its generalizing power and its literary virtuosity, the piece surpasses Plutarch's acclaimed *Consolation to his Wife*. Clearly, the *Charidemus* is by someone very familiar with Dio's works, with his ways of thinking, with his manner of self-projection, which is at once brash and subtle, and with the complex riches of his literary technique. It is far superior to anything produced by Favorinus, whose imitations of Dio in *Orr.* 37 and 64 are flat indeed. If it is

---

[60] I do not accept the determined minimalism of Sidebottom (1996).
[61] Swain (1996) 187–241.
[62] For of course the relationship between the text as transmitted and 'the original(s)' is often particularly problematic in Dio.

by a pupil, we have a single work of supreme quality by a pupil extremely close to Dio of whom we otherwise know nothing. The very possibility seems remote. But in any case, the view that the *Charidemus* may be spurious rests on a simple misconception, for neither of the two great scholars cited in favour of this view, von Arnim and Nilsson (who in fact merely follows von Arnim), denied that Dio wrote the frame of the work; they claimed only the independence of Charidemus' putative contribution. But that claim is, as we have seen, untenable, indeed quite naïve. Yet the *Charidemus* as a whole is anything but naïve.

Let us then unreservedly welcome the *Charidemus* back into the canon of Dio's works and salute its greatness: its immense literary resource, its profound philosophical seriousness, and its deep humanity.

PART FOUR

Philosophy

9

Plato in Dio

MICHAEL TRAPP

Plato's name is not often mentioned in the surviving corpus of Dio's work, occurring only five times in the seventy-six genuine pieces; even if three further thinly veiled allusions are added, that only yields a total of eight.[1] Yet appreciation of his influence is essential to a proper understanding of Dio. Ancient and Byzantine critics give a prominent place to the relationship between the two authors, but consider it in almost purely stylistic terms.[2] As will emerge, this is too restrictive; the reality is more complicated and more interesting. Plato is indeed acknowledged and imitated by Dio as a model of good prose style (in several distinct registers), but the imitation and appropriation extend also to elements of structure and characterization; and besides his stylistic importance, he also inhabits Dio's discourses as an intellectual authority, and as a model for philosophical action. Examination of Plato in Dio will therefore shed light not only on Dio's literary composition—the nature of his building blocks, and the texture of his finished products—but also his self-presentation as thinker and doer, and as upholder of cultivated values. In doing this, it will also, naturally, illuminate the values and expectations, the cultural horizons, of the audiences he addressed. And it will, equally clearly, expand and refine our sense of the importance of Plato in the high culture of the first and second centuries AD.

---

[1] *Orr.* 2. 47, 8. 1, 36. 26–9, 37. 32, and 53. 2; plus 5. 3, 7. 129, and 54. 4. For comparison, there are ten mentions of Aristotle, five each of Xenophon and Zeno, three of Demosthenes, two of Antisthenes, one each of Aeschines Socraticus, Chrysippus, and Cleanthes, and about fifty apiece of Socrates and Diogenes. Two lost works, mentioned by the *Suda*, have Plato's name in their titles; on these, see below, pp. 222–3, 234–5.

[2] Philostr. *VS* 486–8; Menander Rhetor 3. 411. 29 Sp.; Photius, *Bibl.* cod. 209, 106. 25–107. 27 Henry; Arethas, scholion on *Orr.* 1–4 (*Urb. gr.* 124) *ad fin.* For the texts see von Arnim (1893–6) 2: 311–28 and Cohoon and Lamar Crosby (1932–51) 5: 362–417; illuminating discussion in Brancacci (1985) 92–3, 99, 111–22, 211–20, 239–44.

I shall look first at Dio's most overtly Platonizing piece, followed by six other major orations in which Plato's presence, though not quite so pervasive and so close to the surface, is none the less a major constituent. I shall then survey other, more localized instances of imitation and evocation of Plato through the remainder of the corpus, so as to clarify (and classify) the different levels on which the process operates. In conclusion, I shall ask how evenly (or otherwise) the Platonic material is distributed in Dio, and on what particular parts of the Platonic corpus he concentrates his attention; and I shall attempt to place his relationship to Plato against the broader canvas of literary and philosophical activities in the first two centuries.

THE *BORYSTHENITICUS* (OR. 36)

I begin, then, with one of Dio's most richly worked orations, delivered in Prusa, and telling the story of an encounter and a speech in a far-away and rather odd location.[3] Travelling during his exile,[4] Dio reaches the once prosperous, now ramshackle, town of Borysthenes, on the very edges of the Greek world. Strolling by the banks of the river Hypanis, he is met by a group of locals, one of whom is the handsome young Callistratus; engaging him in conversation, Dio teaches him a gentle lesson about the folly of looking for political wisdom in Homer alone, for all that Homer is the only poet generally esteemed in these frontier regions of Hellenism. But a barbarian attack is feared, so Dio and his audience move for safety's sake from outside the city walls to the temple of Zeus, which also serves as the *bouleutērion* of the Borysthenites. Here Dio begins a disquisition about the true city, touching on the cosmic dimensions of this theme, but apparently intending to concentrate on its earthly aspect. He is, however, interrupted by one Hieroson, a venerable individual who identifies himself as a devotee not only of Homer but also—along with some few others of the local populace—of Plato. Hieroson begs Dio to change tack:

[3] Delivery in Prusa is alleged in the title (ὃν ἀνέγνω ἐν τῇ πατρίδι); this is neither supported nor contradicted in the text, but there seems no reason to doubt it. On Dio's evocation of place in this oration, see Trapp (1995). See also Anderson, above, pp. 145–50.

[4] During, not after, the period of exile: μετὰ τὴν φυγήν in 36. 1 is an interpolation, perhaps misplaced from the title line (Russell (1992) 211); the true state of affairs is to be inferred from κατελθεῖν in 25 (ibid. 224).

For although we are unacquainted with this more refined form of philosophy, yet we are, as you know, lovers of Homer, and some, not many, lovers of Plato too. To this latter group I myself belong, for I always read his writings as best I can; and yet it may perhaps seem odd that one who speaks barbaric Greek should delight in the man who is the most Greek and the most wise of poets, and should cultivate that man's society, quite as if a person almost wholly blind were to shun every other light but turn his gaze upward to the sun itself.

. . . [I]f you wish to do us all a favour, postpone your discussion of the mortal city . . . and tell us instead about that divine city or government . . . stating where it is and what it is like, aiming as closely as possible at Plato's freedom of style, just as you seemed to me to be doing a moment ago. For if we understand nothing else, we do understand at least his language because of our long familiarity with it, for it is grand and not far off Homer.[5]

Dio accedes. To the Borysthenites, he reports, he modestly denied any intention to vie with the old masters; but to his Prusan audience he admits in retrospect that mention of Homer and Plato had moved and inspired him. He then launches into his account of the heavenly city, which moves from fairly sober exposition of standard Stoic doctrine[6] to a weird and wonderful myth of the Magi, in which the cosmos is compared to a team of celestial horses. At the very end of the speech, he apologizes if the loftiness of the myth has resulted in unclarity,[7] and begs his (Prusan) audience to blame not him, but the Borysthenites who egged him on to it.

Whatever else is going on in this speech (and there is a great deal), it is clear that Dio is claiming to be following in Plato's footsteps to some extent, and doing so quite openly. But to what extent; and does the explicit claim in fact tell the whole truth?

---

[5] *Borystheniticus* 26–7 (Loeb translation, adapted) τῆς μὲν γὰρ ἀκριβεστέρας ταύτης φιλοσοφίας ἄπειροί ἐσμεν, Ὁμήρου δέ, ὡς οἶσθα, ἐρασταὶ καί τινες οὐ πολλοὶ Πλάτωνος· ὧν δὴ κἀμὲ ὁρᾷς ὄντα, ἀεί ποτε ἐντυγχάνοντα τοῖς ἐκείνου ὅπως ἂν δύνωμαι· καίτοι ἴσως ἄτοπον βαρβαρίζοντα τῶν ποιητῶν μάλιστα τῷ ἑλληνικωτάτῳ καὶ σοφωτάτῳ χαίρειν καὶ ξυνεῖναι, καθάπερ εἴ τις μικροῦ τυφλὸς τὸ μὲν ἄλλο φῶς ἀποστρέφοιτο, πρὸς αὐτὸν δὲ τὸν ἥλιον ἀναβλέποι . . . σὺ δὲ εἰ θέλεις πᾶσιν ἡμῖν χαρίσασθαι, τὸν μὲν ὑπὲρ τῆς θνητῆς πόλεως ἀναβαλοῦ λόγον, . . . περὶ δὲ τῆς θείας εἴτε πόλεως εἴτε διακοσμήσεως . . . εἰπὲ ὅπῃ τε καὶ ὅπως ἔχει, ὡς δύνασαι ἐγγύτατα τείνων τῆς τοῦ Πλάτωνος ἐλευθερίας περὶ τὴν φράσιν, οἷον δὴ καὶ ἄρτι ποιεῖν ἡμῖν ἔδοξας. εἰ γὰρ μηδενὸς ἄλλου, τῆς γε φωνῆς ξυνίεμεν ὑπὸ συνηθείας ὅτι οὐ σμικρὸν οὐδὲ πόρρω τοῦ Ὁμήρου φθέγγεται.
[6] See Schofield (1991) 64–92.
[7] *Borystheniticus* 61 ἐπᾶραι τὸν λόγον οὐκ ὀκνήσαντες . . . εἰ δὲ ἀτέχνως ὑψηλόν τε καὶ ἐξίτηλον ἀπέβη τὸ τοῦ λόγου σχῆμα.

If we restrict our attention initially to the direct mention of Plato's name, which Dio puts into Hieroson's mouth, we see an analysis of Plato that concentrates on the general conceptual and linguistic style of his philosophizing, in particular on his avoidance of mean technicality and philosophical formulae in favour of something more sweeping and free in expression.[8] For Dio's purposes the most important element in this is the stylistic claim, the scope of which extends both forward, to the main set-piece discourse in 29–60 (including the Magian myth), and back to its interrupted 'trailer' in 18–23 ('just as you seemed to me to be doing a moment ago'). Dio spoke for the Borysthenites and the Prusans, and writes for us, in imitation of the Platonic free grand style, that marked by 'the avoidance of regular periods or contrived figures in the interests of producing natural emotive effects',[9] to which Plato himself was supposedly led by his reading of Homer. It is a claim that is amply justified by Dio's actual performance, both in what precedes and in what follows it: see for instance the single-sentence account of cosmic concord that constitutes the whole of 22, or (from among several possible examples) the description of the process of *palingenesia* in 55–7. But what these examples simultaneously make clear is that claiming to follow Plato stylistically means also claiming to follow him in theme: the free grand style goes naturally with exalted subject-matter of just the kind that is in question. Dio himself takes care to draw attention to the loftiness of his subject-matter, not only in his concluding apology for perhaps 'flying too high', but perhaps also, more subtly, in Hieroson's encouragement to him to '*stretch as near as you can to Platonic freedom of diction*'.[10]

But it is also easy to see that Dio is not aiming simply at a generally Platonic effect, either in subject-matter or in style. There are

---

[8] Plato is seen as characterized not only by ἐλευθερία περὶ τὴν φράσιν, but also by the absence in him of ἀκριβεστέρα φιλοσοφία; for the purposes of this oration at least, he is distanced from the more scholastic approach seen as characteristic of Aristotle and the Hellenistic schools. For this perception both of Plato and of later philosophers, compare especially Max. Tyr. 4. 1–7 and 26. 2, with Trapp (1997), pp. xxiv–xxv.

[9] Russell (1992) 225, on 36. 27. This is an analysis of Plato familiar (in disapproving vein) from Dionysius of Halicarnassus *Demosth.* 5–7 and *Ep. Pomp.* 2, and (more positively, together with the link to Homer) [Longinus] *Sublim.* 13 and 32. 5–8.

[10] ὡς ἐγγύτατα τείνων: an exhortation which is itself couched in Platonic phraseology: for τείνω used to express similarity, see *Crat.* 402c, *Tht.* 169a and, especially, *Phdo* 65a and *Resp.* 548d, in both of which it is qualified by ἐγγύς τι; and for frequent occurrences of ἐγγύτατα in Plato, see Ast (1835–8) s.v. ἐγγύς.

specific Platonic precedents at work, with which comparison is being challenged. Most obviously, as I have argued elsewhere,[11] both the 'trailer' in 18–23 and the Magi's curious image of the cosmic chariot-team in 39–60 are built round imitation and reworking of the celebrated myth of the *Phaedrus*, in which not only the broad concept but an extensive series of points of detail and items of vocabulary and phraseology evoke the Platonic original. But even within these two sections, more than one Platonic precedent is in play. The careful distinction between the different colours of the horses in the cosmic team and their relative velocities (43–7) follows the description of the different colours and speeds of the whorls on the spindle of Necessity in the Myth of Er in *Republic* 616c–617b.

Platonic reference, moreover, is not confined to the Magian myth and to 18–23. We see it also in Dio's framing account of his encounter with Callistratus and the other Borysthenites by the Hypanis, outside the city walls, in his preliminary discussion with Callistratus about good and bad poets and their definition, and in his remarks on poetic inspiration at the start of his culminating disquisition (33–5). The master-model in all this is again the *Phaedrus*,[12] but once more other sources are not excluded. The comparison of teachers to sellers of food and drink in 11, and the picture of Dio's and Callistratus' audience working hard to keep in step behind them recall the *Protagoras* (313d–314b, 315b); the question raised in 21 about qualities of rulers and qualities of communities picks up *Republic* 429a; and Callistratus' encouragement to Dio to proceed as much for the audience's sake as for his own[13] recalls a stereotypical moment from the dialogues seen, for instance, at *Gorgias* 458b–d and *Protagoras* 335d. Equally, it is again Platonic style that is in question as well as Platonic substance. As in the myth he imitates Plato's grand style, so in the earlier stages of the oration Dio imitates his equally celebrated skill in scene-setting, and in the recording of dialogue: the former in 1–6 (where the detail, but not the presentation, is Herodotean);[14] the latter in the exchange with Callistratus in 10–15,

[11] Trapp (1990) 148–50.

[12] Ibid. 150–2, adding the further observation that the whole structure of the story told in the oration (encounter; first exchange, centred on a challenge to the interlocutor's favourite authority; first, provisional speech by Dio; second, definitive speech, with myth) also echoes that of the first half of the *Phaedrus* (speech of Lysias; first speech of Socrates; Socrates' palinode).

[13] ἐπεὶ καὶ τούσδε ὁρᾷς πάντας ἐπιθυμοῦντας ἀκοῦσαί σου.

[14] Cf. Russell (1992) 212, on 36. 1.

where Dio takes on the Socratic role of the authoritative questioner, steering the discussion with a gentle but firm hand, and showing up the inadequacy of his interlocutor's comfortable convictions.

Plato is thus for Dio in the *Borystheniticus* a stylistic and literary model, a source of themes, and the creator (in Socrates) of the role of authority that Dio co-opts for himself in this story of his own past achievements. It would, however, be wrong to conclude that the relationship is one that operates on a purely literary level, and that it involves no endorsement of Plato's intellectual status, or of the content of his thought. Besides commenting on his similarity to Homer, Hieroson is made to describe Plato as 'most Greek and most wise', pre-eminent like the sun—a compliment which of course praises Plato in terms borrowed from his own most famous image for transcendent pre-eminence.[15] More subtly, in the first part of his discourse about the true city, before Hieroson's interruption, Dio *in propria persona* begins with a sermon on the need for proper definitions: it is the mark of the truly educated individual 'to discern clearly the distinctive identity of the subject of discussion', that is to say 'what kind of thing it is, and in what respect it is identical to nothing else'.[16] This is a characteristic emphasis of Plato's Socrates, noted particularly in the *Phaedrus* (237b–c, cf. Albinus, *Isagoge* 1), but it is here given as a lesson well learned by all serious thinkers.

The *Borystheniticus*, then, provides a particularly rich instance of Platonizing on Dio's part. The Plato of this oration, if of no other, is both a philosophical and a literary model. Dio's imitation covers both mythological and dialectical modes, and their appropriate styles; it extends from individual phrases and sentence-formulae to the architecture of individual episodes, and indeed to the structure of the whole work; and it allows him to present himself both as a Plato and as a Socrates, challenging comparison with the hero of the dialogues as well as with their author. He takes a particular, cele-brated dialogue as his central point of reference, but blends in a wide range of other Platonic material as well. We now have to ask how far this individual oration is characteristic of Dio's *œuvre* as a whole. Is Plato in fact less important to Dio's endeavours in general than he is in this one privileged instance? The answer seems to be that, while the *Borystheniticus* is indeed an extreme case, it is by no means

---

[15] Cf. Max. Tyr. 11. 1, where the same image is used for the same purpose.

[16] *Borystheniticus* 18–19 γνῶναι σαφῶς ὅ τι ἐστὶν αὐτὸ ὑπὲρ οὗ ὁ λόγος . . . ὁποῖόν τι καὶ καθ' ὃ μηδενὶ τῶν ἄλλων ταὐτόν.

an isolated one. In no other oration do we find Plato as both topic and model, both named and assessed, and made the object of literary mimesis; but it is easy to point to further examples of each phenomenon on its own. We shall look first at the handful of other cases where Plato's qualities as writer and thinker come under discussion, then at the much larger category of Dio's Platonic mimesis outside the *Borystheniticus*.

ASPECTS OF THE *REPUBLIC*: ORR. 7 AND 53

There are in fact only two other cases where Plato is named and his authority put under discussion; both concern aspects of the *Republic*, but they vary interestingly in their tone and focus.[17] In one of them, something like the respect displayed in *Or.* 36 is again on view; in the other, respect is tempered by a measure of self-congratulatory reproof.

Or. 7, the *Euboicus*, is, like the *Borystheniticus*, a work that begins with a scene from the exile years (1–80), from which discussion of a more serious political theme emerges (81–151). This time, however, the presentation of the political matter is more direct, in argumentative rather than mythological mode. Beginning with a defence of the virtues of the life of the poor, formulated as a refutation of a *sententia* from Euripides (*El.* 424–31), Dio turns in 103 to the more limited issue of the proper occupations of the specifically urban poor. This topic almost inevitably conjures up Plato's exercise in city-founding and role-definition in the *Republic*, and sure enough by 107 Dio is already to be found speaking in Platonic tones of theoretical expulsions from the city.[18] It is, however, in 129 ff. that the Platonic reference becomes fully operative, as Dio defends the ample scale and apparently digressive nature of his own political treatise, with a hunting image (good huntsmen follow the best trail available at any given moment, cf. e.g. *Resp.* 432d, *Parm.* 128c) followed by an explicit appeal to the precedent of the *Republic*:

---

[17] The only other places where Plato is named are *Or.* 2. 47, where the young Alexander is made to praise him for his observation (*Resp.* 404b) that Homer's heroes did not eat fish; and 8. 1, where he features fleetingly in a biography of Diogenes. For completeness's sake, note also 5. 3, where a near-quotation from *Laws* 722d is marked as such with the formula ὡς ἔφη τις; and 54. 4, where Plato is present by implication in an allusion to those friends of Socrates who preserved his words and teaching for posterity.

[18] *Euboicus* 107 ἐκβαλεῖν ἐκ τῶν πόλεων τῷ λόγῳ.

Neither should we, perhaps, find fault with someone who set out to discuss the just man and justice and then, having mentioned a city for the sake
of illustration, expatiated at much greater length on the constitution of a
state and did not grow weary until he had enumerated all the variations
and the kinds of constitutions, setting forth very clearly and magnificently
the features characteristic of each; even though he does find critics here and
there who take him to task for the length of his discussion and the time
spent on—for heaven's sake—the illustration. But if the criticism is that his
remarks on the state have no bearing on the matter in hand, and that not
the least light has been shed on the subject of investigation which led him
into the discussion at the start—for these reasons, if for any, it is not altogether unfair to call him to task. So if we too shall be found to be expound-
ing matters that are not pertinent or germane to the question before us, then
we might be found guilty of prolixity. But, strictly speaking, it is not fair
on other grounds to commend or to criticize either length or brevity in a
discourse.[19]

In this interestingly nuanced passage, Dio, elegantly summarizing Books 2–5 and 8–9 of the *Republic*, acknowledges Plato as an
authoritative predecessor in the field of political discourse (method-
ical, ample, clear, weighty), and at the same time claims his authority
for a particular (virtuously 'digressive') mode of presentation. But
the passage is not without a critical edge. While making a show of
defending Plato against one form of criticism, Dio implies that he
is vulnerable to another, and moreover that he himself, while following
what is good in Plato's example, has managed to avoid what is not.
He endorses the criticism—known in modern times too—that, for
all the interest of its political sections, the *Republic* does not in the
end succeed in marrying together its ethical-psychological and its
political matter closely enough to justify the generous allocation of
space to the latter.[20] There may also be further polemical edge to

---

[19] *Euboicus* 130–2 ἴσως οὖν οὐδὲ ἐκεῖνο μεμπτέον, ὅστις περὶ ἀνδρὸς δικαίου
καὶ δικαιοσύνης λέγειν ἀρξάμενος, μνησθεὶς πόλεως παραδείγματος ἕνεκεν,
πολλαπλάσιον λόγον ἀναλώσειν περὶ πολιτείας, καὶ οὐ πρότερον ἀπέκαμε πρὶν
ἢ πάσας μεταβολὰς καὶ ἅπαντα γένη πολιτείων διεξῆλθε, πάνυ ἐναργῶς τε καὶ
μεγαλοπρεπῶς τὰ ξυμβαίνοντα περὶ ἑκάστην ἐπιδεικνύς, εἰ καὶ παρά τισιν αἰτίαν
ἔχει περὶ τοῦ μήκους τῶν λόγων καὶ τῆς διατριβῆς τῆς περὶ τὸ παράδειγμα
δήπουθεν· ἀλλ' ὡς οὐδὲν ὄντα πρὸς τὸ προκείμενον τὰ εἰρημένα καὶ οὐδ' ὁπωστιοῦν
σαφεστέρου δι' αὐτὰ τοῦ ζητουμένου γεγονότος, οὗπερ ἕνεκεν ἐξ ἀρχῆς εἰς τὸν
λόγον παρελήφθη, διὰ ταῦτα, εἴπερ ἄρα, οὐ παντάπασιν ἀδίκως εὐθύνεται. ἐὰν
οὖν καὶ ἡμεῖς μὴ προσήκοντα μηδὲ οἰκεῖα τῷ προκειμένῳ φαινώμεθα διεξιόντες
μακρολογεῖν εἰκότως ἂν λεγοίμεθα. καθ' αὑτὸ δὲ ἄλλως οὔτε μῆκος οὔτε βραχύτητα
ἐν λόγοις ἐπαινεῖν ἢ ψέγειν δίκαιον.
[20] For a modern version of this complaint, see Annas (1981) 146–51.

the last couple of sentences in this little methodological set-piece, in which Dio insists that neither brevity nor prolixity is a virtue in itself. In the context of a discussion of Platonic composition, this could easily be taken as a riposte to the Platonic Socrates' insistence that brevity is always preferable (above all, *Gorg.* 449b–c and *Prot.* 334b–335c). Whether or not this is the case, the whole passage is an interestingly ambivalent evocation of Platonic authority, demonstrating that the awed admiration of Plato put into Hieroson's mouth in *Or.* 36, and implicitly endorsed there by Dio himself, is not the universal rule. Both as political theorist and as composer of discourses, Dio indeed wishes to be seen to be venturing on to the same territory as Plato; but this time he also wishes to suggest that he may have managed the presentation at least rather better.

Or. 53 might seem to offer Dio another opportunity to take up a critical position, and distance himself from at least part of Plato's thinking, but this time the expectation is not fulfilled. The topic is Homer. Dio surveys a range of philosophical approaches to and verdicts on the poet, before moving on to praise the unassuming modesty of his life-style, and summarizing his teachings on the Good King (11–12). The point of all this must be those concluding paragraphs; John Moles is surely right to discuss the piece in connection with the *Kingship Orations*,[21] and it seems plausible to suggest that it is a *prolalia* to a performance of one of them. Plato's celebrated attack on epic and tragic poetry in *Republic* 377b–398b is duly summarized in 2,[22] following on from Democritus, Aristarchus, Crates, Aristotle, and Heraclides Ponticus in 1, and followed by Zeno, Antisthenes, and Persaeus in 5. What is intriguing is the care Dio seems to take to draw the sting from Plato's criticism. For he seems to go out of his way to present it as of limited scope and (apparently) uninfluential, and to underline that he does not take it to reflect badly on its author. He sandwiches his summary of Plato's attack between assertions that Plato had, even so, a deep admiration for the charm and grace of Homer's poetry, and for his mimetic power (2 and 6; as at *Olympicus* 68 Dio blandly ignores the fact that Plato's reference to Homer's mimetic versatility in the *Republic* (397a–398a) was anything but complimentary). The criticism is treated as relating

---

[21] Moles (1990) 362.

[22] As so often in the later tradition, Plato's general attack on all forms of poetry is taken as directed primarily against Homer, on the strength of the apparent reference to him in *Resp.* 398a–b.

only to Homer's portrayal of the gods—nothing is said about the portrayal of human heroes; there is not the slightest hint of the resumption and intensification of the onslaught in Book 10 of the *Republic*. And as for the question of how the criticism might reflect on Plato, Dio urbanely sidesteps, remarking that the issue is a difficult one, as it always must be when 'one of two friends of yours, both worthy of your respect, brings charges against the other' (3). The conciliatory pose is, moreover, gently reinforced at the end of the oration, when Dio attributes to *Homer* a view of the duty of the good king which echoes *Plato*'s doctrine on the end of human life. Homer's portrayal of Minos, Dio says, shows that good kings have a duty to liken their ways to god, as far as is possible for men (11).[23] Plato in *Theaetetus* 176a famously spoke of the duty of the philosopher to flee from the mortal realm as fast as possible, and to do so by likening himself to God as far as possible;[24] the passage supplied Middle Platonism with one of its standard formulae for the human *telos*, and it is this that Dio here echoes.[25] What is more, the very choice of Minos as the key figure in Homer's account of kingship rests as much on *Plato*'s use of him at the beginning of the *Laws* (624a–625b), and perhaps on the pseudo-Platonic *Minos* (318e ff.), as it does on *Odyssey* 19. 178–9. Whereas in *Or.* 7, Dio, summarizing the political aspect of the *Republic*, found a rather unobvious way of taking Plato to task, he seems here to be resisting a much more obvious opening for criticism.[26]

In this connection, it is disappointing not to know more about one of Dio's lost works, known to us by title only from the *Suda*, the four-book *To Plato in Defence of Homer*. This is generally, and plausibly, assumed to offer an allegorizing defence of Homer of the kind Dio alludes to in passing at *Or.* 53. 2, with perhaps also some similarities to the account of him as a moral instructor that he puts into the mouth of the young Alexander in *Or.* 2.[27] What is less clear is what it may have said about Plato: whether it took the same irenic line as *Or.* 53, or whether in this case defending Homer involved a more definite counter-attack on his critic. Looking not only at *Or.*

---

[23] ἀφομοιοῦντας, ὡς δυνατόν ἐστιν ἀνθρώποις, θεῷ τὸν αὐτῶν τρόπον.

[24] φυγὴ δὲ ὁμοίωσις θεῷ κατὰ τὸ δυνατόν· ὁμοίωσις δὲ δίκαιον καὶ ὅσιον μετὰ φρονήσεως γενέσθαι.

[25] Cf. Dillon (1977) index s.v. 'Likeness to God'.

[26] On *Or.* 53, cf. Kindstrand (1973) 139–41.

[27] Cf. von Arnim (1898) 152, Brancacci (1985) 253–9.

53, but also at the comfortable way Plato and Homer are assimilated in *Or.* 36, one might well be tempted to assume the former.

But whatever is assumed about the lost treatise, the surviving works are broadly consistent in the attitude they evince. As author of the *Republic*, as commentator on Homer, and as practitioner of an exalted style appropriate to high cosmic and political themes, Plato is handled with respect. Criticism of his argumentative strategy is possible, and his attitude to Homer is clearly a matter for some regret; but these are details. Dio is far from displaying the kind of hostile and contemptuous attitude we know to have been prominently and regularly represented in writing on Plato from the fourth century BC onwards, and still vigorously alive well after his day.[28]

PLATONIC MIMESIS

Orr. 7 and 36 show Dio not just commenting on Plato, but doing so in order to draw attention to his own imitation of aspects of Platonic style and thematics. There are several other orations in which, although Plato's name is not directly mentioned, and no explicit verdicts are passed on him, the Platonic presence is none the less strong and significant.

Perhaps the most prominent of this further group is *Or.* 30, the *Charidemus*, penetratingly analysed above in this volume by John Moles.[29] It is cast in a familiar Platonic form, as a report of an encounter introduced by a preliminary dialogue, itself set somewhat later in time, in which one speaker asks the other for an account of what was said and done.[30] But the particular nature of the encounter, and of the reported words, tie it closely to one particular model— the *Phaedo* (one of the two texts which, according to Philostratus, Dio took with him into exile). The general reminiscence inherent in the framing scene (inquiry about the manner of a notable individual's death) is first brought into sharper focus in a pair of remarks towards its end, in 4–7: first, the observation that Charidemus, on

---

[28] For this tradition, see above all Dion. Hal. *Demosth.* 5–7 and 23–30; Aristides, *Orr.* 2 and 3; and Athenaeus 186d–192b, 215c–220a, and 540e–509e (with discussion in Düring (1941)).

[29] See Ch. 8. I am happy to endorse his dismissal of any worries about the authenticity of the speech, which seem to me to based on very shaky arguments.

[30] Cf. *Symposium, Euthydemus, Theaetetus*.

his death-bed, was able to converse (*dialegesthai*) until the very last moment (4); then the further detail that, far from others consoling him, he was consoling them with his final words (6). Though there are no close verbal echoes, these details unambiguously align Charidemus with Socrates, and the whole work in which his death is commemorated with the *Phaedo*. The consolatory discourse that follows, recorded by dictation at Charidemus' own insistence, and now read (re-performed) by his father Timarchus for Dio, does not at first sight bear any close relationship to Socrates' arguments on the immortality of the soul, apart of course from the shared insistence that the death of the body is not an evil to be feared. Instead, Charidemus relates a pair of myths, giving alternative perceptions of the nature of human existence, on either of which death is not an evil.[31] The second of them, the relatively more cheerful image of the world as a dining-hall and life as a *symposium*, narrated by a 'rustic', is indeed largely un-Platonic in character.[32] The first, however, with its grimmer vision of the world as a prison-house, in which mankind is bound in chains of pleasure and pain, is both more generally Platonic in tone, and built around crucial details once again lifted from the *Phaedo*: the world as a guard-house (*phroura*, 10, with verbal echo of *Phdo* 62b); the obligation on men to 'remain at their post' until divinity gives the word (17, cf. *Phdo* 62b); the inferior nature of physical objects in the human realm, as contrasted with the world of the gods (11–13, cf. the *Phdo* myth, 109a ff.); and the 'chains' made from alternate links of pleasure and pain (21; cf. *Phdo* 60b–c, where Socrates muses on the interrelationship of pleasure and pain as his chains are taken off). Platonic too, in a way that has specific relevance to *Phaedo*, but a wider resonance as well, is the clear characterization of the first myth as Orphic in tone and overall character: note above all the opening reference to the blood of the Titans, and the subsequent characterization of the teller of the myth as 'the

---

[31] Cf. perhaps the Socrates of the *Apology* (40c ff., cf. *Charid.* 9 and 25), rather than that of the *Phaedo*, arguing that, on either of the two most plausible views of death, it is something for him to welcome.

[32] To be strictly accurate, of course, the rustic's 'song' is divided into a short first and a long second narrative on life as a *symposium*. I find John Moles's reading of this second myth as a recasting of the *Symposium* unpersuasive, in the absence of any clear verbal or conceptual parallels. If any *Symposium* is laid under contribution here, it is Xenophon's (1. 26 perhaps echoed at the end of 36). The most I find on the Platonic account is a possible reworking of *Critias* 109d ff. (as noted in the Loeb, ad loc.) in 26, and a similarity to *Axiochus* 365b in 43.

offspring of some vagabond'.[33] At the same time, in a manner familiar from the *Borystheniticus*, elements from *Phaedo* are combined by Dio with material more reminiscent of the *Republic*: above all the characterization of the passions in 14–15 (cf. *Resp.* 588c–589b), and the vision of the bound prisoners and their means of release (17–25), which echoes both the setting and the narrative structure of the allegory of the cave (*Resp.* 514a ff.).

Or. 4, the last of the kingship speeches, begins with a strategic echo of [Plato] *Epistle* 2. 310e in 2; this allows Dio, speaking before the emperor, to compare himself not only with Diogenes advising Alexander, but also Plato advising Dionysius. The discourse of Diogenes that follows on the three guardian spirits is also Platonic in character, being inspired by the account of degenerate personality types and styles of life in *Republic* 8–9. John Moles, who has drawn attention to these echoes,[34] also suggests evocation of a combination of the Myth of Er with *Laws* 713c–d in the closing paragraph. While agreeing with the analysis of the main body of Diogenes' speech—in which yet more Platonic notes can easily be detected[35]—I would prefer to see the conclusion as staying with the same part of the *Republic* as the preceding sections: just as Plato contrasted his four degenerate types with the truly virtuous adjustment (*harmonia*) of the soul's constituents, so too Dio/Diogenes here glances fleetingly back in conclusion from the spirits that mislead

---

[33] For the Titans in Orphic mythology, see Burkert (1985) 297–8, with refs.; for the popular perception of Orphic priests, Plato, *Rep.* 364b and Eur. *Hipp.* 952–5, with Barrett's note. The (widely shared) perception of Orphic doctrine in *Phaedo* is built chiefly on the reference to the world as a guard-house, labelled by Plato ad loc. as a 'secret doctrine' and connected to the Orphics in *Crat.* 400c, which is followed up later in the dialogue in the picture constructed of the soul's relationship with the body (67d, 81e, 92a); cf. Olympiodorus, *Comm. in Platonis Phaedonem* pp. 2. 19–4. 27 Norvin (and Index Auctorum s.v. 'Orpheus'). For discussion of Orphic elements in Plato in general, Guthrie (1935) 156–71 and 238–44.

[34] Moles (1983*a*), esp. 256–8 and 262–3, and (1990) 348–50. I would if anything see a still closer relationship than Moles does between Dio's three *daimones* and Plato's degenerate psychological types, lining up Dio's avaricious spirit with Plato's oligarch, the hedonist with a combination of the tyrant and the democratic man, and the ambitious spirit with the timarch. This in turn would lead us to see a glancing reference to the perfectly virtuous man (= the philosopher-king) in the last paragraph of the oration (139).

[35] The reference to the need for flattery in pursuit of civic distinction in 125 recalls the *Gorgias* (esp. 462b ff. and 481c–482a); the metaphorical use of ὄχλος in 125, *Phdr.* 229d; and the reference to the inner strife of the soul in 138, the *Republic* again.

to the one that leads to virtue via 'education and reason'.[36] But
to concentrate only on Diogenes' speech and the earlier, fleeting
evocation of *Epistle* 2 is, I believe, to miss what must originally have
been an equally striking Platonic element in the oration. Like the
Borystheniticus and the *Charidemus*, this speech too has a Platonic
master-text, which constitutes a point of reference from start to finish.

This text is the *First Alcibiades*, now generally (and I am sure rightly)
denied to Plato, but in antiquity not only accepted as genuine, but
privileged as, pedagogically, one of his most important works.[37] Two
crucial passages in the initial scene-setting of Alexander's encounter
with Diogenes are enough to establish a relationship between Dio's
account and its prototype: 4 (Alexander's burning desire for his
name to be known the world over) echoes *Alc.* 1. 105a–c; and 11
(Alexander's long-standing desire to speak to Diogenes, and conviction that he had great benefits to confer) picks up *Alc.* 1. 104c–d
and 105d. Thereafter, the Platonic prototype is kept consistently in
view for the remainder of the oration, on the level both of leading
themes and of specific detail. Like Socrates, Diogenes insists to
Alexander that, although he is well-educated in a conventional sense,
he still lacks the truest form of education and is therefore premature in his ambitions (4. 29 ff. and 70; *Alc.* 1. 118a with 106e ff.).[38]
Like Socrates, he insists that the younger man will only qualify as

---

[36] This is not to deny that the concluding paragraph is, as Moles says, 'a brilliant
piece of writing'. Dio contrives an ending that works both for Diogenes concluding
his discourse to Alexander (ending in good pedagogical style with positive protrep-
sis rather than gloomy warning, and making an elegant ring with his earlier reference to the good *daimōn* in 75), and for himself, speaking before and to the emperor.
For, appropriately in a work of implicit panegyric, the conclusion is hymnic: like
Theocritus before him (17. 135–7), Dio adapts the concluding formulae of the
hymnodist (μεταλαβόντες . . . ὑμνῶμεν | μεταβήσομαι ἄλλον εἰς ὕμνον, hHom. 5.
295–4, etc.), as he turns to make a graceful bow to the patron before whom he has
been performing. The two levels of reference (Dio and Diogenes) are held together
by the punning use of the word ἁρμονία, referring both to the constitution of the
soul/personality, which has been Diogenes' theme, and to the 'strains' of Dio's speech,
as it turns in conclusion from warnings about wrong spirits to praise and acknowledgement of a better guardian (the 'good *daimōn* and god' being, as Moles argues,
both the embodiment of moral enlightenment, and the god-like emperor or his *genius*).

[37] Albin. *Isag.* 5; Diog. Laert. 3. 62; Olymp. *In Alc.* 3. 3–4; Procl. *In Alc.* 6. 3–7. 1;
Anon. Proleg. 26 (7. 219. 30–4 Hermann); cf. Segonds (1985), pp. x–xix.

[38] The clear presence of this theme of conventional education versus true (moral)
culture in *Alc.* 1, with which Dio is quite clearly working, is one of the reasons why
I am sceptical of attempts (esp. Brancacci's in this volume, but cf. also Höistad (1948)
156 ff.) to claim special importance for Antisthenes as a model, both here and elsewhere in Dio. See further below, pp. 232–4.

a true leader when he gains this education (4. 24–5 and 53; *Alc.* 1. 121a–124b, esp. 122a). Like Socrates, he exhorts him before all else to 'know himself' (4.57; *Alc.* 1. 124a, 128e ff.),[39] and insists that self-knowledge demands knowledge of the higher aspects of the self (4. 75; *Alc.* 1. 129e ff. and 133c—Diogenes' insistence on the need to know one's *daimōn* parallels Socrates' on the need to know the god-like soul). Like Socrates, he holds forth to his pupil on Homer and the customs of the Persians (4. 39 ff. and 66 ff.; *Alc.* 1. 112b and 121c ff.). When he speaks of Alexander's present servitude of spirit (4. 75), he echoes Socrates at *Alc.* 1. 135b; when he describes the dress habits of the *daimōn* of hedonism, he recalls *Alc.* 1. 122c.[40] And when at the very end he makes his final reference to the good *daimōn* and the path of 'sound culture and reason', he is returning not just to the starting-point of his set-piece oration, but also to the main theme of the Platonic prototype.

My last example of an oration pervaded by Platonic references is perhaps the least expected, the *Olympicus*. There would at first sight seem to be many reasons for thinking of this as a notably un-Platonic piece. The theme of concepts and representations of divinity may be shared with the *Republic* and the *Laws*, but both the external form of the oration (festival speech, enclosing a reported speech of self-defence), and its willingness to admit the legitimacy of both artistic and literary images, seem a long way from Platonic practice. If Phidias' account of the versatility of Homeric mimesis (12. 68) draws on Plato's celebrated criticism (*Rep.* 397a ff.), it does so in order radically to revalue it. Closer examination, however, reveals a steady succession of Platonic references and borrowings. The very first words of the oration repeat the opening of the *Gorgias* (447a). The prologue, in which Dio steps into a version of his Socratic pose, glances again at the *Gorgias*, as well as at *Phaedo* and *Hippias*.[41] When he turns to his main and more exalted theme, his 'hymn' in praise of the King of the Gods, we hear the *Phaedrus* (the locus of one of Plato's own most celebrated 'hymns')—247c3–4 in

---

[39] *Alc.* 1 being, of course, the *locus classicus* for this Socratic injunction.

[40] ἐσθήτων τε μαλακῶν ἕλξεις / ἐσθῆτας ἱματίων θ' ἕλξεις.

[41] *Grg.* in the references to Polus, Gorgias, and rhetorical flattery in 14–15; *Hippias* in the reference to Hippias in 14 (unless this is taken as a glance at *Prot.*); *Phdo* (85a–b) in the reference to swan-song (as an image for a human activity) in 4. Note also the characterizations of Socrates in 13 and the sophists in 10, both of which draw *inter alia* on material in the dialogues (for the former, cf. e.g. *Apol.* 20c, 23a; for the latter, *Apol.* 19e, *Prot.* 315a–b, 316b).

22,[42] a blend of 245c3–4, 246a3, and 246e4 in 27.[43] When along the way he wishes to reflect on the course his argument is taking, or to emphasize the importance of his theme, it is to Platonic turns of phrase and images that he resorts: in 38, the contrast between forensic and philosophical procedure echoes specifically *Theaetetus* 172d–e, preceded and followed by more generally Platonic personification of the *logos*, and seafaring imagery;[44] in 53, the reminder of the importance of the topic recalls (e.g.) *Gorgias* 472c, and is again surrounded by Socratic-sounding dialogue-formulae.[45] In the discussion of poetry, besides the use of the *Republic* already noted, there seems also to be a glance at the *Ion* (534a ff.) in the characterization of poetic inspiration in 70. In 80–3, when he makes his Phidias turn from human skills to the handiwork of the divine Artificer, the language of craftsmanship and of separation and interweaving necessarily recall the *Timaeus*.[46] And at the very end, in 84, Dio's comment that the Greeks would have crowned Phidias for the speech of defence he has scripted for him glances once more at *Rep.* 398a, converting ironic praise for Homer into real praise for his counterpart in the visual arts. No single Platonic model turns out to underlie this oration, but the consistency of reference is striking all the same; its point and its justification are to be found in a combination of Dio's assumption of the Socratic pose as the giver of the oration, and Plato's immense importance as an authority on its chosen subject-matter(s).

PLATO IN DIO

The six orations surveyed in the first part of this chapter have demonstrated, implicitly, that Plato and the Platonic dialogues are important to Dio's own projects on a number of different levels. These may now be summarized, and reinforced with further instances from elsewhere in his work.

First, Plato is an indispensible model in the construction of philosophical myths (even if his mythological motifs and style normally

---

[42] ὑμνῆσαι λόγῳ . . . ἀποδέοντι τῆς ἀξίας (Dio) | οὔτε τις ὕμνησέ πω . . . οὔτε ποτὲ ὑμνήσει κατ᾽ ἀξίαν (Plato); the same Platonic passage is echoed again, I think, in 59, νοῦν γὰρ . . . οὔτε τις πλάστης οὔτε τις γραφεὺς εἰκάσαι δυνατὸς ἔσται.

[43] περὶ δὴ θεῶν . . . ἡγέμονος.   [44] See further Russell (1992) ad loc.

[45] E.g. 52, σκοπῶμεν τὸ νῦν; 54, ἆρ᾽ οὖν οἴει.

[46] δημιουργίας, τελειότατος δημιουργός, δημιουργήσαντα τὸν ἄπαντα κόσμον, διακρίνοντα καὶ ἐμπλέκοντα; cf. *Tim.* 36e.

blend with other, non-Platonic allegorical material).[47] Two other particularly striking specimens may be set beside those from the *Charidemus* and the *Borystheniticus*. The first is the myth of Heracles, told to Dio on his wanderings by 'an old woman of Elis or Arcadia', and reported in *Or.* 1. Much of this is admittedly of other than Platonic inspiration; Dio evidently draws heavily on Xenophon's account of Prodicus' *Horae*, and on either the *Tabula Cebetis*, or at least the same allegorical traditions as the *Tabula* works with. However, I detect also, in the topography of the peaks of Kingship and Tyranny, some imaginative reuse of the myth of the *Phaedo*: specifically, in the booming river flowing round the two peaks in its deep, sheer-sided gully (66); in the distinction drawn between the bright, pure air of Kingship and the murk and mist of Tyranny (68); and in the subterranean passages that honeycomb the ground on which the throne of Tyranny rests (77).[48] Dio co-opts elements of Plato's elaborate allegory for the distinction between higher and lower worlds, and reapplies it to higher and lower forms of government. At the same time, Platonic notes are also detectable in the choice of the narrator for the myth, and of the scene for its telling: the Dorian prophetess is a transposed Diotima from the *Symposium*, and both the circumstances of her encounter with Dio and her preamble about inspiration recall the *Phaedrus*.[49] The second instance in this category is *Or.* 5, the *Libyan Myth*, for which the Platonic germ is provided by the *Phaedrus* again and the *Republic*, with their use of mythological monsters—and specifically multiform monsters—as cautionary images for the blend and interplay between rational and irrational factors within the soul (*Phdr.* 229d–230a; *Rep.* 588c ff.). Two-thirds of the way through the speech, moreover, Dio gently echoes Socrates' words in *Phaedrus* about the folly of spending too much time or effort on this kind of allegorizing (*Phdr.* 229d in 18).

One other observation can be made about Plato in Dio's myth-telling. It is striking how frequently, in framing his myths, Dio takes time to reflect and comment on their utility, truth-value, plausibility, and style (e.g. *Orr.* 1. 56–8; 5. 16–18; 36. 42). This too should be seen as a Platonizing feature, building on such Socratic comments on this kind of issue as can be found in *Gorgias* 523a, *Phaedo* 114d, and *Laws* 872d–e.

---

[47] See further Saïd in this volume, above, pp. 172 ff.
[48] Cf. *Phdo* 110c–111c, 111d–113c.   [49] Cf. Trapp (1990) 143–4.

Secondly, Dio learns from and mimics Plato also in his composition of dialogues. We saw this in considering the *Borystheniticus*,
which for all that it was composed for delivery as an epideictic oration, has the form of a first-person narrated dialogue (complete with
myth) on the model of, say, the *Charmides* or the *Protagoras*. But
the point can be made about almost all the pieces in the corpus that
take dialogue form, whether narrated or mimetic: the conversations
of Alexander and Philip in *Orr.* 1 and 2; the conversations of Diogenes
with Alexander and others in 4, 9, and 10; *Melancomas* II and the
Charidemus (28 and 30); and the large set of short exchanges on
moral-philosophical topics between Dio himself and his anonymous
interlocutor(s) (*Orr.* 14–15, 21, 23, 25–6, 55–6, 60–1, 67, 70, 74, 77).
In almost all of these, a debt to Platonic dialogue-style is detectable;
and in many cases a natural consequence of this imitation is to
reinforce the impression of Socratic role-playing on the part of the
principal speaker. *Orr.* 55 and 56 make a particularly nice pair of
examples, combining as they do familiar Platonic phraseology with
an equally familiar overall argumentative choreography. Thus in 55.
1–6, I note not only such formulaic phrases as (e.g.) 'can you say?',
'tell me and don't hold (it) back', 'is there any way that we can say?',
'but how is it possible?' and 'well then',[50] but also the way that Dio
leads his interlocutor through a series of individual cases to the formulation of a general proposition; and in 56, besides a similar string
of Platonizing (Socratizing) phrases, we find, half-way through, an
insistence on the importance of precise definition (7), and at the end
a discussion of whether to drop the current subject for another, or
pursue it to greater depth (16). Not all Dio's dialogues have as strong
a Platonic colour as these two, but I think that there is only one
(*Or.* 58, young Achilles and Chiron) where it is entirely absent.[51] In
general, his sense of appropriate diction, and of the right sort of inter-
change between the parties to the encounter, rests firmly on Platonic
foundations (things just would not have come out as they do had Plato
not established the conventions as he did)—and the one exception
brings this out all the more clearly by contrast with the remainder.

---

[50] ἔχεις εἰπεῖν, εἰπὲ καὶ μὴ φθονήσῃς, ἔσθ᾽ ὅπως φήσομεν, καὶ πῶς οἷόν τε
and εἶεν.

[51] According to Höistad (1948) 174–6, this draws heavily on Antisthenes. If correct, this would provide a neat explanation of its un-Platonic style; but the grounds
alleged (similarity between Chiron's 'curriculum' and that attributed to Diogenes in
Diog. Laert. 6. 30–2) may not be sufficiently strong to establish the debt.

A further category of Platonizing follows neatly on from the previous one, and indeed overlaps with it substantially. Dio is systematically indebted to the Platonic portrayal of Socrates. He draws on it not only in his own depictions of Socrates (*Orr.* 54 and 55) but also—still more—in his portrayals of Diogenes and of himself. In the material surveyed already, the most striking examples are *Orr.* 12 and 36, where Dio builds the Socratic persona for himself, and 4 and 30, where he assigns it to others (Diogenes and Charidemus). Other instances are not far to seek: *Or.* 4 for another Socratized Diogenes, *Orr.* 13 and 32 for further examples of Dio himself posing as Socrates. The latter two deserve brief consideration.

In *Or.* 13 the Socratic imitation looks to two specific models, in the *Apology* and the *Clitophon*. Like the Socrates of the *Apology*, Dio presents himself as one who came to accept his status as a man of wisdom only gradually, after wrestling with others' opinions about himself that he initially wished to reject. But once he accepted the role, he says, it was to Socrates that he turned for the substance of his exhortations to his fellow-men; and both in the opening words of the discourse Dio quotes, and in what he says about how Socrates delivered it, we recognize the *Clitophon* (407b–e, 408a–c, 409a ff.).[52]

In *Or.* 13, then, we find Dio portraying himself quite directly as Socrates' pupil and heir, and doing so with reference specifically to Platonic accounts. In the other case, *Or.* 32, the Platonic reference is as clear, but the use of the Socratic role is more subtle and indirect. Rather as in the opening of the *Olympicus*, Dio plays ironic games with the Socratic profession of ignorance, and with Socratic shabbiness, contriving simultaneously to play down his own talents and accomplishments and to appropriate the most glorious philosophical role of them all. In the *Olympicus*, the claim to ignorance is made twice in 5 and 9, then repeated again in 14–15, in expanded form (no pupils, no skills, and no good looks, either), and in this third occurrence it is explicitly related to the Socratic precedent. In the *Alexandrian* the evocation is spread over a longer stretch of the oration and is less explicit, in keeping with the still subtler game Dio is here playing with his audience's perceptions and expectations, modulating from the desired and anticipated encomium of the city into a philosopher's call for self-criticism and reform. After an opening

---

[52] For a different view, see Brancacci, below, p. 251.

survey of the Alexandrians' insatiable appetite for entertainment, Dio ventures the suggestion that what they should really be on the look-out for is honest and disinterested advice (11); pivoting on this, he turns to consider what such (philosophical) advice should be like, and what specific benefits it can bring, while at the same time developing a contrast between it and other less profitable kinds of spectacle and performance. Through all this runs the steadily more insistent implication that it is Dio himself to whom the Alexandrians should look to fulfil the desideratum, and indeed that simply by listening to him now they are beginning to do just that. And it is bound up with this that we again find the Socratic thread: the suggestion in 12 that it is as a result of the planning of some *daimonion* that Dio has come to Alexandria; the modest reference in 22 to his own shabby appearance and lack of conventional verbal gifts; the description of the Alexandrian *dēmos* to its face as a 'multifarious and dreadful beast' in the style of a Centaur or Scylla or Chimaera in 28; and the comment on the gap between the prosaic level of his verbal style and the weighty nature of his theme in 39.[53]

There is, however, a problem that needs to be confronted in connection with Dio's Socratic and dialogic material, especially in view of Aldo Brancacci's essay in in this volume (Chapter 10). I have been insisting on the importance of Plato as source and model, and in doing so am clearly open to the charge of neglecting some very obvious alternatives, mentioned several times by Dio himself: Xenophon, singled out from among the Socratics in *Or.* 18 for the grace of his style, and the usefulness of his subject-matter to the aspiring orator;[54] Aeschines and Antisthenes, listed along with Plato in *Or.* 8 as pupils of Socrates encountered by Diogenes in Athens.[55] Dio's Socratic reading must have extended to these authors as well, and it is accordingly inadequate to talk only of Plato as his Socratic source, either for personal and biographical information, or for dialectical style.

It is clearly true and important that Dio's Socrates (including the direct discussions, in *Orr.* 54–5, as well as the Socratic traits portrayed in the speech and behaviour of others) comes to him from

---

[53] For this analysis of *Or.* 32, cf. Trapp (1995).

[54] *Or.* 18. 13–18; it is, however, Xenophon's historical rather than his Socratic works that are principally in view here.

[55] *Or.* 8. 1; note also the general reference in *Or.* 54. 4 to the 'friends' who publicized Socrates' words and teachings for him.

the Socratics as a group, rather than from just one of them; and we have ample evidence, quite apart from Dio himself, of the circulation and appreciative reading of Xenophon, Aeschines, and Antisthenes in his day.[56] Individual biographical details, and particular encounters and topics mentioned, can indeed be traced to non-Platonic sources;[57] and Dio's dialogic-dialectical style is not always infused with distinctively Platonic colour.[58] But equally, as I hope to have shown, there are clearly identifiable places where the Platonic source is overt and secure. Absence of Plato from some Socratic contexts is not a good reason to downplay his importance overall, or to look in other directions sooner than his. In particular, I am sceptical of attempts to establish a heavy use by Dio of Antisthenes, made most determinedly a generation ago by Höistad, and more recently by Aldo Brancacci.[59] The test cases are *Orr.* 3, 4, and 13, which it is suggested draw particularly on Antisthenes' *Archelaus* and *Protrepticus*. In the case of *Or.* 4, I hope to have shown above that the central object of Dio's imitation there is in fact the *First Alcibiades*, which contains many of the themes and images that are claimed as Antisthenic. Some use of Antisthenes cannot be ruled out, but if it is there at all it should be seen as an overlay over a Platonic framework, not itself the main frame. The other two orations, I would go on to suggest, follow the same pattern. In both of them, Dio is not closely following an Antisthenic (or any other) source, but composing freely in a generally Socratizing vein around a set of reference-points of

---

[56] For Xenophon, see esp. Quint. *Inst.* 10. 1. 83 with commentators ad loc.; H. Breitenbach in *RE* IX(a), 1895–7; Münscher (1920); and note the spectacular case of Arrian (Stadter (1980) index s.v. 'Xenophon'). For Aeschines, see Dittmar (1912). For Antisthenes, see the appendix in Dittmar (1912) 299–310. Dio himself, in my view (for a different view, see Brancacci, below, pp. 245–6), will not have thought of himself as following one or another rival version of Socrates, but rather as using a whole range of equally valid sources in combination to gain access to the real, historical Socrates and his teaching.

[57] e.g. the invitation to Macedonia from Archelaus (13. 30), or his hymn to Apollo and Artemis (43. 10), or his rebuke to the Thirty (43. 8, from Xen. *Mem.* 1. 2. 32).

[58] For much of the time, Dio's dialectical style seems closer to the relatively less colourful standard of Xenophon, with its rather monotonous reliance on a very few connecting formulae (esp. οὖν and τί δέ;).

[59] Höistad (1948) 50–61, 150–222; Brancacci (1992) and in this volume, below, pp. 246–54. My doubts concern not only the alleged debts to specific dialogues by Antisthenes, but also the more general claims (Brancacci, pp. 244–8) that (i) two entirely separate (Platonic and Cynic-Stoic) portrayals of Socrates can be distinguished, and (ii) authors like Dio could have made (or would have wanted to make) a conscious and *exclusive* choice between the two alternatives.

Platonic origin.[60] In *Or.* 3 (1 and 29–41), almost all of the Socratic material can be accounted for as free reworking of and embroidery on passages of the *Gorgias* and Xenophon's *Memorabilia.*[61] In *Or.* 13 (14–28), the same job is done by the *Clitophon.*[62] To my mind it is perverse to treat the Platonic parallels, which can be demonstrated to hold with surviving texts, as subsidiary, and to emphasize instead debts to works that depend on reconstructions.[63]

Finally, in this survey of the different levels of Dio's Platonizing, mention should be made of Plato as personal example. In discussing *Or.* 4, it was suggested that the opening allusion to Plato *Epistle* 2. 310e ff. is there, at least in part, to point the parallel between Dio as instructor of the emperor and Plato as instructor of Dionysius. Dio is, like Plato, committing himself to the practical preaching of philosophical values to a particularly important and influential pupil. The *Encomium of Heracles and Plato,* another lost work of Dio's, known only by title from the *Suda,* can perhaps be made to point in the same direction. The normal reaction to this, admittedly somewhat

---

[60] A key text for understanding Dio's procedures in this respect is *Or.* 26, in which he recasts the pseudo-Platonic *Sisyphus.* This cannot perhaps in itself be considered a secure example of Platonizing, as the authenticity of this particular dialogue was aready questioned in antiquity (Diog. Laert. 3. 62), but it does on the other hand show how Dio works when building on a specific model. The two works share a topic (deliberation and advising: 26. 1/387d), and a number of specific details (26. 1–3 + 6–8/388a–391b; 26. 2/388c; 26. 3/387e; 26. 5/390de), but the phrasing, the order of exposition, the length, and the overall thrust of the argument all come out differently in the 'imitation'.

[61] Esp. *Grg.* 470d–e, 490e–494a (where the complaint about Socratic analogies leads on to discussion of self-rule in tyrants), 515c ff. (the topic of the good ruler, for which cf. also *Rep.* 345b–347c); Xen. *Mem.* 4. 4. 5.

[62] *Or.* 13. 14–21 embroider rhetorically on the basic thesis of *Clitophon* 407b–e and 409a ff.; 22 shares the steersman comparison with 408b and 410b, but borrows material also from *Gorgias* and *Protagoras*; 27 picks up on 407c–d and 408a–b; 28 echoes 407d and 408b–c. The only substantial part of the argument that does not have a precedent in the *Clitophon* is that of 23–6, on the reasons for Greek victory in the Persian Wars and the Persians' lack of a true king; this is clearly not Platonic matter and might perhaps be related Antisthenic (or Cynic? or Stoic?) precedent. In favour of the *Clitophon* as Dio's main inspiration, it should be noted that in antiquity it was not only accepted as a genuine Platonic work, but also placed first in some collections of the dialogues (Diog. Laert. 3. 62).

[63] I note one particular point of disagreement with Aldo Brancacci. *Or.* 55. 22 certainly does not preserve the subtitles of a set of Antisthenic dialogues (Brancacci (1992) 313–14, cf. below, pp. 247–8, in this volume). Dio may indeed have had Antisthenes' works in view here, but only as one set of reports among several. The reference to Anytus looks also to *Meno* 90c and Xen. *Apol.* 29–30, and that to Meno to *Meno* 76b; that to Lycon follows from the *Apology*; and that to Lysicles looks to the *Aspasia* of Aeschines (cf. Plut. *Pericles* 24 with Σ Plato *Menex.* and Aristoph. *Eq.* 132).

startling, notice seems to be to wish it away: von Arnim suggested a conflation of titles; Brancacci, following Gallavotti, emends to *'against Plato'* (*kata Platōnos*).[64] Both reactions rest on a perception of Dio, whether 'sophist' Dio or 'philosopher' Dio, as an anti-Platonist, incapable of complimenting him on any sustained scale. Now, it may well be right that the *Suda's* entry is confused, but it is nevertheless worth making a case for its credibility in this respect. For, on the evidence considered so far, quite apart from what remains to be surveyed, it is not clear that Dio *was* an anti-Platonist. Negative reactions to Plato in his work cover just two points, his misassessment of Homer, and the fact that Diogenes did not like him (and the second of these is handled with fleeting brevity and not particularly endorsed by Dio himself). Encomium of Plato does not have to be excluded on principle. Nor, secondly, is the collocation of Plato with Heracles as impossibly bizarre as has been claimed, since there is at least one partial parallel to be found in an author working within a century of Dio, and heavily influenced by him. Twice over, in *Dialexeis* 15 and 34, Maximus of Tyre cites Heracles and Plato in quick succession as exemplars of strenuous lives lived out in pursuit of practical virtue—Heracles for the obvious reasons, Plato by virtue of his hazardous trips to Sicily, and his fortitude in dealing with a savage tyrant in the service of philosophy (15. 6–9; 34. 7–9). This may seem impossibly strained to us, and Maximus is indeed a more straightforwardly Platonizing author than Dio, but it should perhaps make us think twice before dismissing an *Encomium of Heracles and Plato* out of hand (especially from the pen of an author who liked to present himself as a strenuous wanderer and an expert on kingship and tyranny).

OVERALL STATISTICS AND DISTRIBUTION

In the limited sample of Dio's work surveyed so far, we have found evidence of substantial use of six Platonic dialogues (*Republic, Phaedrus, Phaedo, Gorgias, Clitophon*, and *First Alcibiades*), and more sporadic reflections of nine or ten more (*Protagoras, Theaetetus, Timaeus, Critias, Epistles, Hippias, Ion, Apology, Laws*, and (?)*Sisyphus*). In addition, we have seen how Dio can affect Platonic

---

[64] von Arnim (1898) 155; Brancacci (1985) 245–6, citing Gallavotti (1931), cf. 256–9.

style both in his myths and in his accounts of the soul and the cosmos, and in his passages of dialectical debate, and how Platonic turns of phrase can occur at more or less any point. The general picture does not alter much if the angle of vision is widened to take in the whole of the corpus. Two more dialogues—*Euthydemus* and *Crito*—can be added to the list of minor echoes;[65] and a series of further echoes detected to those already listed (most notably, to *Gorgias*).[66] Moreover, a complete account of Dio's stylistic Platonizing (both in the orations discussed above, and over the corpus as a whole) must take account of the word-list compiled by Wilhelm Schmid in his study of Dio's classicizing vocabulary in *Der Atticismus*: even though it might be felt that not all of the forty-six items he lists have an equally strong Platonic aura, his general contention that the dialogues exercise a noticeable influence on Dio's choice of words, even when imitation of specific passages is not in question, is surely sound.[67]

Several important points become clear when the whole of Dio's *œuvre* is taken into account in this way. First, the range of dialogues evoked and referred to is not an unduly broad one for the time; it stays well within the bounds of general culture. These are the dialogues generally known and read by the cultivated person as part of a literate education. The hard, technical dialogues such as *Philebus*, *Parmenides*, *Sophist*, and *Cratylus*, the territory of the real philosopher, are conspicuous by their absence. Moreover, in what he chooses to discuss in those dialogues he does call up, Dio keeps firmly

---

[65] *Euthyd.* 305c in *Or.* 24. 3; *Crito* 52a–d in *Or.* 47. 7.

[66] *Gorgias*: 32. 17 (464b f.), 33. 6–7, 13, 44 (464b ff., 521e), 34. 29–34 (general), 35. 8 (481d–e), 50. 8 (470d–e), 73. 10 (485e–486a, 506b); *Prot.*: 6. 25–6 (320c ff.), 13. 22 (319b–c, 322d–323a); *Phdo*: 8. 12 (117b); *Alc.* 1: 10. 21 ff. (124a ff.); *Tim.*: 11. 37 (21e ff.); *Apol.*: 42. 5 (26d), 43. 8–9 (32c–d, 24b); *Resp.*: 2. 47 (404b), 32. 28 (588c ff.), 49. 9–10 (general). This list is bound to be incomplete; there must be both other reminiscences of specific contexts, and many other instances of Platonic phraseology.

[67] Schmid (1887–97) i: 141–3. His list is: ἀγριαίνω, ἀνασφάλλω, ἀνεπιδεής, ἀπηνής, Ἀσκληπιάδαι, ἄτυφος, ἄφθεγκτον, βδάλλω, γαληνός (metaphorical), γλίσχρως καὶ μόλις (calqued on *Resp.* 553c). δευσοποιόν, διακορής, διακόσμησις, διχόνοια, ἐμμελῶς, ἐντυγχάνω ('study', 'read'), ἐξάντη ποιεῖν, ἐπίπνοια, ἐπιτερπής, ἐρεσχελέω, ἑταιρότατος, εὐανθής, εὐμαρής, εὐπορέω (+ inf.), εὐσχημονέω, θρέμμα, κηδεμονία, κολοφών, κυρίττω, λέγω οἷον, μανότης, μεγαλαυχεῖσθαι, παντοδαπός εἰμι, πενιχρός, προσπαίζω (+ acc.), πρόσρημα, πτοεῖσθαι, κατὰ ῥοῦν φέρεσθαι, σκιρτάω, σοφός (= 'skilful', 'clever'), σταθερός, κατὰ τρόπον, χαῦνος, χαυνόω, ψυχαγωγία, ὡς τὸ πολύ. This contrasts with twenty-four items allegedly traceable to Xenophontic usage (143–4) and twelve to Demosthenic (144). Schmid also comments (179–87) on the conformity of Dio's use of particles to Platonic and Xenophontic usage.

to a grammarian's rather than a philosopher's agenda. The second point is that the distribution of Platonic material across Dio's work is far from even. Some stretches of the corpus rank as decidedly 'low-Plato' zones. Although occasional touches of Platonic colouring can be found in the great city speeches (particularly from the *Gorgias* in *Orr.* 32–5), the Bithynian pieces (*Orr.* 38–51, plus some fragments like *Or.* 79) seem to be almost entirely free of it. Similarly, I draw a relative blank with some of the more uncomplicatedly epideictic pieces, such as the *Troicus* (*Or.* 11),[68] *Melancomas* I (29), and *Orr.* 75–6 on law and custom. There is little or no Plato in some of the literary-critical pieces, such as *Or.* 18 (where Xenophon is preferred to Plato as a stylistic model among the Socratics), and *Orr.* 52 and 59, on the Philoctetes plays. Finally, there are many of Dio's sermonizing pieces where the most that might be claimed is the use of a very generally Platonic-Socratic style (e.g. *Orr.* 8, 16–17, 20, 22, 24, 27, 62, 65, 66, 68–9, and 80—again, many of these are excerpts, not complete works). I make these statements with a little diffidence, as I am aware that another reading would almost certainly suggest a string of minor revisions, but if they are even approximately correct, that gives us already some thirty-five pieces, going on for half of the whole corpus, in which Platonic material and Platonic style are not notably drawn on, except on a purely and rather diffusely stylistic level.

CONCLUSION

The results of a more general survey of Dio's *œuvre* supplement and confirm the impressions created by the limited subset of pieces in which Plato is actually named or addressed directly. Plato's dialogues and his portrayal of Socrates were extremely important for Dio both in the construction of his works and in the creation of the character in which he came before his public. Some of the explanation for this is, as the ancient and Byzantine critics imply, stylistic. A philosophizing (moralizing) orator needs a pose and a stylistic register that, while giving him a creditable literary identity as a composer of prose for oratorical performance, will also set him apart from the austerer, more utilitarian oratory of courts and assemblies. Although not an

---

[68] But note the suggestion that Dio's Egyptian priest of Onuphis (37) may recall *Tim.* 21e ff. as well as Herodotus 2. 113 ff.

Michael Trapp

oratorical author, Plato was an ideal choice for appropriation for this function. Dialogue form in itself provides a kind of non-oratorical oratory, reported speech just waiting to be reconverted into live speech; *Plato's* dialogues, with their interpolated episodes of monologue, their depiction of a resourceful philosophical persuader, and their sheer stylistic richness and variety, made the invitation irresistible. But to these considerations of style and literary form, we have of course to add Plato's status as the greatest and richest of the commemorators of Socrates, and his immense intellectual authority and importance for the shape of the philosophical landscape in Dio's day (and indeed for the preceding four centuries). For all its disagreements, Dio's own formal *hairesis*, Stoicism, was deeply influenced by Plato, sharing with him not only a devotion to the example and ideals of Socrates, but also a large part of its philosophical agenda (its sense of what the philosophical agenda *was*). From an earlier generation, we can point (cautiously) to the figure of Posidonius, in whom we seem to see both a conceptual and a literary engagement with Plato; from nearer Dio's time, to the respectful treatment Plato is accorded in Seneca's *Epistles* and *Essays*, and in Arrian's versions of the teaching of Epictetus.[69] In using Plato, Stoic Dio was using an honoured ancestor of his own philosophical family. He also hoped, surely, that his Platonic echoes and quotations would be recognized by his audience, and appreciated by them as evidence of both his general literary cultivation and, specifically, of his discriminating and insightful familiarity with the Platonic corpus. Not that we need imagine him to have expected all of them to be up with him all the time. The audience of Borysthenites, as described in *Or.* 36 by his character Hieroson, with its 'some few' devotees of Plato, invites the reader of that oration who does catch the full range of Platonic reminiscence to congratulate himself on his unusual perspicacity; and that in turn perhaps provides a model for the anticipated reception of the *Orations* more generally.

The limits of Dio's Platonizing are quite soon reached none the less. As already observed, the Plato he uses in his discourses is mainstream Plato, the works most familiar to rhetorical education and the cultivated general public. His needs and ambitions do not take

---

[69] Seneca: *Dial.* 3. 6. 5, 3. 19. 17, 4. 20. 2, 4. 21. 10, 5. 12. 5–7, etc.; *Epp.* 58 and 65, plus 44. 3–4, 94. 38, 109. 38; Epictetus: 1. 8. 11–13, 2 . 17. 5 (+ 11, 35), 2. 18. 20, and his many quotations from *Crito, Apol., Soph., Laws, Theaet., Phdo, Gorg., Alc.* 1, *Clitoph., Resp.,* and *Smp.* (see the index to Schenkl's *editio maior*).

him on to technical philosophical territory, even to the distance that, for instance, Seneca ventures in *Epistles* 58 and 65 (on Platonic ontology and the Forms). He does not set himself up as a devotee of or an expert in Platonism, as, within half a century or so, generically similar figures such as Apuleius and Maximus will do. Quite apart from questions of personal choice, he belongs to the wrong generation, before the full development of the Platonist revival makes that a role that can intelligibly be taken up ouside the narrow confines of professional schools. But these limits should sharpen our sense of what Dio really did owe to Plato, and of how important he felt it was to display his acquaintance, rather than inducing us to ignore or downplay this side of his literary and intellectual personality.

10

Dio, Socrates, and Cynicism
ALDO BRANCACCI

INTRODUCTION

Socrates is an important literary and theoretical presence in the work of Dio Chrysostom. A quick look at any modern edition of the *Orations* will confirm this. Of all the philosophers mentioned in the writings of Dio, Socrates is the one who receives the greatest number of citations: more than Plato, Aristotle, the Stoics, and the Cynics —more even than Diogenes. And if the Cynic beats him by having four discourses dedicated to him, Socrates holds his own with the two speeches in which he is the protagonist: *On Socrates* (*Or.* 54) and *On Homer and Socrates* (*Or.* 55). To this should be added the notable length of citations about Socrates and the interesting nature of those concerning the Socratics. No less important is the fact that the philosopher is cited in many other writings belonging to different periods of the author's production, for it demonstrates that the interest in Socrates was not a momentary, albeit intense, episode but rather a constant presence in Dio's intellectual and literary development.

One of the reasons for Socrates' ubiquity in Dio's works is undoubtedly the fundamental functionality of the model, its preeminent and unquestionable paradigmatic value, and, even more, the possibility it offered of establishing an effective identification between the ancient philosopher and his modern follower: a possibility that Dio, with his bland but sophisticated rhetoric, does not fail to exploit, as is evidenced by numerous statements which are distributed skilfully throughout his writings.[1] For Dio, however, Socrates is much

---

[1] See for example the long passage in *Or.* 43. 8–10 (= *SSR* I C 121), where Dio admits, Σωκράτης ἐκεῖνος, οὗ μέμνημαι πολλάκις, κτλ. (NB The ancient sources concerning Socrates, Antisthenes, and the Socratics are quoted by the edition of Giannantoni (1990), *Socratis et Socraticorum reliquiae*.) See also *Or.* 47. 7 (*deest* in *SSR*), and *Or.* 51. 8 (*deest* in *SSR*). On the importance of the Socratic *persona* in Dio see Moles (1978) 98–9.

more than a literary and cultural model. And he is not just a prestigious guarantor of Dio's Greek identity. He is a philosopher, indeed the very father of ancient philosophy, a common claim in the historiographic genealogies elaborated during the Hellenistic period: a philosopher whom Dio appears to have encountered through an intricate network of traditions and who may have had a deeper and more wide-ranging influence on his intellectual personality than has been hitherto supposed. Furthermore, Socrates provides a privileged interpretative key that helps to situate Dio in a philosophical perspective and to account for his peculiar approach to philosophical traditions—Cynicism especially, but also Stoicism—which in ancient culture and doxography were seen as deriving directly from Socrates.

In the following pages, I intend to examine the references to Socrates and the Socratics in the *Corpus Dioneum*. I will seek to uncover the matrix of the various traditions discernible in Dio's work in order to identify those that had the greatest influence on him. I shall then carry out a brief comparison with the speeches devoted to Diogenes in order to show how a number of structural elements of Dio's Cynicism are derived from Socrates.

DIO'S SOCRATES

A passage in Synesius, the exact interpretation of which has been the subject of much discussion, appears to go directly counter to the above statement. In *Dio, or On Living by his Example*, the Neoplatonic philosopher writes that in some of his writings Dio 'hurled at Socrates and Zeno the coarse jests of the Dionysiac festival', describing their followers as worthy of being banished 'from all seas and lands in the belief that they are Messengers of Death to states and civic organization alike'.[2] Yet it is quite evident that in this passage Socrates and Zeno are not placed on the same level as their presumed followers, and, in any case, jesting, even if caustic and biting, is not the same thing as a direct and violent attack. It should be added that here Synesius refers to the youthful speeches of Dio and that the speech of which he is thinking is, very probably, the lost essay *Against the Philosophers*. In this sense his observation finds an explanation in the sphere of Dio's opposition to all

---

[2] Synes. *Dio* p. 238. 7–12 Terzaghi τοῖς ἐκ Διονυσίων σκώμμασι, κτλ. On this passage see Jones (1978) 15–16, and Brancacci (1985) 182–5.

philosophers, and especially to the activities of Cynics and Stoics, during the reign of Vespasian, and should be read, in spite of some differences in context, in line with the harsh attack against 'the so-called philosophers' (*hoi kaloumenoi philosophoi*) and 'the so-called Cynics' (*hoi Kunikoi legomenoi*) in the *Alexandrian Oration*.[3] Finally, it is balanced by another comment of Synesius, which we can easily verify, who states that, in other works, Dio praised the two philosophers, presenting them as an 'example' (*paradeigma*) 'of noble and wise conduct' (*gennaiou biou kai sōphronos*). In fact, Synesius himself ends up noting how 'in many speeches' (*en suchnois logois*) devoted to Socrates and Diogenes the two philosophers are presented as models of the perfect and true philosophic way of living, a height that few men can aspire to attain.[4]

Actually, Dio's interpretation of the philosophy of Diogenes and Socrates is somewhat different. On a historical and cultural level, his rediscovery of Socrates is, first of all, part of the general and massive recuperation of *logoi Sōkratikoi* that characterizes the beginning of the imperial period, which, in the philosophical context, entailed a generalized return to Socrates. In this recuperation there is also a reaction against the traditional consideration of Socrates as a literary figure (*prosōpon*), a mere spokesman for Plato's philosophy, which was prevalent in the Platonic tradition at least,[5] a consideration which itself helps to explain the renewed interest of philosophers and men of letters in the images of Socrates disseminated by other Socratic traditions. Dio's familiarity with these traditions is evidenced by numerous explicit statements found in his speeches, on which we may focus as a starting-point.

In line with the citation practice and the attitude common in antiquity, Dio holds that the literary production of the Socratics faithfully follows Socrates' *logoi*, and is in turn indistinguishable from the protagonist of that literature. The distinction between a 'historic' Socrates and a 'literary' one, which for moderns represents a difficult historiographic problem, is present only in episodic and exceptional

---

[3] Cf. *Or.* 32. 8–9. On this passage see Malherbe (1970), and Brancacci (1994) 442–4. The attack on the 'so-called Cynics' and the 'so-called philosophers' can be interpreted as one against rival philosophers and preachers from whose oratorical style and goals Dio wishes to keep his distance. The date of the *Alexandrian Oration* is controversial. The dating of this speech to the age of Trajan has recently been reproposed by Sidebottom (1992). Swain (1996) 429 states that 'a Trajanic date is not secure, but it is preferable'. [4] Cf. Synes. *Dio* p. 240. 3–7 Terzaghi.
[5] Cf. Diog. Laert. 2. 52.

form in ancient literature. Thus, in the speech *On Homer and Socrates*—where Dio argues that Socrates was the pupil of Homer rather than of Archelaus, because both Socrates and Homer discussed the same moral issues—Dio notes that Socrates' exceptional modesty is demonstrated by the fact that, 'Socrates did not even put his words into writing and himself bequeath them to posterity, and in this he outdid Homer. For just as we know the name of Homer by hearing it from others, so too we know the words of Socrates because others have left them to us'.[6]

The state of the Socratic sources available to Dio is more precisely illustrated by a passage in the speech *On Socrates*, where, after having drawn a parallel between the philosopher and his contemporaries, the sophists, Dio notes that,

However, while the words of those sophists, who won such admiration, have perished and nothing remains but their names alone, the words of Socrates, for some strange reason, still endure and will endure for all time, though he himself did not write or leave behind him either a treatise or a will. In fact, Socrates died intestate as to both his wisdom and his estate. Yet though he had no estate that could be made public property through confiscation—as is commonly done in the case of men who have been condemned as criminals—his words in reality have been made public property, not by foes, God knows, but by his friends; nevertheless, though they are even now not only accessible for all but also held in high esteem, few understand them and partake of their wisdom.[7]

Dio's access to the writings of the Socratics is confirmed by the fact that he subjects them to prescriptions and evaluations of a specifically literary nature. In the epistle *On Training for Public Speaking*, addressed to an unknown man hoping to acquire eloquence

---

[6] *Or.* 55. 8 (= *SSR* I C 444) οὐδὲ τοὺς λόγους αὐτὸς [= Σωκράτης] κατέλιπε γράψας, καὶ ταύτῃ γε ὑπερέβαλε τὸν Ὅμηρον. ὥσπερ γὰρ τὸ ὄνομα τὸ ἐκείνου παρ' ἑτέρων ἀκούοντες ἴσμεν, οὕτω καὶ τοὺς λόγους τοὺς Σωκράτους ἄλλων καταλιπόντων. (NB translations of Dio's works are those of Cohoon and Lamar Crosby in the Loeb Classical Library's edition, with a few alterations.)

[7] *Or.* 54. 4 (= *SSR* I C 427) ἀλλὰ δὴ τῶν μὲν θαυμαζομένων ἐκείνων σοφιστῶν ἐκλελοίπασιν οἱ λόγοι καὶ οὐδὲν ἢ τὰ ὀνόματα μόνα ἔστιν· οἱ δὲ τοῦ Σωκράτους, οὐκ οἶδ' ὅπως, διαμένουσι καὶ διαμενοῦσι τὸν ἅπαντα χρόνον, τούτου μὲν αὐτοῦ γράψαντος ἢ καταλιπόντος οὔτε σύγγραμμα οὔτε διαθήκας. ἐτελεύτα γὰρ ὁ ἀνὴρ ἀδιάθετος τήν τε σοφίαν καὶ τὰ χρήματα. ἀλλὰ οὐσίαν μὲν οὐκ εἶχεν, ὥστε δημευθῆναι—καθάπερ εἴωθε γίγνεσθαι ἐπὶ τῶν καταδικασθέντων—οἱ λόγοι δὲ τῷ ὄντι ἐδημεύθησαν, μὰ Δί' οὐχ ὑπ' ἐχθρῶν, ἀλλὰ ὑπὸ τῶν φίλων· οὐδὲν μέντοι ἧττον καὶ νῦν φανερῶν τε ὄντων καὶ τιμωμένων ὀλίγοι ξυνιᾶσι καὶ μετέχουσιν.

in order to take part in public life,[8] Dio puts forward a selection and hierarchy of the most important authors in Greek literature, both in poetry and in prose. After having dealt with the orators, Dio includes the Socratics among the main stylistic models, praises their characteristic grace (*charis*), and writes,

I shall now turn to the Socratics, writers who, I affirm, are quite indispensable to every man who aspires to become an orator. For just as no meat without salt will be gratifying to the taste, so no branch of literature, as it seems to me, could possibly be pleasing to the ear if it lacked the Socratic grace.[9]

Panaetius accepted as authentic, undoubtedly also on the basis of detailed philological analysis, only the Socratic dialogues of Plato, Xenophon, Antisthenes, and Aeschines, expressing reservations on those by Phaedon and Eucleides and rejecting all others.[10] It was probably thanks to his recommendations that the four greatest Socratics were accepted as stylistic models in learned circles and the rhetorical schools.[11] All four are cited by Dio, which shows that he had a particularly wide-ranging and reliable knowledge of Socratic philosophy and of the various related traditions. An examination of the works, however, shows that Dio did not turn to Plato for his portrait of

---

[8] Cf. *Or.* 18. 14 μὴ ὡς ῥήτωρ ἐθέλοι μόνον, ἀλλὰ καὶ ὡς πολιτικὸς καὶ βασιλικὸς ἀνήρ, κτλ. Desideri (1978) 137–9 has proposed that we identify Dio's recipient with Titus, who had not yet become emperor. But see, *contra*, Sidebottom (1996) 450. Nerva, who was an old friend of Dio's (cf. *Or.* 45. 2), might have been the addressee, before becoming emperor: cf. Valgimigli (1912) 72. The tone of great respect, almost of quiet submission, which characterizes the whole letter, becomes more marked towards the end. Cf. *Or.* 18. 20: 'just as expert wrestlers sometimes give way to those who are weaker and make them believe that they are stronger, so you seem to have led me on to write and tell what you, as it happens, know better yourself, just as if you did not know it so well'. Dio's final words (βουλοίμην δ' ἄν, εἴ σοι κεχαρισμένον εἴη, καὶ ἐν τῷ αὐτῷ ποτε ἡμᾶς γενέσθαι, κτλ.) almost sound like timid expressions of a hope to be reinstated in his fatherland and Rome.

[9] *Or.* 18. 13 (= *SSR* I H 24) τρέψομαι δὲ ἤδη ἐπὶ τοὺς Σωκρατικούς, οὓς δὴ ἀναγκαιοτάτους εἶναί φημι παντὶ ἀνδρὶ λόγων ἐφιεμένῳ. ὥσπερ γὰρ οὐδὲν ὄψον ἄνευ ἁλῶν γεύσει κεχαρισμένον, οὕτως οὐδὲ εἶδος ἔμοιγε δοκεῖ ἀκοῇ προσηνὲς ἂν γενέσθαι χάριτος Σωκρατικῆς ἄμοιρον.

[10] Cf. Diog. Laert. 2. 64 (= Panaetius fr. 126 van Straaten = *SSR* I H 17) πάντων μέντοι τῶν Σωκρατικῶν διαλόγων Παναίτιος ἀληθεῖς εἶναι δοκεῖ τοὺς Πλάτωνος, Ξενοφῶντος, Ἀντισθένους, Αἰσχίνου· διστάζει δὲ περὶ τῶν Φαίδωνος καὶ Εὐκλείδου, τοὺς δὲ ἄλλους ἀναιρεῖ πάντας. On this fragment see Alline (1915) 38; Maier (1944) I: 132 n. 2, Patzer (1970) 107, who interpret ἀληθεῖς as 'authentic'. Von Arnim (1898) 131, and recently Alesse (1997) 284, interpret ἀληθεῖς as 'reliable'.

[11] Cf. Longin. *De invent.* p. 559. 13–16 Walz (= *SSR* V A 48). For Antisthenes as a stylistic model see also Dionys. Halic. *De Thucyd.* 51 p. 941 (= *SSR* V A 49), and Phrynic. *ap.* Phot. *Bibl.* 158 (= *SSR* V A 50).

Socrates. The most characteristic and fundamental themes of Plato's interpretation—the basic principle according to which no one errs voluntarily (*oudeis hekōn examartanei*); the theme of *exetazein*, interpreted in an 'aporetic' sense, i.e., as a never-ending process of re-examination rather than as the positive determination of a presumed objective meaning of names; the ideal of *dialegesthai* as *megiston agathōn*; the claim that poets do not possess knowledge; irony; the principle of *beltistos logos*—are all completely absent from the *Orations*. On the contrary, Dio emphasizes a series of opposite motives: the kind of knowledge his Socrates possesses is one of a positive and determinate kind; Socrates is assimilated to the greatest among the poets, Homer; he proves to be willing to spread his teachings among mankind; he almost entirely gives up the atopy, which is inherent in Plato's description. This is a consequence of the fact that of the two philosophic traditions that during antiquity preserved an elaborate and systematic account of Socrates' philosophy, i.e. the Cynic-Stoic one derived from Antisthenes and the Academic-Platonic one derived from Plato, it is evidently the former that Dio refers to.

There are of course in Dio a few echoes of the Platonic Socrates, and it could not be otherwise, because of the importance in ancient literature of Plato's representation of Socrates, as well as the fact that Dio himself was an assiduous reader of Plato.[12] What I should like to emphasize is that philosophically Dio's Socrates has a doctrinal solidity and his own coherent and precise physiognomy because it is modelled on Antisthenes' Socrates. The radical character of Dio's choice is evidenced by comparison with his contemporary Epictetus, who, though relying on a representation of Socrates mediated by Antisthenes and the Stoics, reserves much space in his works to the citation of famous Platonic texts and statements, even while adjusting them, as is shown by a careful analysis, to the Stoic and Cynic temperament that characterizes the *Discourses*.[13]

Dio has certainly read Xenophon's works on Socrates. However, in citing Xenophon, he never mentions Socrates, as one might have expected. Dio mentions Xenophon in the course of his discussion

---

[12] See for example *Or.* 13. 14 (= *SSR* I C 450). The passage at *Or.* 43. 8 (= *SSR* I C 121) refers to Plat. *Apol.* 32c–d or to Xen. *Mem.* 1. 2. 32. The passage at *Or.* 57. 11 (*deest* in *SSR*) does not depend on Plato: cf. Cohoon and Lamar Crosby (1932–51) 4: 426–7 n. 1.

[13] Cf. Calogero (1984), Jagu (1946).

of the Socratics found in the epistle *On Training*. After remarking that to praise them individually would require too much time, he singles out Xenophon, saying that his historical works are perfectly suited to the purposes of politicians. Dio proceeds to discuss the stylistic merits of Xenophon, whom he sees essentially as an historian and an adviser of leaders and statesmen. Even the reference to Xenophon's hortatory speeches (*protreptikois Xenophōntos logois*) has actually no reference to the Athenian philosopher. Finally, Dio confesses having been moved to tears by the account of so many brave deeds.[14]

Antisthenes is cited many times in the *Orations*. Among the Socratics, Antisthenes had the greatest influence on Dio, both for his portrait of Socrates and for his own ethical and political doctrines.[15] As is known, Antisthenes was the author of a particularly ample literary production, including many dialectical and rhetorical treatises, works on ethics, politics, and Homeric criticism, and, from a formal point of view, numerous *logoi Sōkratikoi*, a genre which during the imperial period became common in literary circles and schools of rhetoric, in the Cynic tradition and, perhaps even more so, in the Stoic one. The Stoics were particularly interested in claiming the descent of their school from Socrates and, therefore, claim a connection with Antisthenes, whose dignified moral philosophy was also useful to counterbalance the mediation of Diogenes, upholder of embarrassingly extreme philosophic positions.[16] Particularly important for Dio's knowledge of Antisthenes are: (1) a passage of the speech *On Homer*, which discusses the Antisthenean distinction between *doxa* and *alētheia*, indicating a general knowledge of Antisthenes' writings on Homer;[17] (2) a passage of *Or.* 47 (*Public Speech in his Fatherland*) containing a fragment taken from *Cyrus, or On Kingship*;[18] (3) a long passage from the speech *In Athens, On his Exile*;[19] and (4) a passage in the eighth discourse *Diogenes, or On Virtue*,[20] and certain passages from the third and fourth speeches *On Kingship* which we shall deal with later.

---

[14] *Or.* 18. 14–17. On this passage, cf. Münscher (1920) 115–16.
[15] On this point see Brancacci (1992) 3308–34.
[16] Cf. Mansfeld (1986) 337–9, 346–9.
[17] *Or.* 53. 5 (= *SSR* V A 194). On this passage see Brancacci (1990) 64–6.
[18] *Or.* 47. 25 (= *SSR* V A 86).
[19] *Or.* 13. 14–28 (= *SSR* V A 208). On this passage cf. Giannantoni (1990) 4: 352–3.
[20] Cf. *Or.* 8. 1–4 (= *SSR* I H 2 = V A 1).

Many other examples confirm that Dio had access to a great number of *logoi Sōkratikoi*, the majority of which have not survived and whose paternity is known only exceptionally thanks to parallel traditions. A passage from the oration *On Homer and Socrates* indicates a tradition generically identifiable as Socratic. In this, light is thrown on how the teaching of Socrates has a positive content, both when it expresses itself in the *legein* about the passions and when it proposes to *apotrepein* men from them. The passage is interesting also for the echo we find in it of a debate, not attested by other sources, on the meaning and function of speeches delivered by Socrates' interlocutors:

Most men suppose that such items are purposeless, and they regard them as mere vexation and nonsense. But Socrates held that, every time he introduces a boastful man, he is speaking of boastfulness; every time he introduces a shameless, loathsome man, he is speaking of shamelessness and loathsomeness; every time he introduces an unreasonable, irascible man, he is turning his hearers against unreason and anger. Moreover, in all other cases similarly he revealed the true nature of the passions and maladies of men in the persons of the very ones who were afflicted by the passions or the maladies more distinctly than if he were using mere speeches.[21]

Particularly important is a passage of the same discourse where, in introducing the problem of the significance of Socrates' choice of interlocutors, Dio notes:

Again, it was not without conscious purpose that he represented Gorgias or Polus or Thrasymachus or Prodicus or Meno or Euthyphro or Anytus or Alcibiades or Laches as speaking, when he might have omitted their names. On the contrary, he knew that by this device most of all he would benefit his hearers, if perchance they grasped the point: for to comprehend human beings from their words, and their words from human beings, is not an easy task for any one but philosophers and educated persons.[22]

---

[21] *Or.* 55. 13 (= *SSR* I C 444) οἱ δὲ πολλοὶ μάτην οἴονται τὰ τοιαῦτα λέγεσθαι καὶ ὄχλον ἄλλως καὶ φλυαρίαν ἡγοῦνται. Σωκράτης δὲ ἐνόμιζεν ὁσάκις μὲν ἀλαζόνα ἄνθρωπον εἰσάγει, περὶ ἀλαζονείας λέγειν· ὁπότε δὲ ἀναίσχυντον καὶ βδελυρόν, περὶ ἀναιδείας καὶ βδελυρίας· ὁπότε δὲ ἀγνώμονα καὶ ὀργίλον, ἀγνωμοσύνης καὶ ὀργῆς ἀποτρέπειν. καὶ ἐπὶ τῶν ἄλλων ὁμοίως τὰ πάθη καὶ τὰ νοσήματα ἐπ᾽ αὐτῶν τῶν ἀνθρώπων τῶν ἐχομένων τοῖς πάθεσιν ἢ τοῖς νοσήμασι σαφέστερον ἐδείκνυεν ὁποῖά ἐστιν ἢ εἰ τοὺς λόγους ψιλοὺς ἔλεγε.

[22] *Ibid.* 12 (= *SSR* I C 444) οὐ τοίνυν οὐδὲ τοὺς περὶ Γοργίαν ἢ Πῶλον ἢ Θρασύμαχον ἢ Πρόδικον ἢ Μένωνα ἢ Εὐθύφρονα ἢ Ἄνυτον ἢ Ἀλκιβιάδην ἢ Λάχητα μάτην ἐποίει λέγοντας, ἐξὸν ἀφελεῖν τὰ ὀνόματα· ἀλλὰ ᾔδει τούτῳ καὶ μάλιστα ὀνήσων τοὺς ἀκούοντας, εἴ πως ξυνεῖεν· ἀπὸ γὰρ τῶν λόγων τοὺς ἀνθρώπους καὶ ἀπὸ τῶν ἀνθρώπων τοὺς λόγους ξυνορᾶν οὐ ῥάδιον ἄλλοις ἢ τοῖς φιλοσόφοις καὶ τοῖς πεπαιδευμένοις.

Dio is certainly referring here *also* to Plato's dialogues, but not *only* to them. This is shown by the fact that the subject of the proposition 'it was not without conscious purpose that he represented' is not Plato but Socrates.[23] This means that Dio refers cumulatively, in this passage, to the interlocutors of Socrates in *all* the Socratic literature of which he is aware. That his references are also to non-Platonic dialogues emerges from various details. It is immediately doubtful that Prodicus should be identified with the sophist represented in the *Protagoras*, assuming that all the characters quoted in this passage are to be considered, as the context tells us, as the main interlocutors of Socrates in the corresponding Socratic dialogues. And it is certain that Socratic dialogues named after Alcibiades had been written also by Antisthenes, Aeschines, and Eucleides. Furthermore, the comparison with the passage that ends the speech (quoted below) suggests that the Anytus and the Meno cited in the above quotation were the interlocutors of Socrates in two non-Platonic dialogues, of which Dio has the merit of having preserved for us the subtitles, so to speak. The first, identified as a work of Antisthenes,[24] *Peri burseōn kai skutotomōn*; the second *Peri erastōn kai eromenōn*. From this same passage we also learn the names of the characters and the argument of two other *logoi Sōkratikoi*, known to Dio but no longer extant: *Peri Amniōn kai Kodiōn*, where Lysicles speaks, and *Peri dikōn kai sukophantematōn*, where Socrates' interlocutor is Lycon. The first has been identified by Dittmar and, more recently, by Giannantoni, as a dialogue by Aeschines: 'No more, then, did Socrates employ his words or illustrations at random. On the contrary, when conversing with Anytus he would refer to tanners and cobblers; but if he conversed with Lysicles, it would be lambs and fleeces; if with Lycon, lawsuits and blackmail; if with Meno the Thessalian, lovers and boy-friends.'[25]

Both Antisthenes and Xenophon had insisted on the positive content of Socrates' *logoi*, intending by this to underline both the fact that the philosophy of Socrates had a very precise doctrinal content

---

[23] Michael Trapp, in this volume, above, p. 234 n. 63, misses this point.

[24] By Dittmar (1912) 94–5. Dittmar makes this passage fr. 7 of his edition of the fragments of Antisthenes' *Cyrus*.

[25] *Or.* 55. 22 οὐ τοίνυν οὐδὲ Σωκράτης ἄλλως ἐχρῆτο τοῖς λόγοις οὐδὲ τοῖς παραδείγμασιν, ἀλλ' Ἀνύτῳ μὲν διαλεγόμενος βυρσέων ἐμέμνητο καὶ σκυτοτόμων· εἰ δὲ Λυσικλεῖ διαλέγοιτο, ἀμνίων καὶ κωδίων (= *SSR* VI A 68), Λύκωνι δέ, δικῶν καὶ συκοφαντημάτων, Μένωνι δὲ τῷ Θετταλῷ περὶ ἐραστῶν καὶ ἐρωμένων.

and also the actual ability of Socrates to lead men to virtue.[26] The same position is found in Dio, who in fact is led by this to compare his own teaching to that of his ancient master:

Now to my hearers I used to say practically the same things as Socrates did, things old-fashioned and simple, and when they refused to leave me in peace even on reaching Rome itself, I did not venture to speak any word of my own, fearing lest I be laughed at and regarded as a fool, since I was well aware how completely old-fashioned and ignorant I was; and I said to myself: 'Come now, if I, copying the words of another, use such derogatory words about things which are highly regarded at Rome here, and tell them that not one of these things is a good, if I speak of luxury and intemperance, and tell them that what they need is a thorough and sound education, perhaps they will not laugh at me for uttering such sentiments nor declare that I am a fool. But if they do so, I shall be able to say that those words were spoken by a man whom the Greeks one and all admired for his wisdom (*epi sophiai*), and what is more, whom Apollo actually considered the wisest man (*sophōtaton*) in the world, while Archelaus, the king of Macedonia, who knew a great deal and had consorted with many wise men, tried to get him to come to Macedonia, offering him gifts and fees that he might have the privilege of hearing him say such things.[27]

As one can see, Dio completely ignores the Platonic interpretation of the oracle, according to which Socrates may call himself the wisest of men simply because he knows that he does not know. On the contrary he positively presents Socrates as the wisest man in the world and, consequently, aligns the story of the oracle with the tradition, derived from the *Archelaus* of Antisthenes, according to which Socrates was invited to the court of the king of Macedonia precisely because of his wisdom but declined the invitation. The emphasis on Socrates' *sophia* is not casual and recalls a passage from the speech

---

[26] Cf. Porphyr. *Schol. ad Od.* α 1 (= *SSR* V A 208); Xen. *Mem.* 1. 4. 1.

[27] *Or.* 13. 29–30 (= *SSR* I C 112) πρός τε οὖν τοὺς ἄλλους σχεδόν τι τὰ αὐτὰ διελεγόμην ἀρχαῖα καὶ φαῦλα, καὶ ἐπειδὴ οὐκ εἴων ἐν αὐτῇ τῇ Ῥώμῃ γενόμενον ἡσυχίαν ἄγειν, ἴδιον μὲν οὐδένα ἐτόλμων διαλέγεσθαι λόγον, μὴ καταγελασθῶ τε καὶ ἀνόητος δόξω φοβούμενος, ἅτε συνειδὼς αὑτῷ πολλὴν ἀρχαιότητα καὶ ἀμαθίαν· ἐνεθυμούμην δέ· φέρε, ἂν μιμούμενος τινὰς διαλέγωμαι λόγους περὶ τῶν θαυμαζομένων παρ' αὐτοῖς ὡς οὐδέν ἐστιν αὐτῶν ἀγαθόν, καὶ περὶ τρυφῆς καὶ ἀκολασίας, καὶ ὅτι παιδείας πολλῆς καὶ ἀγαθῆς δέονται, τυχὸν οὐ καταγελάσουσί μου ταῦτα λέγοντος οὐδὲ φήσουσιν ἀνόητον· εἰ δὲ μή, ἔξω λέγειν ὅτι εἰσὶν οἱ λόγοι οὗτοι ἀνδρὸς ὃν οἵ τε Ἕλληνες ἐθαύμασαν ἅπαντες ἐπὶ σοφίᾳ καὶ δὴ καὶ ὁ Ἀπόλλων σοφώτατον αὐτὸν ἡγήσατο· καὶ Ἀρχέλαος Μακεδόνων βασιλεύς, πολλὰ εἰδὼς καὶ πολλοῖς συγγεγονὼς τῶν σοφῶν, ἐκάλει αὐτὸν ἐπὶ δώροις καὶ μισθοῖς, ὅπως ἀκούοι αὐτοῦ διαλεγομένου τοὺς λόγους τοιούτους.

On Homer and Socrates where Dio claims that both the poet and
the philosopher, 'were devoted to the same ends and spoke about
the same things, the one through the medium of his verse, the other
in prose: human virtue and vice, actions wrong and actions right,
truth and deceit, and how the masses have only opinions, while the
wise have true knowledge'.[28]

This passage obviously presupposes a knowledge of Antisthenes'
theory of the *sophos*, which the Stoics inherited. It is this theory that
contains the opposition between *doxa* and *epistēmē* and, therefore,
the opposition between common men, the *phauloi*, who have only
opinions, and the wise men, the *spoudaioi*, who know fundamental
ethical truths.[29] On this subject, Antisthenes' Socrates is remarkably
different from the Platonic one, who in the *Apology* states he was
never the teacher of anyone and that he knows nothing,[30] and to
whom such a sharp distinction between ignorant men and wise men
would have seemed absurd. A survey of the passages by Dio that
discuss the type of philosophy embraced by Socrates confirms
that Dio's reading of Socrates was mediated by Antisthenes' and
Xenophon's interpretation, from which he takes the 'positive' and
'dogmatic' view of Socrates' teaching, which became common later
on among the Cynics and the Stoics. Socrates is presented as, on
the one hand, convinced of his ability to attain moral truth and, from
this point of view, of being a *sophos*, in the technical sense of the
word, and, on the other hand, of being a true teacher of protrep-
tics, bent on confuting and educating men:

For Socrates indeed entered the lists in all kinds of arguments and all sorts
of lectures—against orators, sophists, geometricians, musicians, athletic
trainers, and all the other craftsmen—and, whether in palaestra or symposium or market-place, he was not prevented in any way at all from plying
his calling as philosopher (*philosophein*) or from impelling (*protrepein*)
toward virtue those who were with him, not by introducing any topic of

[28] *Or.* 55. 9 (= *SSR* I C 444) ὑπὲρ τῶν αὐτῶν ἐσπουδαζέτην [sc. Σωκράτης τε
καὶ Ὅμηρος] καὶ ἐλεγέτην, ὁ μὲν διὰ τῆς ποιήσεως, ὁ δὲ καταλογάδην· περὶ
ἀρετῆς ἀνθρώπων καὶ κακίας καὶ περὶ ἁμαρτημάτων καὶ κατορθωμάτων καὶ
περὶ ἀληθείας καὶ ἀπάτης καὶ ὅπως δοξάζουσιν οἱ πολλοὶ καὶ ὅπως ἐπίστανται
οἱ φρόνιμοι.
[29] Cf. Porphyr. *Schol. ad Od.* a 1 (= *SSR* V A 208); Gnom. Vat. 743 n. 6 (= *SSR*
V A 166); Phaen. *ap.* Diog. Laert. 6. 8 (= *SSR* V A 172); Diog. Laert. 6. 5 (= *SSR* V
A 71). On these fragments see Brancacci (1990) 114–17.
[30] Cf. Plat. *Apol.* 33a–b.

his own or any preconceived problem, but rather by consistently employ-
ing the topic at hand and applying it to philosophy.[31]

The protreptic aspect of Socrates' teaching, which was proper to
Antisthenes, and will later on become a characteristic of the Cynic
sage, is illustrated at length in paragraphs 14–28 of the speech *In
Athens, On his Exile*, for which Dio was inspired not by the *Clitophon*, as some scholars suggest, but by Antisthenes' *Protrepticus*, the
work mimicked in the opening of the *Clitophon*,[32] precisely for the
purpose of illustrating that Antisthenes' Socrates is indeed capable
of exhorting men to virtue, but not of explaining what virtue is and
what exactly it consists of. Dio himself, in introducing the discourse
he is about to quote, states explicitly that the *logos* is not his own
and, through the formula *hōs ephē tis* indicates, albeit in an allusive
fashion, the *auctoritas* which lies behind it.[33] The exposition of
Socrates' allocution, which Dio himself presents as 'an ancient
appeal' (*tina logon archaion*), and on account of which he fears being
also viewed as 'old-fashioned' (*archaios*) by his listeners, has the purpose of showing Socrates' attitude towards true education (*alēthinē
paideia*) and towards the principles that must govern the moral conduct of men in both the public and the private sphere. At the end
of the section, Dio specifies that, for Socrates, the goal of moral
science is the lessons one must learn to become *kalos kai agathos*,
and for this reason it is necessary to dedicate oneself to philosophy:
'And speaking in this manner he [= Socrates] would exhort his
hearers to take care to give heed to his words and to pursue philosophy; for he knew that if they sought that which he recommended,
they would be doing nothing less than philosophy. And doing

---

[31] *Or.* 60. 10 (= *SSR* I C 428) ἐκεῖνος [sc. Σωκράτης] γὰρ εἰς ἅπαντας δὲ λόγους
καὶ πάσας διατριβὰς καθίει, καὶ πρὸς ῥήτορας καὶ πρὸς σοφιστὰς καὶ πρὸς
γεωμέτρας καὶ μουσικοὺς καὶ παιδοτρίβας καὶ τοὺς ἄλλους δημιουργούς, καὶ
ἐν παλαίστραις καὶ ἐν συμποσίοις καὶ ἐν ἀγορᾷ οὐκ ἐκωλύετο ἐξ ἅπαντος τρόπου
φιλοσοφεῖν καὶ προτρέπειν ἐπ' ἀρετὴν τοὺς συνόντας, οὐκ ἰδίαν εἰσφέρων
ὑπόθεσιν οὐδὲ πρόβλημα ἐσκεμμένον, ἀλλ' ἀεὶ τῇ παρούσῃ χρώμενος καὶ ταύτην
προσάγων πρὸς φιλοσοφίαν.

[32] Cf. [Plat.] *Clitoph.* 410a–e.

[33] Cf. *Or.* 13. 14. The dependence of paragraphs 14–28 of Dio's oration on a work
by Antisthenes, identified as the *Protrepticus*, has been discussed by many scholars
(from von Arnim to Th. Gomperz to Praechter, from Raeder to Maier to Chroust).
Since I am unable to quote them all here or to take up the entire question from the
beginning, the reader should refer to Giannantoni (1990) 4: 350–3, who includes Dio's
passage in his edition of the sources of Antisthenes. Michael Trapp, in this volume,
above, p. 231, in my view ignores all this.

philosophy is nothing but finding out how to become virtuous men, and aspiring to this.'[34]

The notion of a positive aspect in Socrates' philosophy is evident in certain passages of the third speech *On Kingship* where Socrates is the protagonist. These passages, which even from a literary point of view are noticeably different from the rest of the speech, have a historical basis, in the sense that Dio based them on certain doctrines that actually characterized Antisthenes' Socrates. Very likely these doctrines had been expounded in *Archelaus, or On Kingship*.[35] In this dialogue Antisthenes illustrated his notion of what the good king is by using as a starting-point Socrates' refusal to visit the tyrant Archelaus of Macedon, who had invited him to his court promising gifts and remuneration. I have shown elsewhere that the brief initial dialogue between Socrates and Hippias, found in paragraphs 1–3 and 25–41, is derived from the *Archelaus*. The passage is replete with themes, technical terms, and concepts that are characteristic of Antisthenes. But, more important, the opposition between 'king' (*basileus*) and 'tyrant' (*turannos*), found in this brief Socratic dialogue, is rooted in Antisthenes' logical-linguistic doctrines. Antisthenes had argued that for each thing there is one and one only defining discourse, i.e. the discourse that expresses the proper quality (*poion ti esti*) that pertains exclusively to that object and therefore identifies and defines it, whereas the discourse that does not achieve this identification remains completely foreign (*allotrios*) to the object.[36] In applying this theory to moral concepts, Antisthenes argued that *basileus* is not he who is so *de facto*, because he is entitled to the conventional signs of power, but he who is *basileus de jure*, because he is endowed with the characteristics and attributes that are intrinsic to the notion of *basileia*, and has none of the attributes that contradict or violate the logical consistency of the notion. From this perspective, which Dio adopts as his own, a person can be called *basileus* without establishing an intolerable contradiction between name and thing, only if he is temperate, brave, just, and wise, if he is of noble character, charitable, respectful of the law, if he cares for the well-being of his subjects and gives precedence to their interests

---

[34] *Or.* 13. 28 (= *SSR* V A 208) καὶ οὕτως δὴ παρακάλει πρὸς τὸ ἐπιμελεῖσθαι καὶ προσέχειν αὐτῷ τὸν νοῦν καὶ φιλοσοφεῖν· ᾔδει γὰρ ὅτι τοῦτο ζητοῦντες οὐδὲν ἄλλο ποιήσουσιν ἢ φιλοσοφήσουσι· τὸ γὰρ ζητεῖν καὶ φιλοτιμεῖσθαι ὅπως τις ἔσται καλὸς καὶ ἀγαθὸς οὐκ ἄλλο τι εἶναι ἢ τὸ φιλοσοφεῖν.

[35] Cf. Brancacci (1992) 331₈–34.　　　[36] Cf. Brancacci (1990) 221–6, 231–49.

over his own. The person who loves pleasure, leads a slothful life, avoids any kind of exertion, uses his subjects as tools to satisfy his lust, who is cowardly, foolish, unruly, and does not respect the law, this person does not have any power—note that Socrates does not say that he does not deserve power—and for this reason must be called *turannos* and not *basileus*.[37]

The Socrates presented by Dio in these paragraphs is, therefore, not simply a literary model and even less a pure invention. Rather, according to my thesis, he forms a coherent philosophical model derived from doctrines that were characteristic of Antisthenes' Socrates and that Dio could easily find in his Socratic dialogues. The reason for Dio's choice can be found in the basic motivations of his literary and political activity during these years. Antisthenes' Socrates was the bearer of an ethical-rational approach to politics, as well as of a number of conceptual distinctions, theoretical motifs, and technical terms, that provided Dio with a solid base for his theory of kingship, which he develops at length in the second part of the third speech *On Kingship*, and, more generally, for Dio's effort to elaborate, during the reigns of Nerva and Trajan, his vision of the philosopher as adviser of the prince.[38] Clear evidence that Dio was aware of this relationship and insisted on it is represented by the fact that the political doctrines expounded in the second part of the speech are presented as conforming to the teachings of *hoi meta Sōkratēn*.[39]

The second distinctive feature of Socrates, as presented by Dio, namely his peremptory, but not therefore less peculiar, assimilation to Homer, is perfectly clear within this context. What Dio himself wrote in his speech *On Homer* can be used to illuminate the matter. He opposes two great currents of thought, which in ancient philosophy formed around the evaluation of Homer's poetry. On one side there is Plato, who condemns Homer basically on the grounds of morals and of the obscurities and contradictions which can be found in Homer's text; on the other side, we have Antisthenes, Zeno, and Persaeus, who tried to explain and justify the contents of Homer's poetry which appeared unacceptable, aiming to use the poetry for their own purposes.[40] Despite his observation on the difficulty of

---

[37] *Or.* 3. 38–41 (*deest in SSR*). On this passage see Brancacci (1992) 3326–31.
[38] Cf. Desideri (1978) 287–318.   [39] *Or.* 3. 42.
[40] *Or.* 53. 2–5. For the statement of Dio about Aristotle cf. ibid. 1 and, on this passage, Russell (1981) 33.

having to arbitrate in a dispute between two men he loves equally, Dio essentially places himself within this second tradition as the greater part of his work clearly demonstrates.[41] By this choice, moreover, he takes his place among those authors, not many in number, who, in the ancient world, were able to make a clear and conscious distinction between Socrates and Plato, thereby leading to the reconstruction and revaluation of a Socrates whose ideas on some qualifying theoretical points not only did not coincide with those of Plato but clearly differed from them.

SOCRATISM AND CYNICISM IN DIO

In the light of the above observations it is possible to account for a number of textual elements that have previously been neglected or insufficiently explained. In the discourses *On Kingship*, there is a noticeable distinction between the third piece, where Socrates is at times present, and the fourth, where Diogenes is the protagonist. The presence of these two philosophers in a group of works that are basically homogeneous, even though they might belong to slightly different periods,[42] may be further accounted for if one keeps in mind the fact that the influence of Antisthenes is discernible also in the fourth speech, and that Antisthenes, as is known, was not only the disciple of Socrates but, according to the ancient tradition, also the teacher of Diogenes. Specifically, the influence of Antisthenes is visible in two themes that are central to the fourth speech: the doctrine of *dittē paideia* and the related motif of *kallista basileuein*.[43] Both descend from the principle of the unity of meaning in names and from the restrictive interpretation of moral concepts, connected to the theory of *oikeios logos*, which were characteristic of Antisthenes and which are clearly in evidence in the following passage:

But no one can be a bad king any more than he can be a bad good man; for the king is the best one among men, since he is most brave and righteous

[41] It should be remembered that Dio wrote a treatise in four books entitled *In Defence of Homer against Plato* (Ὑπὲρ Ὁμήρου πρὸς Πλάτωνα). On this treatise and on Dio's use of Homer see Brancacci (1985) 253–9. On the way Dio uses myth see Blomqvist (1989).

[42] On the dating of the orations *On Kingship* see von Arnim (1898) 325, 407 f., 412, 414 f., and Desideri (1978) 272–4 and 285 ff.

[43] Cf. Brancacci (1990) 80–4, 104–9, 164.

and humane, and cannot be overcome by any toil or by any appetite. Or do you think a man is a charioteer if he cannot drive, or that one is a pilot if he is ignorant of steering, or is a physician if he knows not how to cure? It is impossible, nay, though all the Greeks and barbarians acclaim him as such and load him with many diadems and sceptres and tiaras ... Therefore, just as one cannot pilot except after the manner of pilots, so no one can be a king except in a kingly way.[44]

The connection between Socratism and Cynicism that is thus established, and which is evident in the text, offers an additional and more profound justification of the exchange between Socrates and Diogenes found in Dio's speech and suggests that it is something more than a mere whim or a purely rhetorical choice. Consider, for example, the transition from the so-called *Diogenes* speeches (*Diogenics*) to the speeches *On Kingship*. Undoubtedly, one may consider the *Diogenes* speeches as earlier, belonging to the period of exile, and argue that exile induced in Dio a more heartfelt affiliation to Cynicism and consequently the rediscovery of the radical figure of Diogenes, the most sophisticated and suitable model available from both a literary and philosophical point of view.[45] However, one must not forget that even in the *Diogenes* speeches one sometimes finds echoes of Antisthenes, for example in the eighth, where the allegory and the condemnation of pleasure, exemplified through a very peculiar interpretation of the myth of Circe, certainly takes into account what Antisthenes had written in his *On Circe*.[46] This does not mean, of course, that we have to deny the originality of these speeches or ignore the fact that some of their characteristics are derived from interpretations of the figure of Diogenes which were common in the ancient tradition. Rather, the point is to highlight in Dio's

---

[44] *Or.* 4. 25 (= *SSR* V B 582) ἀλλ' οὐδὲ ἔστιν, ἔφη, βασιλεύειν κακῶς οὐ μᾶλλον ἢ κακῶς ἀγαθὸν εἶναι. ὁ γὰρ βασιλεὺς ἀνθρώπων ἄριστός ἐστιν, ἀνδρειότατος ὢν καὶ δικαιότατος καὶ φιλανθρωπότατος καὶ ἀνίκητος ὑπὸ παντὸς πόνου καὶ πάσης ἐπιθυμίας. ἢ σὺ οἴει τὸν ἀδύνατον ἡνιοχεῖν ἡνίοχον εἶναι τοῦτον; ἢ τὸν ἄπειρον τοῦ κυβερνᾶν κυβερνήτην, ἢ τὸν οὐκ ἐπιστάμενον ἰᾶσθαι ἰατρόν; οὐκ ἔστιν, οὐδ' ἂν πάντες φῶσιν Ἕλληνες καὶ βάρβαροι καὶ πολλὰ διαδήματα καὶ σκῆπτρα καὶ τιάρας προσάψωσιν αὐτῷ ... καθάπερ οὖν οὐκ ἔστι κυβερνᾶν μὴ κυβερνητικῶς, οὕτως οὐδὲ βασιλεύειν μὴ βασιλικῶς. That this passage reflects the positions of Antisthenes has been argued by, among others, Weber (1887) 238–53, Höistad (1948) 56–61, Caizzi (1964) 59–60, Giannantoni (1990) 4: 312, Brancacci (1990) 80–4.

[45] On the *Diogenes* speeches see von Fritz (1926) 80–90, Brancacci (1980), Jouan (1993a).

[46] Cf. *Or.* 8. 21–6 (= *SSR* V B 584). On this passage cf. Lulofs (1900) 57, Decleva Caizzi (1966) 84–5, Funke (1970) 459–71.

work certain significant associations, one could almost say structural connections, between Socratism and Cynicism.

In fact, this connection is stated openly in a speech which is presumably earlier than the fourth speech *On Kingship*, in a peculiar passage that has been insufficiently explained hitherto. The passage is the opening of the eighth speech, *Diogenes, or On Virtue*:

> When Diogenes was exiled from his native Sinope, he came to Athens, looking like a complete beggar; and there he found a goodly number still of Socrates' companions: to wit, Plato, Aristippus, Aeschines, Antisthenes, and Eucleides of Megara; but Xenophon was in exile on account of his campaign with Cyrus. Now it was not long before he despised all save Antisthenes, whom he cultivated, not so much from approval of the man himself as of the words (*tous logous*) he spoke, which he felt to be alone true and best adapted to help mankind.[47]

In this passage, Dio incorrectly states that the reason for Xenophon's exile was his participation in the expedition of Cyrus the Younger against his brother Artaxerxes. In this way he anticipates Xenophon's exile by five years. Instead, as is well known, Xenophon was exiled from his native city because of his military and political activity in favour of Sparta and, more specifically, because of his participation in the battle of Coronea in 394 BC. His exile lasted until 365, the year of his return to Athens. By having Diogenes return to Athens before that date, Dio makes his meeting with Antisthenes entirely credible, since Antisthenes was still alive in 366.[48] In so doing, Dio is aligning himself with a tradition, common in antiquity and particularly supported by Cynicism and Stoicism, which, in connecting Diogenes and Antisthenes, highlighted the Socratic origin of Cynicism as well as the Cynic, and therefore Socratic, influence on Stoicism. The fact that Dio's tactic is deliberate and studied is confirmed by two important details. On the one hand, Dio goes as far as positing a meeting between Diogenes and Socrates' followers, whom he

---

[47] *Or.* 8. 1 (= *SSR* V A 1 = V B 584) Διογένης ὁ Σινωπεὺς ἐκπεσὼν ἐκ τῆς πατρίδος, οὐδενὸς διαφέρων τῶν πάνυ φαύλων Ἀθήναζε ἀφίκετο, καὶ καταλαμβάνει συχνοὺς ἔτι τῶν Σωκράτους ἑταίρων· καὶ γὰρ Πλάτωνα καὶ Ἀρίστιππον καὶ Αἰσχίνην καὶ Ἀντισθένην καὶ τὸν Μεγαρέα Εὐκλείδην· Ξενοφῶν δὲ ἔφευγε διὰ τὴν μετὰ Κύρου στρατείαν. τῶν μὲν οὖν ἄλλων ταχὺ κατεφρόνησεν, Ἀντισθένει δὲ ἐχρῆτο, οὐκ αὐτὸν οὕτως ἐπαινῶν ὡς τοὺς λόγους οὓς ἔλεγεν, ἡγούμενος μόνους εἶναι ἀληθεῖς καὶ μάλιστα δυναμένους ἄνθρωπον ὠφελῆσαι.

[48] Cf. Dudley (1937) 3 and n. 1; Giannantoni (1990) 4: 200; Brancacci (1990) 36 n. 23.

names. That is a *unicum* in our tradition. On the other hand, he emphasizes the difference between Diogenes and Antisthenes, while stressing that Diogenes admired Antisthenes' literary production, which is exactly what moderns hold. Socratism and Cynicism are thus closely connected but, as evidenced by the following paragraphs of the speech—passages that insist on the eminently practical character of Diogenes' philosophy, on the pre-eminent concern for 'deeds' (*erga*), and on his rigour[49]—are also accurately distinguished.

From a more literary perspective, Dio stresses the basic affinity between Socrates and Diogenes by suggesting common traits, to do alternately with life-style, character, and doctrines, even while he preserves a distance between the two. Thus, in the opening of the third speech *On Kingship*, Socrates is presented as a poor man (*penēs*),[50] a trait that was adopted and emphasized by the Cynics, while Diogenes, in the opening of *Or.* 8, is presented as 'looking like a complete beggar'. When Diogenes debates with the men he approaches he is said to look at them askance (*hupoblepsas*), just like Socrates in Aristophanes' *Clouds*, or in Plato's *Symposium*, or in the *Phaedo*, a text that Dio was familiar with, where the philosopher is said to gaze upon his interlocutor from below with 'bull's eyes' (*taurēdon hupoblepsas*).[51] Dio presents Socrates as being of a sociable nature and as being 'accessible to all who wished to approach and converse with him', and of Diogenes he says, 'he gave his time to any who wished to interview him'.[52] He notes that the majority of well-known people in Athens affected not to notice Socrates when he walked abroad just as the inhabitants of Corinth avoided Diogenes

[49] After Antisthenes' death Diogenes moved to Corinth, where 'he lived without renting a house or staying with a friend, but camping out in the Craneion' (8. 4); the competitors of Diogenes are the toughest and the hardest to beat, τοὺς πόνους; with hardships he is ever wont to battle day and night (12–15); Diogenes risks his life in another battle more terrible, the fight against pleasure (20–6); he takes as a model Heracles, 'who in his labours' suffered 'wretchedness exceedingly great' (28–35).

[50] *Or.* 3. 1 (*deest* in *SSR*) Σωκράτης Ἀθήνησι, περσβύτης ἀνὴρ καὶ πένης; cf. *Or.* 54. 3 (= *SSR* I C 427) Σωκράτης πένης ἀνὴρ καὶ δημοτικός, κτλ.

[51] For Socrates cf. Aristoph. *Nub.* 362 (τὠφθαλμὼ παραβάλλεις); Plat. *Symp.* 221b, *Phdo* 117b. For Diogenes, Dio *Or.* 8. 12 ὁ δὲ ὥσπερ εἰώθει ὑποβλέψας, κτλ. (= *SSR* V B 584) and *Or.* 4. 24 (= *SSR* V B 582), where the Cynic looks askance (δεινὸν ὑποβλέψας) at Alexander the Great, who, we are told, 'was delighted with the man's boldness and composure in not being awestruck in his presence' (15).

[52] *Or.* 54. 3 καὶ παρεῖχεν αὐτὸν τοῖς βουλομένοις προσιέναι καὶ διαλέγεσθαι, and *Or.* 8. 7 παρέσχε δὲ καὶ αὐτὸν τῷ βουλομένῳ ἐντυγχάνειν.

precisely because they were used to him always being present.[53] Any who approached Socrates, 'like those who have struck something with their foot, got hurt and speedily departed'; analogously, the strangers who crowded around Diogenes at Corinth, 'after speaking or listening for a short time, went their way, fearing his refutation of their views'.[54] Elsewhere the two philosophers are cited together as models for their great intellect, for the lives they led, and for what they said to men.[55] To Socrates' irony, emphasized by all ancient sources, corresponds the harsher sarcasm, mellowed however by a bantering note, that characterizes Dio's Diogenes, who, in the sixth speech, insists without cease on the themes of *paizein* and *gelan*.[56] If Socrates' mission, as presented in Plato's *Apology*, was *exetazein kai elenchein* his interlocutor,[57] Dio entrusts Diogenes with that of *exelenchein kai kolazein* the ignorance and folly of men.[58] Finally, as Dio's Socrates exhorts men to virtue and seeks to instruct them,[59] so Diogenes, with a similar though more decided attitude, studies the behaviour of men and calls himself the physician of souls.[60]

CONCLUSION

The issues raised in this chapter inevitably lead one to the question of what weight should be given to Dio's relationship with philosophy,

---

[53] *Or.* 54. 3 οἱ μὲν οὖν πολλοὶ τῶν δυνατῶν καὶ ῥητόρων προσεποιοῦντο μηδὲ ὁρᾶν αὐτόν, and *Or.* 9. 4 Κορινθίων μὲν οὐδεὶς αὐτῷ προσεῖχε τὸν νοῦν, ὅτι πολλάκις αὐτὸν ἑώρων ἐν τῇ πόλει.

[54] *Or.* 54. 3 ὁ δὲ προσελθών, ὥσπερ οἱ προσπταίσαντες, ἀλγήσας ταχὺ ἀπηλλάττετο, and *Or.* 8. 10 βραχύ τι εἰπὼν ἢ ἀκούσας ἀπῄει, φοβούμενος τὸν ἔλεγχον.

[55] *Or.* 72. 16 (= *deest* in *SSR*); cf. 72. 11 (= *SSR* V B 474).

[56] Cf. *Or.* 6. 7 ταῦτα δὲ εἰώθει μὲν παίζων ἔλεγεν, 13 κατεγέλα, 17 ἀλλὰ παίζων ἔλεγεν, 20 ἔλεγε παίζων (= *SSR* V B 583). On this characteristic of Dio's Diogenes see Brancacci (1996) 418. [57] Cf. Plat. *Apol.* 29e4–5.

[58] *Or.* 8. 5 (= *SSR* V B 584).

[59] *Or.* 60. 10 (= *SSR* I C 428), *Or.* 43. 8–10 (= *SSR* I C 121).

[60] *Or.* 8. 5–8 (= *SSR* V B 584): Diogenes 'observed that large numbers gathered at Corinth on account of the harbours and the *hetairai*, and because the city was situated as it were at the crossroads of Greece. Accordingly, just as the good physician (τὸν ἀγαθὸν ἰατρόν) should go and offer his services where the sick are most numerous, so, said he, the man of wisdom should take up his abode where fools are thickest in order to convict them of their folly and reprove them'. Indeed, the duty of the true Cynic is 'to make a study (ἐπισκοπεῖν) of the pursuits and ambitions of men, of their reasons for being abroad, and of the things on which they prided themselves'.

assuming that one accepts that this does have a real organic unity and coherence. For Zeller, and for those who after him have discussed Dio's usually neglected philosophical side, Dio was an eclectic.[61] Though nowadays this definition seems generic and unsatisfactory, one must admit that Dio can in no way be considered a systematic philosopher—indeed during the imperial period the notion itself of a systematic philosophy had lost force—or one who fully belonged to any given philosophical school. What I would like to suggest at the end of this survey is that the presence of Socrates, seen through the filter of the Antisthenean tradition, and the ensuing connection between Socratism and Cynicism, evident in many of Dio's works, is one of the elements, and perhaps not the least important, that makes it possible to speak of Dio as a philosopher. Even the ancients discussed which school of philosophy Dio could be ascribed to. Better than the judgement of Synesius, who sided Dio with Stoicism but in terms that are too general to satisfy the requirements of modern historiographic consciousness, is perhaps the testimony of Fronto, which was used by Momigliano to claim, in opposition to Synesius (and von Arnim), that Dio had in fact had a philosophical education from his earliest years.[62] In a letter addressed to Marcus Aurelius, Fronto proposes to his imperial disciple, who was taken with enthusiasm for Epictetus, whom the rhetorician judges *incuriosus*, a richer and more thought-out selection of examples. These are four intellectuals, equally famous as philosophers and as masters of style and all pupils of the Stoic Musonius Rufus: Euphrates, Dio, Timocrates, and Athenodotus. They represent, according to Fronto, the modern equivalent of the four great philosophers and men of letters of the past, all disciples of Socrates: Xenophon, Antisthenes, Aeschines, and Plato.[63] Socrates, father of Greek moral philosophy, stands, from this point of view, to Musonius Rufus, father of the reborn Roman Stoicism, as do the refined Socratics *d'antan* to the learned Stoics of today, as—if the parallelism is present even

---

[61] Cf. Zeller (1923) 3. 1: 847–51.

[62] Cf. Momigliano (1969) 258–9, (1975) 971–5.

[63] Fronto, *ad M. Antonin. imp. de eloq.* 1 p. 135 Van den Hout. On this letter see Brancacci (1985) 42–50. For Plato, Xenophon, and Antisthenes as models, cf. also Fronto, *ad M. Antonin. imp. de eloq.* 2, 16 p. 141. 4–7 Van den Hout (= *SSR* V A 47).

between the single members of the two series[64]—Antisthenes does
to his modern emulator, Dio. This construction, in the intention of
Fronto, was designed to justify the synthesis of *eloquentia* and
philosophia in which he believed and on which he based his cultural
programme. The documented recuperation of Socrates and of the
Socratic and Cynic traditions which Dio achieved, while it allows
us to give a more dense and precise significance to this testimony,
invites us to reflect on the complexity of the intellectual and literary background which, carefully reworked and assimilated, at times
visible and at times dissimulated, lies behind Dio's discourses.

[64] Desideri (1978) 9–10, I think rightly, holds this view. Parallelism seems to be
present even between Plato, the prince of philosophers, and Athenodotus, whom Fronto
surely considers the most accomplished philosopher of the four, given that elsewhere
(*ad M. Caesarem et invicem* 1–2 p. 17. 8 Van den Hout; *ad M. Caesarem et invicem*
4, p. 65. 23 Van den Hout) he names him explicitly as his master in philosophy. Thus
Timocrates, who was a philosopher, but also a rhetorician, and the teacher of the
sophist Polemon (cf. Philostr. *Vit. Soph.* 536), corresponds to Aeschines, who, of the
four Socratics, was the most specifically literary.

Dio on the Simple and Self-Sufficient Life

FREDERICK E. BRENK

The wealth you miss, remember this, worthwhile things cannot
 be bought or sold.
The moon belongs to everyone. The best things in life are free.
            (Popular song of the Great Depression)[1]

They suspect that these philosophers look down on them for wasting their
money eating and drinking, for wanting to lie down on a nice bed, to enjoy
the company of young women and boys when they have a bit of free time,
to get rich quick, and to be famous and respected by people, that is, the
philosophers look down upon what they consider the greatest things in life
. . . Therefore, they ridicule them, hoot at them . . . and argue that they are
talking rubbish and out of their minds.   (Dio, *Or.* 72. 7).[2]

This is not a very self-sufficient use of quotations, but I hope it suggests how attitudes towards the simple life are not that simple. Dio
himself is something of a paradox in this matter. Though he was a
member of the upper class of his native city, Prusa, he embraced
aspects of Cynic philosophy. During his exile under Domitian, he
even lived, or imagined himself living, as a poor, travelling Cynic.
His life, then, raises several problems. Among them are his particular understanding of what was called 'self-sufficiency' (*autarkeia*) and
the influence of his Stoic teacher, Musonius, upon him in this matter.[3]
Did Dio sincerely embrace the cause of the poor and identify his own
self-sufficiency with theirs, having real sympathy for the 'victims of
society', and sincerely condemning slavery as an institution? Did his

---

[1] DeSylva et al. (1973).
[2] Desideri (1978) 235–6 notes that Dio did win a few converts (72. 11–12).
[3] Dio does not name Musonius as his teacher, but as Jones (1978) indicates
(12–16), there is no reason to doubt. See also Desideri (1978) 62–3, Russell (1992) 4.

ideas change radically at certain periods of his life? Was his own adoption of radical self-sufficiency during his exile merely a temporary expedient, and not part of a philosophy for the whole of life? Any examination of Dio's attitude towards self-sufficiency depends upon Dio's portrait of Diogenes in the *Diogenes* orations, comments in *In Athens, On his Exile*, and other works referring to his life in that period, and, more importantly, in the *Euboicus*, where he developed some surprisingly radical and progressive views on social justice and society.

<h2 style="text-align:center">FROM MUSONIUS TO DIO</h2>

Dio had philosophical precedents for his attitude towards self-sufficiency. Like others, he puts his own twist on a popular concept. When depicting it in its most extreme form, he sees it through Cynic eyes. He takes a step back into the past in 'reconstructing' Diogenes, the most flamboyant practitioner of *autarkeia*, and a step into the future in anticipating the 'divine men' (or 'itinerant charismatics') and Christian devotees of poverty during the succeeding centuries. Almost all the philosophical schools advocated a simple life, frequently equated with *autarkeia* (getting by with what is 'sufficient' or 'having enough'). The word itself does not appear in Dio,[4] but the notion and the ideas associated with it certainly do. Each school tended to interpret this simple life-style differently or direct it to a particular goal.[5] The radical form advocated by Diogenes consisted in getting by on almost nothing, living as simply as the mouse he took as his instructor and model (Diogenes Laertius 6. 22, citing Theophrastus' *Megarian Dialogue*). Paradoxically, in Greek the same word can imply being filthy rich or poor as a church mouse.[6]

Antisthenes, one of the Socratics, and like Socrates one of Xenophon's characters, might have influenced Musonius here, and through Musonius, Dio. Antisthenes, in Xenophon, goes farther than most philosophers in delineating the specifics (*Symposium* 4. 34–44): self-sufficiency satisfies all our basic needs, helps us to

---

[4] Nor for that matter in Musonius Rufus.   [5] Meikle (1995) 44 f.

[6] Aristotle uses it primarily in the sense of 'having enough' or really, 'having quite a bit' (for independence). The *polis*, for example, needs a sufficiency of wealth, which is part of the 'good life'.

survive by performing the lowest type of work should circumstances require, produces honesty and generosity, and creates leisure for intellectual pursuits. The 'propaedeutic' aspect of Antisthenes' *autarkeia* ('should circumstances require') is normal in Greek authors, though it is here reduced to a minimum. Others, however, held that wealth was necessary for virtue: Panaetius (Diogenes Laertius 8. 128),[7] Posidonius (*ibid.* 7. 103). For Posidonius one needed money to study the literature, which was an essential preparation for philosophy; without philosophy one could not acquire virtue. Others like Seneca, however, were reluctant to admit that *virtus* was not accessible for all.[8]

Not everyone thought that *autarkeia* should be a permanent state. Epicurus lived a rather ascetic life and apparently considered *autarkeia* a permanent, desirable condition for himself. Nevertheless, like many other philosophers, he proposes *autarkeia* not so much as a permanent state as a preparation for the future, should necessity arise.[9] At least the milder form of *autarkeia* seems essential to Epicureanism. For most Stoics, however, *autarkeia* was primarily an interior disposition.[10] The actual practice of the simple life was not essential in itself for the quest of virtue. For a Stoic, sickness or health, poverty or wealth, were 'indifferents' or relatively indifferent.

Musonius Rufus himself was a quite innovative, though in some ways severe, thinker. He had high esteem for manual labour and stressed practice and direct observation over theory.[11] He had, by modern standards, very advanced views on the education of women, marriage, and respect for the poor.[12] Among Musonius' illustrious

---

[7] Though Brunt (1973) 21–3 takes this to be Posidonius' position (Diog. Laert. 8. 128).

[8] *Epistle*, 88. 31; in *On Benefits* 3. 18. 2 (cf. Musonius, fr. 2) he claims that virtue is open to all; see Brunt (1973) 22.

[9] See Long and Sedley (1987), no. 21B 4 (1: 114; 2: 116–17).

[10] Epictetus, another pupil of Musonius, recommended a tortuous *meditatio* in which one lops off in succession bodily members, the body itself, then children, wife, and brother (4. 1. 99–114).

[11] Musonius is cited from Lutz (1947) unless otherwise specified. Moles (1978) 95 n. 135 suggests that Dio may have been influenced by the older Stoic, Cleanthes, who watered gardens.

[12] Laurenti (1989) 2125–8 treats *autarkeia* in Musonius and his relationship to Antisthenes (2167). Brancacci (1989) 4049–75 examines the supposed influence of Antisthenes (4067 and 4069–70) on living frugally (citing Diog. Laert. 6. 105). For Musonius' advanced views on marriage (but not on sleeping with a slave girl), see Goldhill (1995) 133–43 (esp. 135–7); Nussbaum (1994) 323–4, 334, 344; and Saller (1998) 89. Blomqvist (1995) 173–90 suggests that Musonius may be behind Dio's advocacy of equal education for women, in contrast to Plutarch's less enlightened attitude (188).

pupils were both Dio and Epictetus, and to both of them he apparently transmitted his own destiny of going into exile. In *That Exile is not an Evil* (9), Musonius claims that the simpler life forced upon men in exile often restores their health, and that they rarely lack the bare necessities. According to this 'work-ethic' theory, energetic, industrious, and intelligent people will always find suitable employment and do reasonably well wherever they go (10–20). Dio was a little less enthusiastic than Musonius about exile. He claims his health broke down and he had to endure many tribulations. In *What Kind of Employment is Appropriate for a Philosopher* (11), Musonius advocates (reasonably mild) *autarkeia* as a permanent state of life for the philosopher. The philosopher, moreover, should be employed outside teaching, preferably in farming, which is most 'according to nature'.[13]

Some scholars have criticized the Musonius of *On Food* (18A) and *On Clothing and Shelter* (19) for being autocentric in a Stoic vein. However, in the latter work, he advocates self-sufficiency as allowing people to contribute more to charity. Dio, too, would emphasize *philanthrōpia*, but in a different way. In some respects, then, though his *autarkeia* is quite ascetical and autocentric, Musonius does consider its beneficial effects upon society. He addresses an implied upper-class reader. In this sense his teaching resembles his work on marriage as a partnership or on the condemnation of masters sleeping with their slave girls. The bait offered is the benefit, for the reader, of upright moral conduct.[14] Musonius does not, like Dio at times, express solidarity with the victimized or enter into the preoccupations of the poor and marginalized. Still, a faint glimmer of altruism does shine through his Stoic crust, such as the allusion to the great risks acrobats take for their miserable pay (7. 5–15) or the relationship between self-sufficiency and charity (19. 20–30).

Let us turn to Dio. A subject that has drawn much scholarly attention is his apparent 'solidarity' with the masses. Did he have a 'soft spot' for the poor? Writing in 1973, Brunt was struck by the *Euboicus*'s introduction of the reader to the concerns of a poor family. This was very untypical of classical philosophers.[15] Some (the

---

[13] The terminology, like that of Chrysippus on the same subject, strikingly resembles that of the New Testament Epistle to Timothy; cf. Brenk (1990) 39–51.

[14] For the Stoic position in general, see Brunt (1973), esp. 18–19.

[15] Moles (1995) 177–80 outlines the general themes and the problem of reality/fiction in the *Euboicus*.

soft-hearted Dio school?) have held that the profound experience of hardships and suffering during Dio's exile period brought about an interest and sense of solidarity with the *massa damnata*. Others suggest that Dio distanced himself somewhat from the poor and that his views had been essentially formed on an intellectual level before his banishment.[16]

The problem for us is that the chronology is very uncertain.[17] If the *Diogenes* orations were written before the *Euboicus*—which is not at all certain—then Dio's ideas had advanced considerably: the *Euboicus* seems to be a mature reconsideration of both *autarkeia* and contemporary social problems. In any case Dio's main opinions can be found in these speeches together with *In Athens, On his Exile* and related material. In each of them we find a slightly different perspective. The *Diogenes* orations form a major segment of Dio's corpus. Thus, his reconstruction of the Cynic philosopher is very important for studying his own attitude to self-sufficiency. Here we encounter a rather fierce counter-cultural attitude towards luxury and the independence brought through self-sufficiency, but not without a somewhat peculiar social conscience. Dio humanizes the philosopher, though not entirely. In some of these orations Diogenes is not interested in military or civic *aretē*—so esteemed in his society —but in personal *eudaimonia*. Therefore, self-sufficiency, freedom, and insensibility to pleasure or pain (*autarkeia, eleutheria,* and *apatheia*) are important, while wealth, political power, and fame are denounced.[18] In the works which refer to his exile Dio creates a persona—or, rather, multiple persona—in accordance with the ideals of the wandering philosopher.[19] Naturally, his comments on his own exile are the most personal. In the *Euboean Oration* Dio also speaks a great deal about self-sufficiency and the benefits of the simple life. Here, however, he allows the reader to see things from several viewpoints: through himself as omniscient narrator and protagonist/ witness, through the eyes of the Euboeans (in particular, the hunter and some citizens of the town), and finally through his own eyes

---

[16] On the praise of poverty as a Cynic peculiarity, see Brunt (1973) 9, 12. He believes, however, that Dio was probably influenced by Panaetius, Xenophon, and most of all, Musonius (citing Musonius, fr. 11 Hense). See also Blomqvist (1989) 108–14.

[17] Cf. Jones (1978) 135–6.   [18] So Goulet-Cazé (1986) 38–40.

[19] See Moles (1978) 96, 99–100; and Jouan (1993*a*) 393. Brancacci (1985) 31 notes the tension between rhetoric and the philosophical models, Socrates and Musonius Rufus.

again as he presents a manifesto for the cure of unemployment and poverty.[20]

DIO AND DIOGENES

Just what did Dio do with his Diogenes? He does not allow his own real or fictitious personal experiences to intervene.[21] He at least pretends, though, to identify with his famous Cynic protagonist.[22] In any case, he seems to have trimmed him somewhat to the lines of Musonius' ideal philosopher, while giving him a philanthropic mission. Only on rare occasions, such as when lecturing Alexander, does Diogenes forget that his original mission was to convict society's dregs of their 'stupidity and folly' (8. 5).[23] In the fourth *Kingship Oration*, though aiming at the ghost of Alexander, he probably hoped to hit the Roman emperor. Alexander admires Diogenes for all the wrong things and despises his ability to get by with little (*euteleia*, 4. 6). At *Or.* 64. 18 Dio speaks of the staff along with the wallet (*pera*) and cloak (*himation*) as among the characteristic attributes of Diogenes. Earlier he had described the Cynic as wearing the *himation* (6. 14), which at night did double duty as a blanket. Glaring like a lion and not mincing words in ordering Alexander around, Diogenes condemns luxury, self-indulgence, acquisitiveness, avarice, and ambition for fame and glory.[24]

In *Or.* 6, *Diogenes, or On Tyranny*, our Cynic philosopher seems to have studied Musonius' teachings on the benefits of the simple life.[25]

---

[20] Alcock (1993) outlines some of the reasons for poverty in Greece in this period—modified in Alcock (1997*a*), where the reluctance of the elite to interfere is blamed (esp. 110–14). See also Rizakis (1997) 28–33 for rural poverty in Greece.

[21] See Giannantoni (1990) 4: 551–9, citing Brancacci (1977), (1980).

[22] Billerbeck (1996) 211–13 considers Dio's portrait of Diogenes as idealistic but rather non-propagandistic.

[23] For Dio as a source for Diogenes and Cynic doctrine, see, for example, Giannantoni (1990) 4: 551–9; and Desideri (1978) 543–7. Desideri is the most sceptical.

[24] Dio's hero bears little resemblance to the Villa Albani statue of Diogenes, a nude old man. Tired, puffy-fat, and bent over with age, he holds out his hand to beg, while a rather endearing small dog sits at his side: Zanker (1995) 176–7 and fig. 93. In Diog. Laert. 6. 55, Diogenes identifies himself with a vigorous Maltese or Molossian hound. Richter (1984) 113–14, with good reason, is less positive about the attribution of the statue to Diogenes than in the earlier edition (2: 181–5). See also Schefold et al. (1997) 252–3 (*autarkeia* and pride despite sufferings) and Clay (1996).

[25] Goulet-Cazé (1986) 186 f. notes that Musonius was in basic agreement with Diogenes, who believed in permanent *autarkeia*, and was in opposition to Seneca, for whom it was, rather, a temporary ascetical practice.

He reassures us that shivering and going thirsty is healthier than gorging oneself on food. Dio spices his texts, however, with animalistic images not found in Musonius but apt for the 'dog-like' Cynic. When someone protests to Diogenes that animals endure the cold because nature gave them fur coats, Diogenes retorts that frogs, who live in freezing ponds, have none.[26] In one essential point, his begging, Diogenes maintains his independence from Musonius' ideal philosopher. For Musonius, begging is parasitical.[27] The philosopher should at least get a part-time job and preferably in the agricultural sector.[28] Diogenes is, however, an uncontestable beggar in only one passage, where Dio almost disguises it. Here he compares the Cynic to Odysseus. Though scorned as a mendicant and good-for-nothing, Diogenes resembled Odysseus taunted by the suitors (9. 9).[29]

None the less, Dio's attitude towards the poor remains somewhat ambiguous. Blomqvist has noted that in orations which may be dated earlier Dio treats the poor with a certain contempt, if he mentions them at all. Quite different are *Orr*. 1, 7, and 61. Here he contrasts the noble poor with the evil rich, who lack the liberty required to produce *eudaimonia*.[30]

In *Or*. 8 (*Diogenes, or On Virtue*), Diogenes is filled with missionary zeal toward the masses. Like Dr Frankenstein, however, he wishes to keep a little distance from his somewhat unpleasant creation. Antisthenes had called Diogenes a wasp and Plato 'Socrates gone mad'.[31] In Dio's oration, the Cynic philosopher heads for the

---

[26] Rich (1956) 24 treats *autarkeia* in relationship to animals, men, and the gods (*autarkeia* as a 'defence mechanism'); cf. Goulet-Cazé (1986) 47–80 on animals (closer to the gods than men, 61–4), and Moles (1996*a*) 112–14 part of a cosmopolitan world.

[27] For the discrepancy between *autarkeia* and begging, see Branham (1996) 96–7: *autarkeia* is a desideratum, but freedom an imperative.

[28] For the attitude of philosophers towards manual labour, see Brunt (1973) 25–6. Like Plato and Aristotle, the Early and Middle Stoics depreciated manual work. Panaetius, who insisted on 'means' for virtue, was a Rhodian aristocrat. Cleanthes, a poor man, however, did part-time, heavy manual labour (*SVF* 1: 463 (Diog. Laert. 7. 168)). Epictetus, born a slave, also valued labour with one's hands (1. 16. 16) (Brunt (1973) 26; see also 33). Only twice, though, in Diogenes Laertius do we find Diogenes actually begging (6. 46, 6. 56), and in one case he is only asking his due, presumably for his moral advice.

[29] For Dio as Odysseus, see Swain (1996) 231.

[30] Blomqvist (1989) 228 nn. 31–2 for other orations where these contrasts apply; for rich and poor in Dio, see ibid. 56–7, 104–6, 159–62.

[31] Diog. Laert. 6. 54. The words are missing, though, in the best MSS. On the characterization, see Moles (1996*b*) 473.

port of Corinth, where the morally evil and 'sick' are most numerous, 'to convict them of their folly and reprove them (8. 5)'.[32] He
does not, however, regard all of us as morally depraved, but only
certain ones—comparing them to thieves at a banquet (9. 3). In
conformity with his wish to keep a certain prudential (and prudish)
distance from his creature, Dio allows Diogenes to end this oration
by defecating in front of his audience, an act which modern
scholars have charitably interpreted as a symbolic replication of
Heracles' cleansing of the Augean stables.[33]

Or. 10 (*Diogenes, or On Slaves*), concerning a runaway slave,
offered another opportunity to introduce the topic of *autarkeia*.
Here it is the reason for not having slaves. As typical of so much
classical literature, we miss the viewpoint of the 'worthless slave'.
Nor does Diogenes attack the institution of slavery as such. The ex-
owner describes himself as a poor man, but so severe is the *autarkeia*
Diogenes proposes for obtaining *eudaimonia* that it is almost equivalent to possessing nothing. His words recall a famous passage from
the New Testament. The owner should observe the happiness and
freedom from care possessed by birds and beasts. They lack intelligence but they have a great blessing: 'they own no property' (10. 16).

What do these views owe to the experience of exile? The
Diogenes orations as a whole, which seem to belong to that period,
repeat or even exaggerate Musonius' harsh demands regarding
autarkeia. And, as several scholars have noted, in the purely
philosophical sense we cannot speak of conversion during the exile
period, even if we posit a change of emphasis. Later, too, in the
Euboicus, written after the exile, we find views that Musonius had
apparently expressed years before.[34]

---

[32] Moles (1983*c*) 110 finds it 'quite remarkable' that Epictetus (3. 24. 64) should
say Diogenes 'loved everyone', but that in the broad sense such *philanthrōpia* was
'integral to Cynicism'. He sees evidence for this (112–13) in the traditions about
Antisthenes (Decleva Caizzi (1966) 91), Diogenes, and Crates (Diog. Laert. 6. 87–8).
Moles (1996*a*) reaffirms in even stronger fashion his stance on Cynic *philanthrōpia*
and missionary zeal, which he sees as compatible with what often seems to be a contempt for the masses (114–20, esp. 115–16). See also Brancacci (1994) for imperial
Cynics as physicians of the soul (440–1).

[33] Cf. Diog. Laert. 6. 69. Jouan (1993*a*) 391 considers that Dio is too lenient towards
Diogenes' breach of civility. For ancient and modern reactions, see Krueger (1996)
and Döring (1997), esp. 395 (on Julian's view).

[34] For Dio's exile in relation to Musonius and the Cynic Demetrius, who was active
at Rome, see for example Moles (1978) 82–7; Desideri (1978) 94, 211, 547. Recently
Griffin (1996) has tried to reconstruct the role of Demetrius, Musonius, and Dio in
the political events surrounding Dio's exile. She regards Dio's account as unreliable
(esp. 194–8, 204). See, too, Sidebottom (1996), esp. 456; Desideri (1991*a*) 3897–901.

During and after the exile Dio adopted the guise of the Cynic philosopher, though he later seems conveniently to have forgotten Diogenes' austerity. Dio suggests that during his exile people often thought him, like the Cynics, totally impractical, going to extremes, and part of 'a crazy, wretched lot' (*Or.* 34. 2). Nor did exile make him healthier, as Musonius promised. Just the opposite happened. Dio returned to Prusa, exhausted 'from great and unremitting hardship' to lament the ruinous condition of his estate. He could cope with austerity, and even his son resembled him in this respect. It was, however, a necessary evil, not, as Diogenes would have it, 'happiness' or 'blessedness' (*Or.* 40). But there were worse troubles. He had to undergo not only 'perils and hardships', loss of friends, physical infirmity, but the hatred of an emperor—a person called lord and god by the whole world but in reality an evil *daimōn* (45. 1). Even making allowances for rhetorical overkill, Dio's *autarkeia* was no paradise.

IN ATHENS, ON HIS EXILE

Or. 13 (*In Athens, On his Exile*) virtually excludes all but three 'personal' details, but among them is Dio's visit to Rome, where he made a plea for better education, adherence to stricter standards of justice, and railed against what we would call consumerism and the unequal distribution of wealth (13. 37).[35] He offers here a surprising explanation for dealing with the (barely) self-sufficient life. In contrast to Musonius and others, an innovative detail is the lukewarmness towards propaedeutic *autarkeia*. The Stoics had argued that through voluntary *autarkeia* in normal times we can brace ourselves for the exceptional, when *autarkeia* may be a part of survival. Dio's innovation consists in suggesting that the remedy lies outside our control. Thus, propaedeutic *autarkeia* becomes, in a sense, irrelevant. Perhaps the Domitianic period gave him an insight into different responses to sudden adversity. The difference, in Dio's view, is not necessarily philosophical or moral preparation for adversity, but a natural disposition somehow 'assisted by the divine'. Dio seems genuinely intrigued by some persons' innate ability to endure poverty, sickness, old age, and exile. His recourse to divine assistance serves as a 'leader' into his consultation of the Delphic oracle (13. 9–10).

[35] Moles (1995) 180 notes Dio's uncompromising attacks on Roman luxury.

The substance is that perhaps God lightens the burden to suit the strength and will of the individual afflicted (13. 3). Apparently this happened to Dio to some extent, or at least to his 'persona' in these orations. Delphi evidently gave him a sense of mission. Shortly after the consultation, he vested himself in the robes of a beggar philosopher and set out to improve the world. The dividing line between posing and reality is a mystery. The mendicant Cynic was an acceptable, if not respectable, part of early imperial society, something like Homeric kings coming home disguised as beggars, as Dio said of Diogenes. If not totally honourable, becoming a Cynic was at least permissible. Dio had found a role.

THE *EUBOEAN ORATION*

The best of Dio's thought on *autarkeia* has been saved for last. The *Euboean Oration* contains his most developed ideas on the subject and discloses a social and economic dimension.[36] His ideas are not necessarily revisions of his earlier attitude towards the poor or of the role of *autarkeia* in their lives. The apparent severity of the *autarkeia* praised here is, at least at first sight, surprising. But Dio is quick to show his Euboean hunters enjoying themselves, getting up a wedding feast at short notice, and being cheerful and generous.

How did Dio reconcile what he advocates here with the life-style he embraced on his return home from exile? Perhaps he considered the *autarkeia* of this discourse as something 'relative', suitable for himself under the conditions of life at that time, and suitable for the poor peasants he met then. Later, once he had returned to his estate at Prusa and began to live again the life of the local nobility, he may simply have reflected that different kinds of *autarkeia* were suitable for different conditions and statuses in life. Living the life of the wealthy, along with its obligations, would represent a change of circumstances, not necessarily a change of view.

None the less, Dio's extraordinary sympathy and empathy for the poor and unemployed in the *Euboean Oration* and his consideration of programmes for their improvement seem somewhat inconsistent with the normal attitude of the upper classes. The real change, then,

---

[36] On other aspects of the *Euboean* see in this volume Ma; Desideri (esp. pp. 99–100); Anderson, pp. 145–50.

in Dio's philosophical progress seems to have come not necessarily during the exile period, but in the period after the exile, between the *Diogenes* orations and the *Euboicus*.

In the *Euboicus* Dio praises the natural virtues and interdependent *autarkeia* of a Euboean family. They become something of a model for curing the ills of contemporary society. He begins with the claim that this is a 'personal experience', words which immediately arouse suspicion.[37] His ideas come from actual experience of humanity in a particular instance and are not reflections derived from philosophical literature—or so he would have us believe. The Euboean incident could be considered one of those *exempla*, or illustrations of moral conduct, for which the period was so famous. In any case it is a curious mixture of contemporary reality and fictional/mythical themes. The teachings on self-sufficiency are, thus, set with and in a novella. During his exile, though this is not explicitly stated, Dio was shipwrecked while crossing to Greece from Chios. A man 'in a shabby cloak' looking for a deer took him in and introduced him to the almost subsistence level of life at which his family survived. Only twice has this huntsman been to the city, and the second time under compulsion, to respond to an accusation of evading taxes. Dio does not write a condemnation of the city as such. Rather, the man's 'virtue' creates a bond of solidarity between city and country. The two are seen as mutually interdependent, even if the city lurks as a potential threat to rural life. In the tale that the huntsman tells the shipwrecked Dio about his arraignment for avoiding taxes, someone from the city whom he had also saved came to his rescue, praised his style of life, and induced the city to honour him and to promise it would henceforth let him be (7. 54–61). After this story, Dio expounds at some length in the second half of the oration upon the dignity of the life of the industrious poor, the perils that await them in the city, and how they may find legitimate occupations.[38]

---

[37] *Or.* 7. 1 τόδε μὴν αὐτὸς ἰδών. Bertrand (1992) finds the account too utopian and anachronistic to be true, but if true, that it is closely tied to the traditions of 'le mythe politique grec' (82). Less sceptical are Jouan (1993*b*) 195 and Moles (1995) 178. The description of meeting the hunter parallels that of meeting the Elean or Arcadian priestess in *Or.* 1; cf. Blomqvist (1989) 72–4.

[38] As Desideri (1978) 227–8 notes, Dio is inconsistent, both looking for legitimate urban occupations for the poor, and doubting the poor will find them.

Dio has nothing against 'economic development' in itself, though he may harbour a sneaking suspicion that it is inversely proportional to the level of proletarian virtue. Even when Dio first discovers them, the Euboean family are living not much above subsistence level, but they have improved their lot somewhat. Dio wears the shabby cloak (*phaulon himation*) fashionable among Cynic philosophers, something he adopted after his consultation of the Delphic oracle (13. 10). But the huntsman uses a more primitive leather or hide over-garment (7. 8–9). Dio now discovers that poverty breeds 'love of mankind' (*philanthrōpia*), while riches have the opposite effect. *Autarkeia* seems to be a precondition for *aretē*, but in Dio it is not the independent, individualistic type we know from Diogenes. Rather, it is socially oriented towards others in a very humane way quite unlike the very severe, paternalistic *philanthrōpia* of Diogenes. Thus, Dio's new *autarkeia* reflects a state of mutual interdependency and support within the family rather than the rugged independence which Diogenes vaunted. Diogenes' *autarkeia*, in fact, as both ancient and modern commentators love to point out, made him totally dependent on the charity of others. The Euboeans' voluntary acceptance of *autarkeia* not only keeps them from hoarding their few possessions but also allows them to share these with others. Diogenes was not so famous for offering a helping hand, whereas even now the protagonist and his family live mainly from the hunt and also from agriculture and help others by helping themselves. As Musonius would have predicted, however, though their fathers lived only in huts (*skēnai*, 7. 15)—a word popular among autarkicist writers—they died at a ripe old age, still strong and vigorous of body (7. 20).

Dio recognizes *autarkeia* as producing substantial social benefits, the most important of which is 'crime prevention'. Crime and unemployment go hand in hand. The remedy—in modern terminology —is not to build bigger and better prisons, but to find work. Accordingly, he dedicates the final part of the oration to the problem of unemployment and suitable occupations for the poor. To some extent he endorses Musonius' advocacy of agriculture as the best type of employment, in contrast to the idyllic but not so realistic hunting of the Euboeans. He had already introduced the topic at the huntsman's trial in the city earlier. One of the citizens had suggested, as a remedy for unemployment and poverty, that the city should hand over unused public land for cultivation (7. 34–7). The proposal, if accepted, presumably would also keep the unemployed from turning to organized crime, that is, brigandage (7. 40).

In his description of the industrious and self-sufficient ideal community of the Euboeans, Dio stresses their *philanthrōpia*, hospitality, and felicity (*eudaimonia*). They seem, in his view, already to have achieved 'happiness (*eudaimonia*) and the blessed life'.[39] In fact they represent the traditional virtues of a peasant society, above all, family solidarity and sharing. Dio's almost Dickensian sentimentality emphasizes not so much their independence from the city as their simple pleasures and the goodness they show towards others. Their virtues, as in Dickens, naturally bring them an unexpected reward, when the shipwrecked citizen, saved by the hunter, comes to their aid. The rich, in contrast, are the most miserable of human beings. Dio thus combines the traditional themes associated with *autarkeia*, *eudaimonia*, and *eleutheria*, but he also underscores in a remarkable way the social repercussions of these virtues. His *autarkeia*, then, here takes on nuances different from those we find in other philosophers and even elsewhere in his own writings.[40]

Naturally, Dio had an abundance of precedents for the social benefits of self-sufficiency. Earlier philosophers probably subsumed 'avoiding temptation to evil' under the category of *autarkeia* promoting virtue. The association of *philanthrōpia* and hospitality with self-sufficiency may seem somewhat novel, but in the Cynic tradition, Crates gave his money away to charity, and Musonius advocated something similar.[41] But sharing with others and taking in strangers is not particularly characteristic of the Cynic tradition. Like Diogenes, the Cynics generally seem to conceive their *philanthrōpia* in a more abstract, theoretical way, as moral reprobaters, guides, and exemplars. Dio's Euboeans, though, are somewhat like Musonius' ideal students who were supposed to learn virtue not from reading books but by watching their teacher ploughing the fields. The Euboeans have never studied *autarkeia* in articles or books, but have a natural inclination to endure adversity, even flavouring it with good deeds. They also resemble those persons Dio describes in *Or.* 13, who manage to endure

[39] ὥστε ἐμὲ εὐδαιμονίζειν τοὺς ἀνθρώπους ἐκείνους καὶ οἴεσθαι μακαρίως ζῆν πάντων μάλιστα ὧν ἠπιστάμην (7. 65).

[40] Nussbaum (1994) 431–8 sees Stoic *autarkeia* as dehumanizing the human person, and sniffs out a paradox: Stoic suicide is an admission of being implicated in the world and its evils (436).

[41] For Dio's appreciation of the dignity of the poor, see Blomqvist (1989) 58, 74–7, 82–3, 228.

the hardships of banishment without too much difficulty. Living a
life very much 'according to nature', the Euboeans are spontaneously
more generous than the rich, even going so far as to share their costli-
est possessions (or their daughters') with a shipwrecked voyager (7.
82). What a poor excuse it is, Dio exclaims, to desire to be rich in
order to entertain one's friends (7. 97)!

Poverty is not an impediment but rather a stimulus to virtuous
conduct, producing actions more 'in accordance with nature' (7. 103).
Dio, however, avoids a total endorsement of poverty and is careful
not to incite poor against rich, country against city.[42] Perhaps he
inwardly feels that the lower classes will reject his *autarkeia* as an
implicit condemnation of their aspiration to 'a better life'.[43] Nor
is the huntsman, himself, the very perfect model of perfect self-
sufficiency. When accused by a citizen of the town of having fields
and villages, he retorts that he wished it were true—so that 'we could
have given something to you [the townspeople] and also belong to
the "blessed ones" [the wealthy class] ourselves' (7. 42). The huntsman goes on to claim that their possessions are both sufficient for
them and replaceable, should they be given away. One can forgive
the huntsman, of course, for just making a rhetorical point, or a small
slip of the tongue, in wishing to be rich. Like a good Stoic, though,
Dio hedges his bets. He hides somewhat behind the principle of
indifferents: poverty is not worse than wealth and perhaps for many
people is better (7. 115). But Dio's point here is also rhetorical. He
has already demonstrated the superior virtue of the poor, who are
generous though it hurts, and has condemned the stinginess of the
rich, who having so much, give so little.

A striking part of Dio's treatment of legitimate employment for
the poor is his sympathy for the victims of society. His attitude here
contrasts with the usual one found in the Cynic/Stoic tradition. For
example, when discussing prostitution, the Stoics, including even
Musonius, overtly care little about the potential harm to the prostitute. Rather, they fear the moral danger posed by the prostitute
to male virtue or to virtue in general, including that of their implied
reader. In contrast, Dio launches a tirade against the institution of
prostitution itself, an institution which he regards as radically evil,

[42] Desideri (1991*b*) 3952 cautions that whatever Dio may say theoretically about
the country in the *Euboicus*, the *polis* remains the centre of community. Cf. above
in this volume, pp. 103 ff.
[43] So Desideri (1978) 222–3, 236.

and against those who run it. He does not direct his attack against the prostitutes. Prostitution as such fosters the exercise of inhumanity toward its victims, and these are not the male clients.[44] In Dio's own words, the business of prostitution thrives by exploiting lust in a manner both humiliating and brutalizing to the women and children who are employed for this purpose. Their clients are, rather, licentious and dissolute men who respect neither man nor God. At first sight Dio appears to be wearing mythological blinkers in invoking Zeus as the 'god of family life (*Genethlios*), who will punish these malefactors' (7. 135). He is, in fact, following philosophical tradition.[45] Dio's appeal, then, for the abolition of prostitution is based on the victimization and exploitation of what we might call the 'social dead' (7. 138). Prostitution is a crime, however, not only against the prostitutes and children themselves, but also against the dignity of all human beings, 'to whom God gave the power of distinguishing good from evil'.[46] Wealth corrupts. The rich buy sexual favours from creatures (literally 'bodies', *sōmata*) 'of no account' (*atima*) and 'enslaved' (7. 138, cf. 140, 143–4).[47] The words 'of no account' and 'enslaved' suggest again that prostitutes and children drawn into the trade are unwilling victims of evil operators and clients, not corruptors of the virtuous. Dio ends this essay with a bitter condemnation of pederasty. Pederasty forces boys into a humiliating type of subjection. These same persons one day will hold the highest and most responsible positions in society (7. 151–2).[48]

DIO'S *AUTARKEIA*

Like Musonius and others of his time, Dio seems to have returned to the origins of Hellenistic philosophy in challenging some of the institutions of his society.[49] Some scholars have contrasted Diogenes'

[44] Cf. Hawley, above, p. 133.   [45] See Russell (1992) 151.

[46] See Brunt (1973) 17–18. Russell (1992) 153 would say 'having the experience of fair or foul' is something which 'implies an understanding of good and evil'. He thinks Dio is close to Musonius Rufus (frr. 63–7 Hense) in his condemnation of prostitution here (p. 150) and in opposition to Cynic doctrine—citing van Geytenbeek (1963).

[47] Cf. Bradley (1994), esp. 174–6 for a vivid depiction of the degrading effects of Graeco-Roman slavery, in part from the mouth of Epictetus; see also Garnsey (1996) 93–7, 239–40 (on Dio and slavery, p. 66).

[48] Cf. Whittaker (1997).

[49] Jouan (1993a) 397 sees Dio as trying to reattribute to the founder basic principles of Cynicism, which had been lost or changed. See also Krueger (1996) 231–4.

condemnation of slavery with the rather sanguine complacency of
Aristotle, who saw slavery as the justifiable relationship between those
naturally superior and inferior.[50] Brunt thought Dio went further
than any other classical author in subverting the institution of slavery.[51]
Did not the real Diogenes actually go to the dregs of Corinth to
assist these creatures in their moral struggles? Did he not live their
poverty and social stigma? Did he not feel sympathy for them or
somehow identify with them? Diogenes learned to survive on
little, as most of humanity is forced to do even today, but he did
not just make a virtue of necessity. Like Dio among the Euboeans,
Diogenes too must have discovered the surprising generosity of
the poor and discovered virtues often surpassing those of the rich.
Diogenes' teaching, like that of Epicurus, often appears to be popular
morality dressed up in philosophical garb. Both offered philosophical and moral justification, and a sense of self-respect and self-esteem
for the simple life that perforce most ordinary people live. Were
not Diogenes, and Epicurus—who supposedly had *hetairai* in his
community—closer to the pimps and prostitutes of Corinth, than
those philosophers, especially from well-to-do families, who posited
a reasonable amount of wealth as a necessary condition for virtue?
According to the ancient sources, Diogenes was buried near the gate
at Corinth, not far from those dregs of society whose stupidity and
depravity he was busy denouncing. Over the grave the Corinthians
erected a stele topped by a dog, and bronze statues were later
erected, accompanied by the following inscription:

> Even bronze ages with time. But thy glory,
> Diogenes, all eternity will never extinguish.

> Thou alone taught mortals the wisdom of self-sufficiency in
> sustenance and of travelling lightly through life.
> (Diogenes Laertius, 6. 78 (= *Greek Anthology* 16. 334)).[52]

---

[50] *Politics*, 1. See, for example, Long (1974) 4, 'painful defence of slavery', versus
the Hellenistic emphasis on the individual and the sharing of a common human nature.
As Garnsey (1996) 126 notes, Aristotle applied 'inferior' to 'barbarians'; thus, by his
own definition, vast numbers of (non-barbarian) slaves did not merit slavery; see also
Garnsey (1997) 161, 172–4, on the Stoic position.

[51] Brunt (1973) 18. But he believes that authors like Posidonius, the jurist Pius,
and Seneca were not unconcerned about the plight of slaves; rather, these writers
wanted arguments for slaves' protection that would convince their owners (p. 19).

[52] γηράσκει καὶ χαλκὸς ὑπὸ χρόνου, ἀλλὰ σὸν οὔτι
κῦδος ὁ πᾶς αἰών, Διόγενες, καθελεῖ·
μοῦνος ἐπεὶ βιοτᾶς αὐτάρκεα δόξαν ἔδειξας
θνατοῖς καὶ ζωᾶς οἶμον ἐλαφροτάταν

The Cynics and, like the Cynics, Dio gave philosophical justification, dignity, and direction to the simple and autarkic life of the common man. Not everyone wants to be rich. Some like their simple life-style and fear the intrusion of sudden wealth as potentially destructive.[53] However, Dio did not want to leave the poor mired in misery, ruling out the possibility of economic progress and a rise in their standard of living. Unlike Diogenes or Musonius, most people would not want to think of *autarkeia* as an absolute, even if in practice their lives are based on it. Most at least like to believe they are striving for better things.[54]

Dio's *autarkeia*, then, is a composite. It is not the permanent, inflexible norm of the wandering Cynic. Nor are *autarkeia* and the simple life just 'indifferents'. They are very positive factors for virtue. In particular, Dio associates *autarkeia* with *philanthrōpia* and with the solidarity of persons within the family, region, and the community of human beings. He was quite aware from the crowds that insulted him and thought him mad that *autarkeia* does not always 'sell'. So, in a sense, perhaps, he changed his 'pitch'. It was not simply a question of putting fur on the frogs that live in ponds. But the apparent change in his thought undoubtedly reflects some profound transformations. In his own life Diogenes had barely travelled farther than from Athens to Corinth. But the early Empire of Dio was one of tremendous extension, upward mobility, social, economic, and religious vitality. Dio's *autarkeia* is a small reflection of this greater world, with its greater problems and greater possibilities of resolution. Was Dio's teaching on *autarkeia* a failure? Possibly so. Its relative character suggests insincerity, at least in so far as solidarity with the poor is concerned.

Once Dio returned to his estates in Prusa he apparently did not forget the poor. He may still have been their champion. But he no longer lived like them. The stricter approach, advocated by Diogenes and apparently followed by Musonius and other philosophers, required more. At least a mild form of *autarkeia* was an absolute for all those seeking 'virtue'. Dio's own return to upper-class life at Prusa and to managing large estates pulled him back into what we might charitably call relative *autarkeia*, a self-sufficiency fitting his social status and marked by generosity in benefactions, but hardly

---

[53] Greeks in general were always suspicious of the effect of wealth on character. See, for example, Dover (1974) 109, 111–12, 170–5, 180.

[54] Advocating a rather severe *autarkeia* as a goal is something different.

what Diogenes had in mind. Seneca, a Stoic, could consider wealth or poverty as 'indifferents'.[55] He probably never put great weight on the Cynic type of *autarkeia*. Still, his life-style does not fit comfortably with the ideal image of the philosopher. His portrait artist sensed the contradiction.[56] Seneca-like one could ask: If wealth were so indifferent, how did you get so much? But many philosophers, not just the Cynics, and later the Christian preachers and saints— at least in the idealized depiction of their life-style—continued the tradition of the ancient model, even more energetically advocating 'poverty in spirit' and, frequently, solidarity with the poor. Christians and Cynics were sometimes in close contact and both were popular with a large part of the population. There are structural similarities between the thought world of the Christian preachers and the Cynic philosophers, and on the communicative level. At the same time there was an uncrossable divide.[57]

Nevertheless, such philosophers and religious preachers found a door ajar. Dio and the well-to-do philosophical writers might live *autarkeia* for a time, though permanent sacrifice of status, class, and local power was something else.[58] Relatively severe and permanent *autarkeia* might be interpreted as assimilation to the poor and as a form of dedication to them.[59] But Diogenes, Epicurus, and the stereotypical philosopher of art and literature had to remain at odds with the pursuit of wealth and social position. Otherwise, how can one proclaim that money isn't everything or that the best things in life are free? Who wants to admit, with or without fur coats, to being inferior to frogs?[60]

---

[55] Rosivach (1995).

[56] Schefold et al. (1997) 376 (pl. 244) characterizes the Seneca (double herm with Socrates), which has a double chin and rather obese, unathletic look, as 'the complete opposite of the Greek philosophers'.

[57] See Hahn (1989) 172–82. He cites the *Didachē* for similarities with Cynic preaching (pp. 173, 177–8). He notes, however, that known Cynics of the imperial period come from relatively well-to-do families (pp. 180–1). Brancacci (1994) distinguishes between Cynics in the intellectual literary tradition and the non-literary.

[58] Hahn (1989) 173 notes how Dio, like some other upper-class philosophers, felt the need to address the lower classes.

[59] For the Christians, see Downing (1993) and (1996), esp. 461–2; Malherbe (1996) (a reaction against the stern *autarkeia* of Cynics like Demetrius, a contemporary of Paul, 134–5); and Dorival (1993).

[60] Thanks are due to Professor Karin Blomqvist of the University of Lund for suggesting several changes. Mary Hopkins offered her usual help in forcing me to rewrite a good many sentences, and Dr Paul Mankowski, S.J., also kindly looked over the manuscript. I am also grateful for the comments of two anonymous readers, and especially to the editor, Simon Swain, for his corrections and suggestions.

BIBLIOGRAPHY

Note: the Bibliography lists works cited with a few additions.

AALDERS, G. J. D. (1986), 'Cassius Dio and the Greek World', *Mnemosyne* 39: 282–304.

ALCOCK, S. E. (1993), *Graecia capta: The Landscapes of Roman Greece* (Cambridge).

—— (1997*a*), 'Greece a Landscape of Resistance?', in D. J. Mattingly (ed.), *Dialogues in Roman Imperialism* (Portsmouth, RI) 104–15.

—— (1997*b*), 'The Problem of Romanization, the Power of Athens', in M. C. Hoff and S. I. Rotroff (eds.), *The Romanization of Athens* (Oxford) 1–7.

ALESSE, F. (1997), *Panezio di Rodi. Testimonianze* (*Elenchos*, 27; Naples).

ALFÖLDI, G. (1977), *Konsulat und Senatorenstand unter den Antoninen* (Bonn).

ALLINE, H. (1915), *Histoire du texte de Platon* (Paris).

ANNAS, J. (1981), *An Introduction to Plato's Republic* (Oxford).

ALPERS, J. (1912), *Hercules in bivio* (Göttingen).

AMATO, E. (1995), *Studi su Favorino. Le orazioni pseudo-crisostomiche* (Salerno).

AMELING, W. (1983), *Herodes Atticus*, 2 vols. (Hildesheim).

—— (1984*a*), 'Das Archontat in Bithynien', *Epigr. Anat.* 3: 19–31.

—— (1984*b*), 'Cassius Dio und Bithynien', *Epigr. Anat.* 4: 123–38.

ANDERSON, G. (1976), *Studies in Lucian's Comic Fiction* (Leiden).

—— (1982), 'Lucian: A Sophist's Sophist', *YCL* 27: 61–92.

—— (1986), *Philostratus. Biography and Belles Lettres in the Third Century A.D.* (London).

—— (1989), 'The *Pepaideumenos* in Action in the Early Roman Empire', *ANRW* 1. 33. 1: 79–208.

—— (1993), *The Second Sophistic: A Cultural Phenomenon in the Roman Empire* (London).

—— (1994), *Sage, Saint and Sophist. Holy Men and their Associates in the Early Roman Empire* (London).

—— (1997), 'Alciphron's Miniatures', *ANRW* 2. 33. 3: 2188–2206.

ANDREI, O. (1981), 'Il tema della concordia in Dione di Prusa (Or. xxxviii, xxxix, xl, xli). Ceti dominanti ed ideologia nel II sec. d.C.', *Studi e ricerche* (Ist. di Storia, Florence) 1: 89–120.

—— (1984), *A. Claudius Charax di Pergameno. Interessi antiquari e antichità cittadine nell'età degli Antonini* (Bologna).

ARAFAT, K. (1996), *Pausanias' Greece. Ancient Artists and Roman Rulers* (Cambridge).

ARNIM, H. VON (1891), 'Entstehung und Anordnung der Schriftensammlung Dios von Prusa', *Hermes*, 26: 366–407.

—— (1893–6) (ed.), *Dionis Prusaensis quem vocant Chrysostomum quae extant omnia*, 2 vols. (Berlin).

—— (1897), *De recensendis Dionis Chrysostomi orationibus* (Rostock).

—— (1898), *Leben und Werke des Dio von Prusa* (Berlin).

—— (1899), 'Zum Leben Dios von Prusa', *Hermes*, 34: 363–79.

ASMUS, J. R. (1900), 'Synesius und Dio Chrysostomus', *Byzant. Zeitschr.* 9: 85–151.

—— (1895), *Julian und Dion Chrysostomus* (Tauberbischofsheim).

AST, F. (1835–8), *Lexicon Platonicum* (Leipzig).

AUBIGNAC, F. Hédelin, abbé d' (1715), *Conjectures académiques ou Dissertation sur l'Iliade* (Paris; repr. with intro. by V. Magnien, Paris, 1925).

AUJOULAT, N. (1992), 'Sur le débat du *Dion* de Synésios de Cyrène', *Byzantion*, 62: 63–108.

AVEZZÙ, E. (1985), *Dione di Prusa, Il Cacciatore*, ed. E. A. Donadi and F. Donadi (Venice).

BALLAND, A. (1981), *Inscriptions d'époque impériale du Létôon*, Fouilles de Xanthos, 7 (Paris).

BALSDON, J. P. V. D. (1979), *Romans and Aliens* (London).

BARRY, W. D. (1993), 'Aristocrats, Orators, and the "Mob": Dio Chrysostom and the World of the Alexandrians', *Historia*, 42: 82–103.

BASLEZ, M.-F. (1992), 'La Famille de Philopappos de Commagène', *DHA* 18. 1: 89–101.

BECKER, A. S. (1993–4), 'The Theologia Tripertita in Dio Chrysostom's Olympian Oration', *CW* 87: 67–71.

BELIN DE BALLU, E. (1972), *Olbia. Cité antique du littoral nord de la Mer Noire* (Leiden).

BERARDI, E. (1998), 'Avidità, lussuria, ambizione: tre demoni in Dione di Prusa, *Sulla regalità* IV 75–139', *Prometheus*, 24: 37–56.

BERNHARDT, R. (1971), *Imperium und Eleutheria. Die römische Politik gegenüber den freien Städten des griechischen Ostens* (Hamburg).

—— (1985), *Polis und römische Herrschaft in der späten Republik (149–31 v.Chr.)* (Berlin and New York).

BERTRAND, J.-M. (1992), 'Le Chasseur dans la ville', in M.-F. Baslez et al. (eds.), *Le Monde du roman grec* (Paris) 85–92.

BERVE, H. (1967), *Die Tyrannis bei den Griechen*, 2 vols. (Munich).

BIDEZ, J. and CUMONT, F. (1938), *Les Mages hellénisés*, 2 vols. (Paris).

BIELMAN, A. (1994), *Retour à la liberté. Libération et sauvetage des prisonniers en Grèce ancienne. Recueil d'inscriptions honorant des sauveteurs et analyse critique* (Lausanne).

BILLAULT, A. (1998), 'Paysages de Dion Chrysostome', in C. Mauduit and P. Luccioni (eds.), *Paysages et milieux naturels dans la littérature antique* (Lyons) 123–41.

BILLERBECK, M. (1996), 'The Ideal Cynic from Epictetus to Julian', in R. B. Branham and M.-O. Goulet-Cazé (1996) 205–21.

BINDER, H. (1905), *Dio Chrysostomus und Posidonius. Quellenuntersuchungen zur Theologie des Dio von Prusa* (diss. Tübingen).

BIRLEY, A. R. (1997), 'Hadrian and Greek Senators', *ZPE* 116: 209–45.

BLOMQVIST, K. (1989), *Myth and Moral Message in Dio Chrysostom. A Study in Dio's Moral Thought, with a Particular Focus on his Attitudes towards Women* (diss. Lund).

—— (1995), 'Chryseïs and Clea, Eumetis and the Interlocutress. Plutarch of Chaeronea and Dio Chrysostom on Women's Education', *Svensk Exegetisk Årsbok*, 60: 173–90.

BOL, R. (1984), *Das Statuenprogramm des Herodes Atticus-Nymphaeums* (Berlin).

BOWERSOCK, G. W. (1965), *Augustus and the Greek World* (Oxford).

—— (1969), *Greek Sophists in the Roman Empire* (Oxford).

—— (1979), 'Historical Problems in Late Republican and Augustan Classicism', in *Le Classicisme à Rome aux Iers siècles avant et après J.-C.* (Geneva) 57–75.

—— (1997), 'The Second Sophistic Revisited' (Cambridge; unpublished lecture).

BOWIE, E. (1974), 'The Greeks and their Past in the Second Sophistic', in M. I. Finley (ed.), *Studies in Ancient Society* (London) 166–209.

—— (1982), 'The Importance of Sophists', *YCS* 27: 29–59.

—— (1985), 'Dio of Prusa', in P. E. Easterling and E. J. Kenney (eds.), *The Cambridge History of Classical Literature*, 1 (Cambridge) 669–72.

—— (1990), 'Greek Poetry in the Antonine Age', in Russell (1990) 53–90.

—— (1991), 'Hellenes and Hellenism in the Writers of the Early Second Sophistic', in S. Saïd (ed.), *Hellenismos. Quelques jalons pour un histoire de l'identité grecque* (Leiden) 183–204.

BRADLEY, K. (1994), *Slavery and Society at Rome* (Cambridge).

BRANCACCI, A. (1977), 'Le orazioni diogeniane di Dione Crisostomo', in G. Giannantoni (ed.), *Scuole socratiche minori e filosofia ellenistica* (Bologna) 141–71.

—— (1980), 'Tradizione cinica e problemi di datazione nelle orazioni diogeniane di Dione di Prusa', *Elenchos*, 1: 92–122.

—— (1985), *Rhetorike philosophousa: Dione Crisostomo nella cultura antica e bizantina* (*Elenchos*, 11; Naples).

—— (1989), 'I κοινῇ ἀρέσκοντα dei Cinici e la κοινωνία tra cinismo e stoicismo nel libro VI (103–5) delle "Vite" di Diogene Laerzio', *ANRW* 2. 36. 6: 4049–75.

BRANCACCI, A. (1990), *Oikeios logos. La filosofia del linguaggio di Antistene* (*Elenchos*, 20; Naples).

—— (1992), 'Struttura compositiva e fonti della terza orazione *Sulla Regalità* di Dione Crisostomo: Dione e l'*Archelao* di Antistene', *ANRW* 2. 36. 5: 3308–34.

—— (1994), 'Cinismo e predicazione popolare', in G. Cambiano et al. (eds.), *Lo spazio letterario della Grecia antica*, 1: *La produzione e la circolazione del testo*, pt. 3 *I Greci e Roma* (Rome) 433–55.

—— (1996), 'Pericopi diogeniche in *PVindob* G 29946 (= C.P.F. Diogenes Cynicus 8 T)', *Elenchos*, 17: 407–22.

BRANHAM, R. B. (1996), 'Defacing the Currency: Diogenes' Rhetoric and the *Invention* of Cynicism', in Branham and Goulet-Cazé (1996) 81–104.

—— and GOULET-CAZÉ, M.-O. (1996) (eds.), *The Cynics. The Cynic Movement in Antiquity and its Legacy* (Berkeley).

BRASCHINSKY, J. (1977), rev. of Belin de Ballu (1972), *Gnomon*, 49: 617–22.

BRAUND, D. C. (1984), *Rome and the Friendly King. The Character of Client Kingship* (London, Camberra, and New York).

—— (1997), 'Greeks and Barbarians: The Black Sea Region and Hellenism under the Early Empire', in S. E. Alcock (ed.), *The Early Roman Empire in the East* (Oxford) 121–36.

BRAVO-GARCÍA, A. (1973), 'Notas sobre el tema de la concordia en Dio de Prusa', *Habis*, 4: 82–92.

BREITUNG, A. (1887), *Das Leben des Dio Chrysostomus* (Gebweiler).

BRENK, F. E. (1990), 'Old Wineskins Recycled: "Autarkeia" in I Timothy 6.5–10', *Filologia Neotestamentaria*, 3: 39–51.

BRÉQUIGNY, L.-G. Oudard Feudrix de (1752), *Vies des anciens orateurs grecs* . . . , vol. 2: *Dion Chrysostome* (Paris).

BRISSON, L. (1982), *Platon, les mots et les mythes* (Paris).

BRIXHE, C. (1987), *Essai sur le grec anatolien au début de notre ère* (2nd edn.; Nancy).

BRUNT, P. (1961), 'Charges of Provincial Maladministration under the Early Principate', *Historia*, 10: 189–227 (repr. in *Roman Imperial Themes* (Oxford, 1990) 53–95).

—— (1973), 'Aspects of the Social Thought of Dio Chrysostom and of the Stoics', *PCPhS* 19: 9–34 (repr. in *Studies in Greek History and Thought* (Oxford, 1993) 210–44).

—— (1976), 'The Romanization of the Local Ruling Classes', in *Assimilation et résistence à la culture gréco-romaine dans le monde ancien* (Bucharest and Paris) 161–74 (repr. in *Roman Imperial Themes* (Oxford, 1990) 267–81).

—— (1979), 'Divine Elements in the Imperial Office', *JRS* 69: 168–75.

—— (1988), 'The Emperor's Choice of "Amici"', in P. Kneissl and V. Losemann (eds.), *Festschrift für Karl Christ* (Darmstadt) 39–56.

—— (1994), 'The Bubble of the Second Sophistic', *BICS* 39: 25–52.

BUDÉ, G. DE (1916–19) (ed.), *Dionis Chrysostomi orationes* (Leipzig).

BULTMANN, R. (1910), *Der Stil der paulinischen Predigt und die kynisch-stoische Diatribe* (Göttingen).

BURCKHARDT, J. (1864), 'Ueber den Werth des Dio Chrysostomus für die Kenntniss seiner Zeit', *Neues Schw. Mus.* 4: 97–122 (repr. in E. Dürr (ed.), *Gesamtausgabe*, 14).

BURKERT, W. (1985), *Greek Religion* (Oxford).

BURTON, G. P. (1975), 'Proconsuls, Assizes and the Administration of Justice under the Empire', *JRS* 65: 92–106.

CAGNAZZI, S. (1980), 'Demos', *QdS* 6: 297–314.

CAIZZI, F. (1964), 'Antistene', *StudUrb* 38: 48–99. [see also Decleva Caizzi]

CALDERINI, A. (1913), 'Ricerche intorno alla biblioteca e alla cultura greca di Francesco Filelfo', *SIFC* 20: 204–424.

CALLANDER, T. (1904), 'The Tarsian Orations of Dio', *JHS* 24: 58–69.

CALOGERO, G. (1984), 'Cinismo e stoicismo in Epitteto', in id., *Scritti minori di filosofia antica* (*Elenchos*, 10; Naples) 395–408.

CAMERARIUS, J. (1562), *Dionis Dissertatio de Non Temere Credendo* (Leipzig; acc. to Fabricius first published 1551 in Nuremberg).

CAMERON, A. and LONG, S. (1993), *Barbarians and Politics at the Court of Arcadius* (Berkeley).

CAMPANILE, M. D. (1994), *I sacerdoti del Koinon d'Asia (I sec. a.C.–III sec. d.C.)* (Pisa).

—— (1996), 'Città d'Asia Minore tra Mitridate e Roma', *Studi ellenistici*, 8: 145–73.

—— (1997*a*), 'Il culto imperiale in Frigia', in R. Gusmani, M. Salvini, and P. Vannicelli (eds.), *Frigi e frigio* (Rome) 219–27.

—— (1997*b*), 'Un nuovo asiarco da Milasa', *ZPE* 119: 243–4.

—— (1999), 'La costruzione del sofista: note sul βίος di Polemone', *Studi ellenistici*, 12: 269–315.

CAMPBELL, J. B. (1984), *The Emperor and the Roman Army* (Oxford).

CAPELLE, W. (1896), *De Cynicorum Epistulis* (diss. Göttingen).

CARTLEDGE, P. and SPAWFORTH, A. (1989), *Hellenistic and Roman Sparta* (London and New York).

CASAUBON, I. (1798 [1604]), *Diatriba*, in Reiske (1798) 2: 445–542.

CASSOLA, F. (1962), *I gruppi politici romani nel III secolo a.C.* (Trieste).

CELLINI, G. A. (1995), 'La fortuna dello Zeus di Fidia: considerazioni intorno al λόγος ὀλυμπικός di Dione Crisostomo', in *Miscellanea greca e romana*, 19: 101–32.

CHARLES-SAGET, A. (1986), 'Un miroir-du-prince au 1er siècle après J.C. (Dion Chrysostome *Sur la royauté* 1), in B. Cassin (ed.), *Le Plaisir du parler: Études de sophistique comparée* (Paris) 111–29.

CHIRASSI, I. (1963), 'Il significato religioso del XII discorse di Dione Crisostomo', *Riv. di Cult. Class. e Med.* 5: 266–85.

CLAY, D. (1996), 'Picturing Diogenes', in Branham and Goulet-Cazé (1996) 366–87.

COARELLI, F. (1986), 'L'urbs e il suburbio', in A. Giardina (ed.), *Società romana e impero tardoantico*, 2 (Rome) 1–58.

COHOON, J. W. (1939) (trans., ed.), *Dio Chrysostom*, 2 (London and Cambridge, Mass.).

—— and LAMAR CROSBY, H. (1932–51) (trans., eds.), *Dio Chrysostom*, 5 vols. (London and Cambridge, Mass.).

CORRADI, G. (1929), *Studi ellenistici* (Turin).

COULTON, J. J. (1987), 'Opramoas and the Anonymous Benefactor', *JHS* 107: 171–8.

CRACCO RUGGINI, L. (1976), 'La vita associativa nelle città dell'Oriente greco: tradizioni locali e influenze romane', in *Assimilation et résistence à la culture gréco-romaine dans le monde ancien* (Bucharest and Paris) 463–91.

CROISET, A. and CROISET, M. (1899), *Histoire de la littérature grecque*, 5: *Periode alexandrine, periode romaine* (Paris).

CROWTHER, N. B. (1991), '*Euexia, Eutaxia, Philoponia*: Three Contests of the Greek Gymnasium', *ZPE* 85: 301–4.

CUMONT, F. (1896–9), *Textes et monuments figurés relatifs aux mystères de Mithra*, 2 vols. (Brussels).

CUVIGNY, M. (1986), 'Une histoire de langue (Dion de Pruse, 66,5–6)', *REG* 99: 361–6.

—— (1994) (trans., comm.), *Discours Bithyniens (Discours 38–51)* (Paris).

CYTOWSKA, M. (1952), *De Dionis Chrysostomi rhythmo oratorio*, Auctarium Maeandrium 2 (Warsaw).

DAVIES, J. K. (1984), 'Cultural, Social and Economic Features of the Hellenistic World', in *CAH* 7. 1 (2nd edn.; Cambridge) 257–320.

DAY, J. (1951), 'The Value of Dio Chrysostom's Euboean Discourse for the Economic Historian', in P. Coleman-Norton et al. (eds.), *Studies in Roman Economic and Social History in Honor of A. C. Johnson* (Princeton) 209–35.

DEBORD, P. (1998), 'Comment devenir le siège d'une capitale imperiale: Le "parcours" de la Bithynie', *REA* 100: 139–65.

DECLEVA CAIZZI, F. (1966), *Antisthenis fragmenta* (Milan and Varese). [see also Caizzi]

DEININGER, J. (1965), *Die Provinziallandtage der römischen Kaiserzeit* (Munich).

DESIDERI, P. (1973), 'Il *Dione* e la politica di Sinesio', *Atti Acc. Sc. Torino*, 107: 551–93.

—— (1978), *Dione di Prusa. Un intellettuale greco nell'impero romano* (Florence).

—— (1980), 'Religione e politica nell'*Olimpico* di Dione', *Quaderni storici*, 15: 141–61.

—— (1986), 'La vita politica cittadina nell'Impero: lettura dei *Praecepta gerendae rei publicae* e dell'*An seni res publica gerenda sit*', *Athenaeum*, 64: 371–81.

—— (1991*a*), 'Dione di Prusa fra ellenismo e romanità', *ANRW* 2. 33. 5: 3882–902.

—— (1991*b*), 'Tipologia e varietà di funzione comunicativa degli scritti dionei', *ANRW* 2. 33. 5: 3903–59.

—— (1994*a*), 'Dion Cocceianus de Pruse dit Chrysostome', in *Dictionnaire des philosophes antiques* 2 (Paris) 841–56.

—— (1994*b*), 'La letteratura politica delle *élites* provinciali', in G. Cambiano et al. (eds.), *Lo spazio letterario della Grecia antica*, 1: *La produzione e la circolazione del testo*, pt. 3: *I Greci e Roma* (Rome) 11–33.

—— (1995), 'Plutarco e Machiavelli', in I. Gallo and B. Scardigli (eds.), *Teoria e prassi politica nelle opere di Plutarco* (Naples) 107–22.

—— (1998), 'Forme dell'impegno politico di intellettuali greci nell'impero', *RSI* 110: 60–87.

DESSAU, H. (1899), 'Zum Leben Dios von Prusa', *Hermes*, 34: 81–7.

DeSYLVA, B. G. et al. (1973), 'The Best Things in Life are Free', in A. J. Lerner and J. Styne (eds.), *Great Songs of Broadway* (New York) 36–9.

DETIENNE, M. (1967), *Les Maîtres de vérité dans la Grèce archaïque* (Paris).

DE VIVO, A. (1980), *Tacito e Claudio: storia e codificazione letteraria* (Naples).

DEVREKER, J. (1982), 'Les Orientaux au Sénat romain d'Auguste à Trajan', *Latomus*, 41: 492–516.

DIBDIN, T. F. (1827), *An Introduction to the Greek and Latin Classics*, 2 vols. (London).

DIHLE, A. (1977), 'Der Beginn des Attizismus', *A&A* 23: 162–77.

DIJK, G. J. VAN (1997), *Αἶνοι, Λόγοι, Μῦθοι. Fables in Archaic, Classical and Hellenistic Literature with a Study of the Theory and Terminology of the Genre* (Leiden).

DILL, S. (1904), *Roman Society from Nero to Marcus Aurelius* (London).

DILLON, J. (1977), *The Middle Platonists* (London; 2nd edn. 1996).

DINDORF, L. (1857) (ed.), *Dionis Chrysostomi orationes* (Leipzig).

DITTMAR, H. (1912), *Aischines von Sphettos. Studien zur literaturgeschichte der Sokratiker*, Philologische Untersuchungen 21 (Berlin).

DÖRING, K. (1997), 'Kaiser Julians Plädoyer für den Kynismus', *RhM* 140: 386–400.

DORIVAL, G. (1993), 'L'Image des Cyniques chez les Pères grecs', in Goulet-Cazé and Goulet (1993) 419–43.

DOVER, K. J. (1974), *Greek Popular Morality in the Time of Plato and Aristotle* (Oxford).

DOWNING, F. G. (1988), *Christ and the Cynics: Jesus and Other Radical Preachers in First Century Tradition* (Sheffield).

DOWNING, F. G. (1993), 'Cynics and Early Christianity', in Goulet-Cazé and Goulet (1993) 281–304.

—— (1996), 'A Cynic Preparation for Paul's Gospel for Jew and Greek, Slave and Free, Male and Female', *NTS* 42: 454–62.

DUDLEY, D. R. (1937), *A History of Cynicism from Diogenes to the Sixth Century A.D.* (London).

DÜMMLER, F. (1882), *Antisthenica* (diss. Bonn) = *Kleine Schriften*, 1 (Leipzig, 1901) 10–78.

DUNCAN-JONES, R. (1990), *Structure and Scale in the Roman Empire* (Cambridge).

DÜRING, I. (1941), *Herodicus the Cratetean. A Study in Anti-Platonic Tradition* (Stockholm).

ECK, W. (1970), *Senatoren von Vespasian bis Hadrian* (Munich).

EDELSTEIN, L. and KIDD, J. G. (1972), *Posidonius*, 1: *The Fragments* (Oxford).

EMPERIUS, A. (1830), *Observationes in Dionem Chrysostomum* (Leipzig).

—— (1840), *De exilio Dionis Chrysostomi* (Brunswick).

—— (1844), *Dionis Chrysostomi Opera Graece* (Brunswick).

ENGELMANN, H. (1993), 'Celsusbibliothek und Auditorium in Ephesus', *ÖJh* 62H: 105–11.

ESTIENNE (STEPHANUS), H. (1577), *Epistolia, dialogi breves, oratiunculae, poematia* (Paris).

FABRICIUS, J. A. (1796), 'Dio Chrysostomus', *Bibliotheca graeca*, 5, ed. G. Chr. Harles (3rd edn.; Hamburg) 122–37 (rev. from vol. 4, pp. 305–19 of the 1st edn. of 1708).

FEIN, S. (1994), *Die Beziehungen der Kaiser Trajan und Hadrian zu den Litterati* (Stuttgart).

FERRANTE, D. (1981), *La semantica di logos in Dione Crisostomo alla luce del contrasto tra retorica e filosofia* (Naples).

FILELFO, Fr. (1492), [*Dio, Ad Ilienses*] (Cremona; repr. 1494 and 1500 at Paris, 1499 at Venice with Petronius' *Satyricon*).

FOUCAULT, M. (1986), *The History of Sexuality*, 3: *The Care of the Self* trans. R. Hurley (New York).

FRANÇOIS, L. (1917), 'Dion Chrysostome critique d'art: Le Zeus de Phidias', *REG* 30: 105–16.

—— (1921), *Essai sur Dion Chrysostome. Philosophe et moraliste cynique et stoïcien* (diss. Paris).

—— (1922), *Dion Chysostome. Deux Diogéniques* (diss. Paris).

FREEMAN, P. W. M. (1996), 'British Imperialism and the Roman Empire', in Webster and Cooper (1996) 19–34.

—— (1997), ' "Romanization-Imperialism"——What are we talking about?', in K. Meadows, Ch. Lemke, and J. Heron (eds.), *TRAC 96* (Oxford) 8–14.

FRITZ, K. VON (1926), *Quellenuntersuchungen zu Leben und Philosophie des Diogenes von Sinope*, *Philologus*, Suppl. Bd. 18. 2 (Leipzig).

FRÖSÉN, J. (1974), *Prolegomena to a Study of the Greek Language in the First Centuries A.D. The Problem of Koiné and Atticism* (diss. Helsinki).

FUCHS, H. (1938), *Der geistige Widerstand gegen das Römertum* (Berlin).

FUNKE, H. (1970), 'Antisthenes bei Paulus', *Hermes*, 98: 459–71.

GABBA, E. (1955), 'Sulla *Storia romana* di Cassio Dione', *RSI* 67: 289–333.

—— (1959), 'Storici greci dell'impero romano da Augusto ai Severi', *RSI* 71: 361–81.

—— (1974), 'Storiografia greca e imperialismo romano (III–I sec. a.C.)', *RSI* 86: 625–42.

—— (1982), 'Political and Cultural Aspects of the Classicistic Revival in the Augustan Age', *ClAnt* 1: 43–65.

—— (1984), 'The Historians and Augustus', in F. Millar and C. Segal (eds.), *Caesar Augustus. Seven Aspects* (Oxford) 61–88.

—— (1987), review of Gruen (1984), *Athenaeum*, 75: 205–10.

—— (1988), *Del buon uso della ricchezza* (Milan).

—— (1990), 'L'imperialismo romano', in A. Schiavone (ed.), *Storia di Roma*, 2. 1 (Turin) 189–233.

—— (1991), *Dionysius and the History of Archaic Rome* (Berkeley and Los Angeles). [Ital. trans., *Dionigi e la storia di Roma arcaica* (Bari, 1996).]

GALLAVOTTI, C. (1931), 'Sopra un opuscolo perduto di Dione Crisostomo', *RFIC* 39: 504–8.

GARASSE, F. (1625), 'Invective contre Homère', in id., *Nouveau jugement de ce qui a esté dict et escrit pour et contre le livre de la Doctrine Curieuse* (Paris) 106–21.

GARDNER, J. F. (1986), *Women in Roman Law and Society* (London and Sydney).

GARNSEY, P. (1971), '*Taxatio* and *Pollicitatio* in Roman Africa', *JRS* 61: 116–29.

—— (1974), 'Aspects of the Decline of the Urban Aristocracy in the Empire', *ANRW* 2. 1: 229–52.

—— (1996), *Ideas of Slavery from Aristotle to Augustine* (Cambridge).

—— (1997), 'The Middle Stoics and Slavery', in P. Cartledge et al. (eds.), *Hellenistic Constructs. Essays in Culture, History, and Historiography* (Berkeley) 159–75.

GASCÓ, F. (1992), 'Para una interpretación historica de las declamaciones en tiempos de la segunda sofistica', *Athenaeum*, 80: 421–31.

—— (1998), 'Vita della polis in età romana e memoria della polis classica', in S. Settis (ed.), *I Greci. Storia cultura arte società*, pt. 2: *Una storia greca*, 3: *Trasformazioni* (Turin) 1147–64.

GAUTHIER, P. (1985), *Les Cités grecques et leurs bienfaiteurs* (Paris).

—— (1993), 'Les Cités hellénistiques', in M. H. Hansen (ed.), *The Ancient City-State* (Copenhagen) 211–31.

GEELIUS, J. (1840), *Olympicus* (Leiden).

GEFFCKEN, J. (1909), *Kynika und Verwandtes* (Heidelberg).

GEYR, H. (1897), *Die Absichtssätze bei Dio Chrysostomus* (Wesel).

GEYTENBEEK, A. C. VAN (1963), *Musonius Rufus and Greek Diatribe* (Assen).

GIANNANTONI, G. (1990), *Socratis et Socraticorum reliquiae*, 4 vols. (*Elenchos*, 18; Naples).

GILL, C. and WISEMAN, T. P. (1993) (eds.), *Lies and Fiction in the Ancient World* (Exeter).

GINER SORIA, M. C. (1990–1), 'Anotaciones a un dialogo consolatorio', *Faventia*, 12–13: 293–305.

GLEASON, M. W. (1986), 'Julian's Misopogon and the New Year at Antioch', *JRS* 76: 106–19.

—— (1995), *Making Men. Sophists and Self-Presentation in Ancient Rome* (Princeton).

GOESSLER, L. (1962), *Plutarchs Gedanken über die Ehe* (Zurich).

GOLDHILL, S. (1995), *Foucault's Virginity: Ancient Erotic Fiction and the History of Sexuality* (Cambridge).

GOULET-CAZÉ, M.-O. (1986), *L'Ascèse cynique. Un commentaire de Diogène Laërce, VI 70–71* (Paris).

—— and GOULET, R. (1993) (eds.), *Le Cynisme ancien et ses prolongements* (Paris).

GOZZOLI, S. (1987), 'Fondamenti ideali e pratica politica del processo di romanizzazione nelle province', *Athenaeum*, 75: 81–108.

GRAINDOR, P. (1930), *Un milliardaire antique. Hérode Atticus et sa famille* (Cairo).

GREN, E. (1941), *Kleinasien und der Ostbalkan in der wirtschaftlichen Entwicklung der römischen Kaiserzeit* (Uppsala).

GRIFFIN, M. T. (1982), 'The Lyons Tablet and Tacitean Hindsight', *CQ* 32: 404–18.

—— (1996), 'Cynicism and the Romans: Attraction and Repulsion', in Branham and Goulet-Cazé (1996) 190–204.

GROAG, E. (1939), *Die römische Reichsbeamte von Achaia bis auf Diokletian* (Vienna and Leipzig).

GRUEN, E. S. (1984), *The Hellenistic World and the Coming of Rome*, 2 vols. (Berkeley).

—— (1998), ' "Egemonia" romana e continuità ellenistiche', in S. Settis (ed.), *I greci. Storia cultura arte società*, pt. 2: *Una Storia greca*, vol. 3: *Trasformazioni* (Turin) 773–801.

GUTHRIE, W. K. C. (1935), *Orpheus in Greek Religion* (London).

HABICHT, Ch. (1958), 'Die herrschende Gesellschaft in den hellenistischen Monarchien', *VfSWG* 45: 1–16.

—— (1969), *Die Inschriften des Asklepieions*, Altertümer von Pergamon 8. 3 (Berlin).

—— (1975), 'New Evidence on the Province of Asia', *JRS* 65: 64–91.

—— (1995), 'Ist ein "Honoratiorenregime" das Kennzeichen der Stadt im späteren Hellenismus?', in M. Wörrle und P. Zanker (eds.), *Stadtbild und Bürgerbild im Hellenismus* (Munich) 87–92.

HADAS, M. (1953), *Three Greek Romances* (New York).

HAGEN, P. (1887), *Quaestiones Dioneae* (diss. Kiel).

HAHN, C. (1896), *De Dionis Chrysostomi orationibus quae inscribuntur Diogenes* (diss. Göttingen).

HAHN, J. (1989), *Der Philosoph und die Gesellschaft: Selbstverständis, öffentliches Auftreten und populäre Erwartungen in der höhen Kaiserzeit* (Stuttgart).

HAHN, L. (1906), *Rom und Romanismus im griechisch-römischen Osten* (Leipzig).

HALFMANN, H. (1979), *Die Senatoren aus dem östlichen Teil des Imperium Romanum bis zum Ende des 2. Jh. n. Ch.* (Göttingen).

—— (1982), 'Die Senatoren aus den kleinasiatischen Provinzen des römischen Reiches vom 1. bis 3. Jahrhundert (Asia, Pontus-Bithynia, Lycia-Pamphylia, Galatia, Cappadocia, Cilicia)', in *Epigrafia e ordine senatorio*, 2 (Rome) 603–50.

HALPERIN, D. (1990), *One Hundred Years of Homosexuality* (New York).

HANSEN, M. H. (1991), *The Athenian Democracy in the Age of Demosthenes: Structure, Principles, and Ideology* (Oxford).

HARRIS, B. F. (1991), 'Dio of Prusa: A Survey of Recent Work', *ANRW* 2. 33. 5: 3853–81.

HAUPT, H. (1884), 'Dio Chrysostomus als Historiker', *Philologus*, 43: 386–404.

HAWLEY, R. (1998a), 'The Dynamics of Beauty in Classical Greece', in D. Montserrat (ed.), *Changing Bodies, Changing Meaning. Studies on the Human Body in Antiquity* (London) 37–54.

—— (1998b), 'The Male Body as Spectacle in Attic Drama'. in L. Foxhall and J. Salmon (eds.) *Thinking Men. Masculinity and Self-Representation in the Classical Tradition* (London) 83–99.

—— (1999), 'Practising What You Preach: Sources and Treatment', in S. B. Pomeroy (ed.), *Plutarch's Advice to Bride and Groom and Consolation to his Wife* (New York) 116–27.

HEPP, N. (1968), *Homère en France au XVIIᵉ siècle* (Paris).

HERMAN, G. (1980–1), 'The Friends of the Early Hellenistic Rulers: Servants or Officials?', *Talanta*, 12–13: 103–49.

HIGGINS, M. J. (1945), 'The Renaissance of the First Century and the Origin of Standard Late Greek', *Traditio*, 3: 49–100.

HIGHET, G. (1973), 'The Huntsman and the Castaway', *GRBS* 14: 35–40.

—— (1974), 'Lexical Notes on Dio Chrysostom', *GRBS* 15: 247–53.

—— (1983), 'Mutilations in the Text of Dio Chrysostom', in *The Classical Papers of Gilbert Highet*, ed. R. J. Ball (New York) 74–99.

HINGLEY, R. (1996), 'The Legacy of Rome: the Rise, Decline and Fall of the Theory of Romanization', in Webster and Cooper (1996) 35–48.

HIRZEL, R. (1895), *Der Dialog*, 2 vols. (Leipzig).

HÖISTAD, R. (1948), *Cynic Hero and Cynic King. Studies in the Cynic Conception of Man* (Uppsala).

HOLZBERG, N. (1996), 'Rhetoric: Dio Chrysostom', in G. Schmeling (ed.), *The Novel in the Ancient World* (Leiden) 640–4.

HOPKINS, K. (1980), 'Taxes and Trade in the Roman Empire (200 BC–AD 400)', *JRS* 70: 101–25.

HORSLEY, G. H. R. (1987), 'The Inscriptions from the so-called "Library" at Cremna', *AS* 37: 49–80.

HOUSER, J. S. (1998), '*Eros* and *Aphrodisia* in the Works of Dio Chrysostom', *ClAnt* 17: 235–58.

HOUT, M. P. J. VAN DEN (1988), *M. Cornelii Frontonis Epistulae. Schedis tam editis quam ineditis E. Hauleri usus iterum edidit M. P. J. Van den Hout* (Leipzig).

HUEBER, F. (1997), *Ephesos: Gebaute Geschichte* (Mainz).

HUNTER, R. L. (1983), *A Study of Daphnis and Chloe* (Cambridge).

JAGU, A. (1946), *Epictète et Platon* (Paris).

JONES, A. H. M. (1940), *The Greek City from Alexander to Justinian* (Oxford).

JONES, B. W. (1990), 'Domitian and the Exile of Dio of Prusa', *PP* 45: 348–57.

JONES, C. P. (1966), 'Towards a Chronology of Plutarch's Works', *JRS* 56: 61–74.

—— (1971), *Plutarch and Rome* (Oxford).

—— (1973), 'The Date of Dio of Prusa's Alexandrian Oration', *Historia*, 22: 302–9.

—— (1975), 'An Oracle given to Trajan', *Chiron*, 5: 403–6.

—— (1978), *The Roman World of Dio Chrysostom* (Cambridge, Mass.).

—— (1997), 'Egypt and Judaea under Vespasian', *Historia*, 46: 249–53.

JOUAN, F. (1966), 'Dion Chrysostome. Discours Troyen (XI) qu'Ilion n'a pas été prise', 2 vols. (diss. Paris).

—— (1977), 'Les Thèmes romanesques dans l'*Euboïcos* de Dion Chrysostome', *REG* 90: 38–46.

—— (1993*a*), 'Le Diogène de Dion Chrysostome', in Goulet-Cazé and Goulet (1993) 381–97.

—— (1993*b*), 'Les Récits de voyage de Dion Chrysostome: réalité et fiction', in M.-F. Baslez et al. (eds.), *L'Invention de l'autobiographie d'Hésiode à saint Augustin* (Paris) 189–98.

KAHRSTEDT, U. (1954), *Das wirtschaftliche Gesicht Griechenlands in der Kaiserzeit* (Berne).

KAEGI, W. (1942), *Historische Meditationen* (Zurich).

KAIBEL, G. (1885), 'Dionysios von Halikarnass und die Sophistik', *Hermes*, 20: 497–513.

KAIMIO, J. (1979), *The Romans and the Greek Language* (Helsinki).

KALLET-MARX, R. M. (1995), *Hegemony to Empire. The Development of the Roman Imperium in the East from 148 to 62 BC.* (Berkeley).

KAMPMANN, U. (1997), *Die Homonoia-Verbindungen der Stadt Pergamon* (Saarbrücken).

KASSEL, R. (1958), *Untersuchungen zur griechischen und römischen Konsolationsliteratur* (Munich).

KENNEDY, G. (1972), *The Art of Rhetoric in the Roman World 300 B.C.–300 A.D.* (Princeton).

KENNEL, N. M. (1997), 'Herodes Atticus and the Rhetoric of Tyranny', *CPh* 92: 346–62.

KIDD, I. G. (1988), *Posidonius, 2: The Commentary* (Oxford).

KIENAST, D. (1964), 'Die Homonoiaverträge in der römischen Kaiserzeit', *JNG* 14: 51–64.

—— (1971), 'Ein vernachlässigtes Zeugnis für die Reichspolitik Traians: Die zweite tarsische Rede des Dion von Prusa', *Historia*, 20: 62–80.

—— (1995), 'Zu den Homonoia-Vereinbarungen in der römischen Kaiserzeit', *ZPE* 109: 267–82.

KINDSTRAND, J. F. (1973), *Homer in der Zweiten Sophistik* (Uppsala).

—— (1978), 'The Date of Dio of Prusa's Alexandrian Oration: A Reply', *Historia*, 27: 378–83.

KLEINER, D. E. E. (1983), *The Monument of Philopappos in Athens* (Rome).

KOLAKOWSKI, L. (1978), *Main Currents of Marxism*, trans. P. Falla, 3 vols. (Oxford).

KONSTAN, D. (1994), *Sexual Symmetry: Love in the Ancient Novel and Related Genres* (Princeton).

—— (1997), 'Friendship and Monarchy: Dio of Prusa's Third Oration on Kingship', *SymOsl* 72: 124–43.

KOOLMEISTER, R. and TALLMEISTER, T. (1981), *An Index to Dio Chrysostomus*, ed. J. F. Kindstrand (Stockholm).

KRAYERUS, C. (1687), *Homerum a Dione Chrysotomo... vindicabit... respondens Chr. Krayerus* (G. Kirbach *praeses*) (Wittenberg).

KROLL, W. (1915), 'Randbemerkungen XXXI', *RhM* 70: 607–10.

KRUEGER, D. (1996), 'The Bawdy and Society. The Shamelessness of Diogenes in Roman Imperial Culture', in Branham and Goulet-Cazé (1996) 222–39.

LAMBERTON, R. (1997), 'Plutarch and the Romanizations of Athens', in M. C. Hoff and S. I. Rotroff (eds.), *The Romanization of Athens* (Oxford) 151–60.

LARMOUR, D. H., MILLER, P. A., and PLATTER, C. (1998) (eds.), *Rethinking Sexuality. Foucault and Classical Antiquity* (Princeton).

LARSEN, J. A. O. (1938), 'Roman Greece', in T. Frank (ed.), *An Economic Survey of Ancient Rome*, 4 (Baltimore) 259–498.

LAURENTI, R. (1989), 'Musonio, maestro di Epitteto', *ANRW* 2. 36. 3: 2105–46.

LE CORSU, F. (1981), *Plutarque et les femmes dans les Vies parallèles* (Paris).

LAMAR CROSBY, H. [see Cohoon, J. W. and Lamar Crosby, H.]

LEMARCHAND, L. (1926), *Dion de Pruse. Les Œuvres d'avant l'exil* (diss. Paris).

LEOPARDI, G. (1814), 'Commentarii de vita et scriptis rhetorum quorumdam qui secundo post Christum saeculo vel primo declinante vixerunt', pt. 1: 'De vita et scriptis Dionis Chrysostomi commentarius', in G. Cugnoni (ed.), *Opere inedite di Giacomo Leopardi*, 2 vols. (Halle, 1878) 1: 5–42.

LEPPER, F. A. (1948), *Trajan's Parthian War* (London).

—— (1970), review of Sherwin-White (1966), *Gnomon*, 42: 560–72.

LE ROY, C. (1987), 'La Formation d'une société provinciale en Asie Mineure: L'Example lycien', in E. Frézouls (ed.), *Sociétés urbaines, sociétés rurales dans l'Asie Mineure et la Syrie hellénistiques et romaines* (Strasbourg) 41–7.

LETTA, C. (1994), 'Il dossier di Opramoas e le liste dei legati e degli *archiereis* di Licia', *Studi ellenistici*, 4: 203–46.

LEVICK, B. M. (1967), *Roman Colonies in Southern Asia Minor* (Oxford).

LÉVY, I. (1895), 'Études sur la vie municipale de l'Asie Mineure sous les Antonins. I', *REG* 8: 203–50.

LEWIN, A. (1995), *Assemblee popolari e lotta politica nelle città dell'impero romano* (Florence).

LIEBMANN-FRANKFORT, T. (1966), 'Valeur juridique et signification politique des testaments faits par les rois hellénistiques en faveur des Romains', *RIDA* 13: 73–94.

LINCK, M. (1674), *Exercitatio historica de Bello Trojano*... (E. R. Roth *praeses*) (Jena).

LONG, A. A. (1974), *Hellenistic Philosophy* (London).

—— (1996), 'The Socratic Tradition. Diogenes, Crates, and Hellenistic Ethics', in Branham and Goulet-Cazé (1996) 28–46.

—— and SEDLEY, D. N. (1987), *The Hellenistic Philosophers*, 1–2 (Cambridge).

LORAUX, N. (1981), *L'Invention d'Athènes: histoire de l'oraison funèbre dans la 'cité classique'* (Paris).

—— (1995), *The Experiences of Tiresias. The Feminine and the Greek Man* (Princeton).

LOWENTHAL, D. (1985), *The Past is a Foreign Country* (Cambridge).

LULOFS, H. J. (1900), *De Antisthenis studiis rhetoricis* (Amsterdam).

LUTZ, C. E. (1947), 'Musonius Rufus, the Roman Socrates', *YCS* 10: 3–147.

LUZZATTO, M. T. (1983), *Tragedia greca e cultura ellenistica. L'Or. LII di Dione di Prusa* (Bologna).

MANSFELD, J. (1986), 'Diogenes Laertius on Stoic Philosophy', *Elenchos*, 7: 295–382.

MACREADY, S. and THOMPSON, F. H. (1987) (eds.), *Roman Architecture in the Greek World* (London).

MAIER, H. (1944), *Socrate. La sua opera e il suo posto nella storia*, 2 vols. (Florence). [Orig. edn., *Sokrates. Sein Werk und seine geschichtliche Stellung* (Tübingen, 1913).]

MAITTAIRE, M. (1741), *Annales typographici* (London).

MALHERBE, A. J. (1970), 'Gentle as a Nurse. The Cynic Background to I Thess. II', *Novum Testamentum*, 12: 203–17.

—— (1996), 'Paul's Self-Sufficiency', in J. T. Fitzgerald (ed.), *Friendship, Flattery, and Frankness of Speech. Studies on Friendship in the New Testament World* (Leiden) 125–40.

MARSHALL, A. J. (1968), 'Pompey's Organization of Bithynia Pontus: Two Neglected Texts', *JRS* 58: 103–9.

MARTHA, C. (1854), *Dionis philosophantis effigies* (diss. Paris).

—— (1865), *Les Moralistes sous l'empire romain, philosophes et poètes*, 8th edn., (Paris, 1907).

MASON, H. J. (1974), *Greek Terms for Roman Institutions* (Toronto).

MAZON, P. (1943), 'Dion de Pruse et la politique agraire de Trajan', *Lettres d'Humanité*, 2: 47–80; cf. *CRAI* (1943) 74, 85–7.

MAZZA, M. (1974), 'Sul proletariato urbano in epoca imperiale. Problemi del lavoro in Asia Minore', *Sic. Gym.* 27: 237–78.

MEIKLE, S. (1995), *Aristotle's Economic Thought* (Oxford).

MEINERS, C. (1778), 'De Zoroastris vita, inventis et scriptis commentatio secunda', *Comm. Societ. Reg. Scient. Gottingensis, hist. et phil. cl.* 1: 45–99.

MEISER, C. (1912), 'Ueber den Charidemos des Dion von Prusa', *Sitz.-ber. k. Bayer. Akad. Wiss.*, Jg. 1912, Abh. 3.

MEISTER, R. (1933), 'Hans von Arnim', *Bursians Jahresberichte (Jahresb. über die Fortschritte der kl. Alt.)* 241: 56–79.

MENCHELLI, M. (1997), 'La morte del filosofo o il filosofo di fronte alla morte: ἐπιείκεια e πραότης nel discorso XXX di Dione di Prusa', *SIFC* 15: 65–80.

MESK, J. (1920–1), 'Zur elften Rede des Dio von Prusa', *WS* 42: 115–24.

MEYER, E. (1924), *Kleine Schriften* (Halle).

MILAZZO, A. (1978), 'Il discorso περὶ βασιλείας di Dione di Prusa e l'opuscolo περὶ τοῦ καθ''Ὅμηρον ἀγαθοῦ βασιλέως di Filodemo', *Sileno*, 4: 73–107.

MILLAR, F. (1964), *A Study of Cassius Dio* (Oxford).

—— (1977), *The Emperor in the Roman World* (London).

—— (1981), 'The World of the Golden Ass', *JRS* 71: 63–75; repr. in S. J. Harrison (ed.), *Oxford Readings in the Roman Novel* (Oxford, 1999) 247–68.

MILLAR, F. (1987), 'Introduction', in Macready and Thompson (1987), pp. ix–xv.

—— (1993), 'The Greek City in the Roman Period', in M. H. Hansen (ed.), *The Ancient Greek City-State* (Copenhagen) 232–60.

MILLET, M. (1990), *The Romanization of Britain. An Essay in Archaeological Interpretation* (Cambridge).

MITCHELL, S. (1990), 'Festivals, Games, and Civic life in Roman Asia Minor', *JRS* 80: 183–93.

—— (1993), *Anatolia. Land, Men, and Gods in Asia Minor*, 2 vols. (Oxford).

—— (1995), *Cremna in Pisidia. An Ancient City in Peace and in War* (London).

MOLES, J. L. (1978), 'The Career and Conversion of Dio Chrysostom', *JHS* 98: 79–100.

—— (1983*a*), 'The Date and Purpose of the Fourth Kingship Oration of Dio Chrysostom', *ClAnt* 2: 251–78.

—— (1983*b*), 'Dio Chrysostom: Exile, Tarsus, Nero and Domitian', *LCM* 8: 130–4.

—— (1983*c*), ' "Honestius quam ambitiosius?" An Exploration of the Cynic's Attitude to Moral Corruption in his Fellow Men', *JHS* 103: 103–25.

—— (1984), 'The Addressee of the Third Kingship Oration of Dio Chrysostom', *Prometheus* 10: 65–9.

—— (1990), 'The Kingship Orations of Dio Chrysostom', *Papers of the Leeds International Latin Seminar*, 6: 297–375.

—— (1993), review of Russell (1992), *CR* 43: 256–8.

—— (1995), 'Dio Chrysostom, Greece, and Rome', in D. Innes et al. (eds.), *Ethics and Rhetoric. Classical Essays for Donald Russell on his Seventy-Fifth Birthday* (Oxford) 177–92.

—— (1996*a*), 'Cynic Cosmopolitanism', in Branham and Goulet-Cazé (1996) 105–20.

—— (1996*b*), 'Diogenes', in *The Oxford Classical Dictionary* (3rd edn.; Oxford) 473–4.

MOLING, J. (1959), *Dion von Prusa und die klassischen Dichter* (diss. Innsbruck).

MOMIGLIANO, A. D. (1969), 'Dio Chrysostomus', in id., *Quarto contributo alla storia degli studi classici e del mondo antico* (Rome) 257–69 (lecture of 1950).

—— (1975), 'Dio of Prusa, the Rhodian "libertas" and the Philosophers', in id., *Quinto contributo alla storia degli studi classici e del mondo antico* (Rome) 2: 966–75 (part of a review of C. Wirszubski, *Libertas as a Political Idea at Rome during the Late Republic and Early Principate* (Cambridge, 1950), in *JRS* 41 (1951) 146–53).

MOMMSEN, T. (1909), *The Provinces of the Roman Empire* (trans. W. P. Dickson, rev. F. Haverfield, from Bk. 8 of the *Römische Geschichte*), 2 vols. (London).

MOREL, F. (1589), *[Dionis] Περὶ βασιλείας καὶ τυραννίδος* (Paris).

—— (1598–9), *Dionis Chrysostomi oratiuncula de lege* (Paris).

—— (1604), *Dionis Chrysostomi Orationes LXXX* (Paris).

MOROCHO GAYO, G. (1988) (trans.), *Dión de Prusa, Discursos*, 1 (Madrid).

MORR, J. (1915), *Die Lobrede des jüngeren Plinius und die erste Königsrede des Dio von Prusa* (diss. Troppau).

MORTENTHALER, M. (1979), *Der Olympikos des Dion von Prusa als literarhistorisches und geistesgeschichtliches Dokument* (diss. Vienna).

MÜLLER, H. (1995), 'Bemerkungen zu Funktion und Bedeutung des Rats in den hellenistischen Städten', in M. Wörrle und P. Zanker (eds.), *Stadtbild und Bürgerbild im Hellenismus* (Munich) 41–54.

MÜNSCHER, K. (1920), *Xenophon in der griechisch-römischer Literatur*, *Philologus*, Suppl. Bd. 13. 2 (Leipzig)

MURRAY, O. (1990), 'Cities of Reason', in O. Murray and S. Price (eds.), *The Greek City from Homer to Alexander* (Oxford) 1–25.

MUSSIES, G. (1972), *Dio Chrysostom and the New Testament* (Leiden).

NAOGEORGUS (KIRCHMEYER), T. (1555), *Dionis . . . Orationes LXXX* (Basle; repr. 1585 at Venice).

NESSELRATH, H. (1990), 'Lucian's Introductions', in Russell (1990) 111–40.

NILSSON, M. P. (1961), *Geschichte der griechischen Religion* (2nd edn.; Munich).

NOCK, A. D. (1940), review of Bidez and Cumont (1938), *JRS* 30: 191–8.

NOÈ, E. (1996), 'Un esempio di mobilità sociale nella tarda repubblica: il caso di Ibrea di Milasa', in E. Gabba, P. Desideri, and S. Roda (eds.), *Italia sul Baetis. Studi di storia romana in onore di Fernando Gascó* (Turin) 51–64.

NORDEN, E. (1898), *Die antike Kunstprosa von VI Jahrhundert v. Chr. bis in die Zeit der Renaissance*, 2 vols. (Leipzig and Berlin, 2nd edn. 1909).

NUSSBAUM, M. C. (1994), *The Therapy of Desire. Theory and Practice in Hellenistic Ethics* (Princeton).

OBER, J. (1989), *Mass and Elite in Democratic Athens: Rhetoric, Ideology, and the Power of the People* (Princeton).

PALM, J. (1959), *Rom, Römertum und Imperium in der griechischen Literatur der Kaiserzeit* (Lund).

PANAGOPOULOS, C. (1977), 'Vocabulaire et mentalité dans les *Moralia* de Plutarque', *DHA* 3: 197–235.

PATOUSAS, J. (1744), *Δίωνος τοῦ Χρυσοστόμου, Διογένης, ἢ περὶ ἀρετῆς*, in id., *Ἐγκυκλοπαιδεία φιλολογική*, 3 (Venice; rev. G. Patousas) 355–61.

PATZER, A. (1970), *Antisthenes der Sokratiker. Das literarische Werk und die Philosophie dargestellt am Katalog der Schriften* (Heidelberg).

PELLING, C. B. R. (1989), 'Plutarch: Roman Heroes and Greek Culture', in M. Griffin and J. Barnes (eds.), *Philosophia togata*, 1 (Oxford) 199–232.

PERA, R. (1984), *Homonoia sulle monete da Augusto agli Antonini* (Genoa).

PERNOT, L. (1993), *La Rhétorique de l'éloge dans le monde Gréco-Romain*, 2 vols. (Paris).

—— (1997), 'Rhétorique et idéologie politique', in id. (trans.), *Éloges grecs de Rome* (Paris) 5–12.

—— (1998), 'La Rhétorique de l'Empire ou comment la rhétorique grecque a inventé l'Empire romain', *Rhetorica*, 16. 2: 131–48.

PERRY, B. E. (1967), *The Ancient Romances: A Literary-Historical Account of their Origins* (Berkeley).

PFEIFFER, R. (1968), *History of Classical Scholarship. From the Beginnings to the End of the Hellenistic Age* (Oxford).

PICOLHOMINEIIS, Fr. DE (1471), *[Dionis, De regno]* (Rome; repr. 1493 at Bologna).

PINO POLO, F. (1989), '*Ius contionandi* y contiones en las colonias romanas de Asia Menor', *Gerion*, 7: 95–105.

PORTER, J. I. (1992), 'Hermeneutic Lines and Circles: Aristarchus and Crates on the Exegesis of Homer', in R. Lamberton and J. J. Keaney (eds.), *Homer's Ancient Readers* (Princeton) 67–114.

PRAECHTER, K. (1892), 'Dion Chrysostomus als Quelle Julians', *Archiv für geschichte der Philosophie* 5: 42–51.

PRICE, S. (1984), *Rituals and Power: The Roman Imperial Cult in Asia Minor* (Cambridge).

PUECH, B. (1992), 'Prosopographie des amis de Plutarque', *ANRW* 33. 6: 4831–93.

PUIGGALI, J. (1984), 'La Démonologie de Dion Chrysostome', *LEC* 52: 103–14.

QUASS, F. (1982), 'Zur politischen Tätigkeit der munizipalen Aristokratie des griechischen Ostens in der Kaiserzeit', *Historia*, 31: 188–213.

—— (1993), *Honoratiorenschicht in den Städten des griechischen Ostens: Untersuchungen zur politischen und sozialen Entwicklung in hellenistischer und römischer Zeit* (Stuttgart).

QUET, M.-H. (1978), 'Rhétorique, culture et politique: Le fonctionnement du discours idéologique chez Dion de Pruse et dans les *Moralia* de Plutarque', *DHA* 4: 51–118.

—— (1981), 'Remarques sur la place de la fête dans le discours de moralistes grecs et dans l'éloge des cités et des évergètes aux premiers siècles de l'empire', in *La Fête, pratique et discours* (Paris) 41–84.

RADERMACHER, L. (1931), 'Hans von Arnim', *Almanach d. Akad. d. Wiss. in Wien*, Jg. 81: 211–19.

RAHN, H. (1944), *Platon und Dion von Prusa* (diss. Frankfurt).

RAWSON, E. (1989), 'Roman Rulers and the Philosophic Adviser', in M. Griffin and J. Barnes (eds.), *Philosophia togata*, 1 (Oxford) 233–57.

REARDON, B. P. (1971), *Courants littéraires grecs des IIe et IIIe siècles après J.-C.* (Paris).

—— (1983), 'Travaux récents sur Dion de Pruse', *REG* 96: 286–92.

—— (1984), 'The Second Sophistic', in W. Treadgold (ed.), *Renaissances before the Renaissance. Cultural Revivals of Late Antiquity and the Middle Ages* (Stanford) 23–41.

REINACH, T. (1906), 'Inscriptions d'Aphrodisias', *REG* 19: 79–150.

REISKE, J. J. (1798), *Dionis Chrysostomi orationes*, 2nd edn., ed. E. C. Reiske, 2 vols. (Leipzig).

REMY, B. (1986), *L'Evolution administrative de l'Anatolie aux trois premiers siècles de notre ère* (Lyons).

RENOIRTE, T. (1951), *Les 'Conseils politiques' de Plutarque* (Louvain).

RENOUARD, A. A. (1834), *Annales de l'imprimerie des Alde* (3rd edn.; Paris).

REUTER, D. (1932), *Untersuchungen zum Euboikos des Dio von Prusa* (diss. Leipzig).

RHODES, P. J. (1972), *The Athenian Boule* (Oxford).

RHODOMAN(N)US, L. (1585), *Dionis Chrysostomi Oratio Troica* (Rostock; repr. in id., *Quinti Calabri Paraleipomena . . . Homeri* (Hanover, 1604)).

RICH, A. N. M. (1956), 'The Cynic Conception of αὐτάρκεια', *Mnemosyne*, 9: 23–9 (repr. in M. Billerbeck (ed.), *Die Kyniker in der modernen Forschung. Aufsätze mit Einführung und Bibliographie* (Leipzig 1990, 233–9).

RICHTER, G. M. A. (1984), *The Portraits of the Greeks*, rev. R. R. R. Smith (Oxford; 1st edn. 1965).

RIZAKIS, A. D. (1997), 'Roman Colonies in the Province of Achaia. Territories, Land and Population', in S. E. Alcock (ed.), *The Early Roman Empire in the East*, Oxbow Monograph 95 (Oxford) 15–36.

ROBERT, L. (1937), *Etudes Anatoliennes: Recherches sur les inscriptions grecques de l'Asie Mineure* (Paris).

—— (1940*a*), *Les Gladiateurs dans l'Orient grec* (Paris).

—— (1940*b*), *Hellenika*, 1 (Paris).

—— (1965), *Hellenica*, 13 (Paris).

—— (1969), 'Les Inscriptions', in J. des Gagniers et al. (eds.), *Laodicée du Lycos: Le nymphée; campagnes 1961–1963* (Quebec).

—— (1977*a*), 'Documents d'Asie Mineure', *BCH* 101: 43–132.

—— (1977*b*), 'La titulature de Nicée et Nicomédie. La gloire et la haine', *HSCP* 81: 1–39.

—— and ROBERT, J. (1954), *La Carie*, vol. 2: *Le Plateau de Tabai et ses environs* (Paris).

ROCHETTE, B. (1997), *Le Latin dans le monde grec: recherches sur la diffusion de la langue et des lettres latines dans les provinces de l'empire romain* (Brussels).

ROGERS, G. M. (1991), 'Demosthenes of Oenoanda and Models of Euergetism', *JRS* 81: 92–100.

—— (1992), 'The Assembly of Imperial Ephesus', *ZPE* 94: 224–8.

ROHDE, E. (1876), *Der griechische Roman und seine Vorläufer* (Leipzig; 4th edn., ed. K. Kérenyi, Darmstadt, 1960).

—— (1886), 'Die asianische Rhetorik und die zweite Sophistik', *RhM* 41: 170–90 = *Kleine Schriften* (Tübingen and Leipzig, 1901) 2: 75–97.

ROSIVACH, V. J. (1995), 'Seneca on the Fear of Poverty in the Epistulae Morales', *AC* 64: 91–8.

ROSTOVTZEFF, M. I. (1919), 'Proletarian Culture' (Russian Liberation Committee no. 11, by M. I. Rostovtsev) (London).

—— (1941), *The Social and Economic History of the Hellenistic World*, 3 vols. (Oxford).

—— (1957), *The Social and Economic History of the Roman Empire* (2nd edn. ed. P. M. Fraser, Oxford 1957; 1st edn. 1926).

ROUECHÉ, C. (1984), 'Acclamations in the Later Roman Empire: New Evidence from Aphrodisias', *JRS* 74: 181–99.

—— (1989), *'Floreat Perge'*, in M. M. Mackenzie and C. Roueché (eds.), *Images of Authority. Papers presented to J. Reynolds* (Cambridge) 206–28.

RUGE, W. (1932), 'Tarsos', *RE*, IVA: 2413–39.

RUPERTUS, C. A. (1659), *Observationes ad Historiae Universalis Synopsin Besoldianum Minorem* (Nuremberg).

RUSSELL, D. A. (1973), *Plutarch* (London).

—— (1979), 'Rhetors at the Wedding', *PCPhS* 205: 104–17.

—— (1981), *Criticism in Antiquity* (London).

—— (1983), *Greek Declamation* (Cambridge).

—— (1990) (ed.), *Antonine Literature* (Oxford).

—— (1992), *Dio Chrysostom. Orations VII, XII, XXXVI* (Cambridge).

SAID, E. W. (1978), *Orientalism* (London).

STE CROIX, G. E. M. DE (1981), *The Class Struggle in the Ancient Greek World* (London).

SALLER, R. (1998), 'Symbols of Gender and Status Hierarchies in the Roman Household', in S. Murnaghan and S. R. Joshel (eds.), *Women and Slaves in Greco-Roman Culture. Differential Equations* (London) 85–91.

SALMERI, G. (1980), 'Per una biografia di Dione di Prusa', *Sic. Gymn.* (1980) 671–715.

—— (1982), *La politica e il potere. Saggio su Dione di Prusa* (Catania).

—— (1987), review of Gruen (1984), *RSI* 99: 787–93.

—— (1991), 'Dalle province a Roma: il rinnovamento del senato', in *Storia di Roma*, 2. 2 (Turin) 552–75.

—— (1994), 'La *Costituzione degli Ateniesi* aristotelica, l'Atene di età imperiale e l'Italia del Sigonio', in G. Maddoli (ed.), *L'Athenaion Politeia di Aristotele, 1891–1991: per un bilancio di cento anni di studi* (Naples) 40–61.

—— (1998), 'Per una lettura dei capitoli V–VII della *Storia economica e sociale dell'impero romano* di M. Rostovtzeff', *Athenaeum*, 86: 57–84.

SARTRE, M. (1991), *L'Orient romain: Provinces et sociétés provinciales en Méditerranée orientale d'Auguste aux Sévères (31 avant J.-C.–235 après J.-C.)* (Paris).

SASSI (SAXIUS), G. A. (1745), *Historia literario-typographica Mediolanensis* (Milan).

SAUTEL, G. (1956), 'Aspects juridiques d'une querelle de philosophes au IIe siècle de notre ère: Plin., *ad Traian., ep.* 81–82', *RIDA* 3: 423–43.

SAVALLI-LESTRADE, I. (1998), *Les Philoi dans l'Asie hellénistique* (Paris).

SCHEFOLD, K. et. al. (1997), *Die Bildnisse der antiken Dichter, Redner und Denker*, rev. id. and A.-C. Bayard (Basle).

SCHENKEVELD, D. M. (1976), 'Strabo on Homer', *Mnemosyne*, 29: 52–64.

SCHMID, W. (1887–97), *Der Atticismus in seinen Hauptvertretern*, 1–5 (Stuttgart).

—— (1898), *Über den kulturgeschichtlichen Zusammenhang und die Bedeutung der griechischen Renaissance in der Römerzeit* (Leipzig).

SCHMITZ, T. (1996), 'Trajan und Dion von Prusa: zu Philostrat, *Vit. Soph.* 1.7 (488)', *RhM* 139: 315–19.

—— (1997), *Bildung und Macht: zur sozialen und politischen Funktion der zweiten Sophistik in der griechischen Welt der Kaiserzeit* (Munich).

—— (1999), 'Performing History in the Second Sophistic', in M. Zimmermann (ed.), *Geschichtsschreibung und politischer Wandel in 3. Jh. n. Chr.* (Stuttgart) 71–92.

SCHOFIELD, M. (1991), *The Stoic Idea of the City* (Cambridge).

SCHULZ, F. (1951), *Classical Roman Law* (Oxford).

SCOBIE, A. (1977), 'Some Folktales in Graeco-Roman and Far Eastern Sources', *Philologus*, 121: 1–23.

SEECK, G. A. (1990), 'Dion Chrysostomos als Homerkritiker (or. 11)', *RhM* 133: 97–107.

—— (1996), 'Gegenwart und Vergangenheit bei Dion von Prusa', in M. Flashar et al. (eds.), *Retrospektive. Konzepte von Vergangenheit in der griechisch-römischen Antike* (Munich) 113–23.

SEGONDS, A. (1985), *Proclus. Sur le Première Alcibiade de Platon* (Paris).

SHAW, B. D. (1992), 'Under Russian Eyes', *JRS* 82: 216–28.

SHEPPARD, A. R. R. (1982), 'A Dissident in Tarsus? (Dio Chrysostom, Or. 66)', *LCM* 7: 149–50.

—— (1984), 'Dio Chrysostom: The Bithynian Years', *AC* 53: 157–73.

—— (1984–6), 'Homonoia in the Greek Cities of the Roman Empire', *Anc. Soc.* 15–17: 229–52.

SHERWIN-WHITE, A. N. (1939), *The Roman Citizenship* (Oxford; 2nd edn. 1973).

—— (1966), *The Letters of Pliny* (Oxford).

—— (1984), *Roman Foreign Policy in the East (168 B.C. to 1 A.D.)* (Norman, Okla.).

SIDEBOTTOM, H. (1990), 'Studies in Dio Chrysostom On Kingship' (diss. Oxford).

—— (1992), 'The Date of Dio of Prusa's Rhodian and Alexandrian Orations', *Historia*, 41: 407–19.

—— (1993), 'Philosophers' Attitudes to Warfare under the Principate', in J. Rich and G. Shipley (eds.), *War and Society in the Roman World* (London) 241–64.

—— (1994), review of Russell (1992), *JRS* 84: 265–6.

—— (1996), 'Dio of Prusa and the Flavian Dynasty', *CQ* 46: 447–56.

SINCLAIR, R. K. (1988), *Democracy and Participation in Athens* (Cambridge).

SMITH, R. R. R. (1998), 'Cultural Choice and Political Identity in Honorific Portrait Statues in the Greek East in the Second Century A.D.', *JRS* 88: 56–93.

SONNY, A. (1896), *Ad Dionem Chrysostomum Analecta* (Kiev).

STADEN, H. VON (1996), 'L'Idéal de la tranquillité et la construction du passé dans la Seconde Sophistique: Aelius Aristide', in J.-M. André, J. Dangel, and P. Demont (eds.), *Les Loisirs et l'héritage de la culture classique* (Brussels) 147–61.

STADTER, P. A. (1980), *Arrian of Nicomedia* (Chapel Hill).

STAHL, M. (1978), *Imperiale Herrschaft und provinziale Stadt* (Göttingen).

STANFORD, W. B. (1954), *The Ulysses Theme. A Study in the Adaptability of a Traditional Hero* (Oxford).

SWAIN, S. (1994), 'Dio and Lucian', in J. R. Morgan and R. Stoneman (eds.), *Greek Fiction. The Greek Novel in Context* (London) 166–80.

—— (1996), *Hellenism and Empire. Language, Classicism, and Power in the Greek World, AD 50–250* (Oxford).

—— (1997), 'Plutarch, Plato, Athens, and Rome', in J. Barnes and M. Griffin (eds.), *Philosophia togata, 2: Plato and Aristotle at Rome* (Oxford) 165–87.

—— (1999a), 'A Century and More of the Greek Novel', in id. (ed.), *Oxford Readings in the Greek Novel* (Oxford) 3–35.

—— (1999b), 'Defending Hellenism: Philostratus, *In Honour of Apollonius*', in M. J. Edwards et al. (eds.), *Apologetics in the Roman Empire* (Oxford) 157–96.

—— (1999c), 'Plutarch's Moral Program', in S. B. Pomeroy (ed.), *Plutarch's Conjugalia Praecepta and Consolation to his Wife* (New York) 85–96.

SYME, R. (1958), *Tacitus*, 2 vols. (Oxford).

—— (1982a), 'The Career of Arrian', *HSCP* 86: 181–211 (repr. in *Roman Papers*, 4 (Oxford, 1988) 21–49).

—— (1982b), interview in *Epigrafia e ordine senatorio*, 2 (Rome) 650.

—— (1985), 'Hadrian as Philhellene: Neglected Aspects', *HAC 1982/3* (Bonn) 341–62 (repr. in *Roman Papers*, 5 (Oxford, 1988) 546–62).

SZARMACH, M. (1976), 'Les Discours Περὶ Βασιλείας de Dion de Pruse', *Eos*, 64: 163–76 [Polish, with French résumé].

—— (1977), 'Les Discours diogeniens de Dion de Pruse', *Eos*, 65: 77–90.

—— (1978), 'Le "Discours Troyen" de Dion de Pruse', *Eos*, 66: 195–202.

SZEPESSY, T. (1987), 'Rhodogune and Ninyas. Comments on Dio Chrysostomus' 21st Discourse', *AAntHung* 30: 355–62.

THÉRIAULT, G. (1996), *Le Culte d'homonoia dans les cités grecques* (Lyons).

THOMAS, E. (1909), *Quaestiones Dioneae* (diss. Leipzig).

THORNTON, J. (1998), *'Misos Rhomaion o phobos Mithridatou?* Echi storiografici di un dibattito diplomatico', *MedAnt* 1. 1: 271–309.

TIGERSTEDT, E. N. (1974), *The Legend of Sparta in Classical Antiquity*, 2 (Stockholm).

TIMPANARO, S. (1978), *La filologia di Giacomo Leopardi* (2nd edn.; Rome).

TOBIN, J. (1997), *Herodes Atticus and the City of Athens: Patronage and Conflict under the Antonines* (Amsterdam).

TRAPP, M. (1990), 'Plato's *Phaedrus* in Second-Century Greek Literature', in Russell (1990) 141–73.

—— (1995), 'Sense of Place in the Orations of Dio Chrysostom', in D. Innes et al. (eds.), *Ethics and Rhetoric. Classical Essays for Donald Russell on his Seventy-Fifth Birthday* (Oxford) 163–75.

—— (1997) (trans.), *Maximus of Tyre: The Philosophical Orations* (Oxford).

—— (forthcoming), 'Troy and the True Story of the Trojan War'.

TREU, K. (1958), *Synesios von Kyrene. Ein Kommentar zu seinem 'Dion'*, Texte und Untersuchungen 71 (Berlin).

—— (1961), 'Zur Borysthenitica des Dion Chysostomos', in J. Irmscher and D. B. Schelow (eds.), *Griechische Städte und einheimische Völker des Schwarzmeergebietes* (Berlin) 137–54.

TRISOGLIO, F. (1972), 'Le idee politiche di Plinio il Giovane e di Dione Crisostomo', *Il pensiero politico*, 5: 3–43.

TURRISANUS, F. (1551), *Dionis Chrysostomi orationes LXXX* (Venice).

URSINUS, G. H. (1679), *De Ilio Capto oratio, Contra Dionis Chrysostomi ... De Ilio Non Capto...*, in *Observationum Philologicarum*, 1 (Regensburg) 241–73.

VALDENBERG, V. (1926–7), 'The Political Philosophy of Dio Chrysostom', *Izvestija Ak. Nauk SSSR* 6, ser. 20: 943–74, 1281–1302, 1533–54; 21: 287–306 (in Russian).

—— (1927), 'La Théorie monarchique de Dion Chrysostome', *REG* 40: 142–62.

VALENTINI, A. (1903), *Carlo Valgulio, letterato bresciano del XV. secolo* (Brescia).

VALESIUS, H. (1740), *Henrici Valesii... Emendationum libri quinque et de Critica libri duo*, ed. P. Burmann (Amsterdam) Bk. 2.

VALGIMIGLI, M. (1912), *Contributi all storia della critica letteraria in Grecia*, 1: *La critica letteraria di Dione Crisostomo* (Bologna).

VALGULIUS, C. (1497), [*Cleomedis, De motu . . . etc.*] (Brescia).

VEYNE, P. (1975), 'Y-a-t-il eu un impérialisme romain?', *MEFRA* 87: 793–855.

—— (1976), *Le Pain et le cirque. Sociologie historique d'un pluralisme politique* (Paris).

—— (1988), *Did the Greeks Believe in their Myths?*, trans. P. Wissing (Chicago).

—— (1990), *Bread and Circuses* (London; abridged trans. of *Le Pain et le cirque*).

—— (1999) 'L' Identité grecque devant Rome et l'empereur', *REG* 112: 510–67.

VIDAL-NAQUET, P. (1984), 'Flavius Arrien entre deux mondes', in Arrien, *Histoire d'Alexandre* (Paris) 311–94.

VIELMETTI, C. (1941), 'I "Discorsi bitinici" di Dione Crisostomo', *St. Ital. Fil. Class.* 18: 89–108.

VIRGILIO, B. (1993), *Gli Attalidi di Pergamo. Fama, eredità, memoria* (Pisa).

—— (1998), '*Basileus.* Il re e la regalità ellenistica', in *I Greci*, pt. 2, vol. 3 (Turin) 107–76.

WAKEFIELD, G. (1800), *Select Essays of Dio Chrysostom* (London).

WALTON, C. S. (1929), 'Oriental Senators in the Service of Rome', *JRS* 19: 38–66.

WEBER, E. (1887), *De Dione Chysostomo Cynicorum sectatore* (Leipzig) = *Leipz. Stud.* 10 (1887): 77–268.

WEBER, W. (1915), 'Eine Gerichtsverhandlung vor Kaiser Trajan', *Hermes*, 50: 47–92.

WEBSTER, J. (1996), 'Roman Imperialism and the "Post imperial Age"', in Webster and Cooper (1996) 1–17.

—— and COOPER, N. (1996) (eds.), *Roman Imperialism: Post-Colonial Perspectives* (Leicester).

WECHEL(I)US, A. (1554*a*), *Dionis . . . Orationes LXXX* (Paris) (only 7 speeches).

—— (1554*b*), Δίωνος τοῦ Χρ. Τρωϊκός . . . (Paris).

—— (1555*a*), *Diones . . . Orationes quattuor, De Servitate et Libertate II, Libertate I, Servis I* (Paris).

—— (1555*b*), *Dionis . . . Orationes quinque. De Lege, Consuetudine, Fortuna tres*, trans. R. Guillonius (Paris).

WEGEHAUPT, J. (1896), *De Dione Chrysostomo Xenophontis sectatore* (diss. Göttingen).

WELLES, C. B. (1962), 'Hellenistic Tarsus', *MUB* 38: 41–75.

WENKEBACH, E. (1941), 'Beiträge zur Textkritik Dions von Prusa', *Philologus*, 94: 86–124.

—— (1944), 'Die Überlieferung der Schriften des Dion von Prusa', *Hermes*, 79: 40–65.

WHITMARSH, T. (1998), 'Reading Power in Roman Greece: The *Paideia* of Dio Chrysostom', in Y. L. Too and N. Livingstone (eds.), *Pedagogy and Power* (Cambridge) 192–213.

—— (forthcoming), 'Greece is the World: Exile and Identity in the Second Sophistic', in S. Goldhill (ed.), *Being Greek under Rome. Cultural Identity, the Second Sophistic and the Development of Empire* (Cambridge).

WHITTAKER, J. (1997), 'Plato and Professor Nussbaum on Acts "Contrary to Nature"', in M. Joyal (ed.), *Studies in Plato and the Platonic Tradition. Essays Presented to John Whittaker* (Aldershot) 65–79.

WILAMOWITZ-MOELLENDORFF, U. VON (1900): 'Asianismus und Atticismus', *Hermes*, 35: 1–52 (= *Kleine Schriften*, 3 (Berlin, 1969) 223–73).

WILHELM, F. (1918), 'Zu Dion Chrys. Or. 30 (Charidemus)', *Philologus*, 75: 364–83.

WILSON, N. G. (1992), *From Byzantium to Italy: Greek Studies in the Italian Renaissance* (London).

WINDISCHMANN, F. (1863), 'Stellen der Alten über Zoroastrisches', in id., *Zoroastrische Studien* (Berlin) 260–313.

WINKLER, J. J. (1990), *The Constraints of Desire* (New York).

WINTER, E. (1996), *Staatliche Baupolitik und Baufürsorge in den römischen Provinzen des kaiserzeitlichen Kleinasien* (Bonn).

WISEMAN, T. P. (1979), *Clio's Cosmetics* (Leicester).

WOOLF, G. (1994), 'Becoming Roman, Staying Greek: Culture, Identity and the Civilizing Process in the Roman East', *PCPhS* 40: 116–43.

—— (1998), *Becoming Roman. The Origins of Provincial Civilization in Gaul* (Cambridge).

WÖRRLE, M. (1988), *Stadt und Fest im kaiserzeitlichen Kleinasien* (Munich).

ZAMBRINI, A. (1994), 'L'orazione 35 di Dione di Prusa', *ASNP*, 3rd ser., 24: 49–83.

ZANKER, P. (1995), *The Mask of Socrates. The Image of the Intellectual in Antiquity* (Berkeley).

ZELLER, E. (1923), *Die Philosophie der Griechen in ihrer geschichtlichen Entwicklung dargestellt* (5th edn.; Leipzig).

INDEX

Aeschines Socraticus 232, 233
  Alcibiades 248
  On Lambs and Fleeces 248
Albinus 218
Alexander the Great 46, 90, 180, 222,
  225, 226–7, 230, 266
Alciphron 150
Antisthenes 200, 221, 232, 233, 245,
  246, 250–1, 253, 254, 256, 262–3
  Dio, *Diogenes, or On Virtue* 246,
  255, 256
  Dio, *In Athens, On his Exile* 246,
  249, 251–2
  Dio, *On Homer* 246
  Dio, *Fourth Kingship Oration* 254–6
  Dio, *Third Kingship Oration* 252–3
  Dio, *Public Speech in his Fatherland*
  246
  Alcibiades 248
  Archelaus, on On Kingship 249,
  252–3
  Cyrus, or On Kingship 246, 248
  On Circe 255
  Protrepticus 251
Apuleius 150, 160
Aristides, Aelius 33, 42, 81
Arrian (Arrian-Epictetus) 58, 59, 77,
  238, 245, 264
autarkeia 261–5
  Dio, *Diogenics* (Orr. 6, 8, 10) 266–9
  Dio, *Euboean* 270–5
  Dio, *In Athens, On his Exile* 269–70
  Dio's *autarkeia* 277
Athens 112

Bithynia 65
  Dio's *sunoikismos* 33, 43, 69
  Pliny 74

Carystus 109, 120
Chalcis 119–20
Charax, Claudius 59
Christianity 25, 31, 35, 39, 40, 151,
  268, 278

Cynicism 25, 39, 46–7, 241, 242, 251,
  276, 278
  see also Diogenes/Dio as Diogenes;
  Socrates/Dio as Socrates,
  Socratism and Cynicism

Demosthenes, C. Julius 60
Dio, commentators/editors/
  interpreters/translators
  Arnim, von 27, 28–32
  Blomqvist 48
  Brancacci 46–7, 233
  Bréquigny, de 20
  Brunt 35, 264
  Budé, de 28 n.
  Burckhardt 22
  Casaubon 17
  Cohoon 202–3
  Desideri 35–40, 179
  Dessau 32
  Dindorf 21
  Dudley 35
  Emperius 21
  François 32
  Geel 21
  Hagen 25
  Highet 35 n.
  Hirzel 26–7
  Höistad 35, 233
  Houser 48
  Jones 40–3
  Jouan 47
  Kindstrand 178
  Lemarchand 32
  Leopardi 21 n.
  Martha 22–5
  Moles 45–6, 180
  Momigliano 35 n.
  Morel 17
  Mussies 35
  Naogeorgus (Kirchmeyer) 16
  Quet 44
  Reiske 20
  Rostovtzeff 33–4, 45–6, 65

Dio, commentators/editors/
  interpreters/translators (*cont*.):
  Russell 47–8
  Salmeri 43–4
  Schmid 26, 93, 236
  Sidebottom 40 n., 45 n.
  Sonny 28
  Swain 34 n.
  Turrisanus 16
  Valdenberg 34
  Valesius 20
  Whitmarsh 48 n.
  Wakefield 21 n.
  Zenarus 16
  see also Humanists
Dio, literature/writing:
  Charidemus (*Or.* 30), authenticity of
    188, 199–200, 204–10
  ecphrasis 151
  fiction 6, 122, 143–60
  language 26, 188–9, 196–8, 236
  literary criticism 47
  manuscripts 27–8
  novel and 146–7, 148
  Platonic influences 213–39
    see also Plato
  poets 162–4
  quality, form, style 4–5, 49, 147–9,
    152, 159, 164–71, 196, 209, 213,
    216, 220, 230, 236, 238
  socio-political moralism in 143, 149,
    150–2, 154, 158–60, 230
  textual paternity 194
Dio, myth:
  heroes of used by Dio 166–7, 172,
    235
  invented 156, 157–8, 170, 172–3,
    216–17, 228–9
  logos/truth, relation to 155, 161–4,
    181–3, 190, 196
  moralism/ethics 156, 171–4
  political communication 6–7, 39–40,
    144–5, 150–1, 156, 166, 168–71
  rhetoric 164–71
  Troy and Trojan War 138, 40, 52–4,
    176–86
Dio, philosophy/religion:
  autarkeia 261–78
  'conversion' from sophist 22–5, 36,
    41, 261
  Cynic (preaching) 22, 25–6, 30–1,
    35, 36, 39, 46, 166, 259, 270, 272
  Epicureanism 193
  Orphic 190–1

self-image 7–8, 45–6, 166, 172,
    200–4
  see also Antisthenes; Dio, myth;
    Diogenes/Dio as Diogenes;
    Socrates/Dio as Socrates
  Platonic influences 213–39
    see also Plato
  Plato as intellectual source 213, 218,
    238, 245
    see also Plato
  Stoicism 35, 192–3, 207–8, 215, 238,
    259
  Zeus 192, 207, 208
Dio, politics and society:
  Archippus, Flavius 68
  barbarians 37, 102–3
  children 131–2
  cities 95–9, 103–6, 122–3, 271, 274
  concord/civic virtues 42, 43, 77–81,
    111–17, 273, 277
  countryside 99–102, 271, 274
  exile 14, 36, 40, 62–3, 265, 268–9
  Hellenism 36, 59–60, 77
  male effeminacy and homosexuality
    134–8
  male heterosexuality/lust 132–4,
    274–5
  Nerva 66, 253
  poor, care for 74–5, 99–100, 116,
    261, 264–6, 267, 270–5, 276
    see also *autarkeia*
  prostitution 133–4, 274–5
  Prusan politics and infrastructure
    66–9, 70–3, 104–7, 119, 166
  Rome 36, 38, 43, 44–5, 64, 86–92,
    105–7, 178–9, 209
  slavery 268, 276
  socio-political works 4, 36–7, 230
  Trajan 37, 42–3, 44–5, 68, 91, 104,
    205, 253
  wives 129–30, 132
  women 126–9
  women's physiognomy 128–9
Dio, extant works (Note: for titles of
    orations see pp. 8–10):
  Orr. 1–4: 14, 34, 37, 42–3, 45–6,
    89–91, 106, 221, 255
  Or. 1: 101, 150–2, 163, 174, 202, 203,
    229
  Or. 3: 234, 252, 257
  Or. 4: 225–7, 233, 234, 254–6
  Or. 5: 154–6, 163, 172–3, 229
  Orr. 6, 8–10: 25, 36, 255, 266–9
  Or. 6: 98, 172

Or. 7: 21, 31–2, 41–2, 99–100, 108–124, 133–4, 145–50, 165, 219–21, 265, 270–5
Or. 8: 172, 246, 255, 256, 257
Or. 10: 162
Or. 11: 13, 18–19, 30, 38, 152–3, 176–86, 237
Or. 12: 21, 32, 37–8, 86 n., 102–3, 203, 221, 227–8
Or. 13: 97, 231, 234, 246, 249, 251–2, 265, 269–70
Or. 18: 38, 144, 244
Or. 20: 153–4
Or. 21: 4, 137–8
Or. 26: 234 n.
Or. 28: 138
Or. 29: 138, 165, 237
Or. 30 187–210, 223–5
  see also Dio, literature/writing, Charidemus (*Or.* 30), authenticity of
Or. 31: 44, 82, 144–5
Or. 32: 36, 41, 79–80, 82–3, 95–6, 116 n., 156–7, 169–71, 242
Or. 33: 78–9, 83–4, 128–9, 168–9
Or. 34: 33, 78–9
Or. 35: 41, 83, 96–7, 147
Or. 36: 25, 41–2, 85–6, 87 n., 101, 157–8, 214–19, 238
Or. 38: 15, 77–8
Or. 39: 15, 80
Or. 41: 88 n.
Or. 43: 85
Or. 44: 104
Or. 45: 33
Or. 46: 41, 63–4, 98–9
Or. 47: 166, 246
Or. 49: 105
Or. 53: 15, 19, 221–3, 246, 253
Or. 54: 231, 240, 243
Or. 55: 230, 231, 240, 243, 247, 250
Or. 56: 230
Or. 58: 230
Or. 60: 175–6, 250–1
Or. 61: 154, 175
Or. 66: 4, 165
Or. 75: 237
Or. 76: 237
Or. 80: 98
Dio, lost works:
  Against the Philosophers 241–2
  Encomium of Heracles and Plato (Ἐγκώμιον Ἡρακλέους καὶ Πλάτωνος) 234

Is the Cosmos Perishable? 45 n.
On the Essenes 103
On the Getae 102–3
To Plato in Defence of Homer/In Defence of Homer against Plato (Ὑπὲρ Ὁμήρου πρὸς Πλάτωνα) 222–3, 235, 254 n.
Diogenes/Dio as Diogenes 46, 47, 98, 155, 163, 165, 166, 169, 172, 178, 181, 213 n., 225–7, 230–1, 232, 235, 242, 254–8, 266–9, 270, 272, 276
  Dio, *Diogenics* (*Orr.* 6, 8–10) 25, 36, 255, 266–9
  see also Cynicism; Socrates/Dio as Socrates, Socratism and Cynicism
Dionysius of Halicarnassus 94

Elatea 118
Epicurus 263, 276
Epictetus:
  see Arrian (Arrian-Epictetus)

Foucault 139
Fronto 259

Galen 115

Heliodorus 149
Herodes Atticus 60
Herodotus 176, 184, 185
Homer:
  early modern interpretations and Dio 18–19
  in Second Sophistic 18, 38, 164, 180, 215
  see also Dio, myth, Troy and Trojan War; Dio, extant works, *Or.* 11; Dio, extant works, *Or.* 53
Humanists:
  Borgias 15
  Bruni, L. 13–14
  Camerarius, J. 16
  Philelphus, F. 13–14
  Picolhomineiis, F. de 14
  Politian 15 n.
  Tifernas, P. 14
  Valgulius, C. 15

[Longinus] 94
Longus 146, 149
Lucian 154, 155–6, 159, 176, 184, 185, 186

Maximus of Tyre 160, 235
Musonius Rufus 126, 200, 262–6,
    266–7, 268–9, 272, 273, 274, 277
Mylasa 120

Panaetius 244, 263
Pausanias 144–5
Philostratus 23
    Apollonius, (Dio in) 23
    Heroicus 147, 176, 184–5
    Lives of the Sophists, (Dio in) 23
Plato 163, 185, 195, 202, 215, 234, 245,
    248
    Dio, *Agamemnon, or On Kingship* 230
    Dio, *Alexandrian* 231–2
    Dio, *Borystheniticus* 214–19
    Dio, *Charidemus* 223–5
    Dio, *Euboicus* 219–21
    Dio, *First Kingship Oration* 229
    Dio, *In Athens, On his Exile* 231
    Dio, *Libyan Myth* 229
    Dio, *Olympicus* 227–8, 231
    Dio, *On Deliberation* 234 n.
    Dio, *On Homer* 221–3
    Dio, *On Homer and Socrates* 230
    extent/limit of influence on Dio
        232–4, 235–7, 242, 244–3
    Apology 231, 250
    Clitophon (see also [Plato]) 231, 234
    Gorgias 217, 221, 227, 234
    Laws 222
    Phaedo 151–2, 189, 190–1, 196, 202,
        223–5, 227, 229
    Phaedrus 150, 170, 174, 217, 227–8,
        229
    Protagoras 217, 221, 248
    Republic 173, 202, 217, 219–23, 225,
        228, 229
    Symposium 151, 191, 193–4, 198, 229
    Theaetetus 222, 228
    Timaeus 176
[Plato]:
    Clitophon (see also Plato) 251
    Epistle 2: 225, 234
    First Alcibiades 226–7, 233
    Minos 222
    Sysiphus 234
Platonism 24, 105, 213
Plutarch 40, 42, 61–2, 75, 95, 105, 123
    and Dio 4, 61, 62, 84, 126, 130,
        138–9, 163, 182, 209
Polemo 59
polis, post-classical 2–4, 40–2, 43–4, 55,
    61–2, 77

classical *polis* and 110, 112–13, 119,
    120, 123
community values 111–17, 118–120
intellectual class of 65, 91
political culture of 64, 69–74, 78–81,
    108–24
Posidonius 201, 263
Prodicus 150, 152, 229

Roman Empire:
    economy of Greek provinces 2,
        54–5, 108–9, 121, 272
    Latin in Greek East 54
    local loyalties 59
    prosopographical approach 40–1
    provincial and civic life and 38, 44,
        53–60, 71, 74–5, 105–7, 108–9,
        118, 277
    provincial senators 55–8
    'Romanization' 53

Second Sophistic:
    chronology 2, 29, 93–5, 108 n.
    communication and language 5–6,
        24, 26, 29, 36, 39, 76, 94
    literature 3, 23, 29–30, 122, 124,
        215
        see also Dio, literature/writing;
        Dio, myth
    politics and ideology 30, 33–4, 42,
        44, 84, 105–6, 122–4
    sex and gender 125–39
Seneca 263, 278
Socrates/Dio as Socrates 152, 163, 194,
    195, 200, 207, 213 n., 218,
    226–7, 230, 231, 237, 240–60,
    241, 247, 249, 257
    Antisthenic 245, 248–54, 254–8
    'historical' Socrates 242
    logoi Sōkratikoi 242–4, 248
    Socratism and Cynicism 254–8,
        259–60
Stoicism 35, 45, 47, 136, 215, 238, 263,
    269, 274
    see also Dio, philosophy/religion,
    Stoicism
Synesius 22–5, 29, 241–2

Tabula Cebetis 229
Theagenes 144–5
Thespiae 118

Xenophon 144, 232, 234, 245–6, 250
Xenophon of Ephesus 146